rn or renew by
date below

PRINCES AND PAUPERS
IN THE ENGLISH CHURCH
1500–1800

PRINCES
&
PAUPERS
IN THE ENGLISH CHURCH
1500-1800

EDITED BY
ROSEMARY O'DAY AND
FELICITY HEAL

1981
BARNES & NOBLE BOOKS
TOTOWA, NEW JERSEY

First published in the USA 1981 by
Barnes & Noble Books
81 Adams Drive
Totowa, New Jersey, 07512

Designed by Douglas Martin
Phototypeset, printed and bound by
REDWOOD BURN LIMITED
Trowbridge and Esher

British Library Cataloguing in Publication Data

Princes and paupers in the English
church 1500–1800
1. Church of England – Finance
I. O'Day, Rosemary   II. Heal, Felicity
262'.03   BX5150

ISBN 0–389–20200–2

Contents

Erratum
pp. 242–3   Notes to table 15. [1] should precede 'In the *Return*...'; * should precede 'This category includes...'; † should precede 'The totals given here...'.

Tables

Graph

Map

Abbreviations

AgHR	*Agricultural History Review*
AO	Archives Office
Bodl.	Bodleian Library
BI	Borthwick Institute of Historical Research, York
BL	British Library
Add. MS	Additional Manuscripts
Cott. MS	Cottonian Manuscripts
Harl. MS	Harleian Manuscripts
Lans. MS	Lansdowne Manuscripts
BIHR	*Bulletin of the Institute of Historical Research*
CC	Church Commissioners
CJ	*Journal of the House of Commons*
CPR	*Calendar of the Patent Rolls*
CRO	County Record Office
CStP Dom	*Calendar of State Papers Domestic*
DNB	*Dictionary of National Biography*
EcHR	*Economic History Review*
EHR	*English Historical Review*
Hill, *Economic Problems*	C. Hill, *Economic Problems of the Church from Archbishop Whitgift to the Long Parliament* (1956)
HJ	*Historical Journal*
HMC	*Historical Manuscripts Commission*
JEH	*Journal of Ecclesiastical History*
LPL	Lambeth Palace Library
LP	*Letters and Papers, Foreign and Domestic, of the Reign of Henry VIII,* ed. J. S. Brewer *et al.* (21 vols., 1862–1932)
LJ	*Journals of the House of Lords*
PRO	Public Record Office
PROB	Public Record Office, Probate Records
RO	Record Office

Note Places of publication are given only for works published outside the United Kingdom. In abbreviating less frequently cited periodical titles, the commonly accepted usage of *Soc.* for Society, *Trans.* for Transactions, etc., has been followed. Other abbreviations are listed above.

Notes on the contributors

Joel Berlatsky, B.A., Ph.D. (Northwestern), is Associate Professor of History at Wilkes College, Wilkes-Barre, Pennsylvania. He has written numerous articles on the Elizabethan episcopate and is co-editor of *The Letter Book of Thomas Bentham*. He is currently working on British attitudes to Ireland and India in the eighteenth century.

Claire Cross, M.A., Ph.D. (Cambridge), is Reader in History at the University of York. She is the author of many articles in academic journals and essay volumes and of three books: *The Puritan Earl, The Royal Supremacy in the Elizabethan Church*, and *Church and People, 1450–1660*.

Ian Green, B.A., D.Phil. (Oxford), is a Lecturer in Modern History at the Queen's University of Belfast. Author of *The Re-establishment of the Church of England, 1660–1663* and of two articles on the early Stuart parish clergy, he is currently completing a monograph on the function and ideology of the Stuart clergy.

Felicity Heal, M.A., Ph.D. (Cambridge), is a Fellow of Jesus College, Oxford. She is the author of *Of Prelates and Princes: a study of the economic and social position of the Tudor episcopate* and of various articles on the Tudor bishops, and co-editor of two volumes on the sixteenth- and seventeenth-century Church. She is currently studying the concept of hospitality in early modern England.

D. R. Hirschberg, B.A. (Stanford), Ph.D. (Michigan), is Assistant Professor of History at the University of Pennsylvania. He has completed a book, tentatively entitled *Patronage, Professionalization and Social Mobility: The Anglican Episcopate, 1660–1760*, and is currently studying Anglican church courts from the Restoration to the early nineteenth century.

B. A. Holderness, M.A. (Cambridge), Ph.D. (Nottingham), is a Senior Lecturer in Economic and Social History at the University of East Anglia. He has published several articles in academic journals and a textbook, *Pre-industrial England* (1976). His research interests are in agricultural development, rural credit and the structure of landownership in North West Europe from 1500 to 1800.

Ann Hughes, B.A., Ph.D. (Liverpool), is a Lecturer in History at the University of Manchester. She was the winner of the Alexander Prize for History in 1980. Her research is on politics and society in Warwickshire from 1620 to 1650.

C. S. Knighton, M.A., Ph.D. (Cambridge), is the author of a dissertation on Westminster Abbey and a contributor to various volumes, including the Toronto edition of the collected works of Erasmus. He is currently preparing a catalogue of Manuscripts in the Pepys Library, Magdalene College, Cambridge.

Anne Laurence, B.A. (York), is a Lecturer in History at the Open University, and is working on an interdisciplinary course on the seventeenth century. Her research is on sectarianism and propaganda in the Civil War.

David Marcombe, B.A. (York), Ph.D. (Durham), is Director of the Centre for Local History, University of Nottingham. He has published articles on the Durham chapter, and is currently editing volumes on the Tudor North and English cathedrals and researching on the archdeaconry of Nottingham.

Rosemary O'Day, B.A. (York), Ph.D. (London), is a Lecturer in History at the Open University. As well as having written two books – *Economy and Community* and *The English Clergy: the emergence and consolidation of a profession 1558–1642* – and various articles, she is also co-editor of two volumes on the sixteenth- and seventeenth-century Church and is currently working on the emergence of the professions in early modern England.

W. J. Sheils, B.A. (York), Ph.D. (London), is Senior Archivist at the Borthwick Institute of Historical Research, University of York. He is the author of *The Puritans in the Diocese of Peterborough, 1558–1642*, and of various articles on the Church, and is a contributor to the *Victoria County History* for Gloucestershire. Dr Sheils is at present preparing a general study of the Church in the sixteenth and seventeenth centuries.

Michael L. Zell, B.A. (U.C.L.A.), M.A. (Columbia), Ph.D. (U.C.L.A.), is a Lecturer in History at the Thames Polytechnic. He has written numerous articles on the clergy and on Kentish history, and is currently preparing a study of Kentish Wealden society in the sixteenth century.

Introduction

For almost a quarter of a century the attitudes of historians of the early modern English Church and its economic condition have been shaped and determined by Christopher Hill's *Economic Problems of the Church, from Archbishop Whitgift to the Long Parliament* (1956). For specialist and non-specialist alike, this was for a long period the only readily accessible source of information regarding the economic life of the Church. Christopher Hill argued that economic factors were of great importance in moulding both lay attitudes to the Church as an institution and also the views of the hierarchy itself. His book sought an entrée to the problem of the causes of the English Civil War and the relationship between Puritanism and capitalism. Hill was responding to the preoccupation of contemporary historians with the causes of the English Revolution: he was not writing as an ecclesiastical historian analysing the nature of the Church from within.

For long after the publication of *Economic Problems* the work accomplished on the economic condition of the Church and its personnel tended to take the form of footnotes to Hill's monograph and his later book of essays, *Society and Puritanism* (1964). It is perhaps inevitable that when such a powerful study appears it has the effect of persuading scholars that little work remains to be done on this topic. Not until the later 1960s did historians again begin to work seriously on the economic condition of the Church as an institution and to formulate new questions. It was in 1967 that Phyllis Hembry's earlier doctoral dissertation on the bishops of Bath and Wells was published; three years later Claire Cross published a significant essay on the revenues of the archbishopric of York.[1] This renewed interest was to become yet more evident during the 1970s.

This volume of studies in the economic history of the Church is intended neither to demolish nor to replace Christopher Hill's work. Instead it seeks to amend and amplify, drawing upon recent research, especially upon the careful local studies that have become so much more common in the last decade. It also endeavours, where appropriate, to suggest alternative lines of approach to the relationship between Church and lay society during the period 1500 to 1750. The choice of such a long time-span is deliberate: while *Economic Problems* was deeply preoccupied with the prelude to civil war, the present writers are more interested in the continuity of the institutions of the English Church and the relations between the Church and lay society through two and a half centuries of major political change.

The economic fortunes of the princes of the Church have attracted the most sustained interest from their contemporaries and historians alike. The bishops, deans and cathedral chapters of the reformed Church in reality rarely rivalled princes in the range or scale of their resources, but they usually stood apart from their fellow-clerics by virtue of their landed influence as well as their wealth remaining after the Reformation. Land necessitated careful management and management entailed records: consequently we are able to discuss levels of episcopal and capitular income with some confidence, especially in the period after the Restoration. Five of the essays in this volume are concerned primarily with the getting and spending of bishops and chapters and with some of the results of the methods of acquisition that they employed.

From these analyses two important themes emerge. The first is that the bishops had great difficulty, at least until the Civil War, in defining their role and function within a Protestant polity. Of the several possible models available – that of the medieval lordly prelate, that of the Lutheran superintendant and that of the leading pastor in the Calvinist tradition – none wholly fitted the circumstances of the Tudor and Stuart Church. As Christopher Hill argued, and as Felicity Heal has also demonstrated in her book *Of Prelates and Princes*, the Crown and laity effectively hindered the bishops from following any of these patterns wholeheartedly.[2] The first generation of Elizabeth's bishops, in the Grindalian moment of the Church, might have achieved some change of direction with the assistance of the laity, but the Crown interposed and the opportunity for redefinition passed.[3] Consequently, as Joel Berlatsky argues in Chapter 5, most of the Elizabethan bishops continued to reflect a pale imitation of pre-Reformation life styles and social functions, deferring to the Protestant pattern only in their choice of reading and gowns. The more quantitative study that Daniel Hirschberg conducts for the post-Restoration episcopate shows a basically similar set of results: the bishops achieved a grandeur that might not be princely but that continued effectively to reinforce hierarchical values within the Church.

When wealth survived on this scale it had to be justified, especially to a hostile laity urging greater simplicity upon the prelates and to a Crown which always needed new sources of income and found the clergy irresistibly ripe for plucking. It is interesting that the most consistent justification was found not in the need for the bishops to support the work of the Church or in any argument that the clergy had to have wealth to win respect, but in an appeal to the traditional obligation to provide hospitality. Both Berlatsky and Hirschberg show that clerics and laymen alike believed that it was an essential part of the duties of the episcopate that it cared for the poor and offered entertainment. Even in the post-Restoration years some bishops had very high levels of expenditure primarily because of the households they maintained, and large households can usually be equated with lavish hospitality. Other work on the bishops gives support to the argument for the importance of hospitality. Phyllis Hembry's essay *Episcopal Palaces, 1535–1660* shows that 177 palaces were still used as homes by the prelates in the sixteenth century and that one of their prime purposes was to provide an environment for the lavish entertainment of neighbours and tenants.[4] The Act of Exchange of 1559 specifically exempted demesne lands attached to episcopal residences from its provisions in order to guarantee good housekeeping. Seventy years later Archbishop Laud was still preoccupied by the need to see that his bishops had good housing and adequate supplies, and was highly gratified when Bishop Wren returned one of his leasehold properties to demesne. In the intervening period there is ample evidence that the bishops were expected to provide good hospitality and that the laity were not slow to indicate their failure. New sees such as Chester, poor sees such as Coventry and Lichfield, and sees entirely let out on lease such as Bangor, all presented considerable difficulties for their occupants as they struggled to satisfy the demands of local society.[5]

In the early Stuart period it became a major convention of biographical writing that the hospitality of the prelate described should be praised inordinately. Isaacson described Lancelot Andrewes as a paragon in this respect, and men as diverse as Bishop Williams and Bishop Morton were eulogized for their behaviour within their households. Of course the spiritual functions of these men were also praised: only Hacket writing on Williams makes the perhaps pardonable mistake of delighting in a description of his household at the expense of an analysis of his spiritual contribution. But the social availability of the prelates always looms large in these accounts: the generosity remarked was not the monopoly of one wing of the Stuart Church; it is to be found in the behaviour of Abbot as well as Andrewes and of Wren as well as Morton.[6] It is difficult to estimate how important hospitality was to these men; the subject will repay further detailed study, but it does appear that the bishops aspired to live in as open and public a manner as their pre-Reformation predecessors. In so doing they may have preserved a pattern of social behaviour that was rapidly becoming obsolete among laymen of comparable wealth and standing.

One other dimension of the problem of function and role is considered in several of the essays. W. J. Sheils suggests that we should perceive the prelates as office-holders, as men who had certain 'private' claims upon the office which they occupied within the Church, claims which were entirely appropriate within the context of sixteenth- and early seventeenth-century society. Thus the archbishops of York deployed the patronage that they had acquired in northern rectories during the great exchanges of the 1540s for a variety of purposes, including the support of their relatives, friends and chaplains. They also accumulated capital reserves from their estates which were then used for private investment in land. Meanwhile they largely failed to use their resources to further the cause of Protestantism in the North. Even so reform-minded a prelate as Grindal stayed bound within a tradition which allowed, indeed at times encouraged, the use of the wealth of the Church for the benefit of those close to the officeholder. It was the dominance of this type of thinking that Laud assailed in his attempts to tighten the control of the Church as institution over its re-sources. Felicity Heal shows how his obsession with this need to protect the Church as a whole often led him to put inappropriate pressure upon local bishops who understood the constraints within their dioceses and their own circles so much better.

The second theme to emerge from the essays on the higher clergy concerns their management of their lands. This is partly a matter of in-ternal analysis: how well, for example, did the dean and chapter of Westminster handle the inflationary pressures of the mid-Tudor years? In this particular case C. S. Knighton is able to demonstrate that continuity among the lay administrators and skill in circumventing the long leases issued under Henry VIII, plus the unusual advantage of secure possession of most of the estates throughout half a century of upheaval, left the chapter with a relatively comfortable income. Hirschberg assembles very valuable data to show that the rental incomes of the bishops were beginning to rise slowly after the Civil War, with sharper increases from 1700 onwards.[7] But mere income figures are of only limited use outside the context of the episcopate's relationship with the rest of society. Thus, to take an example from Hirschberg's paper, the actual wealth, and hence part of the power and influence, of the post-Restoration bishops was closely correlated with the length of time they were permitted to reside in a see. Only half the bishops studied occupied one office for ten years or more: their opportunities for capital accumulation were therefore very limited and we can presumably infer that they also had little time in many cases to build a network of local political and social alliances. It was this association between wealth and political influence that obsessed Laud: Heylyn suggested that his attempts to restrict leases to 21 years had as their basis the desire to demonstrate to church tenants that the institution still had effective control over them.[8] But Laud was not fundamentally an innovator; he accepted the pattern of church finance and tried to work a policy of 'thorough' within it. In some senses he achieved the worst of all possible worlds: his proposals for the reform of church finance could not be more far-reaching because of the property rights of the laity, and yet his tightening of the system did little more than offend local sensibilities. In the case of his own Canterbury estates Felicity Heal suggests that his difficulties derived from the lack of a local dimension to his policies, the absence of a perception of the value of local contacts with the ruling elite which had been an important part of the management of his predecessor, George Abbot.

Since the princes of the Church were perforce committed to a system of finance that had its rationale in a different world, that of feudalism and Catholicism, they had to ameliorate the worst of its weaknesses as best they could. Alongside a concern for the legitimate profits of office came a concern to protect the Church as institution. Although Laud's immediate challenge to the laity merely issued in disastrous conflict between the clergy and the rest of society, he did at least indicate ways in which the hierarchy could escape from the cycle of dependence and exploitation that had marked the hundred years after the Reformation. Thus in the post-Restoration world, when the triumph of secular values was ultimately assured, Laud's approach to the financing of the bishoprics bore fruit.[9]

II

In chapter 1 Michael Zell presents a study of the economic problems of the parochial clergy in the sixteenth century. He pays particular attention to the problems of the unbeneficed clergy, which were accentuated in the early sixteenth century by the excess of supply over demand for new ordinands. The work of Jo Ann Moran on ordinations in the late fifteenth and early sixteenth centuries confirms this.[10] This situation in itself ensured that very low wages would be offered to assistant curates, stipendiaries or chaplains. In the 1520s such unbeneficed clerics earned about the same as a landless labourer. Many of the unbeneficed were forced to supplement their clerical incomes with by-employments, either of a secular or a religious type. Significantly, few of these unbeneficed clergy found promotion to benefices: those ordinands destined for a benefice normally found one relatively quickly after ordination. Michael Zell's study is especially interesting because it complements work done on the Elizabethan and Early Stuart clergy. In *The English Clergy* Rosemary O'Day argues that the problem of over-supply for the ministry even in the 1620s and 1630s has probably been over-estimated. The real problem of the seventeenth century lay in the fact that almost all new ordinands were graduates or university students who tended to see themselves as more than the ecclesiastical counterparts of landless labourers. Yet even here one must be cautious: there were relatively few unbeneficed ministers in the 1620s and 1630s and some of the positions which these men did hold were reasonably prestigious. As clergymen in the period 1558–1642 were still drawn from below the gentry, it is also debatable whether their expectations in terms of income were raised.

O'Day believes that educated clergy did possess a great sense of self-importance and did stress their status, but suggests that by this time the problem of the unbeneficed was statistically small and not unmanageable. It is true that the post-Reformation Church limited the number of by-employments open to the beneficed and unbeneficed clergy, thus restricting the sources of supplementary income. But there can be little doubt that the Reformation, by removing demand for all but a few assistant clergy, also removed the burden of financing a huge band of hired labourers from the Church's shoulders. The difficulties faced in the seventeenth century (when a number of well-educated clergymen were left without benefices or prospects) were due to the continued insensitivity of the Church's recruitment and training mechanisms. Nevertheless, the situation was very different from that in pre-Reformation England. In pre-Reformation England there was no common career structure for parochial clergy and this situation pertained to the sixteenth century as a whole. By the seventeenth century supply did more equally match demand and the Reformation conception of a unified, pastoral ministry was generally capable of realization at parish level. This ideal was never realized with respect to the clerical elite, at least partly because of the outmoded methods of paying the Church's leading personnel.

Michael Zell also tackles the thorny question of the extent to which the average beneficed clergyman's income was adequate in an age of inflation – an issue which has received some attention in other works. He observes that clerical income was drawn from two main sources, glebe and tithe. The income from neither of these sources was guaranteed and, as the endowments of livings varied very widely between diocese and diocese and between parish and parish, it is impossible to say that *all* the parochial clergy were either poorly or satisfactorily provided for at any one time. We do know that many rectors and vicars were provided with adequate glebe for the support of their families – where a clergyman farmed extensive glebe for himself (and had not leased it out at uneconomic rents) he stood to benefit from rising agricultural prices. Similarly, the cleric who collected tithes in kind, and particularly the owner or lessee of the great tithes, benefited from this aspect of inflation. In general, it seems to have been the vicars who suffered most from inflation because they normally collected only the small tithes which had risen less in value. In their studies of tithing in the sixteenth century D. M. Barratt and Stephen Lander have indicated that relatively few beneficed clergy in the Midlands and the South collected commuted tithes. It appears that this pattern persisted into the seventeenth century. Felicity Heal has stressed the new obligations which the post-Reformation clergy were compelled to meet from their traditional sources of revenue – regular taxation, the payment of first fruits and tenths, requests for benevolences from impoverished bishops and so forth. And, of course, most of the clergy in the period 1558–1642 were married and had heavy family obligations. Despite all this, the signs are that most clergymen managed to keep their heads above water and that some few actually prospered.[11]

The relative prosperity of the beneficed clergy may be assessed also by reference to their standards and modes of living. Comparisons between early and late sixteenth-century clerical wills seem to reveal something more than the raised living standards of the community as a whole. This is undoubtedly the case by the seventeenth century, when more of the parochial clergy are well-educated, own books and clothing and live in fairly opulent fashion. Few of the clergymen in the diocese of Coventry and Lichfield, for example, appear to have been so oppressed financially that they were willing to take their parishioners to court regularly for non-payment of tithes, despite the fact that they could look forward to favourable treatment in the ecclesiastical courts if they chose so to do.

One of the major problems facing the beneficed clergyman in the sixteenth and seventeenth centuries, as today, was that of providing for himself after retirement and for his family after his death. It was difficult for the cleric to accumulate sufficient capital to solve this problem. For example, he was obliged (if a rector) to keep the parsonage and the chancel in good repair. As much clerical housing was already old and decrepit, costs of dilapidations for the unfortunate cleric sued in the ecclesiastical courts might be high indeed. Sequestrations of the fruits of benefices for this reason appear to have been common. In fact, some parishes found it difficult to persuade their ministers to live in the house provided, which added to the problems of upkeep. Understandably, ministers preferred to occupy personal property and keep it in good repair rather than to pour personal money (as they saw it) into church property. In the 1660s, for instance, we see Ralph Josselin building a new house for his family, which cost approximately £200.[12] Clergymen appear to have been more willing to maintain the farm buildings belonging to the Church (from which they obtained a tangible personal return) than the domestic buildings. Wills and inventories of seventeenth-century clergymen indicate that many did accumulate enough property by purchase or inheritance or lease to provide to some extent for the future support of wife and children. These source materials, however, are difficult to use systematically and it would be impossible to state what proportion of the parochial clergy was able to support their dependents satisfactorily.

The economic problems of the urban clergy were in many ways distinctive. Many of the leading cities supported more parish churches and ministers than their populations and resources warranted, while other urban parishes coincided exactly with the boundaries of the township concerned. In most cases the sixteenth-century clergy died in modest circumstances, but it is possible to demonstrate that more of the Elizabethan urban clergy 'achieved a reasonable competency' in economic terms than did their forbears, despite inflation; and that, significantly, the Jacobean and Caroline clergy achieved considerable prosperity (relatively speaking) in a period of reduced inflation. In chapter 3 Claire Cross attributes this rising prosperity in Elizabethan times to an increase in the occurrence of pluralism among urban clerics. The wealthy clergymen of the seventeenth century owned land, bought books and loaned money. Interestingly, many of these prosperous urban clergy were preparing their sons for a career in the Church, reflecting their own attitudes to the Church as a desirable career, which was sufficiently lucrative and not socially 'demeaning. These clergy attained relative prosperity by a variety of means – pluralism; schoolmastering; will-making and accountancy; pursuit of personal tithing rights and so forth. Increasingly important were the gifts of individual patrons and the occupancy of parish lectureships, as W. J. Sheils also observed in his study of 'Religion in provincial towns'.[13] In other words, urban clergy prospered not because the Church reorganized traditional sources of finance in their favour but because they were able to take advantage of the rising tide of urban prosperity in the later sixteenth century and the first two decades of the seventeenth century. There were simply more opportunities for lucrative by-employment in even the smallest market town than there were in the average rural parish.

Anne Laurence draws our attention to the position of one clerical group which stood outside the conventional parochial framework: the army chaplains during the 1640s. She maintains that there was no such thing as a career chaplain. Many of the chaplains were beneficed clergymen (for example, Ralph Josselin) and for almost all the period as chaplain 'was an interlude in an otherwise fairly conventional clerical career'. These chaplains were well paid by the standards of the day. In 1645 the Committee for Plundered Ministers set itself the goal of bringing all livings up to a value of no more than £100 *per annum*:

chaplains were paid at the rate of £146 *per annum*. But such appointments were normally brief.

The problem of reorganizing the financing of the parochial clergy was an intractable one, as Laud and his colleagues had discovered. In some real sense the stumbling block was lay vested interests in existing forms of ecclesiastical property. In a period of crisis, such as that of the Civil War and Interregnum, this stumbling block was partially removed with the sequestrian of delinquent property. Consecutive régimes went some way towards tackling the problems of financing the ministry.

Most historians have tended to the view that parliamentary committees were concerned only with the immediate need to relieve parliamentary sympathizers in poor economic straits. Rosemary O'Day and Ann Hughes argue that from the beginning the Committee for Plundered Ministers was concerned not only with this issue but also with that of financing the entire ministry in England and Wales in a more equitable and religiously acceptable fashion. It was Parliament rather than its Committee which concentrated upon the political aspect. It appears that the Committee had even gone some way towards securing parliamentary support for their approach to the national problem of a poorly financed parochial ministry before the end of the war. When a new survey of benefices was produced in 1650 in accordance not only with the impact of inflation on church livings but also with the post-Reformation view of the ministry as primarily concerned with pastoral care, and when in 1654 Oliver Cromwell remodelled the Trustees for the Maintenance of Ministers and gave them immediate access to this survey, the interregnum governments were building upon the ideas of the Committee for Plundered Ministers. The essay shows that Cromwell's State Church was to have been more than a chimera.

The experiments of the 1640s and 1650s do constitute in some ways a movement towards the modernization of church finance at the parochial level. The Trustees adopted a bureaucratic and centralized approach to their work. They envisaged a method of augmenting cures which would have relieved the individual ministers of the need to resort to leasing and improved relations with their parishioners. Parishes would have been smaller and more rational in design so that each community would have received adequate and accessible pastoral care and so that the Church's wealth would have been more equitably distributed. Nonetheless, the attitudes of the various committees and of the Trustees were still dominated by traditional thinking. For example, there was little idea of financing individual livings from a central fund until the 1650s and even then much of the work continued to be funded from local tithes. Moreover, even the Trustees commanded a very small total central revenue for the work at hand. Both collection and accounting techniques were outdated. Yet because the augmenters certainly believed that there was a need for church income to be distributed equitably as a result of central direction and because there was a clear feeling that the revenue from clerical taxation should be invested in the clergy as a body, the work of the Trustees for the Maintenance of Ministers (and of the committees which they followed) was not devoid of significance for later projects of reforming church finance.

The wealth of the parochial clergy in the later seventeenth century has been studied elsewhere by John Pruett.[14] He maintains that there were great variations still in the income of the parish clergy: inequality of endowment was heightened by the inequality of benefits from such ploys as pluralism. The real income of the individual cleric depended not so much upon the endowment of his ecclesiastical living as upon his ability to find a lucrative supplementary source of income. Because of such additional by-employment, less than 20 per cent of Leicestershire clergy in 1706/7 received less than £50 *per annum* despite the fact that in the same year about a third of Leicestershire benefices were valued at less than that sum. (It seems probable, however, that at least some of this discrepancy was accounted for by underestimation of the value of a benefice and by pluralism.) According to Pruett, the Late Stuart clerical proletariat was made up of vicars, stipendiaries and assistant curates drawing less than £50 *per annum*. At the same time, the plight of the urban clergy seems to have been particularly acute, so that the livings in Leicester itself were held in plurality for much of the later seventeenth century.

Nevertheless, the drift of clerical incomes was definitely upward. 'In 1714 parsons were getting more from their glebes and were collecting tithes on greater yields than were their predecessors in the 1530s.' Despite the slowing down of inflation in the later part of the century, there is evidence that clerical incomes continued to rise. This directly contradicts the usual view that the later seventeenth century constituted a period of 'stagnation or decline in the economic condition of the clergy', which has been reiterated by G. V. Bennett.[15] Even the incomes of perpetual curates, technically tied to a fixed stipend, rose by 94 per cent in Leicestershire between 1603 and 1707 and by 58 per cent in Buckinghamshire, Hertfordshire and Huntingdonshire between 1650 and the end of Anne's reign, apparently because patrons augmented the curacies.

As Pruett observes, this rise in the gross real value of clerical livings did not necessarily mean that the net position of the clergy was much improved. The indications are that, after 1690, the clergy were much more heavily taxed than previously. Window taxes, poll taxes and excise taxes alike hit the clergy hard while a heavy land tax fell on both tithe and glebe. By the early eighteenth century at least some clergymen were paying 20 per cent of their income in taxation, much of it in the form of land tax, and this despite the cessation of clerical subsidies and the exemption of all of the poorer clergy from payment of first fruits and tenths. These heavy rates of taxation appear to have cut into the personal estates of late seventeenth- and eighteenth-century clergy after 1690, offsetting the apparent gains in clerical income made since 1650 if not obliterating the real gains made between 1530 and 1650.

Perhaps the best-known project to tackle the problem of financing the parochial ministry in England and Wales is that known as Queen Anne's Bounty. Ian Green's study of the problems met by church reformers in this measure indicates that the scheme finally met with great success simply because of the wide degree of co-operation achieved between Crown, ecclesiastics and laity. He certainly makes clear the problems involved even in discovering which were the poor livings and what their incomes were. The work took 15 years to complete (between the setting-up of the royal corporation and the granting of the first augmentation). The problems of the corporation were increased because the sources of revenue against which the augmentations were to be charged – first fruits and tenths – had been used as a source of royal patronage over the years and because the collection system itself was archaic and inefficient. Eventually all livings worth less than £50 were exempt from payment of first fruits and tenths (after examination) while the wealthier clergy were won over by the welcome realization that their livings would not be reassessed upwards and that they would maintain payments according to the *Valor Ecclesiasticus* assessment. After a number of surveys the Governors of the Bounty of Queen Anne finally published a report to Parliament in 1736 which estimated that a depressing 5,600 churches and chapels (out of a total of approximately 11,000) were below £50 in value – that is, below the poverty line. Probably the survey presented an unduly pessimistic picture of the financial position of the parochial ministry, for it omitted consideration of the alleviating effects of pluralism, clerical by-employment and outright underassessment. However, as the scheme was designed to enable the parochial clergy to fulfil their pastoral obligations without recourse to such ruses, one may consider that such exaggeration was legitimate. Ian Green's study certainly bears out earlier studies in confirming the uneven distribution of clerical incomes both within and between dioceses. The Bounty gave help where it was most needed, in the North, the Midlands and in the Severn Valley. Urban livings also received handsome augmentation.

The study of Queen Anne's Bounty indicates that, once co-

operation was achieved between ecclesiastics and laymen, the problems of financing the ministry equitably were not insuperable. More
work is needed to explain why this co-operation was possible in the
1700s whereas it was not in the 1600s. Ian Green suggests that many
laymen involved in the surveys were eager that the augmentation be
granted because this would absolve them of the need to pay their dues
in full or bear personal responsibility for augmentation. The Act of
1715 made it clear that no proprietor was bound to accept an augmentation for a living if he did not wish to abide by the corporation's rules.
Favourable terms were offered those patrons who chose to donate as
much as the Governors, immediately or in a will. To many the carrot
of obtaining patronage to a living proved irresistible at a time when
numbers of the gentry and the middle classes were entering the
Church. The essentially voluntary and non-punitive nature of the
scheme was made abundantly clear. But we must dig deeper to discover why this scheme succeeded where earlier proposals for voluntary donations of impropriate tithes had failed. Was it simply that this
was the first occasion when both hierarchy and laity converged in
their belief that a centralized effort was required to tackle a major
problem? There can be little doubt that seventeenth-century experiments in centralized administration made their contributions to the
scheme as it stood. Or did its success have something to do with the
less ambiguous involvement of the laity in church property by this
date? In the early seventeenth century many advowson and tithe
holders were torn between the desire to protect their property and the
desire to reform the Church, in a way which the hierarchy found un-
congenial and inconvenient. By the later seventeenth century was lay
society so much less involved in theological and ecclesiastical issues
that the issue of financing the ministry had become one more simply of
defending property interests?

By the end of the period, then, there were signs that the Church was
at last getting to grips with the problem of financing its parochial ministry adequately if not munificently. Significantly enough, this situation came about because of the eventual discovery of a scheme in
which both churchmen and laity could join with alacrity.

III

Whereas a group of historians is exploring in detail the economic condition of the Church itself, rather less attention is being given to the
place of the Church of England in the *national* economy. For this
reason, the contributions to this area from David Marcombe and
B. A. Holderness are all the more welcome.

David Marcombe argues in chapter 12 that the Church gave its tenants such advantageous terms that they were able to emerge as a distinct rural elite in the eighteenth century. This work relates well to a point raised by Christopher Hill in *Economic Problems of the Church* (pp. 36–7). Hill observes that when confiscation of church property was debated in 1640–1 some objected to it on the grounds that tenants of bishops and deans and chapters enjoyed beneficial arrangements which they would forfeit if the church lands were to be sold. Recent studies of episcopal leasing policies show that the bishops did not extract even an approximately economic rent from their properties, relying instead upon entry fines for income: Hacket's comment in 1641 that ecclesiastical leaseholders enjoyed 'six parts in seven of pure gain' on their leases seems to be borne out by the evidence. On the other hand, J. U. Nef urged that ecclesiastical ownership, especially as leases tended to become shorter in duration, deterred leaseholders from the sort of heavy capital investment necessary for industrial development.[16] In a similar vein, T. S. Willan argued that enclosure and other capitalist farming methods were delayed because of ecclesiastical ownership.[17]

David Marcombe is fully aware of the dangers of producing an average leaseholder while also acknowledging the difficulties presented in locating sufficient data to study a whole community of leaseholders: in the event he examined the economic activity of one family and its kin connections. He established that, technically speaking, tenants of the dean and chapter and of episcopal lands received advantageous treatment. During the post-Reformation period traditional tenants were worried that they would be turned off their lands by married clergy hungry for leases of church property. There ensued a fight with the chapter for rights of renewal, low entry fines and low rents in exchange for fulfilment of military and other obligations. In 1626 the chapter decreed that tenants would thereafter pay the equivalent of three years' improved value as a fine every 21 years (1 in 7). Reserved rents meanwhile scarcely changed between 1541 and 1700, at a time when rentals on lay leaseholds were much higher. It was virtually impossible to evict an ecclesiastical tenant as long as he met very limited obligations. Such tenants did well, then, when compared with their lay counterparts or with tenants leasing land directly from individual prebendaries.

But did ecclesiastical tenants introduce modern farming techniques and improvements? Did the levy of fines on 'improved values' deter such enterprise? David Marcombe shows that individual farmers were eager to manage their church leaseholds well so that they could invest in more of the same. A church leaseholder had the necessary contacts to ensure favourable treatment when it came to granting of other church leases, for as long as he was a good tenant. At least those tenants who held leases on secure terms and land which held promise for re-investment were engaging in agricultural improvement. Given the ambitions of the tenant class this probably constituted a large proportion of church leaseholders. Improvements were traditionally ignored in the renewal period (and fine) immediately following the making of the improvements, thus allowing the tenant a chance to recoup his own expenses. In this way reclamation and embankment of the Tyne was encouraged. Ecclesiastical landlords, also, on occasion reduced fines to encourage improvement. The lack of building on leasehold lands may be explained in terms of the close interaction of freehold and leasehold property ownership in the eighteenth century. Most of the leaseholders also owned freehold land and they tended to erect permanent buildings on the freehold sections of their farms. This in no way precluded the efficient farming of the leasehold lands as both types of property were farmed as one unit. Although timber can be shown to have been in short supply on church leaseholds this problem was common on freehold and other leasehold land throughout the country. Indeed, ecclesiastical landowners were more active than most in encouraging the replacement of cut timber. The family which David Marcombe studied engaged in considerable entrepreneurial enterprise in connection with its lime-works. He also points out that ecclesiastical tenants were led to emphasize livestock improvement because this was one area for which they could not be held accountable. The Boazmans were instrumental in the evolution of the shorthorn breed of cattle. David Marcombe suggests that the levy on improvements may have caused the tenantry to focus on this form of investment rather than others. Such activity may have held back industrial development but it can surely not be ignored as of no importance to the economy as a whole.

David Marcombe's essay contributes to a more general debate concerning the conditions necessary for improved agricultural management and techniques. One school of thought is that landholders need the pressure of high rents to push them into exploitation of their land; another is convinced that agricultural advance is dependent upon the type of capital surplus available to farmers who have low overheads in the form of rent and upkeep. In general David Marcombe seems to belong to the latter school. The essay is of great significance also because it calls for a more thorough examination of the mixed nature of landholding in eighteenth-century England and its possible effects upon agricultural development.

Eric Evans' *Contentious Tithe* also casts some light on the possible effects of ecclesiastical concerns upon the course of agricultural development.[18] Tithe constituted a tax not on profit but on produce: as such it hit hardest arable rather than pasture farming, and those farmers still obliged to pay in kind more than those paying a commuted tithe. When one realizes that even in 1813 at least 18 per cent of the total value of tithes was still taken in kind, one senses just how important this fact was to the total economy. It appears that tithing practices did make a considerable difference to the choices for cultivation placed before landholders and in 1816 some of the respondents to a Board of Agriculture questionnaire actually made specific reference to tithe as a factor in their decision-making process.

B. A. Holderness's study of the clergy as money-lenders points to another respect in which the Church formed an integral part of the economy. To what extent were the clergy instrumental in providing rural credit? To what purposes was such credit put? Was clerical participation systematic or done on an *ad hoc* basis? What was the Church's attitude to the situation? Did the position of the clergyman as money-lender affect adversely or positively his relations with his parishioners? What light does the activity of the clergy as a source of rural credit throw upon the economic position of the parochial clergy themselves?

B. A. Holderness disentangles the question of the place of the clergy in the rural credit system from the issue of the moral defensibility of usury in the first part of his essay and in the second faces squarely the issues outlined above. He concludes that between one-quarter and one-third of the English clergy acted as creditors to friends, relatives or neighbours before the eighteenth century, although none appear to have acted in this capacity on a large, money-making scale. In fact most clergy seem to have contributed to rural credit resources in much the same way as did yeomen and tradesmen, although perhaps to a slightly greater extent. The gap between the clergy and the gentry as money-lenders was wider than that between the clergy and yeomen or tradesmen. The evidence seems to support the view that the clergy increased their wealth during the sixteenth and seventeenth centuries, although not to any great extent. Holderness argues that, to the extent that clergymen did become wealthier in the post-Reformation period, they did so as a result of tithes on increased agricultural productivity among their parishioners and the improved prices which they were receiving for produce of the glebe. In the eighteenth century, however, there were some very wealthy clergymen who were able to engage in money-lending to a much larger degree and with more motivation towards profit.

Clerical money-lending, because of the plebeian origins of most of the sixteenth-and seventeenth-century clergy, says Holderness, was geared towards the support of non-capitalistic enterprise. Recent work on the status of the parochial clergy as a professional group may make the equation suggested more complex, but the fundamental point appears to be that the clergy helped finance, on an *ad hoc* basis, the day-to-day farming enterprise of the members of the community in which they lived, including fellow clergymen. This credit was offered 'in neighbourly fashion to kinsfolk or fellow-villager' rather than as part of the usurious exploitation of status. Even when some eighteenth-century clergymen appear as more business-orientated money-lenders, the old pattern continued for the most part unspoiled. As Alan Macfarlane suggested in the case of Ralph Josselin's money-lending ventures, it is probable that seventeenth-century clergymen used lending as a form of banking when surplus funds were available.[19] A form of symbiosis existed between the creditor and the debtor.

Any volume of essays, to be worth publishing, raises many more questions than it answers. This is no exception. Further work is needed in several fundamental areas, some of which are already receiving attention. For instance, we look forward in pleasant antici-pation to Molly Barratt's extensive study of tithe in the sixteenth and seventeenth centuries and to Eric Evans' work on the economic re-sources of Lancashire clergymen. But the way is still open for those who wish to view the Church of England as an integral part of the English economy.

Above all, the essays in this volume make it clear that the economic condition of the Church should not be dissociated from a study of the changing functions of the Church within society. For example, whereas the property interests of the laity in the Church and in patronage have usually been seen to be the chief stumbling block in the way of financial reform, some of the essays here presented suggest that it may well have been the religious views of these lay property owners which constituted the prime obstacle in the way of such reform. When the laity lost interest in religious issues or felt that their religious opin-ions were being adequately represented by church reformers, they were willing enough to join forces with Crown and hierarchy to improve the lot of the clergy. Attitudes to the rightful role of the insti-tutionalized Church in the State underwent considerable revision both at the Reformation and afterwards. He who ignores these changes in order to concentrate exclusively on 'economic conditions' *per se* is certainly in danger of not seeing the wood for the trees. The ad-equacy of the Church's financial resources must be assessed in the light of changing expectations as well as of the comparability of cleri-cal incomes with lay incomes. Equally, a simple comparison with the economic condition of the later medieval Church is unsatisfactory. What is called for is a careful study of the interaction between chang-ing views of the role of the State Church and her economic capacity to discharge the expectations placed upon her. The economic history of the Church cannot and should not be divorced from her development as a religious institution.

NOTES

1. P. M. Hembry, *The Bishops of Bath and Wells, 1540–1640* (1967); C. Cross, 'The economic problems of the See of York', in *Church, Land and People*, ed. J. Thirsk (1970).
2. F. Heal, *Of Prelates and Princes: a study of the economic and social position of the Tudor episcopate* (1980).
3. On the general expectations of change aroused by this Elizabethan generation see P. Collinson, *Archbishop Grindal, 1519–1583* (1979).
4. P. M. Hembry, 'Episcopal palaces, 1535–1660', in E. W. Ives, J. J. Scarisbrick and R. B. Knecht (eds.), *Wealth and Power in Tudor England* (1978).
5. C. Haigh, 'Finance and administration in a new diocese: Chester, 1541–1641', in *Continuity and Change: personnel and administration of the Church in England, 1500–1642*, ed. R. O'Day and F. Heal (1976); M. R. O'Day, 'Thomas Bentham: A case study in the problems of the early Elizabethan episcopate', *JEH*, xxiii (1972).
6. H. Isaacson, *The Life and Death of Lancelot Andrewes* (1829); Baddiley, *Life of Bishop Morton* (1669); J. Hacket, *Scrinia Reservata* (1693); P. Heylyn, *Cyprianus Anglicus* (1719).
7. Contrast Hembry, *Bishops of Bath and Wells*; Heal, *Of Prelates and Princes*, and G. Alexander, 'Victim or spendthrift? The bishop of London and his income in the sixteenth century', in Ives et al., *op. cit.* All three indicate a general fixity of rental income, though with a few increases towards the end of the sixteenth century.
8. Heylyn, *op. cit.* pt ii, 46–7.
9. For a further discussion of the problems of financing the clergy by the traditional methods see R. O'Day, *The English Clergy: the emergence and consolidation of a profession, 1558–1642* (1979).
10. J. A. H. Moran, 'Educational development and social change in York diocese from the fourteenth century to 1548' (Ph.D. thesis, Brandeis University, 1975).
11. D. M. Barratt, 'Conditions of the parish clergy from the Reformation to 1660 in the Dioceses of Oxford, Worcester and Gloucester', (D. Phil. thesis, University of Oxford, 1950); Stephen Lander, 'The diocese of Chichester, 1508–58' (Ph. D. thesis, University of Cambridge, 1974); F. Heal, 'Clerical tax collection under the Tudors: the influence of the Reformation', in O'Day and Heal (eds.), *Continuity and Change*.
12. A. Macfarlane, *The Family Life of Ralph Josselin* (1970).
13. W. J. Sheils, 'Religion in provincial towns: innovation and tradition', in *Church and Society in England from Henry VIII to James I*, eds. F. Heal and R. O'Day (1977).
14. J. Pruett, *The Parish Clergy Under the Later Stuarts* (1978).
15. G. V. Bennett, 'Conflict in the Church', in Geoffrey Holmes (ed.), *Britain After the Glorious Revolution, 1689–1714* (1968).
16. See C. Clay, '"The Greed of the Whig Bishops"? Church landlords and their lessees, 1660–1760', *Past and Present*, LXXXVII (1980), 128-57. J. U. Nef, *The Rise of the British Coal Industry* (1932).
17. T. S. Willan, 'The parliamentary surveys for the North Riding of Yorkshire', in *Yorkshire Archaeological Journal*, xxxi.
18. E. J. Evans, *Contentious Tithe* (1976).
19. Macfarlane, *op. cit.*

1

Economic problems of the parochial clergy in the sixteenth century

Michael L. Zell

The English Reformation was, in many senses, a stunning discontinuity in ecclesiastical life in the sixteenth century. Nevertheless, certain fundamental realities seemed unchanging: the institutional structure of the Church with its hierarchy of officialdom and courts retained its traditional appearance, and – more to the point here – the organization of parochial life showed significant continuities. Perhaps the most important of these was the relative poverty of many parochial clergy, and the chorus of complaint which was raised on their behalf. From Hugh Latimer in the reign of Edward VI to Whitgift and Bancroft at the end of the century, the complaint retained its basic premise: that many benefices were too poorly endowed to support the kind of cleric whom the complainants felt was necessary. However, it is worth noting at the outset that such expressions of concern about clerical poverty generally limited themselves to the problems of the beneficed cleric, and tended to ignore the plight of the unbeneficed. As will become clear, the problems of the parish clergy were not only those of poor rectors and poor vicars, but even more so the lot of those ecclesiastics who had no rights in a living, nor even the likelihood of steady employment. To a very large extent the problem of the unbeneficed was a problem of supply and demand, which diminished as the balance shifted in the second half of the sixteenth century. Given the vastness of these questions, this essay will focus mainly on the early sixteenth century and on the Reformation decades, although it will, I hope, indicate several lines of approach to the late Elizabethan and Jacobean debate on the maintenance of the clergy. It will examine first the supply of priests in the early sixteenth century and the prospects of an ecclesiastical career. To confront the question of clerical poverty it must look below the ranks of the incumbents to the underworld of the unbeneficed. Only then will it be appropriate to examine the economic conditions of parochial incumbents. In doing so it will become apparent that both before and after the Henrician–Edwardian Reformation a relatively large minority of the permanent parochial livings were under-endowed.

The study of the parish clergy in the Tudor period is – like so many other areas of investigation – bedevilled by the unevenness of the sources. To begin with, far more evidence survives about the beneficed than the unbeneficed. A thorough study of all parish clergy is impossible; far less material is extant for some dioceses than for others, and for some chronological periods as compared to others. Moreover, it is far more difficult to discover what clerics actually earned and spent than it is to know the formal income on which they were taxed. The single outstanding source for incumbents' income, the *Valor Ecclesiasticus* of 1535, presents a bewildering array of material which is not consistently detailed from one diocese to another, or even from one deanery to another. It contains estimates of the average values of each living 'from one year to another', but there is no reliable way of checking its accuracy in a systematic way. And, of course, it must be remembered that the *Valor* was compiled at the beginning of what was to be a long period of price inflation, and therefore its assessments may bear little relationship to the reality of clerical incomes in the 1580s or 1590s. My impression is that if the *Valor* errs at all (for 1535) it is more in the direction of under- than over-assessment. Actual accounts kept by sixteenth-century incumbents of their income and expenditure have rarely survived: several have been described by Peter Heath.[1] In contrast, the sources for the income of the unbeneficed are much less full. They appear sometimes on ecclesiastical tax-lists, especially in the 1520s, and the salaries of curates can occasionally be extracted from churchwardens' accounts, accounts of monasteries and particulars of Crown land sales. But little or nothing survives concerning their expenditure. The salaries of chantry priests are often found in last wills and testaments of men and women who endowed either permanent or temporary chantries, while the Edwardian chantry certificates give a systematic source for the basic minimum income of chantrists in the late 1540s.[2] But with chantry priests, as for all the unbeneficed, the basic problem lies in the difficulty of even retrieving the names of all the men concerned.

I

The reality of clerical poverty in the first half of the sixteenth century can be explained in a number of ways. Perhaps the most fundamental of these can be given in terms of the supply of and demand for secular priests. Put most simply there were – at least until the 1540s – far more ordained priests than there were benefices, of whatever value. That situation was only made worse by the practice of pluralism: anywhere from 15 to 25 per cent of the endowed livings were served by incumbents who held more than one benefice each.[3] It follows then that most men who were ordained priest could not look forward to a career in which they rapidly stepped into a permanent, endowed post after ordination. Most would have had to make a much more precarious living as chantry priests, stipendiaries or curates. In fact, in the first three or four decades of the century the typical priest was not a vicar or rector, but one of the unbeneficed. The sources from which the number of unbeneficed clergy can be claculated give only a minimum estimate since invariably they are lists of *employed* clerics at a given time. As will become clear, there are good reasons to believe that there were, in addition to the large number of unbeneficed on tax-lists and visitation books, other ordained priests in every region who were virtually unemployed. But even the numbers of unbeneficed clergy in employment are impressive. In the archdeaconry of Leicester in 1526, for example, there were about 200 parish clergy with benefices, but in addition 250 unbeneficed – but employed – priests.[4] In Oxford archdeaconry at the same time there were 186 unbeneficed clergy in various posts, but only 164 endowed livings (some held in plurality). Approximately the same ratio was to be found in Huntingdon archdeaconry.[5] Some years later, in 1541, 324 unbeneficed clerics were employed in the diocese of Winchester, serving in about 280 parishes and chapels.[6] This last example points up the distinction between parish churches and dependent chapels. In general, the dependent chapel, although it might serve a population as large as many parish churches, did not have a permanent incumbent. In the more populous areas of southern England, East Anglia and the Midlands, where parishes had been laid out early in the Middle Ages, there were relatively few dependent chapels compared to the number of parish churches, but in other areas of the country this might not be the case. The extreme example is perhaps Lancashire, with its 100-odd dependent chapels, and only 58 parish churches. In such areas the ratio of unbeneficed to beneficed was far greater than in Lincoln or in Canterbury dioceses: Lancashire county churches and chapels were served by over 400 secular priests in the 1540s, but of those only about 10 per cent were beneficed. In the East Riding of Yorkshire in 1525 there were only about 200 beneficed clergy to the 364 without benefices but in some post.[7]

The implication of these examples is plain: up to the 1540s most parishes in the Midlands, East and South of England supported more than one cleric, although as we shall see, many of these priests lived in very poor circumstances indeed. This is not to say that all parishes had, in practice, two or more priests present and available for parochial work. Perhaps one-fifth of these were served by a curate alone, whose salary was provided by an incumbent who resided elsewhere or by a monastery which owned the rectory and did not appoint an endowed vicar. In the same Winchester diocese survey quoted earlier, a large majority of the churches listed returned the name of a curate. The churches and chapels of all the Hampshire deaneries, for example, reported curates in about 85 per cent of those listed.[8] The number of posts for curates in Kent at about the same time was somewhat less: the 1521 archdeaconry visitation of Canterbury diocese revealed curates in almost half the churches, and a 1533 subsidy list for Rochester diocese showed curates in about 44 per cent of parishes.[9] But in addition to the curates, many parishes from time to time (and more rarely, permanently) had the benefit of chantry priests as well. All of this together suggests that the demand for secular clergy up to the 1540s was far greater than the number of benefices, although not necessarily greater than the supply of ordained clergy. It is to that subject of supply that we must now turn.

A number of obstacles stand in the way of the historian who seeks to determine the total number of ordained clergy available for posts in the sixteenth century. Most damaging is the lack of complete lists of those ordained in the various dioceses. And even when ordination lists have survived without gaps for a reasonable run of years, it is impossible to know how many of those ordained remained in the diocese of their ordination to join the pool of available clergy, and how many migrated elsewhere. From the few dioceses where lists have survived one receives the impression, at least, that large numbers of men were presenting themselves for ordination in the early sixteenth century. The bishop of Lincoln, for example, was ordaining to the priesthood during the years 1514 to 1521 an average of 126 seculars and 48 regular clergy every year – that is, far in excess of the number of benefices that were likely to become available in his diocese in any given year. By the early 1530s the numbers ordained at Lincoln had dropped somewhat: between 1530 and 1535 only about 117 men per year became priests, of whom almost one-third were religious.[10] After 1536, as has been pointed out by Margaret Bowker, the numbers fell off rapidly, in Lincoln as well as in several other dioceses.[11] A similar trend, although on a smaller scale, can be seen in the lists of ordinands in the diocese of London. There during the four years from September 1522 to August 1526 over 50 priests were ordained each year (somewhat less than half of whom were religious). In the early 1530s the numbers ordained dropped: only an average of 15 per year during 1532 to 1536, more than half of whom were religious.[12] Evidence of this sort suggests that in the two or three decades before the Henrician Reformation there was in existence a very large pool of ordained clerics, not all of whom found posts and many of whom may have been frequently unemployed or at least under-employed. The realization of this surplus of priests over jobs seems to have begun to have an effect on recruitment even before 1536.

To prove that there was such a surplus of priests the historian would, ideally, compare the total number of priests available in a number of neighbouring dioceses (on the basis of complete lists of ordinands) with the number of clerics known to be in posts, beneficed or unbeneficed. Unfortunately this ideal is unattainable, because of the dearth of sources, and because of the geographical mobility among clerics: in effect the whole country would have to be the survey unit. Since systematic proof of the supply of clergy is unlikely, estimates may be attempted and circumstantial evidence of the surplus brought to bear. Something of an estimate has been made of all the clergy in Kent, as a crude sample. The method chosen provides only a minimum estimate of the numbers of priests available, and works on the assumption that emigration and immigration balanced each other. The data from the two Kentish dioceses are not exactly contemporary, but probably close enough for this exercise. In Canterbury diocese there were about 225 rectors and vicars in 1538–41 (with a death rate over the three years of less than 5 per cent). The visitation records reveal another 293 unbeneficed clergy who held posts during the period (whose mortality was unlikely to be higher than the incumbents). Rochester diocese was served by another 118 unbeneficed clerics as well as about 85 incumbents during 1533–5. Finally the archibishop's peculiar of Shoreham deanery provided posts for 35 incumbents as well as perhaps 25 unbeneficed clergy. More clergy could have been identified if all Kentish wills had been searched. But from these basic sources alone it is possible to count upwards of 750 priests holding office of some kind during a short period of years, as well as at least 175 ex-religious who were dispensed to hold secular cures between 1535 and 1541. Some idea of the over-supply of clergy can be perceived when one compares the 700 or 800 known and employed *during* the short period of years with the much smaller number of men – only 490 – who signed the acknowledgment of royal supremacy in 1534. Only that number were holding office in Kent at the same time.[13]

The surplus of clergy in the early sixteenth century can also be inferred from a different kind of evidence: that which shows the high degree of mobility among unbeneficed clergy, as well as the rapid turnover in unbeneficed posts. Here again an example is taken from parallel sets of visitations, tax-lists and curate lists from Rochester and Canterbury dioceses. The table below compares the lengths of tenure of beneficed and unbeneficed clergy, in Canterbury from lists of 1538–41 and 1550–2, and for Rochester from records of 1533–5 and 1544–6. The unbeneficed who are known to have died within the first period have been excluded. There remains a total of 269 men from the Canterbury sample and 105 from the Rochester lists.

Table 1: *Clerical longevity*

	no.	%
1. Unbeneficed clergy of Canterbury, 1538–41*		
Missing or dead by 1550–2	186	69
In same place in 1550–2	18	7
Other unbeneficed post, 1550–2	33	12.5
In a benefice in 1550–2	32	11.5
2. Unbeneficed clergy of Rochester, 1533–5†		
Missing or dead by 1544–6	77	73
In same place in 1544–6	6	7
Other unbeneficed post, 1544–6	11	10
In a benefice in 1544–6	11	10
3. Rochester beneficed clergy of 1535‡		
Missing or dead by 1544–6	28	40
In same living, 1544–6	37	54
In a different benefice, 1544–6	4	6
4. Canterbury livings in 1550–2§ (total 191 rectories, vicarages)		
Held by incumbent for 10 years or more	101	53
Held by incumbent for 5 years or more	59	30
Held by incumbent for less than 5 years	31	17

* *Source*: Canterbury Cathedral Library, MSS. Z/3/5, 6.
† *Source*: Kent AO, DRa/Vb/4 and DRc/R/8.
‡ *Source*: Kent AO, DRa/Vb/4 and DRc/R/7–8; *Valor Ecclesiasticus*.
§ *Source*: Canterbury Cathedral Library, MS. Z/3/6;LPL, Regs. Warham and Cranmer. There were less than 191 individuals as some were pluralists.

The instability in the careers of the unbeneficed, as compared to the incumbents, is quite marked; it is even more pronounced if the chantry priests are distinguished from the rest of the unbeneficed. On average the holders of endowed chantries seemed to have retained their positions longer than did most curates. Thus of the 18 Canterbury diocese unbeneficed who did remain in the same place over the period 1538–41 to 1550–2, only 12 were curates or their equivalent, chaplains with cure of souls for a dependent chapel. R. A. Christophers has found a similar situation in sixteenth-century Surrey: 'the most notable feature of the records of curates is how short a time they spent in any one parish'. Of the 34 named curates in the 1517 Leicester archdeaconry visitation, 28 had moved by 1526.[14] It is unfortunate that complete series of annual visitations for extended periods have not generally survived, for from them an historian could present systematic evidence of the turnover in unbeneficed posts. An alternative source on this question is the witness lists found at the end of last wills and testaments. A continuous series of wills from a populous parish may sometimes provide a running list of most of the unbeneficed who served even for short periods in the parish. They and the visitation books reveal a very rapid turnover of 'chaplains' and 'parish priests'. In Halden, a small parish in Kent, there were four different curates during the years 1501 to 1506.[15] In another Kent parish, Smarden, the curate in 1510 was Athelstan Astley, in 1512 it was William Carnell; during 1513 to 1515 the parish priest was John Glasier; in 1517 the curate was a Thomas (or William) Gervase, followed by Richard Wakefield and John Edgeworth in 1521.[16] The imperfect evidence of wills and visitation call books from Kent at least suggests that most parishes were introduced to a new curate every two or three years, although tenures of five-years or so were not uncommon. All of this material indicates that clergy were easily found and just as easily sacked.

The life of the unbeneficed was characterized by geographical but not economic mobility. Normally he moved from one parish to another in the same diocese. George Jeffrayson moved from Mereworth to Hadlow to Luddesdon (all in Kent) during the years 1544–6. His colleague Martin Huggard, curate of Kingsdown in Rochester diocese in 1544, moved in the following year to be curate of Trottiscliffe, four or five miles away.[17] Many unbeneficed seem to have been employed in one parish and subsequently disappear from the surviving records. Common sense suggests that not all of these clerics had died. Many must have moved out of the diocese; some were probably without a full-time post for periods of years, and others would have moved to similar posts for equally short periods, although the record of their tenures do not survive in the extant records. Only a few obtained benefices.

That a surplus of clergy existed in the early sixteenth century may also be inferred from one other fact: the very meagre salaries necessary to attract them to a post. The normal wage of a curate, a stipendiary or the chaplain of a dependent chapel was no more than incumbents or appropriators might offer, and in many cases the stipends appear to be barely at subsistence level and occasionally below that. Stipends were regulated only by an early fifteenth-century statute, which set a *maximum* level of eight marks (£5 6s. 8d.) *per annum*.[18] Evidence from the first half of the sixteenth century, from all regions of England, indicates that very rarely were curates and chaplains given more than that, while the general level of prices had risen considerably since the mid-fifteenth century. In different parts of the country the usual stipends varied by as much as one-third, with those in the South-East obtaining the highest salaries, if salaries of £5 or £6 can be thought of as 'high' at all. In Kent during the 1520s to 1540s the norm for curates was in the range of £5 to £6 *per annum*, but there were frequent exceptions, usually below that norm in the 1520s and 1530s, and above £6 *per annum* in the 1540s and 1550s. In the 1520s in Lincoln diocese the average stipend was comparable, at just over £5 *per annum*.[19] But in regions more distant from the metropolis the stipends were usually less munificent. The average salary of about 100 curates and chaplains in north Lancashire in 1524 was just £2 9s. 6d. *per annum*. In the East Riding in 1525–6 the normal wage for curates and chaplains was about £4 *per annum*. Speaking about the salaries of curates and chantry priests in Rutland in the 1520s, which averaged over £5 *per annum*, Julian Cornwall has pointed out that at that level unbeneficed clerics with a post were little better off than labourers, and decidedly poorer than resident vicars in the county. An annual stipend of £5 or £6 would correspond to a daily wage rate of 4d. *per diem*, no more than unskilled labourers were receiving before the 1530s.[20] In 1538 Archbishop Lee of York thought that eight marks was an insufficient stipend for a cleric with cure of souls, even in the North. In practice many assistant clergy were receiving substantially less than that at the time he was writing.[21]

Amongst the unbeneficed, chantry priests, especially those who held posts in permanently endowed foundations, appear to have been slightly better off. In distant Lancashire the average chantry priest received about £4 *per annum* in the early sixteenth century, substantially more than the assistant chaplains. In Gloucestershire by the 1540s, almost all chantrists received wages of between £5 and £7 *per annum* and in Kent the normal annual wage of a chantry priest, at the end of the fifteenth century as in the 1520s, was ten marks (£6 13s. 4d.). A Lincoln diocese tax-list of the early sixteenth century shows also that chantrists frequently obtained slightly higher stipends than other unbeneficed.[22] Given the additional fact that the duties of a chantry priest were normally far less onerous than those of a curate, appointment as a chantrist may have been more desirable a post than a curacy. Nevertheless it is probable that the great majority of clerics who served as chantry priests did so for relatively short periods, and that the holders of posts in permanent foundations were in a minority.

How did the unbeneficed survive on salaries like these? The short answer is, probably with great difficulty. It must have been a struggle for many of them in the 1520s and 1530s just to find steady employment. Even in the 1540s, though the number of new ordinands added to the labour pool decreased substantially, the supply of available clerics probably remained high because of the large number of former monks, canons and friars who joined the scramble for ecclesiastical posts.[23] Priests without benefices, even in employment, sought to augment their basic salaries by a variety of means, some involving part-time ecclesiastical jobs and others wholly lay occupations. The minimal stipends paid to assistant clergy in Lancashire drove many to secular pursuits. Christopher Haigh discovered a number of unbeneficed clerics there working as farmers, one employed as a sheep merchant and several who turned to fraud for a living. Many a curate who worked for an absentee incumbent may have earned more than his basic stipend if he received the incidental offerings of his parishioners or bequests in their wills. It seems likely that many non-resident incumbents leased their benefices to local men, who sometimes included the curate. In 1508 the curate of Biddenden, Kent, William Stamyden, was one of the joint farmers of the rectory. Forty years later the curate of All Hallows, Bread Street, London 'farmeth the parsonage'. Their share in such leases must have improved their livings considerably. How exceptional these examples are is anyone's guess.[24]

Unbeneficed clerics most commonly augmented their basic earnings with incidental religious duties. Up to the 1540s extra income would have come most commonly from occasional masses paid for by bequests of parishioners who had recently died. Even relatively poor men left small sums of money for their funerals and month's minds. Half a mark (6s. 8d.) for each occasion was commonly left by countrymen and their widows to hire a few priests (the usual fee was 6d. or 8d. for the day) and to provide a few shillings' worth of food doles to the local poor. Somewhat more wealthy testators left larger sums for their funerals, month's and year's minds – perhaps £1 or £2 in all – and in addition left conventional amounts for extra intercessory masses for their souls. In Kent in the first 30 years of the century a trental of masses – that is 30 masses – cost 10s. The less wealthy could emulate their richer neighbours by hiring chantry priests for periods of less than a full year: the going rate in the 1520s was £1 13s. 4d. for 3 months and five marks for 6 months.[25] The very frequency with which these bequests appear in wills suggests that there would have been no difficulty at all in obtaining the part-time services of secular priests in the vicinity, whether the masses were sung by employed but underpaid curates and chantrists, or by unemployed clerics in search of any income at all. There appear to have been no stringent rules about how these extra duties were allotted. Occasionally testators specify a particular cleric in their testaments; sometimes they give their curate or incumbent the first refusal to do the services and stipulate that if he will not take on the job he should appoint some other acceptable priest. In most cases it was left to executors to find a priest for these short periods and they must have turned to the parish priest for advice, unless a relation of theirs or of the deceased was himself a priest. Apparently there was nothing in canon law to prevent a cleric from taking on more than one of these contracts as 'soul priest'. That they often moved beyond the parish church in which they were first employed to sing masses for other men is suggested by the requests in two wills of 1521. Thomas Woodnett of Ospringe, Kent, left £7 to hire a chantry priest for one year, 'with condition that he shall go to none other obits during the said year.' A Rolvenden man specified that the chantry priest hired for him shall 'keep the parish church of Rolvenden for the most part, unless it be at the desire and request of some trusty friend, the space of iii, iiii or v days in a quarter to be at liberty'.[26] Inspection of a large number of early sixteenth-century wills from three or four neighbouring parishes will show that during most years there was enough extra employment of this nature to occupy several clerics in at least one or two of the parishes. The likelihood of being selected to perform such services was probably greater for natives of the parish or district, and some clerics may have eked out a living in this manner until they obtained a curacy or permanent chaplaincy, or if they were exceptionally lucky or well-connected, a benefice.

The death of a wealthy squire or nobleman must have been of enormous value to the neighbouring clergy, since it usually entailed elaborate and costly burial rites with many anniversary masses and obits, all employing extra priestly labour. Sir William Crowmer, a Kentish squire who died in 1539, left 20 marks for clerics and alms at his burial, the same amount at his month's mind and £5 for masses and doles at his first anniversary. Beyond that his executors were instructed to pay five priests 4s. each to sing masses for his soul at a neighbouring parish church.[27] The scale of a nobleman's funeral arrangement would have been correspondingly greater and almost certainly would have included provision for one or more chantry priests for periods of one year at least.

One other source of extra income for the unbeneficed did survive the 1540s: additional clergy might be employed by a parish or incumbent at the busiest times of the ecclesiastical year, although the need for extra clerical labour at Easter and Christmas and the like was probably limited to the more populous parishes. At St Mary's, Dover, for example, the churchwardens hired two additional priests in 1542 or 1543 to help out at Easter, at a cost of 3s. 4d. plus meals. They also hired a priest on All Hallow's Day and on All Soul's Day, at a cost of 6d. *per diem*.[28] The continued requirement of taking Easter communion, throughout the period under consideration, may have been beyond the resources of many churches, and thus provided extra clerical employment. Before the late 1540s there was no lack of available clergy to take up such part-time employment.

Nothing has been said about benefices thus far, and with good reason. By and large, at least until the 1550s, the unbeneficed clergy (employed or unemployed) formed a distinct layer in the clerical hierarchy, below the class of parochial incumbents. Most incumbents do not seem to have spent a significant period of their careers as curates or chaplains, and most unbeneficed clerics were likely to remain without a permanent living for most or all of their careers. Expressed in modern terms, there was no common career structure shared by all entering clergy by which a new ordinand could advance from unbeneficed to beneficed post. As can be deduced from the examples given above of the large supply of ordinands and of the greater number of unbeneficed than beneficed posts, the yeoman's son who became a cleric in his twenties had no guaranteed prospect of a benefice in the future. He could most likely look forward to a life of narrow income and minimal job security. There would be periods in his career when he lived in real poverty, although many poor priests may have received financial support from their families. The poverty can be inferred from the tiny stipends, the lack of security and from the frequency with which a given cleric appears once or twice in the extant records and then disappears without a trace. When the records are exceptionally full many clerics can be traced through a succession of posts, often with long gaps between appearances. Take Adam Arrowsmith of Kent, for example. He appears first as a stipendiary priest at Wateringbury in Rochester diocese in 1523; his second and last appearance occurs 15 years later, when he was curate of Frittenden in Canterbury diocese. After that, nothing. Perhaps 10 or 15 per cent of the unbeneficed clergy managed to acquire a living in mid-career, and it is at this level that one finds the only movement of significant numbers of clerics between the levels of the clerical hierarchy. The career of William Barforth, a Kentish priest, typifies this mobility. He is found first as chaplain of Hoo, St Werburgh, in Rochester diocese, in 1524. By the early 1530s he had moved to Ospringe deanery in Canterbury diocese, where he signed the oath against the Pope. He disappears again, to reappear in 1541 as curate of Newenham in the same region. Finally two years later he was presented by the Crown to a poor benefice in the same deanery, which he was to hold for two years before he died.[29] The figures set out in the table above give an equally clear idea of how little upward mobility could be expected by the unbeneficed in the 1530s and 1540s. That most unbeneficed clergy could not expect to find a benefice is borne out by the number of institutions to benefices each year. In Canterbury diocese (with Shoreham peculiar) between 1534 and 1552 there were slightly less than 400 institutions, about 20 per year, of which about two-thirds were because of the death of an incumbent. But even these 20 notional livings were reduced by the fact that some were due to exchanges between two incumbents, and others went to men who already held one or more benefices. Given the number of available priests in Kent, these figures suggest only very limited opportunities before the end of Edward VI's reign.

Similar findings about the limits of clerical mobility are reported from other dioceses and countries. In Leicestershire, for example, 'promotion to a benefice appears to have absorbed only a small proportion' of the unbeneficed. Taking as his sample the unbeneficed clergy who appeared in visitations between 1517 and 1536. J. F. Fuggles found that only nine of the curates in the whole archdeaconry found a benefice between 1520 and 1547. A similar lack of advancement was the lot of the unbeneficed in Surrey. Of the 137 men who appear in Bishop Horne's ordination lists in the 1560s, only ten could be traced to benefices in Surrey. Taking in a much longer period of time, R. A. Christophers discovered only 36 curates who managed to acquire benefices during the century, 1520–1620, half of whom moved into livings between 1550 and 1570. In the diocese of Lincoln as a whole most ordinands of the first two decades of the century did not obtain benefices. In the North-West, as we have seen, the prospect of obtaining a benefice for most clergy was next to nil, due to the exceptionally small number of endowed livings and the attractiveness of so many of them to well-connected pluralists from outside the county. For most Lancashire ordinands the best chance of obtaining a benefice was to emigrate. In general then, it seems that throughout England until almost mid-century, the balance of supply and demand worked against the prospects of advancement for most clergy. The average ordinand, without a university education and without influential relations, found himself in competition with thousands of his fellows for the small number of benefices which became vacant each year, and was most likely happy indeed to be settled in a chantry post, a chaplaincy or a curacy with a stipend of between £4 and £6 *per annum*, even if the chances of holding that post for many years were not high. They only rarely became vicars or rectors, and were, in Fuggles' phrase, the 'professionally unbeneficed, who spent all their lives as deputies'.[30]

Taking a much longer view, the first decades of the sixteenth century may well have been a period of exceptionally high recruitment into the clergy, with all the consequences described above lasting well into the 1540s. As has already been noted, the period of high recruitment came to an end in the 1530s, a time which ushered in two decades of great uncertainty and flux in ecclesiastical life, which in part helps to explain the drastic fall-off in ordinations. The theological concomitant of the Reformation also reduced the demand for a major form of clerical employment – intercessory masses for the souls of the dead – while at the same time it set forth a new model of the Protestant parochial clergyman as a highly-educated, resident, preaching minister. The middle decades of the century may still have been difficult for the already-existing clerical labour force, augmented as it was by several thousand ex-religious seeking employment. There was always a good deal of slack to take up, for as well as the ex-monks and friars, there were also all those who had been chantry priests or who had lived from hand to mouth by singing masses for short periods (though the permanent chantry priests as well as most ex-monks received pensions from the Crown until they found new ecclesiastical employment). Nevertheless, the indications are that in the course of the 1540s and 1550s the log-jam began slowly to break up. Margaret Bowker found that of the men ordained at Lincoln in 1537, 18 per cent had obtained a benefice by 1544, and of those ordained in 1538 more than one-fifth had a benefice by 1544: still a minority of ordinands, yet a much larger minority than would have obtained livings so quickly ten years earlier.[31] Given the reduced number of ordinations, many men who had been in unbeneficed posts for years may have found new opportunities in the Edwardian and especially the Marian years (if the religious changes did not put them off). In the mid-1550s the log-jam was further broken by the deprivations of many incumbents who had taken the opportunity to marry between 1547 and 1553. Further vacancies were caused by the widespread epidemic mortality of the last few years of Mary's reign, so potent that 'divers places were left void of ancient justices . . . at this time also died many priests, that a great number of parish churches in divers places of the realm were unserved and no curates could be gotten for money.'[32] To complete this reversal of the earlier situation, the first few years of Elizabeth's reign saw further deprivations of non-conforming incumbents.[33] By 1559 the total number of clergy had fallen considerably, the number of unbeneficed declined enormously. Some churches could be found ministers only with great difficulty and rare indeed was the parish with more than one cleric. Of course it was not only the economic equation of supply and demand; many conservative clerics would not serve under the new Elizabethan Protestant dispensation. But willingness to blow with the prevailing theological winds was an outstanding trait of most sixteenth-century parish clergy, and the relative dearth of willing ministers in the 1560s was in the main not the result of tender consciences but of an absolute decline in numbers due to a combination of short-term demographic circumstances and the medium-term fall-off in recruitment to what was seen as not the most attractive profession. The Queen's Injunctions of 1559 admitted that 'in these latter days many have been made priests, being children, and otherwise utterly unlearned, so that they could [only] read to say matins or mass.' This evident insufficiency of Protestant clergy resulted in mass-ordinations of hundreds of ordinands by several bishops during 1559–61, and in the widespread appointment of 'readers', laymen hired for short periods to read from the Bible and the new prayer book.[34] Given this changed situation, most ordinands who sought clerical employment obtained a benefice or at least a semi-permanent post quite quickly in the early Elizabethan period. The use of unbeneficed clergy in general declined, partly due to the universal fall in numbers, and partly because of the more strict enforcement of the rules against pluralism.[35] Ironically, in some districts pluralism continued to be a necessity in the 1560s and 1570s because of the dearth of qualified clergy and the unwillingness of clergy to accept appointment to some of the very poor benefices. And where dependent chapels still existed in large numbers, or where there was a high concentration of ecclesiastics, the stipends of the unbeneficed remained very low. In a survey of south Lancashire parishes in 1590 it was found that the 17 chapel curates had average incomes of less than £4 *per annum*, that is, in real terms, less than their predecessors 50 years earlier. The wages of ministers of unendowed parishes and of suburban curates in Surrey too had not kept pace with rising prices, the norm in 1603 being between £10 and £12 *per annum*.[36] In the second half of the sixteenth century there remained in existence a clerical proletariat, even though far reduced in numbers from the thousands in that position in the 1520s.

II

Clerical poverty in the second half of the sixteenth century appears to have been less the consequence of an over-abundant supply of ministers, than of a relatively large number of under-endowed livings, some of which simply could not support an Elizabethan incumbent and his family. That this situation had evolved could be blamed, historically at least, on the vagaries of the original endowments of many parish churches from Anglo-Saxon times onwards, on the changes in the geographical distribution of population and of different types of agriculture, and on the fact that neither the State nor the Church in earlier centuries had found it either necessary or useful to demand a minimum level of endowment for all parochial livings. In theory all parish churches were endowed with certain revenues: the main sources being the tithes of all the produce of husbandry in the parish,

various regular offerings and irregular fees paid by parishioners for
the spiritual services provided, and finally, a house and glebe land for
the priest's basic subsistence needs. However, the level of endowment
varied enormously from parish to parish, and the inequality of provision was made more complicated by the diversion of a large share of
the income of many churches to monasteries, hospitals and colleges
which *owned* them. For a church and its revenues were in common
law units of real property, and thus could be bought or exchanged by
individuals or persons corporate – such as abbeys. Canon law in the
Middle Ages only obliged the owner of a church – in the case of a monastery he was referred to as the *appropriator* – to provide an ordained
priest to serve the cure of souls, and nothing more: the law did not
require the abbey to allow its priest to receive the full revenues of his
church. A major part of the income was thus 'appropriated' to the
monastery or college. To control the inevitable abuses which this
practice entailed, the Church in the course of the Middle Ages increasingly required appropriators to set aside part of the income of such
churches as a permanent endowment for the priest on the ground: he,
the deputy, or vicar, then became possessed of the *vicarage*. The
division of a parish church's revenue was not identical in all cases of
diversion: in fact it varied widely. The most common practice was for
the appropriator to retain the tithes of grain and hay (the rectorial
tithes), which were usually the largest component of tithe income in
the parish, as well as frequently holding on to the glebe as well. The
vicar was then left with all manner of other tithes, a house and the
offerings and fees paid by parishioners. Frequently all or part of the
glebe was part of the vicarage as well. But other combinations are frequently found, as well as the arrangement by which the appropriator
collected all the revenues and then paid the vicar a cash stipend. No
general rules can be made about the division of parochial revenues
between appropriator and vicar, but all the various combinations resulted in the parish incumbent not receiving all the revenues paid by the
parishioners, in theory, to support him. Table 2 shows the different
types and proportions of revenues received by a number of relatively
poor incumbents in 1535.

By the sixteenth century about one-third of all parish churches were
appropriated and their revenues diverted. The churches that
remained, the rectories, tended to be worth, on average, at least
several pounds *per annum* more than the value of vicarages in the
same area. In Lancashire the disparity was much greater: £34 *per
annum* average for rectories as against £12 *per annum* for vicarages.
On the other hand, in Surrey the average difference was less than £2
per annum[37]. But in this case averages are somewhat misleading: in
any diocese there was a large minority of poor benefices, many of

Table 2: *Types of revenue of some parochial benefices, 1535*

Sutton Nicholas (Herefords.) rectory		Sandon (Staffs.) rectory	
	%		%
Grain tithes	45	Grain tithes	29
Wool/lamb tithes	11	Wool/lamb tithes	40
Other tithes	6	Other tithes	40
Offerings	15	Offerings	24
House/glebe	23	House/glebe	1

Total £8 17s. 6d.

(*Valor Ecclesiasticus*, III, 36)

Total £8 6s.

(*Valor Ecclesiasticus*, III, 121)

Wellington (Herefords.) vicarage		Upton Episcopi (Herefords.) vicarage	
	%		%
Grain tithes	20	Grain tithes	25
Wool/lamb tithes	18	Wool/lamb tithes	18
Other tithes	15	Other tithes	27
Offerings	42	Offerings	9
House/glebe	5	House/glebe	15
		Annual pension	1

Total £6 13s. 4d.

(*Valor Ecclesiasticus*, III, 35)

Total £9 1s. 10d.

(*Valor Ecclesiasticus*, III, 24)

Pattingham (Staffs.) vicarage		Wadworth (Yorks.) vicarage	
	%		%
Grain tithes	nil	Hay tithes	3
Wool/lamb tithes	44	Wool/lamb tithes	17
Other tithes	7	Other tithes	13
Offerings	25	Offerings	50
From annexed chapel	17	House/glebe	17
Annual pension	6		

Total £8

(*Valor Ecclesiasticus*, III, 100)

Total £4 2s. 6d.

(*Valor Ecclesiasticus*, V, 53)

them rectories, in which the incumbent did receive all the revenues. In these cases the problem lay not with greedy monks or overfed scholars, but with the endowment itself: the parish was either too small or too poor, or possibly the church had not been endowed with sufficient glebe in the first place. Perhaps not atypical of this wide variation in the value of benefices were the livings in Kent in the 1530s. In Canterbury diocese 31 (or 13 per cent) of the 230 normally-served livings were worth less than £6 *per annum*, according to the *Valor Ecclesiasticus*, and another 49 were worth between £6 and £8 *per annum*. In Rochester diocese 13 per cent were valued at under £6 *per annum* and a further 22 per cent at between £6 and £8 *per annum*. Even if these livings were under-assessed by 10 or 15 per cent, the figures nevertheless suggest that upwards of one-third of the livings in the county were worth less than what might be considered a minimum income for an incumbent who attempted to fulfil the various duties expected of him — about £10 *per annum* gross. A comparable situation existed in the large diocese of Coventry and Lichfield, where 10 per cent of all livings were rated at less than £5 *per annum*, and 60 per cent at less than £10 *per annum*. As in Kent, the poor benefices were almost as frequently rectories as vicarages: half of the rectories and 72 per cent of the vicarages were valued at less than £10 *per annum*. Poor livings were likely to be concentrated in large towns and cities, and in areas which had been more populous or more wealthy in the Middle Ages than they were in the sixteenth century. In Canterbury in 1535 five of the town livings were rated at £5 *per annum* or less. York too had many poor urban benefices, and in Chester all but two of the town livings were worth considerably less than the majority of benefices in the surrounding countryside.[38]

The consequences of this maldistribution of parochial revenues, as between appropriator and vicar and between one living and another, came to be fully appreciated and commented upon in the sixteenth century, especially in the context of the Protestant emphasis on the need for an educated minister in every parish. No longer could the uneducated priest be tolerated, the priest described in unflattering terms by Thomas Lever in 1550:

> Yes, forsooth, he ministreth God's sacraments, he saith his service and he readeth the Homilies . . . but the rude lobs of the country, which be too simple to paint a lie, speak foul and truly as they find it, and say: he minishes God's sacraments, he flubbers up his service, and he cannot read his Humbles.

It was assumed by all parties to the Elizabethan debate on the clergy that graduate, preaching clerics would only take up livings which were reasonably endowed, and the converse, that only a Church with well-endowed parochial livings would attract into its ranks the kind of educated men it desired in the first place. In the course of the 1540s and 1550s appropriate rectories had often become *impropriated* rectories as the great bulk of ex-monastic livings were transferred by the Crown to the laity (and to a lesser extent to bishops and cathedral chapters). Nothing had changed fundamentally from the point of view of the vicars holding those livings: for one thing, most monasteries had farmed the rectorial tithes and glebes of the churches they owned to laymen before 1536, and so in many cases only the legal ownership changed at the time of the Dissolution.[39]

By the 1560s several important changes had occurred which affected all incumbents, whether vicars or rectors. To begin with, the amount of money extracted from the parochial clergy in the form of royal taxation grew as a result of the Act of First Fruits and Tenths: from the late 1530s all livings were obliged to pay a tenth each year in tax to the Crown (calculated on the basis of the assessments of 1535) and all incumbents had to pay first fruits upon their institution to a living, a sum equal to one year's revenue of the benefice. Prior to that the parochial clergy had been subject only to irregular royal taxes.[40]

All parish clergy were also bound to feel the impact of the price rise of the mid and late sixteenth century, although the consequences for some might be vastly different than for others. In the face of rapid inflation the parochial incumbent was similarly placed as lay landowners: if his revenues were leased or in the form of fixed or commuted money payments, he was in dire trouble. If, on the other hand, his land was in hand and directly farmed, and other revenues received in kind, he was in a position to ride with the tide of rising prices, or in some cases even to benefit by the extra demand for agricultural produce. As a loose rule, also, the more glebe an incumbent had during this period, the more likely was he to be cushioned from the impact of rising prices. At this point the historian attempting to assess the results of these changes in expenditure and cost of living for the average incumbent must avoid simple answers; for there was no *average* incumbent, and there are no systematic data available on the economic conditions of all or most clergy. The most damaging gaps in the evidence are the lack of records about the leasing of revenue and land by incumbents, and, equally important, the lack of any systematic evidence about the extent of commutation of tithes for money payments by impropriators and incumbents.

Some generalizations, however, can be ventured about the capacity of benefices to keep pace with prices over a much longer period by comparing the 1535 values with the values given for the same livings in the parliamentary surveys of the Interregnum period. Christopher Hill's study of a sample of benefices over that time-span showed that the rectories had grown in value (in money terms) faster than the sample vicarages – 549 per cent as compared to 404 per cent. Both types of livings had more than kept pace with the long-term price rise of common consumables over the same period.[41] Interesting as these findings are, they cannot inform us about how late-sixteenth century clerics were coping with the economic climate of their time. Were the increases Hill reveals continuous or did they come only in the seventeenth century? For the Elizabethan incumbent the availability of glebe land must have been of cardinal importance. Something is known about the extent of parochial glebes in a number of areas of England, but how typical these samples are remains open. In Warwickshire, for example, the vast majority of rural livings were endowed with some glebe; and, more specifically, 87 per cent of the rectories and 40 per cent of the vicarages had substantial glebe lands. The average country living in Warwickshire possessed 25 to 75 acres of land. In Sussex most of the rectories and 40 per cent of the vicarages had at least 5 acres of glebe. In another sample, taken from the exceptionally detailed valuations given in the *Valor* for four deaneries in Gloucestershire, only seven of the 60 livings had little or no glebe in 1535; 13 others had less than one virgate or less than 25 acres, while two-thirds of all benefices had a virgate or more of land. Twenty-six of the 60 livings had quite considerable lands.[42]

The values given for land in the Gloucestershire sample can be translated, even if crudely, to other assessments in the *Valor* where the value of the glebe is stated, but not the acreage. A typical glebe in Gloucestershire of around 25 acres of arable and two or three acres of meadow was valued by the commissioners at about 15 shillings *per annum*. Glebe lands valued at £1 per annum or thereabouts represented a substantial smallholding of more than a virgate along with a reasonable amount of meadow and pasture. This shorthand method of estimating the extent of land is hardly foolproof, because the *Valor* never gives a breakdown of the revenues of a living if it has been leased to a farmer, and thus a large share of livings must be left out of the calculations. But even with these dangers, the method is worth applying. Take the deaneries of Honiton, Kenne and Dunkswill in Devon. There the great majority of livings for which specific values are given had moderately extensive lands attached: only four of 29 livings possessed no glebe or glebe valued at less than £1 *per annum*. It is possible, but unlikely, that all the livings that were farmed had no glebe. A much more patchy picture is found in two Herefordshire deaneries, where 14 of 23 rectories and vicarages had glebes valued at under 15s. *per annum*. But only four – three rectories and one vicarage – reported no income from glebe land at all.[43]

Besides glebe land, the other sources of incumbents' income were exceedingly varied. For most rectories, tithes were the largest single source of revenue, and of these the 'great tithes' of grain and hay were usually the most valuable. As can be seen from table 2 or any of the more detailed valors of benefices in the pages of *Valor Ecclesiasticus*, vicars rarely received more than a small share of the great tithes, and usually depended heavily on the tithes of wool and lambs. If collected in kind, tithes of all sorts would have provided incumbents with a bulwark against inflation. But even before the mid-sixteenth century certain tithes on perishable goods and on newborn livestock (where the number was not usually divisible by ten had been commuted to fixed money equivalents, which were unlikely to rise as prices in general rose. Urban incumbents were normally the greatest sufferers

from tithe commutation, because the personal tithes on income were
the most subject to evasion, and most likely to have been commuted
early. In the countryside the picture was not all one of gloom for
incumbents. The studies of D. M. Barratt on the west Midlands and of
Stephen Lander on Sussex both indicate that most tithes of husbandry
had not been commuted for fixed money payments in the sixteenth
century.[44] And, since most incumbents did not hold urban livings,
most would not have suffered the consequences of commuted personal tithes or from the fixed payments arranged in lieu of tithe on
rental income from urban land and houses, as for example in London.
In the countryside the most seriously at risk were vicarages with little
or no glebe, or where the vicar had little or no share in the tithes, or –
the worst case – where the vicar was paid a stipend in cash. The more
an incumbent depended on parishioners' offerings and fees, the more
likely was he to suffer from the fall in the value of money. However,
probably only a small minority of vicars depended on a money stipend
alone: most got at least a share in the tithe income. Without doubt,
though, the rector whose benefice was not leased out was in a better
position to cope with economice changes than was a vicar in the same
circumstances. For one, rectors tended to have more glebe than vicars.
Even more important, the value of the grain tithes received by rectors
was likely to rise more steeply than the value of the tithes on lambs and
wool, in a period when food prices were generally running ahead of
meat and wool prices. To the extent that farmers in his parish converted from livestock to arable farming in the course of the sixteenth
century, the vicar would again tend to be the loser, while the rector or
the owner of the rectorial tithes would be the beneficiary.

Looking over the whole of the century, most poor livings remained
so although the money value had risen. In Surrey an increasing gap
between poorer and richer benefices had opened up by the early seventeenth century; the wealthier livings were worth £100 to £200 *per
annum* in the Jacobean period, while many poor livings received not
very much more than they had done in the 1540s.[45] That this should
have been the case follows from what has been said about the relative
size of glebes and the importance of the great tithes. But it should be recalled that poor livings were not novel in Elizabethan England: there
were plenty of poor livings in the first half of the sixteenth century, but
much less likelihood that they would go begging for lack of candidates
to sue for them. The economic problems of the clergy did not begin
with the arrival of 'Tawney's century'. The controversy in the Elizabethan period on issue of inadequately-endowed livings was as much the
result of the fact that the dearth of qualified ministers meant that the
poorest livings could not find incumbents – or were only held in plurality – as it was based on Protestant theological ideas about a well-paid

and well-educated parish clergy. As was reported in 1563, 13 vacant livings in Ely diocese could not be filled 'for the exility of the living'.[46]

Archbishop Whitgift's assertion in 1585 that half the livings in the country were worth less than £10 *per annum* must be seen in its context before the simple, but erroneous, conclusion is reached that half of all English incumbents were starving in the 1580s, as they would have been if their incomes had actually been less than that amount. Whitgift here was not talking utter nonsense, but had in mind the values of livings given in the *Valor* of 50 years earlier.[47] Since the historian has no foolproof sources for the actual incomes received by the parish clergy in the later sixteenth century, it is perhaps not unjustified that he turn to less than perfect evidence for some crude estimates rather than admit total defeat. One such source is the great survey of the clergy, compiled by Puritan clerics in many parts of the country with the intention of influencing the Parliament of 1586. It has been used by ecclesiastical historians for the material it contains about the morals and educational attainments of the parish clergy. But in addition, some of the compilers added to their 'findings' about the incumbents a note of the contemporary value of the livings. Such coverage of livings in Berkshire and Cornwall is among the best in the Puritan survey and, when compared with the 1535 valuations in the *Valor*, give a rough and ready guide to the increase in money values of the livings in the intervening period. Livings whose value had less than doubled by 1586 were obviously falling behind, those that trebled in value were certainly holding their own, and those that more than trebled were probably becoming more valuable to their holders.

The results of this comparison between 'official' valors from 1535 and unofficial estimates of 1586 differ somewhat between Berkshire and Cornwall, but both samples reinforce the claim that most livings were improving in value in money terms and at least, on average, keeping pace with inflation. In the Berkshire sample, of 36 vicarages and 30 rectories, the average rectory rose in value by over 300 per cent, whereas vicarages increased in value by only 220 per cent. There the difference in average value between rectories and vicarages in 1535 had been less than £3 *per annum*. In Cornwall, with a sample of 45 vicarages and 31 rectories, the average rise in the value of both types of living was more than three-fold, with the vicarages increasing slightly more than the rectories. The significant difference between the two samples was that the Cornwall rectories had been substantially more valuable than the vicarages in 1535, but had subsequently risen in value less than the vicarages. Of course these figures are just averages, and the data for individual churches reveal much greater variation. Some benefices grew five-, six- or even seven-fold over the 1535 values, while some few had not even doubled. In the four

Cornish deaneries, seven of the 76 livings for which there are valuations in both years failed to double in value. However, all but one of these were not among the poorest livings in 1535. In the two Berkshire deaneries 11 out of 66 livings failed to double in value, some of which benefices had been among the poor livings in 1535. There remained, as there had been in 1535, a minority of obviously poor livings in both counties: in Cornwall nine livings out of 76 were assessed by the Puritan ministers at less than £30 *per annum*. In Berkshire the percentage was higher: 14 livings out of 66 rated at less than £30 *per annum*. The poor livings of 1586 had also been poor livings 50 years earlier, although in some cases they had increased in money value by three- or four-fold during the five decades. The individual benefices which had increased least in value since 1535 were mainly vicarages, though not all the vicarages shared this distinction. The exercise suggests one moral: although in general parochial benefices at least doubled in value between 1535 and 1586, some few had been so poor already in 1535 that even a doubling or trebling in their incomes could not raise them to what might be thought a minimum standard of maintenance for a resident, preaching minister.[48]

III

Any conclusions about clerical poverty can only be tentative and tenuous, for what is most striking is the amazing variety of economic conditions over time and from place to place in England. The reader will already have perceived from the material offered here that the poor clergyman was a reality in Tudor England, especially in the decades before 1560 when the abundance of ordained clerics made any benefice, no matter how poor, the object of intense competition. Although it is likely that very few, if any, actually starved, thousands joined the ranks of the clergy with little prospect of job security or even a modicum of wealth: the average country priest could not have been a person of high social status. The small number of moderately-endowed and wealthy livings were in practice reserved for those with either social connection or university education. In the Elizabethan period, the balance of supply and demand was at least temporarily reversed, the number of unbeneficed dropped steadily and hundreds if not thousands of prospective clerics began to emerge from the universities. In the meantime, however, the inequality of livings still prevailed, even if the income of most just managed to keep pace with the rising level of prices. The economic structure of parochial organization had not been modified to fit the new demands of Protestant theology. In more practical terms there were not enough of the type of benefice which had previously satisfied the minority of well-educated clerics in 1535 to support what was becoming a majority of clerics in the 1580s and 1590s.[49] The economic problems of the Church had not changed so much as the expectations of the clergy and of some of their more articulate Protestant parishioners. The exploitation of the revenues of parochial livings by laymen was not a post-Reformation phenomenon. Nor was the diversion of parochial endowments into the coffers of other ecclesiastics much less important than it had been before the Dissolution: many Elizabethan bishops and colleges depended heavily on their revenues from rectorial tithes. There was no single solution. Lay Puritan critics asserted that the blame was to be laid at the door of 'wealthy' bishops and their chapters, while the bishops claimed that the heart of the problem lay in the greed of laymen. With such powerful interests in near-total disagreement, is it surprising that the sixteenth century failed to find a solution to the problem of clerical poverty?

NOTES

1. *Medieval Clerical Accounts*, (1964), 5.
2. For permanently-endowed chantries see K. L. Wood-Legh, *Perpetual Chantries in Britain* (1965). Many of the Edwardian chantry certificates have been printed by local record societies, as have a number of churchwardens' accounts.
3. See, for example, M. Bowker, *The Secular Clergy in the Diocese of Lincoln, 1495–1520* (1968), 73, 90; M. L. Zell, 'The personnel of the clergy in Kent, in the Reformation period', *EHR*, LXXXIX (1974), 531–2.
4. J. F. Fuggles, 'The parish clergy in the archdeaconry of Leicester, 1520–1540'. *Trans. Leics. Arch. and Hist. Soc.*, XLVI (1970–1), 26.
5. *A Subsidy Collected in the Diocese of Lincoln in 1526*, ed. H. Salter (1909), 249 ff., 171 ff.
6. *Registra Stephani Gardiner et Johannis Poynet*, ed. H. Chitty, (Canterbury and York Society, 1930), 174–85.
7. C. Haigh, *Reformation and Resistance in Tudor Lancashire* (1975) 31–3; 'East Riding clergy in 1525–6', *Yorks. Arch. J.*, XXIV (1917), 62–80.
8. *Registra Gardiner*, 174–85.
9. Zell, *op. cit.*, 517.
10. Lincs. RO, Bishop's Registers 25, 26.
11. Lincs. RO, Bishop's Register 26; M. Bowker, 'The Henrician Reformation and the parish clergy', *BIHR*, I (1977), 34.
12. Guildhall Library, London, MSS. 9531/10–11.
13. Zell, *op. cit.*, 516 for sources.
14. R. A. Christophers, 'The social and educational background of the Surrey clergy, 1520–1620' (Ph.D. thesis, University of London, 1975), 146.
15. *Sub* Halden in Canterbury Cathedral Library, MS Z/3/2 and Kent AO, Maidstone, PRC 17/10/16 and 152v.
16. Kent AO, PRC 17/12/4v, 98, 168v, 395, 585, 588v; 17/13/119v, 17/15/34v, 74.
17. Zell, *op. cit.*, 519–20.
18. 2 Henry V 2; priests without cure were limited to seven marks *per annum*.
19. Zell, *op. cit.*, 522; Bowker, *op. cit.*, 144–5.

20. Haigh, *op.cit.*, 35; 'East Riding clergy in 1525–6', *Yorks. Arch. J.*, xxiv (1917); Julian Cornwall, 'The people of Rutland in 1522', *Trans. Leics. Arch. and Hist. Soc.*, xxxvii (1961–2), 19.

21. *LP* xiii.i.94.

22. Haigh, *op.cit.*, 33–4; Nicholas Orme, *English Schools in the Middle Ages* (1973), 160, Zell, *op. cit.*, 523, and Kent AO, wills in classes PRC 17 and 32, *passim*; Lincs. RO, Subsid. 1/7a.

23. In Kent there were at least 175 ex-religious in the 1540s; on these men see *The State of the Ex.Religious and Former Chantry Priests in the Diocese of Lincoln, 1547–74*, ed. G. A. J. Hodgett. (Lincolnshire Record Society, LIII, 1959), and *Faculty Office Registers, 1534–49*, ed. D. S. Chambers, (1966).

24. Haigh, *op. cit.*, 35–6; PROB 11/16/12; London Chantry Certificate for All Hallows Bread Street: Dr C. J. Kitching kindly showed me his calendar of the 1548 returns for London and Middlesex, which is to appear as a volume in the London Record Society series.

25. Kent wills as in n. 22 above.

26. Kent AO, PRC 17/15/21 and 43v.

27. Zell, *op. cit.*, 523.

28. *Ibid.*, 524.

29. *Ibid.*, 515.

30. Fuggles, *op. cit.*, 31; Christophers, *op. cit.*, 146–9; Bowker, *op. cit.*, 35–6; Haigh, *op. cit.*, 40–1.

31. Bowker, *op. cit.*, 46.

32. Summarized in John Strype, *Ecclesiastical Memorials* (1822), III pt 2, 156–7; also F. J. Fisher, 'Influenza and inflation in Tudor England', *EcHR*, 2nd ser., xviii (1965).

33. On Marian deprivations see W. H. Frere, *The Marian Reaction* (1896); A. G. Dickens, *The Marian Reaction in the Diocese of York*, I (1957); for Elizabethan deprivations see H. Gee, *The Elizabethan Clergy and the Settlement of Religion, 1558–64* (1898) and for an example Zell, *op. cit.*, 531.

34. Edward Cardwell, *Documentary Annals of the Reformed Church of England* (1844), I, 227, 302–4; M. R. O'Day, 'Clerical patronage and recruitment in England during the Elizabethan and early Stuart periods', (Ph.D. thesis, University of London, 1972), 235.

35. Bowker, *op. cit.*, 40ff.

36. Haigh, *op. cit.*, 238; Christophers, *op. cit.*, 153.

37. Haigh, *op. cit.*, 23; Christophers, *op. cit.*, 216.

38. *Valor Ecclesiasticus*, 27–118; Heath, *op. cit.*, 24; D. M. Palliser, *The Reformation in York, 1534–1553* (Borthwick Papers no. 40, 1971), 3; D. Jones, *The Church in Chester, 1300–1540* (Chetham Society, 3rd ser. VII, 1957), 14.

39. Lever's sermon quoted by G. R. Elton in *The English Commonwealth, 1547–1640*, eds. P. Clark, A. G. T. Smith, N. Tyacke, (1979) 218; evidence of rectories farmed can be found in the *Valor Ecclesiasticus* entries under monasteries and in the entries of parochial benefices. Both appropriators and incumbents farmed livings: see e.g. Lincs. RO, Vj/6 fos. 84ff. In general see H. M. Smyth, *Pre-Reformation England* (1938), 37.

40. J. J. Scarisbrick, 'Clerical taxation in England, 1485–1547', *JEH*, xi (1960) and F. Heal, 'Clerical tax collection under the Tudors' in *Continuity and Change: personnel and administration of the Church in England*, eds. R. O'Day and F. Heal (1976).

41. Hill, *Economic Problems* (1956), 111 and *passim* on the debate about the maintenance of the clergy.

42. *Ecclesiastical Terriers of Warwickshire Parishes*, ed. D. M. Barrett (Dugdale

Society, XXII, 1955), introduction; S. Lander, thesis quoted in *Church and Society in England: Henry VIII to James I*, eds. F. Heal and R. O'Day (1977), 104; *Valor Ecclesiasticus*, II, 436ff.: Cirencester, Fairford, Winchcombe and Stow deaneries. See also W. G. Hoskins, 'The Leicestershire country parson in the 16th Century', *Trans. Leics. Arch. and Hist. Soc.*, XXI pt 1 (1939).
43. *Valor Ecclesiasticus* II, 302ff; III, 19ff.
44. Quoted in Heal and O'Day, *op. cit.*, 109.
45. Christophers, *op. cit.*, 224, 261–2.
46. Quoted in Heal and O'Day, *op. cit.*, 108.
47. J. Strype, *Life of Whitgift* (1822), I, 371.
48. Sources: *Valor Ecclesiasticus* and *The Seconde Parte of a Register*, ed. A. Peel (1915), II, 98–110, 143–5.
49. O'Day thesis (see n. 34), *passim*.

2

Economics and economies of a royal peculiar: Westminster Abbey, 1540–1640

C. S. Knighton

The church of St Peter in Westminster had a uniquely variegated history in the sixteenth century. The Benedictine abbey founded by Edward the Confessor and richly endowed by several of his successors was dissolved in January 1540. In the following December there was erected in its place a secular cathedral, the seat of one of Henry VIII's six new bishoprics, staffed by a chapter of a dean and 12 canons, together with 12 minor canons and numerous subordinate persons.[1] The diocese of Westminster lasted less than a decade, being merged back into that of London in April 1550.[2] The cathedral church retained its capitular organization and endowments, but its exact status was in question until 1552 when by Act of Parliament it was declared to be a second cathedral for the Bishop of London.[3] This arrangement lasted until 1556 when Queen Mary restored the Benedictine observance and with it Westminster's ancient extra-diocesan and extra-provincial exemption.[4] The monks left again within eight months of Elizabeth I's accession, and after a year of uncertainty – though not of complete inanition – a secular chapter was re-established on 21 May 1560.[5] In most respects this second collegiate church was similar to the Henrician foundation of 20 years before, though with the important exception that this time there was no diocese. From this date Westminster has been a royal peculiar, owing direct obedience to the Crown as visitor – the royal free chapel of St George in Windsor Castle being the only comparable institution.

It might have been supposed that such a succession of constitutional upheavals would have had damaging effects on the economy of the Church and the livelihood of its members. But in contrast to most similar establishments Westminster Abbey (as for obvious convenience the church must be called) received a substantial endowment and was able to retain it largely intact throughout the century between the Dissolution and the Civil War. The abbey's special links with the

Crown – as coronation church, royal mausoleum (of the Tudor monarchs only Henry VIII was buried elsewhere) and the scene of much other state ceremonial – ensured its preservation. Its status was indeed enhanced when Westminster's other royal church, St Stephen's Chapel, fell victim to the Edwardine Chantries Act. Stories that St Peter's might have suffered a similar fate are without substance.[6] Westminster canonries were often given to royal chaplains, as those of St Stephen's had been before. And the abbey secured the patronage of several courtiers – most notably Lord Burghley who, as High Steward, protected the abbey's legal, financial and educational interests.

As with all Henry VIII's new foundations there was a good deal of continuity between old and new.[7] The last abbot became the first dean, six former monks became canons, five received minor clerical appointments, and four were placed as students in the universities on the cathedral foundation.[8] As well as reducing the pension bill of the Court of Augmentations this arrangement helped to provide an orderly transfer of power: it is notable that most of the fiscal and administrative officers in the early years of the new cathedral were ex-monks rather than outsiders. Each re-establishment did, of course, involve considerable expenditure. The Henrician foundation was assisted by a £200 grant from the Court of Augmentations, part of which was used to build a new schoolhouse.[9] This helped Westminster School in its development from being an unremarkable adjunct of the monastery to become, by the end of the century, the rival of Eton and Winchester. Famous Head Masters such as Alexander Nowell and William Camden played their part in this achievement; so too did the patronage of monarchs (especially Elizabeth I, whom the school now reveres as *fundatrix*) and courtiers (particularly, again, Burghley). The school was not affected by the Marian changes; indeed only members of the chapter were displaced. In 1554 Protestants were ejected, and two years later their Catholic successors had to give way to the monks. The restoration of Catholic ceremonial was predictably expensive: the queen made some contribution to these costs by providing jewels, but the church accounts for the first two years of her reign show that the dean and chapter spent considerable sums on cleaning, repairs, and the purchase of new vestments, plate and service books. Even so, much remained to be done on the occasion of the monastic re-foundation, an operation which cost in excess of £1,150.[10] The new abbot and convent were also obliged to pay pensions to the honourably dispossessed members of the secular chapter. Most of these were, however, beneficed elsewhere or soon received other preferments, and only one ex-canon continued to receive his pension into the early years of Elizabeth's reign (not without some resistance from the restored dean and chapter). That restoration in 1560 cost a modest £154 11s. 5½d.[11]

That the abbey was able to survive these changes with remarkable economic stability may be in part explained by the permanence and efficiency of its lay administrative officers. Monks and canons came and went, but the men who kept the books in order remained. Of special importance was John Moulton, formerly the steward to Abbot Boston, who was appointed receiver-general in 1544 and retained this post until 1563, serving successive monastic and secular administrations with seemingly indifferent loyalty.[12] His predecessor, William Russell, had cooperated closely with John Carleton, the augmentations official who had charge of the Westminster revenues between the dissolution of the abbey and the endowment of the dean and chapter, and forms of accountancy and estate administration practised in the Court of Augmentations were introduced into the new institution. The financial system adopted in the new foundations was centralized, differing considerably from the multiple financial responsibilities of the greater monasteries and the old secular cathedrals and colleges.[13] This allowed the possibility of one official overseeing the receipt of all revenues. The men who devised statutes for the new foundations – Richard Cox, George Day and Nicholas Heath – were more familiar with university colleges than with the old cathedrals. Most of the new cathedrals received their statutes in 1544; although no copies of the Westminster version survive, it is evident from the chapter acts and accounts that they were received at this time, and there is no reason to suppose that they differed significantly from those issued elsewhere.[14]

In cathedrals of the new foundation canons were paid equal stipends; there were no prebends as in the old secular establishments (although the canons were invariably termed 'prebendaries' in the sixteenth century). At Westminster the canons each received a stipend of £28 5s. 0d. a year – slightly less than their counterparts at, for example, Winchester (£31 11s. 8d.) but a good deal more than those at Peterborough (£20). These payments may be contrasted with the widely differing prebendal incomes in the old foundations, assessed (according to the 1291 taxation) at sums from 2d. to 250 marks.[15] Although canonries did not involve cure of souls, their holders were forbidden to occupy canonries in other Henrician foundations; royal chaplains were exempted from this rule.[16] Even so some Westminster canons found themselves in financial trouble. Edward Leighton, a protégé of Thomas Cromwell, clerk of the closet, and holder of several other preferments, was imprisoned for debt in 1546. At this time he bargained with Edward Keble, the then Earl of Hertford's chaplain, to resign his stall in consideration for an unspecified sum. He later claimed that Keble had forged the bond of payment, but was unable to reclaim his canonry; Keble was duly admitted in 1547, by which time his patron had become Lord Protector.[17] Within six years Keble was himself in debt, being admitted to the privileges of Westminster sanctuary by the dean and chapter. It was said that his misfortune came from standing surety for the bad debts of others, but the financial difficulties which attended almost every stage of his clerical career suggest that he was a man of exceptional irresponsibility and malevolence.[18]

Most of the Henrician cathedrals received letters patent of endowment within weeks or days of their several erections. For reasons which remain unexplained Westminster had to wait from 17 December 1540, when the cathedral church was established, until 5 August 1542 for its endowment charter.[19] During this period the dean and chapter had no properties: all members of the collegiate body were the pensioners of the Court of Augmentations. In these months the old monastic obediences were wound up – a process which had to some extent been foreshadowed in 1536 when Abbot Boston was authorized by Cromwell to gather several obediences under his personal control.[20] Only when the new cathedral was endowed could chapter business properly begin.[21] Financial affairs were then committed to two of the canons: a receiver, who took in revenues from the various bailiffs, farmers and collectors, and a treasurer, to whom the bulk of this income was passed on for distribution to the members of the foundation and for the upkeep of the church and its services. The new foundation treasurer had, therefore, a much greater responsibility than his namesake in the old cathedrals, who was concerned only with custody of the ornaments of worship.[22] In other new foundations canons continued to exercise the duties of receiver and treasurer, but at Westminster the post of canon receiver was soon eclipsed by the activities of the lay official of (confusingly) the same title. After John Moulton was appointed receiver-general in 1544 the chapter decreed that no canon receiver was to be appointed during his tenure, and no provision for such an officer was made in the Elizabethan establishment.[23]

As a result the receipt of revenue came to be the responsibility of a skilled lay officer, assisted by an equally assiduous lay auditor. During the transitional periods which preceded and followed the brief restoration of monastic life Moulton also discharged the functions of the treasurer, ensuring that the choir, almsmen and others received their stipends, and that the fabric and services of the church were properly maintained.[24] Not all Westminster's lay officers were so reliable: the chapter clerk, Robert Allott, absconded in November 1570 and was never heard of again. His absence interrupted chapter business for some months.[25] But for the most part the church's officials were competent men who, as far as can be gathered, were free from serious incompetence or corruption.

The treasurer was normally elected from among those canons who resided most regularly, rather than from among the clerical careerists to whom a Westminster stall was merely a stepping stone to higher advancement. In its deans, too, Westminster was fortunate. William Benson, the former abbot (1540–9) was something of a nonentity. He was certainly no careful custodian of the muniments, for he was unable to recall whether the pre-Dissolution register book had been returned from the Augmentations Office.[26] His successor Richard Cox (1549–53), though simultaneously Chancellor of Oxford University, Dean of Christ Church and a prominent figure at Court, resided frequently at Westminster and did much to regularize the religious, educational and financial life of the church.[27] Mary's dean, Hugh Weston (1553–6) seems to have taken a closer personal interest in the mechanics of administration: his signature is frequently found on the routine bills and receipts of his decanate. Several members of his family received generous grants of Westminster property.[28] During the brief monastic revival there was no restoration of the obedientiary system; one of the monks held the old title of cellarer, but he was in fact the secular treasurer under another guise, with Abbot Feckenham exercising a role in financial matters similar to that of Dean Weston.[29] The first Elizabethan dean, William Bill (1560–1) did not long survive the onerous responsibility of being at the same time Provost of Eton and Master of Trinity College, Cambridge. He was succeeded by Gabriel Goodman (1561–1601) whose long reign, although not wholly peaceful, was one of benign consolidation. The deans of the early seventeenth century were men of wider fame: Lancelot Andrewes (1601–5), Richard Neile (1605–10) and John Williams (1620–42) being the most celebrated. The two latter did much to restore the fabric of the church and its surroundings, and to bring back the physical accoutrements of dignified worship.[30] The collegiate church from which Archbishop Williams fled on the outbreak of the Civil War differed little from the cathedral which Henry VIII had established a century before. The religious reformation had clearly altered the nature of its ministrations, but the basic economic structure remained the same, and hardly any change had occurred in the nature or extent of its endowment.

This endowment, which the dean and chapter received in August 1542, was assessed at £2,598 4s. 5d. The income was about £1,000 less than that of the old abbey, and £500 below that originally designed for the new foundation.[31] Westminster received back a substantial proportion of the former monastic estates, accounting for 83 per cent of the new endowment. The remaining properties came from other dissolved houses in various parts of the country, from Surrey to

Yorkshire. These new acquisitions caused special difficulties in the early days of the capitular administration as the church's officers had to discover their precise perquisites and responsibilities.[32] Many of the lands granted to the dean and chapter had belonged to the church of Westminster from Saxon times, including the benefactions of Edward the Confessor in Worcestershire, Gloucestershire and Oxfordshire as well as Middlesex. Edward I, Richard II and Henry V had added to the rent-roll, and the most recent augmentations had come from the chantry bequests of Henry VII and Lady Margaret Beaufort, which included the royal free chapel of St Martin-le-Grand and its dependencies. This last grant gave Westminster large interests in the City of London; together with existing properties in Westminster itself these urban rents amounted to 24.6 per cent of the 1542 endowment.[33]

The urban income was by no means the more easy to realize because of the proximity of the properties; the collectors for London and Westminster had a daunting and unenviable task, and their accounts are filled with details of decayed tenements and unpaid rents. Soon after the Dissolution it was calculated that £50 had been lost in urban rents because of the demise of the abbey, and a further £16 as a result of the dissolution of other religious houses in London which had paid rents to Westminster.[34] It proved impossible ever to levy the whole urban income; one early account shows a deficit of £68 16s. 7d. in a single year because properties were vacant or decayed. A common complaint was that the assessed rent was so high that no tenant could be found. There were, for example, some unrepaired cottages close to the abbey of which some were empty and others 'inhabited with so pore folkes that they be not able to pay any rent' – and this meant that the collector remained charged with £1 3s. 0d. Another tenement was vacant for two years at a charge of £2 6s. 0d. because the tenant, Thomas Green, was 'brought so poor that he went a begging.' Another debtor fled in the night. Similar distress stories are to be found in the accounts of the London collector. Each year the collectors of London and Westminster had to write off between one-quarter and one-third of their collections for such causes. In such circumstances they stood to lose personally; in 1556 the Westminster collector, William Rosey, had to be prosecuted for a debt of £208 18s. 6d., the equivalent of two-thirds of his collection.[35]

By comparison the country properties of the dean and chapter were more successfully administered. They were very widely dispersed, the largest concentrations (about 31 per cent) lying along the Thames Valley and on into Gloucestershire and Worcestershire. There were also clusters of holdings in East Anglia and the east Midlands, with some manors as far away as Lincolnshire, Nottinghamshire and

Yorkshire. In this Westminster differed from the other new foundation cathedrals, even the richer ones (Canterbury, Durham and Winchester), whose estates lay almost wholly within their respective localities.[36] Westminster's dispersed manors, rectories and other rural properties had to be visited each year to receive rents, hold manorial courts, inspect chancels and generally survey the estates. The first such progresses were made in the summer of 1543 by one of the canons and a lay officer (the steward of the lands), when it was necessary to take stock of the new endowment. During May they visited the West of England, and a second excursion in July took them to the Midlands and the North; the total expenditure on these journeys was more than £20.[37]

All these properties were held at farm – the culmination of a gradual reduction in demesne during the later Middle Ages.[38] Geography and economy combined to produce this exclusively *rentier* economy. Except in so far that the surveyors were accommodated and entertained in manor houses and rectories on the annual progresses, capitular bodies were necessarily stationary. Unlike other landowners (such as bishops) they could not take advantage of lands held in demesne to soften the effects of inflation by moving from place to place, eating their way through their lands. Westminster's rent-roll was, furthermore, almost wholly in cash. From two Hertfordshire properties, Sawbridgeworth and Wheathampstead, came quantities of wheat and pepper, and the farmer of Yeoveney in Middlesex provided a boar for the Christmas table; but in all these instances the revenue in kind was only part of the total due. Save for such sums which might be collected during the progresses, the rents were delivered to the receiver at Westminster, theoretically on the normal quarter days, and the annual audit took place in November. Throughout the sixteenth century the rents remained constant in almost every case, and the fluctuations in the receiver's charge were accounted for only by casualties.[39]

The profits of feudal jurisdiction in manorial courts made up a very small part of the income of the dean and chapter. The actual sums so collected might be as much as £54 18s. 8d. (including arrears) as in 1550/1, or as little as 15s. 10d. (1558/9); but between 1550 and 1570 the average amount was only £21 6s. 6d., or less than 1 per cent of the total income. And against these sums had to be set the expenses of the church's officers who travelled to preside at the courts. A sum of £13 6s. 8d. had been allowed for this purpose at the foundation. In 1555/6, for example, the expenses were £8 7s. 6d. and the gross receipts only £17 3s. 1d.[40] The sale of wood, so profitable to some ecclesiastical landlords such as the bishops of Ely, did not play a great part in the Westminster economy. Before 1570 the receivers' accounts record wood sales on only three occasions, when the yields were £17 5s. 0d., 5s. and £2 respectively. Later in the century some larger woods were sold, though without substantially augmenting the corporate revenue.[41]

The bulk of the dean and chapter's income came, therefore, from the fixed rents of its country properties – approximately £1,500 being due from these sources. The conventional solution to the problem of fixed rents in an age of inflation was the entry-fine. In the years before the Dissolution many monastic houses had issued long-term leases in order to raise immediate cash through entry-fines and to buy favour in high places. The aim was not so much to postpone the inevitable surrender as to ensure adequate compensation thereafter.[42] The Westminster muniments, which are largely silent on the subject for the monastic period, do furnish some evidence on these exactions during the early years of capitular administration, mainly for the years 1542 to 1570.[43] When the act book of the dean and chapter was first written up in March 1543 records of fines and fees for the chapter seal were made in the rear of the volume.[44] This systematic registration was not maintained beyond the end of the year, but thereafter the sums charged as fines are occasionally mentioned in the main part of the act book. The inference from such figures as are available is that Westminster fines were not excessive by contemporary standards. Of 339 leases of rural and urban properties made during the time of the first collegiate church there is record of the fines in 39 cases.[45] No obvious correlation is found between rent, term and fine, but only where the rent was small (£5 or under) did the fine exceed twice the annual rent. In most properties worth £20 a year or so the fine was normally between one and two years' rent. Fewer figures survive for the second collegiate church – that is, after the Elizabethan re-establishment; but of nine fines recorded the highest is that of £100 for the rectory of Godmanchester, Huntingdonshire, which was valued at £50 a year. These indications may be compared with the customary fine of three years' rent charged by many lay landlords, such as the Duchy of Lancaster.[46] For urban leases the fine was generally a good deal less than one year's rent: in 1543 a fine of 10s. was standard for rents of between 30s. and 50s. In some cases the fine might be waived or commuted to some useful work such as paving the street. In special cases even a valuable country lease might be made without fine; this happened with the rich rectory of Godmanchester in 1548 at the request of the Duchess of Somerset.[47]

The income from fines and sealing fees was shared among the members of the chapter; the same was true of the wheat rents and other casualties such as wood sales. On 10 February 1543 the relatively large sum of £94 18s. 8d. was split up in this way. A more typical dividend was the £59 available in December 1555, which would have given each member of the chapter £4 4s. 0d. These dividends were supposed to take place quarterly (though they are by no means so regularly noticed in the chapter acts) and it might therefore be reasonable to assume that an individual canon might expect to receive something between £10 and £15 a year from this source, thereby augmenting his stipend of £28 5s. 0d. by as much as one-third. It is clear from one transaction in 1587 that the fines were taken and shared out before all the formalities were completed, since the canons were told that they might have to pay back money they had already received should the lease in question not take effect. Only those actually present in chapter when a lease was agreed or sealed were entitled to this bounty – a measure which was designed to encourage canonical residence. As with many other statutory requirements (especially those which concerned residence) the recurrence of this order in the chapter acts suggests that it was as frequently ignored. As late as December 1591 the chapter found it necessary to call attention to the matter; yet six years later the rule was broken to allow all ten canons of the day to share in the £100 fine from the Godmanchester lease although only six had been present at its sealing on 20 April 1597.[48]

These fines were supposed to redress the balance between a fixed corporate income and rising prices. Since, however, they were shared only by the dean and canons the system did nothing to assist the economic difficulties of the rest of the collegiate body and the church as a whole. A chapter order of 8 November 1550 declared that dividends encouraged hospitality; but we cannot tell whether or not canons used their additional emoluments to offer entertainment to their poorer colleagues. A further act of 15 December 1554 which asserted that the dividends were made 'so that the state of the church be preservyd' suggests that the dean and chapter felt themselves to be coterminous with the collegiate body of which in fact they were numerically only a small part.[49]

Entry-fines could be levied, as their name implies, upon entry into tenure. But the dean and chapter made very long leases, particularly of their country properties. The Henrician statutes had sought to restrict terms for country leases to 21 years and for urban tenements to 60 years.[50] But much longer terms were as common after the dissolution of the abbey as they had been before. Long terms are traditionally and correctly seen as being principally to the advantage of the tenantry, although it should not be forgotten that extended tenancies (where the tenants were competent and trustworthy) might also benefit lessors. But while deans and chapters might have been glad of the continuity afforded by long tenures – and this is particularly true of Westminster with its far-flung estates – the statutory restriction on terms was de-

signed to protect the interests of the capitular bodies. It was not a regu-
lation which the dean and chapter of Westminster managed to obey.
In the first year of their administration (1542–3) not one lease for a
term below 21 years passed their seal. Notably generous grants of
Westminster properties were made to officials of the Court of Augmentations – Sir Richard Rich, Walter Mildmay and Griffin Tyndale
– for terms of 80, 89 and 90 years respectively. Admittedly these
grants were made before the statutes were received in 1544, but the
pattern thereafter was much the same. During the 15 years of the first
collegiate church the average term for manorial leases was 54 years,
with only six out of the 84 such leases registered being within the statutory limit of 21 years or under. Urban leases were better contained; the
average term was 59 years, just under the statutory limit of 60, with
which 153 out of the 255 registered leases complied.[51] It may be noted
that the term of three lives, common on many estates, was unknown at
Westminster before 1570, and is thereafter found only occasionally.[52]

The Henrician statutes also prohibited the granting of leases in
reversion – a rule which was completely ignored at Westminster as
elsewhere. The dean and chapter at first showed some scruples. In
March 1545 they were requested by Queen Catherine Parr to make a
reversionary lease of Stanford rectory, Berkshire, to a page of her
privy chamber. They complied, but found it prudent to register a
protest in the act book.[53] Reversions, both of properties and offices,
were thereafter granted in profusion.

Long terms of leases meant infrequent entry-fines, but the dean and
chapter were able to resort to other measures to secure immediate
capital gains. When a lease with years in hand passed to an heir the
new tenant was obliged to make a new lease and deliver a new fine.
Existing tenants were also encouraged to seek extension of tenure;
this was doubly advantageous to the dean and chapter as it provided
further cash while assuring continuity of tenure. This was, nevertheless, another contravention of the statutes.[54] A further lucrative ploy
was to find some technical fault in the original lease and to charge the
tenant for its rectification. Most leases (statute notwithstanding) included a clause allowing for renewal of tenure, and in 1556 the
chapter announced that any leases made thereafter without such a
clause would be void. Even so the chapter interpreted its order retro-
spectively. The tenant of one prebend of St Martin-le-Grand whose
1553 lease contained no renovation clause was required to have a new
lease sealed in February 1556 at a cost of £10, together with 26s. 8d. in
fees and a fine of £6 13s. 4d. Conversely in December 1564 the chapter
allowed another tenant to pay a fine of £10 in order to be dispensed
from the inclusion of a renovation clause in his lease.[55]

Westminster was in a stronger position than many other ecclesiastical landlords in the sixteenth century because its income derived so largely from manors. The spiritual income, mostly from rectories which had been appropriated to Westminster Abbey, cannot be exactly calculated because rectory and manor often formed part of a single tenancy. But it is evident that the *spiritualia* could not have accounted for much more than a quarter of the dean and chapter's total revenue. This proportion is remarkably low when compared, for example, with that of the income of St George's Chapel, Windsor, which had been endowed very largely with rectorial revenue.[56] It was, moreover, Tudor policy to press bishops into exchanging manors and other temporalities for less desirable and less profitable rectories – a policy which was given statutory basis in 1559. As a result of this Act the pattern of many episcopal estates changed dramatically, as has been shown by recent studies of the lands of the bishops of Bath and Wells and Ely.[57] By contrast the properties of the church of Westminster remained virtually unchanged between 1540 and 1640. The only major reduction in its income occurred in 1545 and 1546 when properties valued at £568 18s. 11½d. were surrendered to the Crown in exoneration of the obligation to maintain readers and students at Oxford and Cambridge. Much of this property was subsequently used to endow Christ Church and Trinity College, Cambridge, and many of the scholars formerly maintained by Westminster and other new foundation cathedrals were found places in the two new colleges.[58] The disbanding of the system by which readers and students were financed from cathedral revenues should not be seen as an assault on the newly established cathedrals themselves but as a rethinking of the government's plans for educational patronage. The original scheme was devised with the creditable intention of linking ecclesiastical and educational establishments – even if it allowed Henry VIII to pose as a patron of learning without loosening his own purse-strings. But the arrangement proved unnecessarily complicated; a certain lack of communication between the scholars and their cathedral paymasters at Westminster is suggested by the reply of the dean and chapter to a government enquiry: 'And what euery of the seyd scolers do professe the seyd deane and chapyture can not tell.'[59]

Some of the cathedrals none the less had cause to complain about the loss of the students' lands. The dean and chapter of Peterborough claimed to have lost £9 2s. 10¼d. as a result of these transactions, and the issue was still alive in 1550 when Sir Richard Sackville was appointed chancellor of the Court of Augmentations. In 1551 the dean and chapter of Ely received a grant of lands from the Crown to compensate for losses at the time of the surrender of their lands. At Westminster the chapter could only complain of being out of pocket by £1 5s. 7½d., but made repeated representations to the government on this score, and because of what they held to be their generally impoverished circumstances. There is no evidence that their petitions were heeded.[60]

The only other important exchange of Westminster property in the sixteenth century took place in 1548 when Sir Anthony Denny purchased the rectory of Cheshunt in Hertfordshire from the dean and chapter. In return he granted them the rectory of Shoreham in Kent. This was originally valued at £6 more than Cheshunt, and so the exchange was theoretically in the chapter's favour. In fact this new acquisition proved to be a considerable liability. The church and rectory house were found to be in ruins, and over the next 20 years almost £50 had to be spent in repairs there – nearly half the amount spent by the chapter on repairs in all its rectories during that period.[61] Rectorial incomes also involved burdens in the way of pensions to vicars and curates, procurations, synodals and other ecclesiastical dues – an annual total of £63 12s. 11½d. to be subtracted from the £500 or so gross income from *spiritualia*.[62] The dean and chapter seem to have been reasonably attentive to their rectorial duties. The accounts regularly mention repairs to chancels and rectory houses. In 1548 the chapter provided copies of Erasmus's *Paraphrases*, at 5s. each, for three of its parishes. In the following year the farmer of Shoreham was allowed 12s. to buy copies of the same work for Shoreham church and its dependent chapel of Otford. In 1563 a bible was given to Shoreham at a cost of 15s.[63] The churches were regularly visited, both officially and pastorally, by members of the chapter. In 1553 Canon Andrew Perne was sent down to preach at Shoreham in the curate's absence. In Elizabeth's reign there were regular sermons by members of the chapter in the abbey's two London churches of St Bride, Fleet Street and St Botulph-without-Aldersgate.[64]

Appropriation of a rectory normally carried with it the advowson of the vicarage where one was ordained. When leasing rectories the dean and chapter of Westminster normally reserved to themselves these advowsons, thereby retaining useful patronage.[65]

The revenue from all these properties, rural and urban, spiritual and temporal, came into the hands of the receiver-general who, on deducting the expenses of his own office (normally around £450, which included administrative charges, repairs, fees to manorial officials, ecclesiastical stipends and dues, and tenths to the Crown) passed on the remainder to the canon treasurer. The receipts recorded in the treasurers' accounts varied considerably during the 30 years after the Henrician foundation – from £951 16s. 11½d. in 1548/9 to £2,030 6s. 1¾d. in 1563/4; but by the end of this period they had settled at about £1,800, of which all was generally consumed.[66] The principal charge on the treasurer was the payment of the stipends of the collegiate body, from the dean at £232 10s. 0d., the 12 canons at £28 5s. 0d. each, down to the under-porters at £5 6s. 8d. each. In addition the treasurer was responsible for ordinary repairs and running expenses and for providing for the liturgical services of the church. Another canon held the office of steward and had general charge of the domestic arrangements.

The treasurer's income from the receiver came at irregular intervals and by odd amounts. But he was obliged to make regular payments to the collegiate body as well as to workmen and tradesmen from outside. The difficulty of his position, particularly when set against the background of debasement and inflation, is highlighted by a chapter minute of 19 March 1552:[67]

> Forasmuche as the cathedrall churche of Westm' hathe had suche losse by the late fall of the money that at this present ther ys not ynough in the treasorers handes to pay the charges of this next our ladye day quarter, yt ys therefore decreed . . . that certeyn plate and stuff shalbe furthewithe sold to make money whearwithe to pay the ministers and other officers wages and other charges now presently to be borne.

Similar measures illustrating the expeditious alliance between economy and puritanism were frequently taken at Westminster, as elsewhere. In January 1549 a number of lecterns and candlesticks, described as 'monymentes of idolatre and supersticyon' were sold in order to raise money for the library. In November 1550 further plate was disposed of to pay for structural alterations.[68] The Marian revival necessarily reversed this policy, and much was expended in restoring the paraphernalia of worship. At least £31 7s. 4d. was paid for Catholic service books, some of which were bought back from members of the choir, who had presumably appropriated them in Edward's reign.[69] When the ecclesiastical tide turned once more the Elizabethan chapter was able to economize by converting copes procured in the previous reign into cushions and a canopy for the queen at her visit in 1571.[70] Other occasional economies are revealed in the chapter minutes. In June 1549 the commons of the grammar scholars – the boys of Westminster School – were reduced, and in the following month the minor canons were allowed to opt out of commons altogether: a measure which reflects domestic penny-pinching as much as it does the decline of communal life. But the common table retained its attractions, for in 1584 the chapter was understandably concerned about the number of guests being brought in by the college servants.[71]

The treasurers' accounts are unfortunately missing for the middle years of Edward VI's reign, and it is therefore impossible to assess pre-

Table 3: *Summary of Westminster treasurers' accounts,*
1544–71 (figures corrected to nearest £)

Year	Arrears	Receipts	Total charge	Expenses
1544/5	–	2268	2268	1891
1545/6	177	1872	2459	1622
1546/7	250	1617	1868	1537
1547/8	331	1352	1683	1441
1548/9	242	952	1194	–
1549/50	–	–	–	–
1550/1	–	–	–	–
1551/2	–	–	–	–
1552/3	0	1499	1499	1499
1553/4	0	1840	1840	1566
1554/5	275	1680	1955	1559
1555/6	–	–	–	–
1560/1	–	–	1934	1761
1561/2	172	2082	2255	2070
1562/3	106	2025	2131	2058
1563/4	98	1943	2041	1758
1564/5	58	1692	1750	1711
1565/6	105	1874	1979	1921
1566/7	31	1761	1792	1780
1567/8	11	1867	1878	1845
1568/9	23	1752	1775	1772
1569/70	3	1691	1694	1683
1570/1	3	1760	1763	1761

Sources: Westminster Abbey Muniments 37064, 37060, 37112, 33603,
37382, 37387, 33604, 37660, 37551, 33618, 33619, 33620, 33622,
33624, 33625, 33626, 33627, 33628, 33629, 33631.

cisely how the dean and chapter's income was affected in these difficult years. Figures for the rest of the reign show that considerably
lower sums were received and expended by the college than had been
before or would be again. Although matters improved in Elizabeth's
reign the treasurer's budget of around £1,800 paid for less and less.
The relative cheapness of the Protestant liturgy was an advantage, of
course; not only could plate, furnishings and vestments be sold, but a
smaller clerical establishment was required. The Henrician cathedral
had maintained 12 minor canons, whose functions were purely liturgical. By 1556 (despite the restoration of Catholic ceremony) five of
these places were being held by laymen, who could be paid £2 less than
their clerical counterparts. The Elizabethan foundation included only
five minor canons in all. Similarly the epistoler and gospeller established in 1540 when masses were still sung with deacon and subdea-
con were no longer needed in 1560, and no such appointments were
made in the second collegiate church.[72]

This pruning of the clerical staff should have produced a saving of £88 a year, but there was a corresponding increase in payments to lay officials and servants. Some stipends were increased – that of the Under Master of Westminster School, for example, from a miserable £2 13s. 4d. to £6 14s. 4d. *per annum*, while the laundress received a rise from £1 to £4. There also appeared in the Elizabethan college a variety of other functionaries such as a keeper of the water-conduit, a horse-keeper, two gardeners and a barber, who had never been on the foundation of the first collegiate church. The sum allowed for servants in 1540 was £36 a year: by 1570 they were costing £200.[73] The treasurer also had to meet rising costs of wages and materials. Fortunately there was no need of major work on the fabric of the abbey church during the sixteenth century. In the muniments, however, are found indications of constant expenditure on minor repairs and building activities in the church and its precincts. Bills prepared by the clerk of the works show that the average daily rate for a carpenter, glazier or other skilled workman rose from 10d. a day in the 1550s to 1s. a day a decade later, while a common labourer's daily pay increased from 6d. to 8d. over the same period.[74] At least the rates were cheaper than in London: in 1561 the dean and chapter of St Paul's paid labourers 9d. a day and craftsmen between 1s. and 1s. 4d.[75] In addition, of course, there were substantial rises in the prices of all manner of materials and foodstuffs. But the conclusion from the treasurers' accounts must be that the dean and chapter managed to live for the most part within their income.

The treasurer could only hope to balance his account by reducing expenditure on some of the services which the collegiate church was intended to provide. Economies in church furnishings and ritual have already been mentioned; but the new foundation cathedrals were also established as centres for a wide range of social purposes, from the education of the young and the care of the old to the mending of roads.[76] At Westminster £100 was allocated in the Henrician scheme for almsgiving (in addition to £80 a year for the 12 resident almsmen); the first collegiate church spent on average only £56 on such benefactions each year and the Elizabethan college £30. And although £40 was set aside for road repairs around the church, only £26 *per annum* was spent on average under the first collegiate church, and nothing at all after 1560. It is therefore understandable that even in the reigns of Henry VIII and Edward VI the dean and chapter were accused of negligence in this respect.[77] In 1545 a royal commission was appointed to consider the responsibilities of the new foundation cathedrals for highways and alms, and to divert the allocated sums to other uses should this be found desirable. This commission was still active in Edward's reign, for in January 1549 the dean and chapter of

Westminster received a sharp rebuke from the commissioners for failing to report to them. It is unclear whether Westminster's reduced expenditure on highways and alms was an occasion or a result of this commission.[78]

Protestant ritual made for economy; but the Reformation also introduced clerical marriage, which had special social and economic repercussions for cathedral closes and collegiate establishments. The first canons of Westminster were, of course, celibates; but by Edward's reign wives and children had begun to intrude upon the precincts and communal life started to disintegrate. Whereas the monks had been accommodated in a dormitory the canons (and minor canons) needed houses. This was a persistent difficulty for the dean and chapter; the canons could not fulfil their residence requirements without adequate housing for themselves and their families. Westminster's location meant that houses in the precincts were much sought after by courtiers and other public figures, to whom they could profitably be let. In the first year of capitular administration attempts were made to recover nearby premises for college use. Dean Cox tried to establish order in the matter, but the problem was still there in 1581. At this time several of the canons were having to share houses, and were therefore less disposed to reside in them or to take up the offices of treasurer or steward. It was therefore forbidden to lease any residence which had formerly been a canon's house. Yet later in the same year Sir John Goodwin took a lease for 21 years of Vaughan's House, one of the principal canonical residences, and this lease was renewed in 1587. The 1581 order was repeated in 1590, but at the same time Sir John Fortescue, Chancellor of the Exchequer, was permitted to keep his house for life; in 1592 he was granted a lease for 21 years, which was renewed in 1596 for 21 more years or three lives. The dean and chapter were clearly under strong pressures to abrogate the rules which they had themselves made to encourage canonical residence.[79]

It is fair to say that, save for the withdrawal of the maintenance of readers and students at the universities, there was no reduction on educational expenditure. Indeed special attention was given to the school in the early years of Elizabeth's reign, when the dean and several of the canons acted as the boys' tutors.[80] The links with Trinity and Christ Church, foreshadowed in the first collegiate church, were formalized in the Elizabethan statutes. Lord Burghley defended the rights of Westminster scholars to be elected to Henry VIII's two academic foundations, and was also a considerable pecuniary benefactor to the school.[81]

The effects of the Reformation at Westminster are neatly illustrated by the division of the old monastic dormitory to form two large rooms, one for the use of the school and the other to serve as a chapter library. Yet for all the new emphasis on scholarship and preaching the central function of the church of Westminster remained its daily round of choral worship – an activity on which it would be pointless as well as impertinent to set a price. The dean and chapter curtailed expenditure on their liturgical and charitable operations, while increasing spending on lay servants who ministered to their own comforts. Sale of plate and treasure was in keeping with the ideals of the reformed Church, but neglect of alms and other 'social' duties seems less excusable, and left the institution open to the criticisms of those to whom corporate religious life was in any case a vain anachronism. It was by royal intervention that many great monastic houses were preserved and reconstituted as secular colleges, but they occupied an uneasy place in the protestant climate of the age. It was inevitable that the deans and chapters should share the temporary fall of the monarchy in the seventeenth century. Of all the new foundations Westminster depended most closely upon royal patronage; this, together with the careful custody of its deans, canons and lay officials, ensured a century of stability before the dereliction occasioned by the Civil War.

NOTES

I am indebted to the dean and chapter of Westminster for permission to make use of records in their custody.

1. PROE 322/260 (*LP*, XV, 69), *LP*, XVI, 379(30).
2. *CPR 1549/50*, 171–2.
3. Westminster Abbey Muniments (hereafter cited as WAM), 6490; *Statutes of the Realm*, IV, i, xiii (index entry only).
4. WAM 7344.
5. *CPR 1558/60*, 397–403.
6. See *A House of Kings*, ed. E. F. Carpenter (1966), 115–16, and C. S. Knighton, 'Collegiate churches, 1540 to 1560, with special reference to St Peter in Westminster' (Ph.D. thesis, University of Cambridge, 1975), 104–5.
7. See, for example, D. Marcombe, 'The Durham dean and chapter: old abbey writ large?' in *Continuity and Change, Personnel and Administration of the Church in England 1500–1642*, eds. R. O'Day and F. Heal (1976), 125–44.
8. WAM 6478, fos. 2–4. See Knighton, *op. cit.*, 28–31.
9. PRO SC6/Henry VIII/2421, m. 5; E 315/104, fos. 77v–78.
10. *Chronicle of the Grey Friars of London*, ed. J. G. Nichols (Camden Society, old series, LIII, 1852), 94, 104n.; WAM 37412, 37413, 37417, 37426, 37448, 37456, 37457, 37458, 37564, 37567, 37710, 37712, 37716, 37717.
11. WAM 33617, fos. 2–2v. Knighton, *op. cit.*, 159–63.
12. WAM Chapter Act Book I, fos. 19, 22; Register III, fos. 27–8.
13. For monastic finances see M. D. Knowles, *The Religious Orders in England* (1948–59), II, 309–10; H. F. Westlake, *Westminster Abbey* (1923), II, 273–417; and cf. R. B. Dobson, *Durham Priory, 1400–1450* (1973), 66–9. For secular foundations see K. Edwards, *The English Secular Cathedrals in the Middle Ages* (2nd

edn., 1967), and A. K. B. Roberts, *St George's Chapel, Windsor Castle, 1384–1416* (1947).

14. *The Statutes of the Cathedral Church of Durham*, ed. A. H. Thompson (Surtees Society, CXLIII, 1929), xxxix–xl; WAM 37047, f. 8; 37048, fos. 12v, 13. For convenience the Peterborough statutes, printed in *The Foundation of Peterborough Cathedral*, ed. W. T. Mellows (Northamptonshire Record Society Publications, XIII, 1941), 75–104, are used, hereafter cited as *Statutes*.

15. WAM 6478, f. 2; *Documents relating to the Foundation of the Chapter of Winchester*, ed. G. W. Kitchin and F. T. Madge (Hampshire Record Society, I, 1889), 55; Mellows (ed.), *op. cit.*, 71; Edwards, *op. cit.*, 38–9; M. Bowker, *The Secular Clergy in the Diocese of Lincoln, 1495–1520* (1968), 158–9.

16. *Statutes*, 82.

17. WAM 9418; Chapter Act Book I, fos. 20v, 272v.

18. WAM Chapter Act Book I, fos. 73v, 83. For Keble's other troubles see PRO C 24/27 (Keble v. Sutton); Salisbury Diocesan RO, Chapter Act Book 14, 56, 65, 73, 74, 114; *CPR 1557/8*, 347; C. Haigh, *Reformation and Resistance in Tudor Lancashire* (1975), 181.

19. *LP*, XVII, 714(5). See *Durham Statutes*, xxxi–xxxiv. A full table of foundation and endowment charters is given in Knighton, *op. cit.*, 25.

20. WAM 12787.

21. For evidence that the chapter minutes begin in March 1543 and not March 1542 (as claimed in Westlake, *op. cit.*, I, 208; Carpenter (ed.), *op. cit.*, 113 and elsewhere), see Knighton, *op. cit.*, 48–51.

22. Edwards, *op. cit.*, 216–22; *Statutes*, 87–8.

23. WAM Chapter Act Book I, f. 58v (7 December 1549).

24. WAM 37713, 33198E, 33198G, 37718.

25. WAM Chapter Act Book I, fos. 139–42.

26. PRO C 24/27 (Lambe v. Burton, 1548/9), f. 6.

27. WAM Chapter Act Book I, fos. 56–7, 58v, 64v–65v, 72v.

28. WAM 37417, 37431, 37451, 37558, 37585, 37592, 37684, 37685; Chapter Act Book I, fos. 84, 95, 98; Register III, fos. 256–257v, 286v–287v, 298.

29. WAM 18961, 33198C–G, 37788A, 37845, 37872.

30. Carpenter (ed.), *op. cit.*, 141–67. Neile's achievements are catalogued in WAM Book 7.

31. WAM 6478, f. 8–14v; *Valor Ecclesiasticus* (1810–39), I, 424; PRO E 315/24, fos. 5–6.

32. WAM 37047, f. 8; Chapter Act Book I, f. 26v.

33. For a complete account of the monastic revenue see B. F. Harvey, *Westminster Abbey and its Estates in the Middle Ages* (1977).

34. WAM 43951, 43952.

35. WAM 43723, 37170, 33209; Chapter Act Book I, f. 100v.

36. Harvey, *op. cit.*, 26–36; Knighton, *op. cit.*, 179–84. Canterbury's medieval estates were studied by R. A. L. Smith in *Canterbury Cathedral Priory* (1943); for Durham see Dobson, *Durham Priory* and D. Marcombe, 'The dean and chapter of Durham, 1558–1603', (Ph.D. thesis, University of Durham, 1973).

37. WAM 37048, fos. 5–11v.

38. See B. F. Harvey, 'The leasing of the abbot of Westminster's demesnes in the later middle ages,' *Ec HR*, 2nd ser. xxii (1969), 17–27.

39. WAM Registers III, IV, V.

40. WAM Receivers' accounts; mainly in the series 33192–232 (full list in Knighton, *op. cit.*, 188, and see 189–91).

41. WAM 37423*, 33227, 33229, Chapter Act Book I, fos. 181, 185, 220. Cf. F. M. Heal, 'The Tudors and church lands: economic problems of the bishopric of

Ely during the sixteenth century', *EcHR*, 2nd ser., XXVI (1973), 209.
42. See J. Youings, *The Dissolution of the Monasteries* (1971), 57–60.
43. Cf. Harvey, *op. cit.*, 158–9.
44. WAM Chapter Act Book I, f. 312v.
45. Knighton, *op. cit.*, 193–6, including tables based on figures in WAM Chapter Act Book I and Register III.
46. WAM Chapter Act Book I, fos. 115v, 116, 144, 145, 146v, 206, 209v, 247v. Cf. J. Thirsk (ed.), *The Agrarian History of England and Wales*, IV (1967), 267, 270, 336.
47. Knighton, *op. cit.*, 196. WAM Chapter Act Book I, fos. 312v, 44v.
48. *Ibid.*, fos. 312v, 98v, 208v, 223, 247v.
49. *Ibid.*, 64v–65, 92v.
50. *Statutes*, 80.
51. Based on calculations from WAM Register III.
52. WAM Chapter Act Book I, fos. 180v, 184, 219v, 242.
53. *Statutes*, 80. WAM Chapter Act Book I, f. 25.
54. *Statutes*, 80.
55. WAM Chapter Act Book I, fos. 99, 100, 115v.
56. WAM 6478, 33185. Roberts, *op. cit.*, 14.
57. Heal, *op. cit.*, 107; P. H. Hembry, *The Bishops of Bath and Wells 1540–1640* (1967), 129–48.
58. WAM 12960; Register III, fos. 76–7v. For the readers and students see F. D. Logan, 'The origins of the so-called regius professorships: an aspect of the renaissance in Oxford and Cambridge', in *Renaissance and Renewal in Christian History*, ed. D. Baker (1977), 271–8, and Knighton, *op. cit.*, 301–21.
59. B. L. Cott. MS Cleopatra E.IV, f. 366 (*LP*, XIV, i, 868(2)); WAM 43048.
60. Northants. RO, Peterborough Dean and Chapter Records, MD/62; PRO SP 10/14, no. 48; *CPR 1549/50*, 214–16; *CPR 1550/3*, 173; WAM 6481, 6482, 6483, 43933; Chapter Act Book I, fos. 16, 36.
61. WAM Chapter Act Book I, fos. 45v. *LP*, XIX, I, 278(25). WAM 33192, 33194–33198J, 33205, 33219, 33222–33231, 37243*.
62. WAM 6478, fos. 7–7v.
63. WAM 33192, f. 7v, 33193, f. 12v, 33620, f. 5v.
64. WAM 33223, m. 4, 33224, m. 4d, 33227, 33228, 32321, 37563; Chapter Act Book I, fos. 56, 106v.
65. Knighton, *op. cit.*, 330–4.
66. See table, which is simplified from the treasurers' accounts.
67. WAM Chapter Act Book I, f. 72.
68. See, for example, S. J. Lander, 'The diocese of Chichester 1508–1558: episcopal reform under Robert Sherburne and its aftermath' (Ph.D. thesis, University of Cambridge, 1974), 161; WAM Chapter Act Book I, fos. 48, 65v.
69. WAM 37437, 37459, 37460, 37634, 37637, 37642A.
70. WAM 33631, f. 5; Chapter Act Book I, f. 141v.
71. WAM Chapter Act Book I, fos. 50v, 51, 187.
72. Based on WAM treasurers' accounts; a table comparing the establishments of the first and second collegiate churches is given in Knighton, *op. cit.*, 221.
73. WAM 6478, 33618, 33619.
74. WAM 37217–38, 37287–313, 37357–67, 37423–5, 37552, 37557, 37633–55, 37659, 37855–93, 37923, 38243–50, 38546–53, 38653–61.
75. St Paul's Cathedral Library, MS WB 64.
76. B. L. Cott. MS Cleopatra E.IV, f. 366 (*LP*, XIV, i, 868(2)).
77. WAM 6478, f. 4v, 6593, 37462–548, 50781, f. 2, 50782, f. 3 and treasurers' accounts.

78. *LP*, XX, i, 1335(52); WAM 6590, 6591, 6592.
79. WAM Chapter Act Book I, fos. 14, 56–56v, 57v, 64v–65, 174–174v, 177, 210v, 218, 224, 243.
80. WAM 54003–18; see J. Sergeaunt, *Annals of Westminster School* (1898), 15, 36–50.
81. WAM 32446, 32447; Chapter Act Book I, f. 221v; Knighton, *op. cit.*, 279–83.

3

The incomes of provincial urban clergy, 1520–1645

Claire Cross

In a highly individual will made in 1642 Robert More, M.A. 'preacher of God's word' and rector since 1581 of the West Riding township of Guiseley, commented generally upon the state of the English Church and in particular upon its economic difficulties.

But most woeful and lamentable above all other abuses are those dangerous and sacrilegious robberies and spoils of our churches both in the south and in the north parts whereby our rectories and parsonages are impropriated and wrongfully turned into the possession of covetous worldlings, and so into vicarages and miserable curateships of £5, £10 or 20 marks pensions per annum, or the like: which most fearful and bloody robbery the devil first devised and practised by the robbing Romish usurped power under pretence of holiness and charitable relieving of his cloistered monkeries, abbots and nunneries etc., most grievously wronging thereby the majesty of God himself with the princes and people also of the world. This monstrous crying abuse hath been so suffered and continued ever since the death of king Henry the 8th, as that all the godly endeavours and zealous care of our famous kings and queens with our most reverend bishops and honourable nobles and whole estate could never reform the same. And upon this woeful spoil and decay of our church livings Satan hath too violently and necessarily drawn in another mischief worse, if possible, than the former, which is our blind guides or ignorant reading ministers, the very poison and plague of our churches, the disgrace and shame of the gospel and destruction of our people, for insufficient maintenance hath bred insufficient ministers, and these two are the most woeful and dangerous in our English church and most necessary to be reformed.

Shorn of hyperbole, More's argument that inadequate remuneration produced inadequate clergy rings true, if only for its very obviousness, and nowhere is it more likely to have applied than in towns where impropriations and ill-endowed livings abounded. This essay sets out to assess the financial position of the urban clergy in the provinces in the period between the beginning of the Henrician Reformation and the Civil War and to examine how they coped with their especially adverse circumstances.[1]

When contemporary churchmen attacked the poverty of urban cures they seem to have had in mind those ancient towns which had inherited a multiplicity of parishes from the early Middle Ages. London would obviously have headed such a list followed by the populous cities of Norwich and York. On the eve of the Reformation York had more than 50 parishes and even after an amalgamation undertaken on civic initiative in the reign of Henry VIII still retained 25 at the century's close. Towns much smaller than Norwich and York had to contend with very many small parishes within their walls: Lincoln, Stamford, Worcester and Winchester, to name but four, faced the problem at its most acute. Often the earlier a town's settlement the more numerous and badly endowed its parishes seem to have been. Not all towns, however, resembled Norwich or York, and in fact urban cures fall into fairly distinct categories none of which have been excluded from this survey. The new towns of the High Middle Ages entered the Reformation period with a very different ecclesiastical structure from that of the old urban foundations: here the parish frequently coincided with the boundaries of the township. Boston comprised one such parish, as did Leeds and many other northern towns. Some rural townships like Guiseley in Yorkshire, or in the South, Bromsgrove with its chapelry of King's Norton, had more in common with neighbouring villages than they did with the major corporate towns, though even here there were comparisons as well as contrasts. To cite three further instances from York, the apparently entirely urban parishes of St Mary, Bishophill Junior, St Michael-le-Belfrey and Holy Trinity, Micklegate, actually took in whole villages some distance from the city. The port of Hull, on the other hand, had not yet achieved its ecclesiastical emancipation and its two parishes continued as chapelries of adjacent villages. In upland areas of the West Riding parochial distribution diverged even more substantially from the norm, several churches holding sway over a number of subservient townships. Halifax with two dependent churches and as many as ten chapels all under the jurisdiction of its one vicar departs most strikingly from the situation prevailing in most lowland towns. Clearly an incumbent in a town like Halifax with several thousand parishioners from a very large rural region stood to gain much more from congregational giving than did the vicar of a small urban parish of between

200 and 300 souls. Urban parishes could, and frequently did, deviate far from the conventional stereotype.[2]

Just as in the sixteenth century there was geographically no sharp division between urban and rural parishes so, too, no clear differentiation can be made concerning the sources from which urban and rural clergy derived their incomes. By far the greater part of the clergy, irrespective of whether their parishes happened to lie in a town or in the countryside, drew their stipends from tithes and offerings. If rectors, incumbents had the right to both the greater and lesser tithes, that is tithes payable on crops arising directly from the ground, such as corn and hay, and tithes on creatures nourished by the land, cattle, sheep, pigs, poultry and their produce, wool, milk, cheese and eggs. They could also take personal tithes on the profits of trade and industry, offerings and certain fees. Vicars normally had no entitlement to any of the greater tithes, but only to the lesser tithes, personal tithes, fees and oblations. Both rectories and vicarages might possess glebe land which the incumbent could either farm himself or lease. Although More particularly criticized the extent of impropriations (perhaps as many as one-third of all parishes in England were impropriate in 1603) it seems that the impropriators had absorbed the whole of the tithes in a very small minority of these parishes, leaving the curate merely with a pension. Nevertheless, in a period of rapid inflation, the lot of such incumbents was a most unenviable one, as the experiences of the vicars of Warwick and Stratford-on-Avon demonstrate. The impropriators of these former collegiate churches, in both cases the town corporations, allotted the vicars £20 a year in the reign of Edward VI; they were still paying them exactly the same sum in 1586. Similarly, the curates of chapels of ease, usually appointed and paid by the incumbents of the mother churches, also made little headway against fixed stipends in the early modern period.[3]

Although monasteries had appropriated a disproportionate number of urban rectories in the Middle Ages, which had then come to the Crown at the Dissolution, some towns still retained rectories, and these, if they had kept rights to tithe in the adjacent countryside, were among some of the most sought-after of urban livings. More himself held one such rectory; Bury in the diocese of Chester was another. Because of the number of its parishes individual rectories in York had a much lower value than those in single-parish market towns, but the rector of St Saviour which included much of the village of Heworth nevertheless enjoyed a considerable income from tithe of both crops and livestock. In contrast, his fellow York rector of St John del Pike apparently gained nothing from his rectorial rights as this tiny parish had no lands outside the city walls. Contrary to previous assumptions, recent research suggests that rectors still usually levied the

greater part of their tithes in kind, and that they had agreed to comparatively few money commutations. Consequently well-endowed
rectories kept pace with, if they did not exceed, the spectacular rise in
the cost of living between 1500 and 1650. In the same way incumbents
with glebe who either farmed their parsonage land or let it on short
leases might at the very least have stayed abreast of inflation during
this period.[4]

The value of urban vicarages, like that of rectories, depended upon
the physical nature of the parish. In city vicarages with no extra-mural
land the lesser tithes might well have been confined to the produce of
gardens and yards. After energetically pursuing his tithes of apples,
pears and onions, pigs, chickens and pigeons, the vicar of St Martin's,
Coney Street in York in 1567 still failed to obtain an annual income of
more than £10. The more fortunate York vicars of St George's (which
contained much of the village of Naburn) and St Lawrence's (which
took in part of the fields of Heslington) in Elizabeth's reign benefited a
great deal more from their tithes of sheep and wool. In market towns,
especially where the vicar possessed considerable tithing rights,
incomes seem to have increased substantially between 1550 and
1650, though at a rather slower rate than those of rectors, largely
because the price of corn and hay rose more rapidly over the century
than did the prices of livestock and wool.[5]

As rectors and vicars of town parishes with some agricultural
interests, these incumbents might, therefore, well have found that their
incomes followed in the wake of their rural counterparts. In one important respect, however, in the matter of personal tithes, urban
clergy with only exiguous rights to lesser tithes fared very differently
from sixteenth-century country clergy. In the early thirteenth century
the Bishop of London had instituted a rent-charge in lieu of predial
tithes, and by the fifteenth century Londoners had established that
this charge, then 3s. 6d. in the £, also covered tithes due on the profits
of trade and industry. An Act of 37 Henry VIII subsequently reduced
London tithe payments from 3s. 6d. to 2s. 9d. in the £ on house rents.
Apart, it seems, from Canterbury where the inhabitants paid 2s. 6d. in
the £ on house rents, Londoners appear to have been exceptional in
accounting for their personal tithes in this form in the early Reformation period, though in Winchester and Southampton some citizens
calculated their oblations, by this time almost indistinguishable from
personal tithes, in proportion to the rent of their houses. Somewhat
later, in the reign of Philip and Mary, Coventry procured a private Act
of Parliament providing for the payment of tithes at the rate of 2s in the
£ on house rents, but few other towns appear to have employed a
similar manner of assessing personal tithes in the first half of the sixteenth century. If the *Valor Ecclesiasticus* can be seen as a reliable

guide, personal tithes of the profits of trade and industry still formed a
sizeable amount of an incumbent's stipend in both cities and market
towns in the 1530s. In Worcester, for example, well over half the
income of the 11 city clerics came from this source alone, and in York,
too, the total may have been about the same.[6]

When gathering personal tithes an incumbent must have relied far
more on the honesty and goodwill of the merchant and manufacturer
than when taking a tithe of agricultural produce and this problem of
collection may have led some clergy even before the Reformation to
consent to the substitution of a customary payment bearing little relation to an inhabitant's actual profits. Certainly a commutation had
taken place on the tithe of wages before the price rise had seriously got
under way (menservants, or their masters, commonly paid 4d. at
Easter, maidservants 2d., and this had the effect of negating any realistic tithe on wages, particularly since an Act of 1548 had exempted
day-labourers completely from this kind of tithe. As early as the reign
of Mary Tudor some clergy were complaining about the refusal of tradesmen to pay personal tithes and their protests became more strident
under Elizabeth, but the trend towards customary monetary payments continued unabated. By the end of the sixteenth century a
nominal 2d. a head at Easter in addition to 2d. for oblations may – as
at St Martin's in Worcester – have been all that remained in many
parishes of personal tithes. Even where the incumbent still tried to levy
personal tithes – as in the town of Ledbury in Hereforshire – most tradesmen only gave between 1s. and 1s. 6d. a head each year. In general
the incumbents of single-parish market towns with rights at least to
the lesser tithes do not seem to have suffered greatly from the loss of
personal tithes, but their virtual disappearance affected some city
clerics severely. In Worcester, in marked contrast with some neighbouring market towns, not only did the incomes of most city livings
not rise, in some cases they were actually less in nominal value in the
mid-seventeenth century than they had been in 1535. A similar situation seems to have pertained in York.[7]

In two other related fields town clergy seem also to have been at a
financial disadvantage when compared with rural clergy, because of
their greater dependence on other monetary payments which again
did not increase with the cost of living. Before the Reformation parishioners had customarily made offerings, often of ½d., at the four
major festivals of the year; during the course of the sixteenth century
these became fixed at the single payment of 2d. per communicant at
Easter. In regard to occasional fees charged at churchings, marriages
and burials some incumbents appear to have had a little more success
in raising their rates. In the diocese of Worcester some Elizabethan
clerics obtained 1s. for a wedding whereas a century later other incum-

bents received 2s. 6d. for a marriage with banns, 5s. for one with a licence. By the seventeenth century, burial in the chancel brought a rector a hefty fee of between 13s. 4d. and £1. On balance, however, the various sixteenth-century Acts of Parliament had a universally dele-terious effect upon an incumbent's income from fees. The abolition of chantries, obits and prayers for the dead put an end to small but regular sums for requiem masses. An Act of 1529 imposed a fixed rate of payments varying between 10s. and 3s. 4d. in place of the custom-ary mortuary of the deceased's second-best beast or garment; and once more no attempt was made to adjust the scale when prices began to rise. The more populous a parish, the more an incumbent forfeited by these changes. By no means all urban rectors and vicars counted upon personal tithes, oblations and fees for the major part of their income, but when they did, their financial position bordered on the desperate in the later sixteenth and early seventeenth century. How the differently situated urban clergy managed during a period of mounting inflation forms the subject of the remainder of this essay.[8]

Probate records supply extremely valuable details concerning the incomes of individual urban incumbents, though as evidence both wills and inventories are liable to certain drawbacks. An inventory of the deceased's personal property made within a few days of death can provide the most diverse information concerning the cleric's house-hold goods, his clothing, livestock, crops and equipment, his money and plate, and the debts both owing to him and which he himself owed. How accurately relations and friends appraised these goods must be a matter for conjecture, rare court-cases tending to confirm the supposition that goods were fairly generally valued at prices below those they might have fetched on the open market. From their everyday experience neighbours should have had little difficulty in setting a figure upon a cleric's household goods or farming stock, but they seem to have been somewhat disconcerted when confronted by the particular tools of his trade – his books – which feature very infre-quently in other than clerical households, at least until the end of the sixteenth century. These they often assessed on size alone, their pricing seeming especially erratic, as in Spalding in 1625 when valuers estimated the '15 great books and 120 lesser books' of John Hutchin-son, clerk, as worth a mere £4 out of a total personal estate of £318.[9]

As required by the statute of 21 Henry VIII inventories took account of a deceased's personal estate; they did not record his real property which could be very important and therefore cannot furnish a complete statement of a man's financial standing. To some extent wills can be brought in to supply this deficiency, since in the course of making a will a testator might refer to real property, though he had no obligation to do so. Wills rarely give a valuation for a property, and are obviously not open to statistical treatment, but nevertheless they reveal highly significant material not available in inventories. The inventory of Richard Bracket, for example, who died as the incumbent of St Augustine's in Norwich in 1633, sets his personal estate at £113 18s. 8d., a substantial sum, but an underestimate of his total wealth as his will makes clear. In addition to his personalty he owned a messuage and lands just outside the city in Wreningham and two other tenements in Norwich which enabled him to provide generous settlements for his daughter and two sons. Wills also occasionally supplement inventories in other respects, exposing lapses in recording a personal estate as is the case with a Worcester priest, William Rice. The appraisers of his goods returned the paltry total of £3 5s. 10d. in 1553, giving absolutely no indication of the fact that he had a further £32 14s. 2d. out on loan, only disclosed in a schedule attached to his will.[10]

Yet further disadvantages stand in the way of employing probate material to assess the wealth of urban clergy. By no means all clergy left wills or had inventories made of their goods, and even if they did, these records may no longer be in existence. There are now wills or inventories for less than half the clergy thought to have been resident in the archdeaconry of Lincoln in the second part of Elizabeth's reign. Work in York and Worcester confirms this impression of the failure of the clergy to make wills and of their heirs to have their goods appraised; there appears to have been a similar lack of concern to preserve these wills and inventories. The very poorest clergy are probably the ones most likely to have had virtually nothing to bequeath, and so to have gone unnoticed, and any account of the finances of the clergy in the sixteenth and seventeenth centuries must take into account this unknown (but almost certainly substantial) number of poor urban incumbents. Survival of probate records, moreover, varies greatly from diocese to diocese. In some towns it is impossible to make any estimates of the wealth of the local clergy because of the destruction of their wills and inventories. The loss of all clerical probate material for Bristol and Exeter in the early modern period precludes any consideration of the incumbents in these two cities, but for certain towns in the North-East, in East Anglia and in parts of the Midlands probate records are relatively abundant.[11]

While, therefore, the information derived solely from inventories can never give a completely accurate account of a cleric's wealth, and wills need to be consulted to provide a check upon the figures supplied by the inventories, the very bulk of the probate records for some English regions allows approximations to be made of the economic state of certain provincial urban clergy at particular points between 1520 and 1645. For the present purpose this century and a quarter has been divided into three almost equal periods of approximately 40 years, from 1520 until the death of Mary, the reign of Elizabeth, and from the accession of James I until *c.* 1645, and the analysis covers the wills and inventories of some 323 urban clerics (excluding cathedral prebendaries unless they also had town livings) from the dioceses of York and Worcester, the counties of Lincolnshire and Berkshire, and from Newcastle-on-Tyne, Durham and Norwich. The sample is perforce a very haphazard one because of the accidents of record preservation even within this area. While both Worcester diocese and Lincoln county have very full series of wills and inventories from before 1520, there are no inventories for Norwich before the 1580s and the situation is almost the same for Newcastle, Durham and the Berkshire towns. The diocese of York has very many registered wills from the late Middle Ages, but with the exception of dean and chapter livings, practically no inventories at all for the entire period. Consequently, for the 323 clerics there are 117 wills with inventories, 63 inventories without wills (in some of these cases the cleric had died intestate), and 114 wills without inventories.

Table 4: *Clergy inventories, 1520–59*

Inventories	1520–9	1530–9	1540–9	1550–9	Total
over £80	–	–	1	1	2
£70–80	–	–	1	–	1
£60–70	–	–	–	–	0
£50–60	–	–	–	–	0
£40–50	–	–	–	3	3
£30–40	–	–	4	3	7
£20–30	–	–	4	6	10
£10–20	–	3	3	7	13
£5–10	2	–	7	7	16
under £5	–	2	4	3	9
Total	2	5	24	30	61

Despite the random nature of this sample of urban clergy a fairly clear pattern emerges from the inventories even for the earliest of the three periods (table 4). As might have been anticipated, the inventories suggest that most urban clerics died with very modest assets, 48 out of the 62 being of goods of less than £30 including 9 of less than £5. For comparison, of the 51 inventories proved in the Southwell probate court between 1512 and 1559, 32 were of personal estates of under £30. An analysis of 69 Lincolnshire farming inventories for the decade 1530–40 gives 60 estates of under £30, 51 of these being of less than £20.[12]

A further examination of the evidence, however, yields less predictable results. The priest with the most highly valued goods, Richard Rundall with over £84, had held the relatively poor living of St Saviour's in York. This parish admittedly contained a large part of the village of Heworth, and Rundall had certainly been vigorous in his collection of the tithes of lambs pasturing in Heworth fields, but he could scarcely have accumulated goods on this scale from the income of this living alone: part of his wealth must have come from his former office of prior of Healaugh Park and from the state pension he gained on the priory's dissolution.[13]

It seems more than probable that other urban clergy died with personal estates similar to Rundall's, and here wills need to be brought in to supplement the inventories, especially since almost no inventories remain for the clergy of the rich one-parish Yorkshire towns. In the *Valor Ecclesiasticus* Halifax received the very high valuation of £84, Leeds of £38, Doncaster of just over £30, the livings of Wakefield, Guiseley, Dewsbury and Bradford of between £20 and £30 and those of Huddersfield, Rotherham and Pontefract of a little under £20. The career-minded clergy of the late medieval English Church regarded these as among the best urban livings in the northern province. Conspicuous among such men was Thomas Knowles, a native of Wakefield. As he approached death in 1547 he devised a scheme for an inscription to be placed over his grave in Wakefield church recording the fact that he had been 'doctor of divinity, and the vicar of this church, subdean of York, president of Magdalen College in Oxford, prebendary of Apesthorpe pertaining to the church of York, and also vicar of South Kirby.' Through pluralism Knowles had clearly built up a fairly considerable estate in goods, plate and real property; he left a messuage and half a burgate in Kirkgate for the upkeep of Wakefield bridge and the repair of local highways.[14]

While by and large the inventories of men of the stature of Knowles have not survived, those of humbler urban priests figure prominently in this early Reformation period. Some years ago K. L. Wood-Legh pointed out that financially there might be very little difference in income between chantries and benefices with cure of souls and that many two-way exchanges took place between rectors, vicars and chantry priests. Several inventories made between 1520 and 1559 tend to confirm her observation. Six if not seven of the 13 priests with goods worth more than £30 held chantries in Boston, Lincoln, Worcester and York, rather than cure of souls. Richard Cooke, priest of the important Corpus Christie guild of Boston, died in 1540 with a personal estate of over £80, though the debts he had incurred on the guild's behalf reduced this sum to a little more than £43. Five years later, even after the deduction of outstanding debts, his fellow priest, Thomas Crawes, had goods of over £70. William Utting, a former chantry priest of St George's chapel in Lincoln cathedral, in 1556 possessed goods worth £42 and a tenement and copyhold land in Braunstone. In York two chantry priests who both died in 1547 had personal estates of over £30: John Hixon had been a chantry priest in York Minster and a member of St William's College; his fellow priest, John Watson, had served a chantry in the parish church of St Saviour. The greater part of Watson's inventory, £25 out of a total of £35, consisted of money on loan which he had taken pains to set down in a special book. Obviously some urban priests lost a comfortable living when Parliament decreed the abolition of chantries in 1548.[15]

Wills demonstrate that a number of priests in easy circumstances, besides Utting, owned lands and houses at their death. John Bushby, priest probably of St Helen's in Worcester, in 1520 passed on a tenement with appurtenances in Tysoe to his brother, Nicholas, who had also entered the Church, while in Kidderminster 26 years later William Walker left a holding in the North Field to his two sisters, Elizabeth and Sybil. These may well have been family properties which had descended to the priests in the normal course of inheritance, but John Hall, the vicar of Huddersfield, who died in 1526, could have found sufficient resources from his living to purchase property: he had a sizeable estate of messuages, lands and tenements which he enfeoffed to the use of his will. Even in the city of York, where the generality of beneficed clergy might have been expected to have been rather poor, some priests owned real property. The Vicar of St Lawrence, Thomas Barton, had a cottage and garden in Stockton which went to his brother in 1523. Christopher Petty, the former chantry priest in St Mary, Bishophill Senior, had definitiely bought, and not inherited, a little house in Trinity Lane.[16]

The churchwardens' accounts of St Michael, Spurriergate, York, show how one York priest, Thomas Worral, who at his death had goods worth more than £20, had acquired this modest competency without ever joining the ranks of the beneficed clergy. Worral seems to have acted as a stipendary priest in St Michael's from before 1518 until his death in 1550, receiving small payments at obits and funerals as well as serving a poorly-endowed chantry. In addition he managed the extensive property which belonged to the church and drew up the accounts for which the parish paid him an annual wage of £5 as well as, later, allowing him a house rent free. His inventory exceeded by almost £7 that of a neighbouring vicar who held the living of All Saints, North Street.[17]

Many of the urban clergy of the Reformation period must, like Worral, have added to their finances by undertaking 'clerkly' duties such as keeping accounts and making wills and, like him, have been rewarded with gifts in money and kind by their parishioners. Even in populous towns, a few clerics augmented their incomes by engaging in farming. Thomas Logan, the vicar of Hessle and Hull, in 1538 owned a large flock of sheep in addition to a few cows and horses. The priest of the much less valuable vicarage of St Martin's, Lincoln, had at least 40 sheep when he died in 1548. Judging from wills and inventories, however, these farming ventures do not seem to have been very common. Far more usual in an urban context was the practice of money-lending, in some cases on a quite considerable scale given a priest's total resources. Besides Rice, another Worcester cleric, Humphrey Fawnes, who died in 1545 with goods of a mere £3 15s., had £33 owning to him in small debts and a third Worcester priest, Richard Davyth, in 1556 had £22 of an estate of £44 out on loan. Thomas Crawes, one of the Boston chantry priests, was owed £20 in 1545, his total personal estate amounting to £74: the estate of another Boston priest, which came to £35 14s. in 1550, included a total sum due to him of over £17, though this comprised some desperate debts.[18]

Other priests seem to have made money from teaching. In his will Richard Oliver, the vicar of All Saints, North Street, in York, who died in 1535, expressed a decided interest in education, bequeathing money to improve the boarding house of the Minster school and requesting permission for the scholars to attend his funeral. Since he had among his belongings humanist school books like Cicero's *Epistles* and *Offices* and the *Adages* of Erasmus he may well have undertaken some teaching himself. Robert Morres, who ended his life as rector of St Mary, Bishophill Senior, with goods of over £28, had conducted a school in connection with St John's guild in 1531 and some 20 years later had been appointed master of the civic school on Ouse bridge. The valuers of the goods of John Lee, priest of Boston, recalled the fact that Robert Sheppard in 1549 owed him 8s. 8d. for teaching his children. More affluent clergy like Simon Robinson, the vicar of Doncaster, or the Master of the Calendars of Bristol, John Flooke, showed their concern for education by leaving money to maintain children at school, or, like Edward Field, vicar of Evesham, by making gifts of books to the local schoolmaster.[19]

While a study of the wills and inventories of the clergy of the sample dying between 1520 and 1559 indicates that the majority of the priests lived reasonably comfortably, it equally demonstrates that the really poor urban priest did exist, and in some numbers. Twenty-six of the 62 priests died worth less than £10, and of these ten had goods worth under £5. Significantly, many of these men were beneficed, not stipendary or chantry priests. The vicar of St Lawrence's York, Thomas Barton, had goods of only £7 in 1523; the possessions of Peter Mudde, the vicar of Grimsby, just reached £6 nearly ten years later; the parson of St Alban's, Worcester, John Bayle, owned goods amounting to a

mere £3 3s. in 1538 and those of George Bellerby, the parson of St
Wilfrid's, York, only totalled £2 in 1546. Below these clerics must
have come those priests with virtually nothing to leave who do not
appear in the records at all.[20]

The impression given by the inventories of the second period in the
sample does not markedly differ from the first. Despite the five- to six-
fold increase in food prices between 1500 and 1600, the decades of the
1550s and 1590s witnessing particularly spectacular inflation, the
value of the goods left by urban clergy rises very little, certainly not in
proportion with the cost of living (table 5).[21]

Table 5: *Clergy inventories, 1560–1602*

Inventories	1560–9	1570–9	1580–9	1590–1602	Total
Over £100	–	1	–	–	1
£90–100	–	–	1	–	1
£80–90	1	1	–	–	2
£70–80	–	2	–	1	3
£60–70	–	2	–	–	2
£50–60	–	–	–	1	1
£40–50	–	–	2	2	4
£30–40	–	1	1	4	6
£20–30	1	2	2	2	7
£10–20	2	4	1	5	12
£5–10	–	4	3	4	11
Under £5	–	1	1	–	2
Total	4	18	11	19	52

In an innovatory article published some years ago F. W. Brooks put
the average inventory of the largely rural Lincolnshire clergy in the
1530s at just under £30 and then went on to register a quadrupling of
this average during the remainder of the century to £120 in the 1590s.
W. G. Hoskins has shown that Leicestershire country rectors (though
not vicars) seem to have been as prosperous as those in Lincolnshire at
the end of Elizabeth's reign. In his work on the clergy as money-
lenders, which brings in a rather wider spectrum of clerics, B. A. Holderness finds that in the 1570s many died with personal estates of
around £50. In this sample of urban clergy, however, only ten out of
52 clergy had personal estates of over £50. The picture, nevertheless,
seems a little less black when these urban clergy are compared with
other sectors of Elizabethan society. Of 248 inventories from Oxfordshire from between 1560 and 1590, 46 were for more than £50 (nine
being for over £100) while 202 were for below £50 and 159 of these
for below £30. Similarly, of 75 Lincolnshire farming inventories for
the decade 1590–1600 33 were for more than £50, four being for over

£100, while 42 were for below £50, and 24 of these of less than £30.[22]

Another noteworthy feature of this second period is the fall in the overall number of inventories which must surely reflect the abolition of the office of chantry priest. The new paucity of clergy in towns like Boston and Hull, one- and two-parish towns respectively, stands out especially sharply, but is also present – though masked – in the multi-parish cities of York, Lincoln and to a lesser degree, Worcester. The reluctance of men to enter the ministry in the early years of Elizabeth's reign, the financial unattractiveness of many urban livings to incoming clergy once the (subsidized) generation of former chantry priests had gone would have led to a sharing of clerical duties among a much smaller group of men. Perhaps for this reason, despite inflation, a handful of the clergy in the sample seem to have attained a resonably adequate standard of living. One urban cleric in his middle period, Richard Hall, with assets of over £172 appears far ahead of all his fellows, and there can be little doubt that he had obtained his prosperity from extensive pluralism. He had been a prebendary of Worcester cathedral since 1549 and served as vicar-general to the Marian bishop of Worcester. At his death, which probably took place late in 1560, he apparently also retained the rectories of both Stourbridge and St Swithin's, Worcester, as well as being vicar of the lucrative parsonage of Bromsgrove. Of the nine other clergy who left goods valued at over £50, one other, Robert Chauntler, ministered at Bromsgrove, one in Grantham, one in Boston and one in Spalding, all single- or at the most double-parish towns.[23]

Very interestingly, there are also signs that a few clergy who held livings in the multi-parish cities and towns were beginning to gain a similar economic competency. Again, some clergy clearly achieved this only through pluralism. In York fairly regularly now vicars-choral alternated between their office in the minster and a dean and chapter living in the city or in one of the Ridings. Robert Mell, who died in 1573 with goods assessed at over £66, may have been a pluralist of this kind, as his colleague, John Steel, who died in the same year with goods of a little over £60, certainly was: a vicar-choral since 1547, Steel had ministered in a succession of York city cures. In addition, some other towns and cities could produce other relatively affluent urban incumbents. In Norwich Thomas Roberts, clerk of St Clement's, had goods worth over £98 in 1584 and Richard Butt, preacher at St Andrew's, goods of some £44 in 1596. In Lincoln James Gayton, M.A., preacher at St Peter's, had £49 in moveables in 1596 together with leases of a mill and houses, while in the much smaller town of Stamford which also contained several poorly endowed benefices, John Walkewood, parson of All Saints, in 1575 had possessions of over £70.[24]

Moving from the inventories to the wills of these Elizabethan clerics, it seems that rather more than in the earlier period owned real property and this appears especially to have been the case in the North of England. In Bradford in 1596 the vicar, Christopher Taylor, bequeathed several tenements and lands there and in Horton to his wife and children. Edward Maude, the vicar of Wakefield who died in 1598, also had messuages in his parish and elsewhere in Yorkshire to pass on to his family. In Newcastle-on-Tyne the vicar of St Nicholas, Richard Holdsworth, had acquired a house in Pilgrim Street, and another Newcastle cleric, John Morehouse, whose goods alone came to more than £77 in 1596, had a lease of the lordship of Kelton. As in the earlier period some of these clergy may well have inherited their property, but on the most conservative estimate at least Maude and Holdsworth seem to have been purchasing property in their towns of adoption.[25]

Some of the incumbents of these urban cures continued to farm as some town clergy in the previous period had done. In 1581 at Halesowen the vicar, William Ellin, gave several separate bequests of sheep and a heifer in his will, and farm animals and crops together made up a considerable proportion of his inventory which amounted to a little over £38. Some Norwich clergy also kept livestock: Henry Lynye, who died as the minister of St Edmund's in 1601, besides horses and cattle had two acres of wheat, three of barley and half an acre of rye, comprising almost half of his inventory of over £37. In Boston Lawrence Colles had more cattle and sheep, but no crops. Other clergy had money to invest. Of an inventory amounting to £66 Robert Mell, the York vicar-choral, had no less than £25 out on loan in 1673. In the same year his fellow vicar, John Steel, had lent £14 out of a total of £60. In 1575 Thomas Pentland, a former Durham monk and after the Dissolution incumbent of St Oswald's in Durham, had £13 owing to him out of a personal estate of £37, and from an almost exactly comparable estate Lawrence Colles of Boston had £13 in debts in 1601. In addition to his two houses in Boston, John Gamble, clerk of Grimsby, had £38 in bonds when he died in 1582.[26]

Whatever their financial standing, far more of the urban clergy in this middle period owned books. Whereas in the first half of the sixteenth century only very enterprising priests like Richard Oliver of York had procured new humanist books, the great majority contenting themselves with the necessary service-books, missals, breviaries, processionals, and an occasional *Golden Legend,* a *Catholicon* or a medieval handbook for priests, such as the *Pupilla Oculi,* now very many more had both acquired more books (and notably more modern books) and showed a new pride in their possession. As early as 1565 John Bretchgirdle, the vicar of Stratford-on-Avon, distributed

Musculus on Matthew and a homily to the local schoolmaster, Eliot's dictionary to the school, and numerous books in English and Latin, ranging from Josephus on the Jewish War, Virgil, Sallust, Cicero and the *Enchiridion* of Erasmus, to Aesop's *Fables*, the Acts of the Apostles, the Psalms and dictionaries for beginners to a whole host of children who may have been Bretchgirdle's pupils. In 1572 Edward Rhodes, the vicar of Newark, bequeathed Fox's *Acts and Monuments* to the parish church, and the works of Chrysostom, Ambrose, Basil, Gregory, and Bernard together with Luther on the Epistles and Gospels to his successor in the living, adding for good measure a gift of Suetonius to Gabriel Close's student son. In Stamford in 1575 the appraisers of John Walkwood's study listed 60 great books, 20 lesser books, and 20 yet smaller ones, setting them at a total of £15, and another Stamford incumbent, John Mossey, much less wealthy, still had 32 books plus some little books, though they were rated at no more than £1 in 1587. John Morehouse's library in Newcastle, apparently much more realistically valued at £24 in 1596, contained the writings of Whitgift, Jewel, Harding and Fulke, a Tremellius Bible, Calvin's *Sermons*, Beza's New Testament as well as Erasmus's *Adages*, a *Golden Legend* and a lexicon. His assistant, Clement Cookson, who perhaps supplemented his curacy at St John's with some school teaching, had obtained the sermons of Cooper, Smith and John Udall, a book of precedents and Beza's *Questions*, and left a dictionary to the Newcastle schoolmaster for the use of his scholars.[27]

Now that they might legally marry, some clergy understandably in their wills paid great attention to the upbringing of their children. In 1569 John Clark, the vicar of the north side of Grantham, gave all his books worth 40s. to his son, John, 'beseeching the Almighty that he may use them well', and provided a further £24 in money 'for his better education in the Lord'. If John died before reaching his majority he wished his house to go to Christ's College in Cambridge to fund a scholarship there for a poor man's son from Grantham. (Two generations later the vicar of Kendal, Ralph Tyrer, made a very similar bequest, giving over his whole estate to establish scholarships at Trinity College, Cambridge, if his only son died a minor.) Edward Maude, who for a time acted as headmaster of the grammar school in addition to being vicar of Wakefield, in 1598 bestowed an annuity of 10s. on the school and also revealed in passing that in compliance with his father's dying request he had maintained his younger brother at Oxford university. Four of Maude's sons matriculated at Cambridge, Edward going on to become a vicar in Lincolnshire, while Daniel emigrated with Richard Mather to New England, taught first in Boston Latin School, and subsequently accepted the charge of the church at Dover in New Hampshire.[28]

Whereas ten of these Elizabethan urban clergy seem to have accumulated a reasonable competency with goods of over £50, and a
further ten attained a degree of financial independence with goods of
over £30, still 32 out of 52 had goods of less than £30, and of these the
13 with goods valued at under £10 must have been considered poor by
any standard. As might have been expected, a disproportionate
number of these clergy held inadequately endowed livings in Worcester, Reading, York, Norwich and Lincoln. As late as 1589 the
wealth in moveables of Garvin Browne of St Clement's, Norwich,
barely exceeded £4. In 1593 the clerk of St Margaret's, Norwich,
Robert Read, had a personal estate of only £5 13s., and two decades
earlier the goods of Thomas West, vicar of St Martin's, Lincoln, and
those of Edward Baker, vicar of St John's, Worcester, had been assessed respectively at a little over and a little under £5. The poverty and
anonymity of these particular Elizabethan city incumbents supplies
yet further support for More's contention than insufficient livings
produced insufficient clergy.[29]

Table 6   *Clergy inventories, 1603–45*

Inventories	1603–12	1613–22	1623–32	1633–45	Total
Over £1,000	–	1	–	2	3
£500–1,000	–	–	–	–	0
£400–500	–	–	–	–	0
£300–400	1	–	1	1	3
£200–300	–	–	1	4	5
£100–200	2	3	3	9	17
£90–100	–	2	–	2	4
£80–90	–	1	–	3	4
£70–80	–	1	–	2	3
£60–70	–	1	1	1	3
£50–60	1	–	–	3	4
£40–50	1	1	–	–	2
£30–40	1	–	1	1	3
£20–30	1	1	–	1	3
£10–20	3	2	–	1	6
£5–10	1	2	–	1	4
Under £5	–	1	1	1	3
Total	11	16	8	32	67

The overall picture derived from Elizabethan inventories, of a
group of clerics in only a minority of cases coping adequately with the
rise in the cost of living, contrasts dramatically with that of the third
and final period of the survey which takes in the first 40 years of the
seventeenth century (table 6). This table leaves little room for doubt
that more clergy had now achieved a greater prosperity than in either

of the two previous periods, and they had done this at a time when inflation had not been increasing at anything like the same extent as in the sixteenth century. Of the 67 inventories 46 are for clergy with possessions of over £50, including three of men with personal estates in each case amounting to well over £1,000. These figures are all the more significant when compared with the inventories of other sections of Early Stuart England. In the first half of the seventeenth century merchants in smaller towns in the South-East were dying with inventories of between £30 and £40, in medium towns of between £80 and £90, few merchants outside London having estates of over £600. At the very other end of the scale, in Somerset some labourers were thought to have had comfortable cottage estates if they possessed goods of between £7 and £12. After the Restoration Lichfield vicars-choral in the 1660s and 1670s still had no more than £30–£35 in moveables. Even at the beginning of the eighteenth century out of some 1,000 Worcestershire inventories 45 per cent were for under £50 and only 32 per cent for over £100: nearly half of all labourers whose inventories have been preserved had personal estates valued at under £10.[30]

Pluralism must again be the chief explanation for how two out of the three clerical plutocrats in the sample amassed fortunes of over £1,000. William Morton, B.D., who may have originated from Leicestershire, and who died worth £1,853 in 1620, was archdeacon of Durham and vicar of Easington as well as being vicar of Newcastle-on-Tyne. Without question he had been living the life of a cultured gentleman at his two elegantly furnished vicarages in Newcastle and Easington: the appraisers of his goods put his library of 2,500 books alone at £300, that is at exactly half the sum of the great library of archbishop Toby Matthew which his wife presented to York Minster in 1628. Richard Perrot, another B.D. and a Londoner by birth, who died in 1641 with a personal estate of over £1,900, combined a prebend in York Minster with his benefice of Hessle and Hull. He had landed property in both Hessle and Hull in addition to this personal estate, and had acquired at least one advantageous lease, that of Osbaldwick, through his membership of the York chapter. Besides his household goods, his books, plate and money secured by bonds together came to £1,215. The most intriguing, however, of these rich clerics is John Okell, vicar of Bradford, for unlike Morton and Perrot, he does not seem to have indulged in pluralism, nor to have belonged to the clerical establishment of the day. A convinced Calvinist Protestant at a time when his archbishop was leading the Arminian revival, Okell quietly built up an estate of over £1,000 which, dying childless, he ordained should be divided between his wife, three brothers and three sisters. Since he had grown up in Cheshire, it seems

probable that he had purchased at least some of his lands in the West
Riding from the profits of his cure, which his executors sold for £200,
and it may well be that other Yorkshire vicars, whose inventories have
not survived, also enjoyed a somewhat similar standard of living in the
early seventeenth century. Certainly the will of Joshua Smith, vicar of
Huddersfield, reveals that he had lands and houses in South Owram
and Halifax to pass on to his family on his death in 1619: again from
their wills it is clear that another vicar of Bradford, Caleb Kemp, who
died in 1614, owned lands in both his parish and far afield in Sussex,
while Robert Clay, D.D., the vicar of the immense parish of Halifax,
had a very large sum of money in stock and bonds on his death in
1624.[31]

Outside this small band of very wealthy clergy the inventories disclose a larger group of clerics, some 43 out of 67, with goods between
£50 and £360. Among these, as might be predicted, appear the incumbents of the one-or two-parish towns of Spalding, Bromsgrove,
Rotherham, Halifax, Pershore, Evesham, Droitwich and Skipton.
Significantly, some vicars of multiple-parish cities, such as Norwich,
Worcester, Lincoln and York, feature almost as prominently.
Thomas Newhouse, for example, 'preacher of God's word' in the
parish of St Andrew in Norwich, had possessions of £368 in 1611 and
had secured over £200 of this sum with bills and bonds. Among the
books in his library, which he gave to the curate of St John's, Ber
Street, was a Geneva Bible, Calvin on Job, and Calvin's *Institutes*. A
man of very different churchmanship, Ralph Hansby, who in 1635
arranged a deliberately 'medieval' funeral for himself, with tapers and
singing boys to conduct his body to the grave, also had goods worth
over £312. As vicar simultaneously of St Mary's, Nottingham, and
the rural parish of Barton-in-the-Beans in the patronage of the archbishop of York, Hansby again had clearly profited from pluralism. In
York Henry Ayscough, whose goods were valued at £158 in 1643,
had for years held his cure of All Saints, Pavement, in conjunction with
a civic lectureship of £40 per annum. Two other York clergy,
however, who died in 1644, George Leadall, vicar of St Denys in
Walmgate, and John Perins, vicar of the equally poorly endowed cure
of St Mary, Castlegate, without such sponsorship by the corporation
could still acquire goods of £138 and £89 respectively.[32]

This middling group of clergy also seems to have had more money
than previous groups in the sample to put into bills and bonds. In
Norwich alone, in addition to Thomas Newhouse, Ralph Same in
1635 had half his personal estate of £88 in a 'good' debt, Robert Gell
£95 in bonds three years later, Richard Gammon, rector of St
Lawrence's for nearly 40 years, £54 out on loan in 1640 and John
Barnham, minister of St John's since 1627, £140 invested for the

benefit of his little granddaughter. Another Norwich clerk, Thomas Drake, with personal property exceeding £100 in 1617 also had tenements in St Margaret's parish. Similarly, in Lincoln in 1604, Adam Gartside had £100 out of an estate of £190 in bills and bonds, his successor at St Peter at Arches, Thomas Bishop, £98 out of £127. In Worcester also in 1644, George Druman of St Andrew's died with loans of £83 out of a total estate of £96; William Cotterell of St Andrew's of £87 out of a total of £115; and in 1647 John Harvey of St Clement's of £44 out of £55. With incumbents such as these in Norwich, Lincoln and Worcester attaining this modest prosperity, it is less surprising that in 1632 the vicar of Leeds, Alexander Cooke, could set aside a jointure of £100 for his daughter and leave a further £100 and his books to be divided between his two sons.[33]

By now a considerable number of these urban clergy were preparing their children for ecclesiastical careers, another indication that they looked upon the Church as a worthwhile and perhaps in economic terms even a lucrative profession. In 1632 Alexander Cooke, who already had a nephew studying at Oxford, wished one of his sons to be brought up as a scholar, the other to be apprenticed to the godly lord mayor of York, Thomas Hoyle. The vicar of Halifax, Robert Clay, made equally careful plans for his son's education, first with a Buckinghamshire preacher and then at either Magdalen or Merton College in Oxford. As was only consistent in a critic of ill-qualified clergy, Robert More lavished his attention on his 'hopeful' grandson, Jeremy Levett, whom he intended should follow him as rector of Guiseley. Across the Pennines, Thomas Coller, rector of Malpas, donated the advowson of Swettenham to his grandson, John Dod, for his better preferment. While few clergy like More actually owned the living where they ministered, others had acquired presentation rights, as Coller had done, in order to make sure of places in the Church for their descendants. Matthew Stoneham of Norwich left the presentation of Eyke in Suffolk to his daughter on the understanding that she should give the rectory to one of his sons when it became vacant. Some clerical dynasties passed through the female line. In 1616 the vicar of Grimsby, Robert Lord, bequeathed a book in which he had recorded the Easter duties to his 'son' (almost certainly his son-in-law) Dalby who succeeded him as vicar. William Dalby in his turn at his death gave to his nephew the next presentation to St James's church in Grimsby.[34]

Not all the clergy in the sample, however, had arrived at this level of prosperity and some still died poor, though there seem to have been rather fewer really poor urban clergy in the first half of the seventeenth century than in either of the two earlier periods. Sixteen of the 67 clerics had goods of less than £30, and 13 of these, almost without exception beneficed in the cities of Durham, Lincoln, Norwich, Worcester and York, goods of less than £20. Two Lincoln ministers, William Taylor and Robert Rawlins, died in 1609 and 1619 with estates respectively of just under £13 and just under £12. Thomas Ganderton, the parson of St Clement's, Worcester, in 1618 left possessions valued at less than £7; his companion in poverty, James Aingel, minister of St Helen's, in 1642 had a personal estate of only just over £5. In Norwich in 1613 the goods of Lancelot Pease of All Saints amounted to a scant £7 and in York in 1605 those of the rector of St Crux, William Thompson, only cleared £6.[35]

Even when due allowance has been made for this continuing poverty among some urban clergy, the question still remains as to how the generality of these men had attained their relative degree of prosperity by the outbreak of the Civil War. Pluralism in 1640 as in 1520 accounts for the wealth of some of the clerics, but by no means all. The halting of the price rise allowed some urban incumbents, particularly though not exclusively those of one-parish towns who derived a substantial proportion of their income from rural tithes, to catch up with, if not to overtake, the cost of living. Clergy and laity alike benefited from this direct link between ecclesiastical endowment and agricultural market forces, hence the vehemence of More's denunciation of those 'covetous worldlings' who were withholding profits from the Church. Had impropriations been restored in the Church ŏn any scale during Laud's archiepiscopate it would have been well on the way to becoming a very rich institution indeed, and, under farsighted leadership, much might have been done to improve the lot of the poorer clergy. Lay rectors, consequently, offered an easy target to embattled clerics, and without doubt some clergy, urban as well as rural, did suffer under unworthy lay patrons. Richard Langford, the vicar of St Peter's, Droitwich, referred to one such patron in his will of 1640, asserting that the guardians of Sir John Packington had defrauded him of as much as £100 in tithes.[36]

Granted the political and social impossibility of a wholesale egalitarian re-endowment of the Church, the urban clergy in general nevertheless probably gained as much as they lost by the attentions of the laity in the later sixteenth and early seventeenth century. Some of this came about through the enterprise of the clergy themselves. Better-educated ministers (and far more of the clergy in the sample had university degrees at the end than at the beginning of the period) had even wider opportunities for adding to their incomes by their own efforts. Besides the traditional 'secretarial' activities such as will-making and accountancy, clerics took advantage of the growing demand for education, and more town clergy, like Maude in Wakefield, may have taught in a grammar school at some stage of their careers. The clergy of urban parishes without a rural hinterland, moreover, did not supinely acquiesce in the disappearance of personal tithes. Looking to London as a precedent the ministers of Norwich as a body petitioned Parliament in 1607 for a bill to enforce the payment of 2s. in the £ on every house and shop in the city. They failed to obtain their Act, but the Privy Council intervened to order the mayor and corporation to levy a graduated tax on inhabitants for the annual maintenance of ministers 'according to their difference in gifts, sufficiency and diligence in their function.' A later award of Charles I in 1638 did fix the rate at the desired 2s. in the £, though the outbreak of the Civil War prevented its implementation. As the result of another petition from the York clergy the Privy Council in 1629 authorized the taking of a rate on house rents in the city after the example of Norwich. Apparently on their own initiative the chamber of Exeter in 1582 had required every household according to its size to pay either a penny or halfpenny to the parish minister each week, and in Oxford from the late sixteenth century at least houses of a rentable value of 30s. *per annum* and above were paying a penny a week to the incumbent or the impropriator.[37]

Popular evangelical clerics probably received more financially from the voluntary gifts of individual patrons than from these obligatory contributions. Robert More described at length in his will how a group of the Protestant nobility which included the Countess of Cumberland, her father, the Earl of Bedford, Peregrine Bertie, Lord Willoughby and the Earl of Oxford, had collaborated to buy the advowson of Guiseley, installed him as rector and given him the presentation in perpetuity, and even in this sample of clergy he did not stand alone as a beneficiary of this sort of noble patronage: John Beech, clerk of St Peter at Arches, Lincoln, died in 1634 in receipt of a legacy of £18 10s. from the Countess of Warwick. The civic élite of some towns displayed just as much eagerness to promote Protestantism as certain members of the nobility. At the very beginning of Elizabeth's reign some inhabitants of Boston pledged themselves to pay sums varying from £5 to 20s. a year to the preacher Melchior Smith, before emissaries of Hull town council enticed him away with an offer of the living of Holy Trinity. In Leeds in the 1580s the 'better sort' of the inhabitants bought the advowson of St Peter's, presented Robert Cooke and later paid for a lecturer to assist him in his ministry. The corporation of Northampton acquired the rectorial rights of All Saints in 1619 for £200 and set up trustees to appoint the incumbent. These councillors realized quite as clearly as More that to obtain the type of cleric they wanted they had to pay an adequate stipend.[38]

Almost all towns of any size had created a civic lectureship by the end of the sixteenth century, and the grant of a lectureship, or even of a regular preaching commission, could very usefully, as in York, add some £40 or more to the income a local incumbent drew from his parish cure. The governors of York, in company with those of Lincoln and Exeter (and in this respect very different from the 'forward' corporations of Hull and Norwich) developed an active commitment to Protestantism rather late in the sixteenth century, but they hastened to make amends for their predecessors' lack of zeal. Few leading citizens died after 1600 without requesting a funeral sermon, and this alone would have given a favoured minister a fee of £1, £2 or £3: over the years some clerics might gain a competent sum from a source such as this. Some lay-people went further and began taking measures to supplement permanently the income of certain incumbents. In York in 1640 Mrs Moseley gave an annuity of £40 to support a preaching minister at St John's, Ousebridge; two years earlier alderman Thomas Hoyle had made over land in Drax to augment the living of St Martin's, Micklegate; a Mr Cotter had left a rent-charge of £8 to increase the stipend of the rector of St Michael's, Spurriergate, and numerous citizens bequeathed money to their clergy in their wills. Evidence for these sorts of activities will always be elusive and impossible to quantify, but urban clergy on poorly endowed cures who managed to gain a reasonable sufficiency of goods probably owed more to the direct and indirect giving of the laity than has yet been fully acknowledged.[39]

While the causes of the amelioration of the living standards of many provincial urban clergy in the first part of the seventeenth century must remain to some extent conjectural, the fact of this improvement seems to be well attested both by the increasingly generous provision these clerics made for their families in their wills and by the valuation of their personal estates. Any conclusions drawn from probate records can only be impressionistic, but it seems that in respect of the urban clergy More spoke more accurately than perhaps he knew when he lauded the 'godly endeavours and zealous care' not so much of the English monarchs or of the English bishops, but of the 'honourable nobles and whole estate' of the commonalty. Town incumbents may well have lost quite valuable rights to certain income and fees in the course of the Reformation, but at least in some towns where the need was greatest they fairly soon started receiving forms of voluntary maintenance from the laity. From his Arminian standpoint Laud in the 1639s had indeed good reason for his fear of this economic 'dependence of the clergy'.[40]

NOTES

1. BI Original Chancery wills 1642 and Archbishop's Register 32, fos. 107r–108v (More); the very long preamble is printed in full in R. A. Marchant, *The Puritans and the Church Courts in the Diocese of York 1560–1642* (1960), 212–14. The spelling of all quotations has been modernized.
2. W. J. Sheils, 'Religion in provincial towns: innovation and tradition', in *Church and Society in England: Henry VIII to James I*, ed. F. Heal and R. O'Day (1977), 160–2; M. E. François, 'The social and economic development of Halifax 1558–1640', *Procs. Leeds Philosophical and Literary Soc.*, XI pt viii (1966), 217–80.
3. D. M. Barratt, 'The condition of the parish clergy between the Reformation and 1660, with special reference to the dioceses of Oxford, Worcester and Gloucester' (D.Phil. thesis, University of Oxford, 1949) 180–1, 198; I am most indebted to Dr Barratt for the loan of her thesis and for her advice; R. Houlbrooke, *Church Courts and People during the English Reformation 1520–1570* (1979), 122–50.
4. Barratt, *op. cit.*, 196–7, 200, 210–21; E. Kerridge, 'The movement of rent 1540–1640', in *Essays in Economic History*, ed. E. M. Carus Wilson, II (1962), 216–17, 219–20.
5. BI CPG 1331, CPG 494, CPH 1174; Barratt, *op. cit.*, 196–7, 224.
6. Barratt, *op. cit.*, 320–1; A. G. Little, 'Personal tithes', *EHR*, LX (1945), 67–88; D. M. Gransby, 'Tithe disputes in the diocese of York 1540–1639' (M. Phil. thesis, University of York, 1966), 41–4; Houlbrooke, *op. cit.*, 123–4.
7. Barratt, *op. cit.*, 298–321; Gransby, *op. cit.*, 54, 353–7.
8. Barratt, *op. cit.*, 286–98.
9. F. W. Steer, 'Short guides to records: 3 probate inventories', *History*, XLVII (1962), 287–90; J. Thirsk (ed.) *The Agrarian History of England and Wales*, IV (1967), 277–8; M. Cash (ed.), *Devon Inventories of the Sixteenth and Seventeenth Centuries* (Devon and Cornwall Record Society, N.S. XI, 1966), viii-ix; Lincs. AO, Inv 136/16 (Hutchinson).
10. Norwich RO, NCC wills 226–31 Playford and CN Inv 41/068 (Bracket); Hereford and Worcester RO, 008.7 BA 3585/16b wills 1554 no. 32 (Rice).
11. See Below, B. A. Holderness, 'The clergy as money-lenders', p. 200; Cash (ed.), *op. cit.*, viiff.; P. McGrath and M. E. Williams (eds.), 'Bristol wills 1546–1593' (Bristol, typescript, 1975).
12. P. A. Kennedy (ed.), *Nottinghamshire Household Inventories* (Thoroton Society, Record Series XXII, 1963); J. Thirsk, *English Peasant Farming* (1957), 45.
13. BI Archbp Reg 29, f. 104r-v and Original Chancery wills 1550 (Rundall); J. S. Purvis, *Select XVIth Century Causes in Tithe* (Yorkshire Archaeological Society, Record Series, CXIV, 1949), 9–16.
14. BI Archbp Reg 29, fos. 82r–84r (Knowles).
15. K. L. Wood-Legh, *Perpetual Chantries in Britain* (1965), 207; Lincs. AO, LCC wills 1541/21 and Inv 10/29 (Cooke); Inv 14/115 (Crawes); LCC wills 1553–6/202 and Inv 25/48 (Utting); BI, D and C Original wills 1547 (Watson, Hixon).
16. Hereford and Worcester RO, 008.7 BA 3590/1 vol. II, f. 68r-v (Bushby); 3585/16b wills 1555, no. 47 (Walker), and J. S. Roper (ed.), *Worcestershire Clergy Wills and Inventories 1541–1558* (1972), 21–2; BI Archbp Reg 27, f. 153r (Hall); D and C Prob Reg 2, f. 136r and D and C Original wills 1523 (Barton); D and C Prob Reg 3, f. 44r-v (Petty).
17. BI D and C Original wills 1550 (Worrall); PRY/MS 3 and MS 4 (St Michael, Spurriergate churchwardens' accounts); Original Chancery wills [1535] (Oliver).
18. Lincs. AO, LCC wills 1545–9, 310 and Inv 17/161 (Ellis); Inv 14/115 (Crawes); Inv 19/150 (Wells); BI Archbp Reg 28, f. 178v (Logan); Hereford and Worcester RO, 008.7 BA 3585/15b wills 1554 no. 32 (Rice); 3585/8b wills 1545 no. 390

(Fawnes); 3585/17b wills 1556 no. 95 (Davyth).

19. BI Archbp Reg 28, f. 168r–69r (Oliver); Original Chancery wills 1559 (Morres); Archbp Reg 27, f. 163r-v (Robinson); J. A. Moran, *Education and Learning in the City of York 1300–1560* (Borthwick Paper no. 55, 1979), 13; Hereford and Worcester RO, 008.7 BA 3585/4b wills 1540 no. 61 (Flooke); 3590/1 vol. V f. 125r-v (Field); Lincs AO Inv 17/177 (Lee).

20. BI D and C Prob Reg 2, f. 136r and D and C Original wills 1523 (Barton); Archbp Reg 29, f. 99v and Original Chancery wills 1546 (Bellerby); Lincs AO Inv 9/241 (Mudde); Hereford and Worcester RO 008.7 BA 3585/3b wills 1538 no. 377a (Bayle).

21. E. H. Phelps Brown and S. V. Hopkins, 'Seven centuries of the prices of consumables', in *Essays in Economic History*, ed. E. M. Carus Wilson, II (1962), 179–96; Y. S. Brenner, 'The inflation of prices in England 1551–1650', *Ec HR*, 2nd ser., xv (1962–3), 266–78.

22. F. W. Brooks, 'The social position of the parson in the sixteenth century', *J. British Arch. Assoc.*, 3rd ser. x (1945–7), 23–37; W. G. Hoskins, 'The Leicestershire country parson in the sixteenth century', in *Essays in Leicestershire History* (1950), 1–23; see below, Holderness, 'The clergy as money-lenders', p.204 M. A. Havinden (ed.), *Household and Farm Inventories of Oxfordshire 1550–1590* (HMC and Oxfordshire Record Society, XLIV 1965), 8; Thirsk, *op. cit.*, 45.

23. Hereford and Worcester RO, 008.7 BA 3590/2, vol. VI pt II, f. 289v-90r (Hall) and A. B. Emden, *A Biographical Register of the University of Oxford AD 1501 to 1540* (1974), 260–1.

24. BI D and C Prob Reg 5, f. 67r and D and C Original wills 1573 (Mell, Steel) Norwich RO, CN Inv 02/106 (Roberts); Inv 13/032 (Butt); Lincs. AO LCC wills 1596 153 and Inv 87/168 (Gayton); Inv 82/226 (Walkwood).

25. BI Original Chancery wills 1598 (Taylor); Original Chancery wills 1599 and Archbp Reg 31, f. 134v-5r (Maude); Durham University, Dept of Palaeography and Diplomatic, Durham Probate Records Holdsworth 1596; Morehouse 1596 A and B.

26. Hereford and Worcester RO, 008.7 BA 3585/17a wills 1581 no. 94 (Ellin); Norwich RO, CN Inv 17/121 (Lynye); Lincs. AO, LCC Admon 1600/30 (Colles); LCC wills 1582 24 and Inv 67/376 (Gamble); BI D and C Original wills 1573 (Mell, Steel); Durham University, Dept of Palaeography and Diplomatic, Durham Probate Records, Pentlande 1574.

27. Hereford and Worcester RO, 008.7 BA 3585/40b wills 1565 no. 34 (Bretchgirdle); BI Archbp Reg 30, f. 178v (Rhodes); Lincs. AO, Inv 58/226 (Walkwood); LCC Adm 1587/1153 (Mossey); Durham University, Dept of Palaeography and Diplomatic, Durham Probate Records Morehouse 1596 A and B; Cockson, 1598.

28. Lincs. AO, LCC wills 1574 i 337 and Inv 56/235 (Clark); J. P. Earwaker (ed.), *Lancashire and Cheshire wills and inventories*, II (Chetham Society, XXVIII, 893), 197–9 (Tyrer); BI Original Chancery wills 1599 and Archbp Reg 31, f. 134v-5r (Maude); J. and J. A. Venn, *Alumni Cantabrigienses*, pt I, vol. II (1922), 163.

29. Norwich RO, CN Inv 05/098 (Browne); CN Inv 10/211 (Reade); Lincs. AO, LCC wills 1577 i 60 and Inv 61/90 (West); Hereford and Worcester RO, 008.7 BA 3585/60b wills 1576 no 92 (b) (Baker).

30. R. Grassby, 'The personal wealth of the business community in seventeenth century England', *Ec HR*, 2nd ser. xxiii (1970), 231–2; Thirsk (ed.), *Agrarian History*, IV, 419–21; D. G. Vaisey (ed.), *Probate Inventories of Lichfield and District 1568–1680*, Collections for a History of Staffordshire, 4th ser. 5 (1969), 143, 154, 178–9, 247–8; J. A. Johnson, 'Worcestershire probate inventories 1699–1716', *Midland History*, iv (1978), 198.

31. Durham University, Dept of Palaeography and Diplomatic, Durham Probate

Records Morton 1620; BI Original Chancery wills 1628 (Matthew); Original Chancery wills 1641/2 (Perrot); Original Chancery wills 1636 (Okell); Marchant, *op. cit.*, 266; BI Original Chancery wills 1619 (Smith); Original Chancery Wills 1614 (Kemp); Original Chancery wills 1624 (Clay).

32. Norwich RO, CN Inv 24/284 (Newhouse); BI Original Chancery wills 1635 (Hansby) Original Chancery wills 1643 (Ayscough); Original Chancery wills 1644 (Leadall, Perins).

33. Norwich RO, Inv 41/137 (Same); Inv 44/082 (Gell); Inv 46/031 (Gammon); NCC wills 34 Calley and Inv 47B/042 (Barnham); Inv 28/159 (Drake); Lincs. AO Inv 99/100 (Gartside); Inv 144/257 (Bishop); Hereford and Worcester RO, 008.7 BA 3585/239 wills 1644 no. 37 (Druman); no. 30 (Cotterell); 3585/243 wills 1647 no. 99 (Harvey); BI Original Chancery wills 1632 (Cooke).

34. BI Original Chancery wills 1632 (Cooke); Original Chancery wills 1624 (Clay); Original Chancery wills 1643 (More); Earwaker (ed.), *op. cit.* II, 31–3 (Coller); Norwich RO, NCC wills 351–3 (Spendlove) (Stoneham); Lincs. AO, LCC wills 1617 i 529 (Lord); LCC wills 1616 663 and Inv 119/546 (Dalby).

35. Lincs. AO, LCC Adm 1609/170 (Tayler); LCC wills 1618 ii 463 and 121/331 (Rawlings), Hereford and Worcester RO, 008.7 BA 3585/182 wills 1618 no 25 (Ganderton) and 3585/233a wills 1641 no. 2 (Aingel); Norwich RO, CN Inv 26/183 (Pease); BI Original Chancery wills 1604/5 (Thompson).

36. Hereford and Worcester RO, 008.7 BA 3585/231b wills 1640 no. 141 (Langford).

37. F. Blomefield, *Norfolk*, III (1806), 361–2, 244; C. Hill, *Economic Problems*, 275 80, 285–8; W. T. MacCaffrey; *Exeter 1540–1640*, (Cambridge, Mass., 1958), 178–9; Barratt, *op. cit.*, 317–18.

38. BI Original Chancery wills 1643 (More); HC CP 1567/8 (Smith); Lincs AO Inv 141/201 (Beech); R. Thoresby, *Vicaria Leodiensis* (1742), 51–3; J. C. Cox, *Records of the Borough of Northampton*, II (1898), 383–97.

39 MacCaffrey, *op. cit.*, 199–202; J. W. F. Hill, *Tudor and Stuart Lincoln*, (1956), 96–108; York City Library Housebook 1638–50, f. 235 (Elizabeth Moseley); R. H. Skaife, 'Civic officials of York', MS vol. II, 519 (Hoyle); LPL MS 919, fos. 566–7 (Cotter).

40. I. M. Calder, *The Activities of the Puritan Faction of the Church of England 1625–33* (1957), xii.

4

Profit, patronage, or pastoral care:
the rectory estates of
the archbishopric of York,
1540–1640

W. J. Sheils

Most reverend father in God; right trusty and right entirely beloved counsellor, we greet you well. We have late taken the state of our several archbishoprics and bishoprics into our princely consideration, that we may be better able to preserve the livelihood which as yet is left unto them. Upon this deliberation we find that of later times there hath risen a great inconvenience then by turning leases of one and twenty years into lives, for by that means the present bishop puts a great fine into his own purse to enrich himself, his wife and children, and leaves his successors, of what desert so ever to us and the church, destitute of that growing means which else would come in to help them. By which course, should it continue, scarce any bishop could be able to live and keep house according to his place and calling. We know that the statute makes it alike lawful for a bishop to let his lease for one and twenty years or three lives, but time and experience have made it apparent that there is a great deal of difference between them, especially in church leases where men are commonly in great years before they come to those places. These are therefore to will and command you upon peril of our utmost displeasure and what shall follow thereon that, notwithstanding any statute or any other pretence whatsoever, you presume not to let any lease belonging to your archbishopric in lives which is not in lives already. And further that where any fair opportunity is offered you, if any such be, you fail not to reduce such as are in lives into years.

The terse letter from Charles I to Archbishop Neile, sent with similar letters to all the bishops of the realm,[1] struck at the heart of the problem facing all office-holders in early modern society, how to strike a balance between exploiting the opportunities for gain which were considered the just rewards of office and discharging the responsibilities placed on the office-holder by the institution which he served. The dilemma was particularly acute, as it often had been, for the conscientious churchman. Serving an institution whose proclaimed purpose was other-worldly, but which was endowed with great estates over which it exercised lordship, the place enjoyed by the bishops of the Church was full of contradictions. A period of high inflation and price-rises increased the bishops' problems for, by attempting to mitigate the financial consequences of such a situation they made the gap between their vocations and their practices more obvious to those critical of their exploitation of the temporalities of the Church. And criticism there was. The political consequences of the economic policies of ecclesiastical landlords in general were discussed as long ago as 1956 by Christopher Hill in his pioneering *The Economic Problems of the Church*. Since then there have followed a number of studies of the activities of individual bishops or institutions.[2] These shed light on the economic, as well as the political consequences for the Church and so some justification is required for adding to that number.

A study of the leasing policy of the York archbishops in this period can be justified on three counts. Firstly, there is already some disagreement in current writing about the actual economic fortunes of the see of York in this period.[3] Secondly, the archbishop was an especially important owner of impropriate rectories, having 35 in all, most of which he received in exchange with the Crown following the dissolution of the monasteries. Impropriations figure prominently in Hill's book and in contemporary literature detailing the evils besetting the Church. It was estimated by some that, through this medium, some £100,000 *per annum* was diverted from its original purpose of providing for parochial clergy into the hands of laymen and senior ecclesiastics. Such was the force of the complaints that James I briefly considered wholesale reform but his attempts, like other wide-ranging schemes, foundered on the rock of property.[4] Any reform would have necessarily infringed the property rights of large numbers of people, yet in addition to profit, impropriations brought responsibilities to the owner. In the case of the archbishops of York it has been said that the proper discharge of those responsibilities, chiefly the repair and maintenance of some church fabric and ornaments and the provision of services and adequate ministers, 'materially increased their [the archbishops'] power over their clergy and the whole ecclesiastical system of the North'.[5] Examination of the impropriate rectories, therefore, illustrates sharply the choice between personal gain and the discharge of responsibilities faced by successive archbishops of York. Finally, and more generally, studies of the economic activities of the bishops have been principally concerned with the debate over the state of the Church in early modern England; that is to say, far more attention has been devoted to exploring the consequences of episcopal fiscal policy for the institution they served than for the bishops and their families. Yet the bishops, and indeed other higher ecclesiastics, formed an important segment of the office-holding class in early modern England and the importance of office to them and their dependents deserves some consideration. Although

> It is impossible to calculate what seventeenth-century civil servants made out of their positions over and above their direct gains as officials . . . it would be a mistake to exclude the exploitation of office for private advantage because it cannot be quantified. More difficult and interesting is to try and draw any kind of line between fair and reasonable behaviour . . . and conduct which, even by seventeenth-century standards, shades off into the impermissible.[6]

A study of the impropriate rectories owned by the see of York between 1540 and 1640 therefore illustrates the attitude of bureaucrats to the profits of office and examines the politically most contentious source of income available to senior ecclesiastics.

Most of the English bishoprics exchanged properties with the Crown in the years following the dissolution of the monasteries, from which the Crown had acquired vast reserves of 'spiritual' properties in the form of rectory estates. These exchanges were often forced on the dioceses, and at Exeter and Bath and Wells they resulted in a considerable diminution of the rental value of the episcopal estates, which in turn led to great financial problems for the bishops in the century following 1540.[7] In other dioceses the effects of the exchanges were not so obvious, and at Canterbury, Ely and York parcels of land were granted to the Crown in return for rectories without greatly altering the rental value of episcopal property.[8] However, the real value of a fixed rental income during a period of high inflation decreased, though perhaps not quite as dramatically as the Phelps Brown index might indicate, and it is undeniable that the seventeenth-century archbishops of York had less purchasing power at their disposal than had their predecessors in the mid-sixteenth century.[9] This fact encouraged a tradition that the exchange of property undertaken by archbishops Lee and Holgate during the 1540s led to a despoilation from which the see never recovered, despite the restoration of some properties granted by Queen Mary. This local tradition, ignoring the fact that a fixed-rent income was bound to lead to economic decline, has fortunately been subject to recent modification. Claire Cross has pointed out that the rental revenue of the exchanged lands of the archbishop amounted to £939 16s. in 1597 and thus almost replaced the value of the lands granted to the Crown which, in 1535, were worth £985 1s. 3d.

The loss of income from rents was a mere £45 5s. 3d., representing 2.5 per cent of the rental income as assessed in 1535 but, stated in this way, the figures underestimate the economic consequences of the exchanges.[10]

If the exchanges were to be held responsible for the economic decline of the see it was not because they resulted in a reduced rental income, but rather because they changed the nature of the property owned by the archbishop. In 1535 the archiepiscopal income was almost wholly derived from landed estates; 20 years later over 25 per cent of the income came from the 33 rectories, known as 'the Great Collection', which had come to the see by exchange to add to the two rectories, at Lythe and Kinoulton, Nottinghamshire, which were part of the estate prior to the Reformation. The rectories which the archbishop received reflected their monastic origin and included one group in Cleveland, formerly belonging to Guisborough priory, and another in Ryedale between Thirsk and Malton where a number of monastic houses had held estates. Elsewhere a group of four rectories in Holderness had been part of the possessions of Meaux Abbey, and five rectories in the West Riding made up the total.[11] They represented a dramatic change in the source of archiepiscopal wealth and the effect of that change on the profitability of the estates, on the patronage of the archbishops and their capacity to discharge their pastoral responsibilities requires discussion.

The question of profit is the most complex one and cannot really be answered very satisfactorily. Annual rents were generally a poor guide to likely real income from property at this time for, as E. Kerridge has shown, the chief vehicle for adjusting income from land at this period was not the rent paid by the tenant but the entry fine,[12] that is to say the sum payable by the tenant on the renewal of a lease or when changing the terms of a lease. Studies of the sees of Ely and of Chester suggest that the level of entry fines payable by tenants increased as the sixteenth century progressed.[13] This practice was also common to the larger lay estates, but was likely to be particularly attractive to bishops who only held the temporalities during their period of office. A heavy entry fine, usually payable as a lump sum, and a relatively low rental would certainly appeal to the bishop making a lease when compared to a low entry fine and higher annual rent. His successor, of course, might have had a very different view of the transaction, as the letter to Archbishop Neile suggests. In such circumstances it is not difficult to explain the conservatism of the Church in respect to its property; for the bishops, the system of negotiating entry fines rather than rents had obvious attractions despite the fact that, as Archbishop Young was to find out, it could work against some individuals.[14] On the other hand, if a bishop was lucky with the way

Impropriate rectories of the archbishop of York in Yorkshire

leases fell in, as Archbishop Frewen was in the 1660s his income from
entry fines could be far in excess of his income from rents.[15] This calculated risk created a system of estate management in the Church which
placed the short-term gains likely to accrue to a particular bishop
before the long-term benefits of the office he held and the institution
he served. Whatever the effect of the few notorious cases of avarice
and nepotism among bishops of the Reformation period upon the
declining fortunes of the Church, it was probably far less than that resulting from the perfectly acceptable, quite legal, but economically

conservative practice of maintaining the large entry fine as the regulator of incomes from land. This was quite within the law and, as long as lands were not leased for more than three lives or 21 years and they were not alienated or the husbandry altered in a way prejudicial to his successor, the archbishop's responsibility was fulfilled. In this respect it is rather misleading to describe the estates as belonging to the Church for, with the limitations noted above, they were at the disposal of the archbishop during his period of office in just the same way as the income from a parish living was in the hands of the incumbent. The income was not provided principally to increase the standing of the Church, but to pay its servants for their labours.

Unfortunately for the period under discussion, we have no details of the fines exacted for leases and so cannot determine how much archiepiscopal income derived from that source. Nor can we say with any confidence whether entry fines on rectorial estates, with their sometimes cumbersome responsibilities to the parish and the difficulties of tithe collection, kept pace with the entry fines on manors and granges with similar rental values. We can demonstrate, thanks to the Parliamentary Commissioners who surveyed the estates during the Civil Wars, that the real values of the rectories were considerably in excess of their rental values in 1641. At Easington the rectory was said to be worth £178 *per annum* to the tenant who paid a rent of £43 5s. 8d. and the rental value of all the Cleveland rectories was less than one-sixth of their assessed value of £1,020 8s. 2d. in 1645.[16] These figures give some idea of the discretion which successive archbishops could exercise in the fixing of fines when rents were so low. The Commissioners also surveyed the landed estates of the archbishops and there the ratio of real to rental values was similar; for example, at Angram Grange a rent of £13 6s. 8d. was paid on an estate assessed at £85 17s. 6d. *per annum*, and the large collection of properties known as the lordship of Marton, said to be worth £737 14s. 4d. *per annum*, brought in a rental income of £112 3s. 8d.[17] It would seem therefore, that the ratio of rents to real values on rectory estates was broadly similar to that on the archiepiscopal landed estates in the 1640s and this suggests, albeit tentatively, that there was little difference in the two types of property in economic terms. The differences which did distinguish the two derived from the spiritual responsibilities attendant upon rectory estates and from the needs of the archbishops to provide for their families and dependents.

Although legally enjoying the same status as real property, impropriations cannot simply be discussed in terms of fines and rents, for rectory estates at this date were usually accompanied by the ownership of the advowson, or rights of patronage, to the parochial living, and this was the case with the York rectories. They therefore provided an opportunity to place able clerics in the parishes in the hope that their example could further the Reformation. Indeed, in defending the exchanges forced upon Archbishop Holgate, A. G. Dickens made this very point. Certainly, as a result of the exchanges the number of advowsons in the gift of the archbishop almost doubled, but he still controlled less than 10 per cent of the parochial appointments in the diocese.[18] Compared to most other bishops, such as those of Norwich or Peterborough,[19] this represented a substantial amount of patronage which could, in theory at least, be used by a conscientious and determined archbishop to secure a corps of able and dedicated ministers to form a Protestant élite among the parochial clergy of the region. In addition to these advantages rectories carried with them the responsibilities of maintaining the fabric of the chancel of the parish church and providing services regularly during vacancies in livings. For all these reasons, the way in which provincial ecclesiastics managed their impropriate rectories is worthy of some attention, but the story is also important because, as the century progressed, the issue of impropriations in general occupied an increasingly important part in the conflict between the puritan clergy and the hierarchy over reform of the Church.

In the 1560s Richard Coxe, bishop of Ely, voiced the concern of many churchmen over the ownership of rectory estates when he wrote: 'It will be unto us a grievous burden to take benefices impropriated, because we are persuaded in conscience that the parishes ought to enjoy them, in such sort, and for such godly ends, as they were appointed for at the beginning'.[20] What he was worried about was the diversion of tithes and glebe originally designed to finance the parish clergy, into the pockets of higher ecclesiastics and, although he did not say so, of laymen. Coxe's reservations were later taken up by the Puritans, who saw one of the chief weaknesses of the church in the great inequality of incomes for the clergy. A regular feature of Puritan attacks on the episcopate was their ownership of rectories, whilst the related issue of lay ownership was less frequently raised.[21] The consequences of any redistribution of rectorial income, however appealing as a political platform, would have been disastrous for the higher clergy and would have done nothing for the economic well-being of the Church as a whole unless something was also done about lay impropriations. The political and legal implications of such action made it impossible to carry out; nevertheless the bishops were in the unfortunate position of having been forced into exchanging their landed estates for a type of property to which a number of them felt not strictly entitled. Their opponents within the Church and the Puritan gentry shared that view and, in the struggles over ecclesiastical policy, episcopal ownership of impropriations was a political embarrassment but an economic necessity to the hierarchy throughout the period. Against this political background was the necessity of furthering the Reformation in the conservative North. How far did the archbishop use his rectories and patronage for this?

The dispersed nature of the rectories owned by the archbishop has already been mentioned and, for the most part, the exchange of lands provided him with influence in the less populous, less wealthy and remoter regions of the diocese where recusancy was to become a problem, and not in the prosperous West Riding with its industrialized villages and growing dependent chapelries. In addition to the remoteness of the livings their poor level of endowment made them unattractive to the ambitious or able cleric, and only at Doncaster do we find a well-endowed benefice in a strategically placed market town which might influence its hinterland. The opportunity to augment parochial livings by the transfer of some rectorial income was not taken by any of the archbishops of the period, but in this respect they were no worse than their colleagues. Such augmentation was to remain a pious hope and such fragmentary evidence as survives shows that where augmentation did take place, as at Market Weighton in 1577, it was through the initiative of a pious layman and usually of a temporary or conditional nature. A reforming archbishop like Grindal responded to lay initiatives in 1573 and, on the suit of the corporation at Hull, diverted the income of a vicarage towards the maintenance of a town preacher, but little was done on archiepiscopal livings, except at Kirk Leavington where Archbishop Heath granted a lease of the rectory to the incumbent of the parish in 1557, in order to increase the parochial income.[22]

One can only examine the appointments made by successive archbishops to see if pastoral affairs in archiepiscopal livings were better than elsewhere. The mid-century crisis of manpower within the Church meant that the recurring problems of non-residence, failure or inability to provide regular services, catechizing and preaching were as common in archiepiscopal parishes as elsewhere in the North until the latter half of Elizabeth's reign. In addition the notorious neglect of church fabric by the monastic houses left the archbishops with a legacy which, in a parish like Keyingham, they were never able to discharge: the chancels of livings impropriate to the Crown and archbishops were regularly presented for being in a poor state of repair throughout the period.[23] However, from 1580 the visitation presentments suggest that the basic pastoral needs were being provided in all but two archiepiscopal livings: at Easington, where the conservative vicar Henry Jackson had been at loggerheads with his congregation in the early part of the reign, the incumbent at the end of the reign, Joseph Craike, was presented for absenting himself from the parish and leaving his 12-year-old son in charge to perform services;[24] in the very poor living of Marton-in-Cleveland, it proved impossible to find an incumbent able to preach or for the archbishop to find a substitute to provide the quarterly sermons.[25]

These two examples apart, the general improvement in clerical standards reflects what we know of national affairs from the work of P. Tyler and R. O'Day: pastoral care within the parish seems to have been maintained and in the 1630s Archbishop Neile actively pursued his 'beauty of holiness' ideas in his impropriate churches. These parishes were in the vanguard of the Arminian campaign.[26] However, to influence the ecclesiastical system of the North of England (as A. G. Dickens has suggested) the archbishop had to find clerics who could evangelize beyond the parish and reach a wider audience. The nature of the livings in the hands of the archbishop made this difficult, but there were a few examples of archiepiscopal intervention to provide able men to important livings. As early as 1567 the conservative St Quintin family and their tenants at Harpham were withdrawing from their parish church of Burton Agnes where 'commonlie Sermons be on Sondaies and holicdaies preached' by the graduate incumbent Robert Paley. Paley provided a preaching platform in a strongly recusant area and in 1572 John Baites, the curate of St Michael's, New Malton, was pursuing the same ends in a market town church.[27] Baites' views inclined towards Puritanism and he probably owed his appointment to Archbishop Grindal who would have seen the advantage of a preaching ministry in a market town. The living was not a valuable one but another Puritan, Francis Proude, was to serve there in the 1620s. At that date the principal supporter of the Puritans in the North Riding was Sir Thomas Hoby, who later made Proude a curate of his chapel at Hackness. Hoby, whose work with the Council of the North and the Eccesiastical Commission would have brought him into close contact with archbishops Hutton and Matthew, was an important Protestant patron and two other clerics associated wth him found their way into archiepiscopal livings in Cleveland, a recusant stronghold. William Ward was a graduate and curate of Guisborough between 1615 and 1624, having previously been noted for holding exercises at Scarborough. At approximately the same time Thomas Wood was curate at Marton-in-Cleveland and during the Interregnum took up Ward's old position at Guisborough.[28] The position of these men was paralleled in the more receptive climate of South Yorkshire where Grindal used the valuable living of Doncaster to place a preacher, Henry More, who could act as rural dean, to be responsible for the exercise of local discipline at visitation, and act as examining chaplain to the local clergy. More's influence and reputation continued in the person of his successor as vicar and rural dean, Arthur Kay, who made Doncaster a noted preaching centre until his death in 1604. Kay's curate at Doncaster in the 1590s, Richard Stainforth was also offered support by Sir Thomas Hoby,[29] whose efforts, allied to those of archbishops Grindal, Hutton and Matthew, did much to place a few chosen men in archiepiscopal parishes from which they could evangelize the neighbourhood. They met with some success but the majority of the livings were poor, the spiritual soil infertile, and their planting too sparse. What was really required was a reorganization of the archbishop's patronage.

With one notable exception such a reorganization was not attempted, but that exception itself calls for comment. It originated with the Puritan Earl of Huntingdon, in whose household Lady Margaret Hoby, wife of Sir Thomas, had been educated. Huntingdon was President of the Council of the North and tenant of the archiepiscopal rectory of Whitby, an enormous parish with six isolated dependent chapelries to serve, none of which could provide a reasonable income and several of which remained unattended for much of the period. The pastoral difficulties of this moorland area had long been a source of concern to the authorities, but the rapid advance of recusancy in the neighbourhood during the 1580s made the problem acute. Huntingdon took a 21-year lease of the rectory on 20 November 1593 on terms which were unique and deserve quotation at length; the earl was to have the profits of the rectory

> to the intent that a godlye learned and sufficiente preacher may contynue to be there resydente duringe the tyme and terme aforesayde to preache the worde of god truelye to the inhabitantes dwellynge within the lymyttes of the syde Rectorye or parsonage and chapells aforesayde, and to abolishe all Idolatrye, supersticion, and ignoraunce, doth for him [the earl] his executors and assignes covenaunte and graunte to and with the sayde most reverende father in god and his successoures, that he the sayde Henrye Earle of huntingdon, his executors and assignes shall yearely durynge the contynuance of the said term contente, satisfye and paye, or cause to be well and truely contented, satisfyed and payde, unto the handes of such godly learned and sufficiente preacher for the tyme beinge . . . twentye poundes of lawfull englishe money . . . and it is agreede betweene the sayde partyes by these presentes that the sayd most reverende father and his successours shall have the nomination, gyfte and puttinge in and further of any preistes or curates to serve in any of the sayde chapells . . .

Here the object was to provide a preacher, with a reasonable salary taken from the profit of the rectory, to evangelize the area; the strategy being that one able man could accomplish more in this respect than several poorly paid curates. Indeed it was impossible to find curates, and the earl, in return for making over part of the rectory profits, required the archbishop to finance the cost of any curates that were found. Whether the terms of the lease were acted on or not is not known, and the death of the earl in 1595 may have led to a short-lived experiment in any case.[30] The clause however remained in subsequent leases of the rectory, though the references to godly preaching were removed from those leases made by the Arminian Archbishop Neile. Despite these attempts the history of recusancy in the area suggests that it had very little effect and, at best, was a praiseworthy attempt to tackle an intractable problem.[31] The weight of the evidence suggests that the influence the archbishop could exert on the ecclesiastical life of the North was due to the normal activities associated with his office rather than the patronage he had acquired in the 1540s. Although some success was met with at Doncaster, and a few other praiseworthy attempts were made, the exchange of landed estates for rectories did little to improve archiepiscopal control over the clergy or to enhance the progress of the Reformation.

So far attention has been focused on the profitability of and the pastoral responsibilities which accompanied impropriate rectories. We have seen that although the successive archbishops for the most part were diligent in the discharge of those responsibilities, they did little to resolve the fundamental problems created by the scattered nature and poor endowment of the parochial livings of which they were impropriators. In some cases indeed, they even signed away the patronage rights to lessees.[32] The problems of pastoral care in the diocese were considerable and the archbishops conscientious, but the 'Great Collection' did not provide them with much opportunity to alleviate the problem. Reforming archbishops had recourse to other measures, such as appointing a cadre of committed Protestants to cathedral livings, as did Edmund Grindal, or establishing close political contacts with the few Puritan gentry of the area, as did Matthew Hutton.[33]The question of the profitability of the rectories is more complex; the indications are that, at the end of the period, the rectory estates were financially as advantageous to lessees as were the archiepiscopal manors and granges. But was this advantage converted into money by the archbishops? To try and answer this one needs to look at the leasing policy of the archbishops during this hundred-year period.

Charles I's letter to Neile commented on the needs of bishops to provide for their wives and families and, of course, one of the aims of office-holders would be to ensure that, as far as the law allowed, the profits of their office endured beyond the period of their tenure. Two stratagems were available to the archbishops: one was to acquire as much capital as possible during the period of office and to transfer it to other purposes such as the acquisition of land; the other, available when property was part of the endowment of office, was to dispose of leases to family and friends on favourable terms, thus ensuring income from land for a long period of time. Patronage always played an important part in church estate policy[34] and of the two stratagems available to the archbishop, the first was more commonly used in dealing with landed estates such as manors, whilst the second was more often applied to the rectory estates. The impropriations were not really looked upon as sources of direct revenue by the archbishops but as a store of patronage which could ensure that their families and servants enjoyed some of the profits of office long after an individual archbishop had died or moved elsewhere. It is therefore sterile to look at these possessions in narrow economic terms; it is probably true to say that the rectories brought in less income by way of fines and rents than did the landed estates of the archbishops, but this was due more to the attitudes of successive archbishops than to any characteristics inherent in rectory estates. This point requires demonstration, but is nicely illustrated in the terms of a 30-year lease made by Archbishop Holgate to Sir Nicholas Fairfax of Gilling on 23 March 1550/1. The lease concerned Sheriff Hutton rectory and included a clause forbidding the tenant to sub-let the property 'except to such other person or persons as is the friends of the said archbishop'.[35]

The friends and relatives of the archbishop did indeed profit from the rectories throughout our period. Of the 11 archbishops of York between 1540 and 1640 four were unmarried and two others, Holgate and Harsnett, had no immediate dependents by the time they became archbishop.[36] Despite this, the information we have from surviving leases shows that the archbishops viewed their impropriations essentially as a source of family patronage. There were some variations between the practice of individual archbishops, reflecting the different levels of their family commitments, and also a change of emphasis as time progressed; as we shall see, the practice of giving leases to one's servants and relations was less marked in the seventeenth century than in the sixteenth century. Of 82 leases granted before 1606, when Matthew Hutton died, exactly half went to members of families closely connected with the successive archbishops, and it is worth while giving some details.

Archbishop Holgate made 12 leases in eight years, six of them being reversionary and, therefore, strictly illegal without licence. Of the 12 two were in favour of Crown officials and one each went respectively to a member of his immediate family, a brother-in-law, some servants, and a near neighbour of his family. The remaining six were unexceptional, but here again previous connections with the archbishop were important. Prior to the Dissolution, Holgate had been Master of Sempringham and he had profited substantially from the disposal of Gilbertine lands. It is worth remarking that some former Gilbertine property came to the see as a result of the exchange with Holgate and that three leases, those of the rectories of Malton and Lythe and of the tithes at Burton Agnes, went to gentry who had also profited from the sale of Gilbertine estates and may well have been tenants of the order in its final phase. This earlier connection must have been valuable to both the Herbert and the Dakyns families; in addition George Dakyns received a number of preferments, including the archdeacony of the East Riding, from Holgate.[37] Holgate's successor, Nicholas Heath, was a bachelor who granted seven leases in four years, one of them to a Cambridge friend John Blythe, and three to members of his household (two of these after Elizabeth's accession when Heath must have known his tenure of office was to be short).[38] Heath and Holgate had been so busy with leasing rectories that the first Elizabethan bishop, Thomas Young, was apparently unable to make any further leases during his seven years of office, but Edmund Grindal, a bachelor, inadvertently benefited from Holgate's policy of granting 30-year leases and Heath's policy of getting rid of his leases when he foresaw his deprivation. As a result of their actions 19 rectory leases fell in for renewal during Grindal's six years at York, 16 of them in the last year of his pontificate. (A fortunate circumstance which was repeated in the landed estates.) As one would expect from his pastoral reputation he was more scrupulous about his leasing policy, and he only passed one rectory over to a relation, an unmarried niece, and three others to household servants. Some of his friends also got leases: Richard Bunney of Newland received Kinoulton rectory, and William Marshall of Much Hadham, his deputy receiver-general as Bishop of London, was granted Nafferton.[39] For the rest Grindal made grants to people with local connections or to the tenants in occupation. The flood of leases which fell in during Grindal's last year cannot have pleased his old friend and successor Edwin Sandys, whose large and growing family required support. However, during his 12 years in office 22 leases were renewed, most of these in the last half of his pontificate. Of these leases ten went to members of his family, two to his steward and controller of the household, and one to a Crown official.[40] The fortunes of the family were greatly increased by the leases they received, and Sandys was the first archbishop to divert much real estate to his family. A number of Nottinghamshire properties near Southwell, where the archbishop spent a lot of his time, were granted to his sons.[41] On the death of their father the Sandys sons were quick to renew their leases from the bachelor John Piers, although most of the leases still had 16 years to run. Of the ten leases made by Piers, two were to members of his predecessor's family, one went to his own nephew, and two were granted to household servants.[42] Most notable of the rest was the attempt by Piers and the Earl of Huntingdon to regularize the provision of services at Whitby. As one might have expected, given the date of the original exchanges and the activities of Holgate and Heath, the years between 1575 and 1595 were good ones in which to exploit the revenues of the see and 54 of the 82 leases granted between 1540 and 1606 were renewed during those years. During Matthew Hutton's tenure of office the availability of rectorial leases dropped to less than one a year again. Of nine leases granted by him two were to members of the Sandys family, who also renewed their grants of Nottinghamshire lands, and three others were due to kinship ties or close friendship, those to Ralph Lord Eure, Richard Bowes and Timothy Whittingham, some of whom had worked closely with him at Durham.[43] Another lease was made to Miles Dalston, one of his servants, leaving two grants to local landowners, that of Sheriff Hutton rectory being to Thomas Fairfax of Gilling, whose ancestor had received a grant of the same from Robert Holgate in 1550.[44]

It is worth while to stop and pause at this point as the sources for the later period are rather less informative. The lease registers at York are much less full and only record 20 leases between 1606 and 1640; fortunately the parliamentary survey of the estates gives details of tenants in occupation in 1641 and although the information is more sketchy some *lacunae* can be filled.[45] It is not merely the sources, however, which call for some review at this point. It is clear from the details of leases already given that the extent of the patronage afforded by the rectories was diminishing. The exchanges had provided the see with 33 properties, some of which had not been let out on lease before and in which the landlord/tenant relationship had seen great changes between 1535 and 1545. In the buoyant land-market following the Dissolution, the rectory estates were not the most attractive properties available to purchasers and this fact itself probably encouraged the Crown to make the exchanges. For these reasons the rectories provided the archbishop with something of a *tabula rasa* for leasing with few contractual obligations, much more so than in the ancient properties of the see where the rights and privileges of traditional tenants had to be respected. Archbishops sometimes leased small parcels of demesne land near their residences at Cawood and Bishopthorpe to their servants, and Sandys installed some of his family in Nottinghamshire properties, but the extensive estates at Otley and Ripon and in Ryedale were largely left in the hands of traditional tenants and their families. As time progressed and more rectory estates were leased to members of episcopal households, the recipients began to look upon themselves as traditional tenants and, like the sons of Archbishop Sandys, were concerned to renew their leases under succeeding archbishops—so much so that in 1641 descendants of Archbishop Holgate were in occupation of the tithes at Darrington and Wentbridge, various members of the Sandys family held leases of the rectories of Nafferton and Skipsea, to tithes at Owston and Haxey and at Yarm, and Lady Anne Hutton was the tenant of rectories at Sutton-on-the-Forest and Poppleton.[46] In this way opportunities for patronage gradually became restricted for the later archbishops, but the pattern nevertheless persisted. Among leases made by Toby Matthew were grants of the tithe hay at Guisborough to Richard Metcalfe, his servant, and leases of tithes at Knapton and Crambe to other servants, John Newsame and George Kitingale respectively. The lease to Kitingale did in fact replace an earlier lease to him of the valuable rectory of Whitby, which had been rescinded after six months in favour of Sir Henry Guildford.[47] Matthew's successor George Montaigne died on the very day of his enthronement by proxy in the Minister and so was scarcely in a position to profit from his office. Nevertheless, his kinsman Isaac Montaigne moved sufficiently smartly to procure a lease of Westow rectory, where the family held other lands, from Archbishop Harsnett, this being the only lease we know of during the latter's short pontificate.[48] We have little evidence surviving from Neile's primacy and, although a few leases were granted to kinsmen of his friends in the chapter, none of his family or servants appeared to have rectory estates in 1641.[49] Nevertheless, in the 28 rectories for which we have information at that date, 15 were occupied by individuals who were members of episcopal families or had close connections through service with one or other of the archbishops, and this figure might be larger, for in some cases the detail is sketchy. In any case the figure demonstrates the importance of church estates in establishing the fortunes of the archiepiscopal families. In 1616 Sir Timothy Hutton, son of an archbishop, estimated that over one-third of his income of £1,449 *per annum* was derived from church leases.[50]

The rectory estates therefore provided the archbishops with a sizeable if unpredictable area of patronage, though not in the sense thought of by A. G. Dickens. Into these properties they could intrude members of their families on favourable terms. In doing this they did decrease their income for surely, in such circumstances, entry fines were waived or significantly lowered. In this respect it is fair to say that the exchanges of the 1540s did impoverish the see of York, but it was an impoverishment to the advantage of the archbishops as individuals. The rectories were advantageous to the archbishops partly because of their unattractiveness, when compared to landed estates, to investors in the land market. They carried with them responsibilities for church fabric and the tedious problem of collecting tithes, an

activity fraught with the trap of litigation, a trap which ensnared a
number of tenants in our period.[51] For this reason, and perhaps also
because of their monastic origin, landlord/tenant relationships were
not stable in these properties and few families stayed in occupation of
a particular lease for more than two generations (few, that is, except
for archiepiscopal families such as the Sandys).[52] Because of this the
exchanges were also, I think, advantageous to the Church. Without
them the archbishops would have been forced into the expedients
tried by many of their episcopal colleagues in less well-endowed sees:
they would have either had to trample on the sensitivities of ancient
tenants in order to grant landed estates to their own families, or they
would have had to resort to flagrant abuse of ecclesiastical office by
granting preferment to their relations irrespective of merit. The latter
was in fact resorted to by Archbishop Young who, through the accidents of fortune, had little opportunity to grant leases, and also by
Edwin Sandys, whose numerous family received several grants of
offices and manors in addition to rectories.[53]

Impropriations were disliked by many churchmen, but the opposition they engendered touched on fundamental questions of Church
and State. Even their opponents had no practical alternative income
to offer senior churchmen, and really sought a general levelling of
clerical incomes, the consequences of which were never fully worked
out. To Matthew Hutton, a conscientious reformer, the rectorial
tithes and other sources of income represented the legitimate rewards
of learning without which learning could not be sustained. Sure in the
knowledge that members of his family would continue to enjoy
church leases after his own death, Hutton could still honestly claim
never to have hurt any ecclesiastical living in his life.[54] Despite this,
however, the policy of granting leases to one's family gradually
eroded the patronage available to successive archbishops and,
although this was not the case at York, it sometimes forced later generations into more questionable use of their position. Bishop Davenant
of Salisbury incurred the opprobrium of the laity of the county by pre-
ferring his numerous relatives to valuable offices and livings in the
diocese during James I's reign and at Bath and Wells local pressure
probably forced Bishop Godwin to withdraw a lease of West Buck-
land manor to his son and son-in-law in 1587.[55] At York, however,
the actions of the archbishops did not shade off into the impermissible
or scandalous.

It has recently been written of this period that 'men assume public
office for two reasons, first, because they wish to serve the public in
office and secondly, because they wish to enjoy the benefits of office
either in prestige, power, wealth or all three'.[56] The exchanges of the
mid-sixteenth century, by giving rectory estates to the archbishops,

did little to increase the opportunities for service to the public but, if they did diminish the revenues of the see, they compensated for that by providing a valuable store of family patronage which ensured that men of ability would be happy to serve there. The archbishops of York at this period generally discharged their responsibilities honourably and pursued their own purposes with moderation yet, by their actions, they gradually impoverished the institution which they served. The blame lay not with them but with the structural fault of tying the durable to the transitory – of linking property to office. This resulted in sustained criticism of the Established Church and its officers during this period, but the force of that criticism must not obscure the fact that the Church was served at York, as in many other places, by men like Edmund Grindal, Matthew Hutton, Toby Matthew, and, in a different way, Richard Neile whose pastoral, devotional, and theological concern outstripped that of most other occupants of the see. At the highest level the standards of probity among this section of the office-holding class was better than that found in most other walks of life,[57] and the administration of the rectory estates shows that these standards could be sustained whilst, at the same time, the estates of the Church could be used to aid the tranquil emergence of a few new families among the armigerous gentry of Yorkshire and Nottinghamshire. In economic and political terms the rectory estates were a hindrance to the Church, but they were an asset to senior churchmen whose service brought distinction to that same institution.

NOTES

An early draft of this paper was read before Dr D. M. Loades' seminar at Durham University and I am grateful to members of that seminar, particularly Dr D. Marcombe, for their comments.
1. York Minster Library (hereafter cited as YML), Wd, f.121; C. Hill, *Economic Problems*, 310–14.
2. Hill, *op. cit.*; P. M. Hembry, *The Bishops of Bath and Wells, 1540–1640* (1967); F. M. Heal 'The Tudors and church lands: economic problems of the archbishopric of Ely during the sixteenth century'. *EcHR* (1973), 198–217; M. R. O'Day 'Cumulative debt; the bishops of Coventry and Lichfield and their economic problems c. 1540–1640', *Midland History* (1976), 76–90; C. Haigh, 'Finance and administration in a new diocese: Chester, 1541–1641', in *Continuity and Change: personnel and administration of the Church in England 1500–1642*, eds. R. O'Day and F. Heal (1976), 1455–66; G. Alexander, 'Victim or spendthrift? The bishop of London and his income in the sixteenth century', in *Wealth and Power in Tudor England. Essays Presented to S. T. Binoff*, eds. E. W. Ives, R. J. Knecht and J. J. Scarisbrick (1978).
3. M. C. Cross, 'The economic problems of the see of York: decline and recovery in the sixteenth century', *AgHR* (suppl., 1970), 64–83 and see the correspondence between Cross and Lawrence Stone in *AgHR*, xix (1971), 87, 111–12.

4. Hill, *op. cit.*, 132–67, esp. 145, 150.
5. A. G. Dickens, *Robert Holgate, Archbishop of York and President of the King's Council in the North* (1955), 19.
6. G. E. Aylmer, *The State's Servants* (1973), 129; Alexander, *op. cit.*, Table I. Hembry, *op. cit.*, 167–72, 192–6.
7. *Ibid.*, 67–71, 105–23; F. R. H. Du Boulay, 'Archbishop Cranmer and the Canterbury Temporalities', *EHR*, LXVII, 19–36.
8. Heal, *op. cit.*, 199.
9. See letter from L. Stone, *AgHR*, (1971), 87 and F. Heal, 'Economic problems of the clergy' in *Church and Society in England from Henry VIII to James I*, eds. F. Heal and R. O'Day 109–10, and 'The Tudors and church lands', *op. cit.*, 208–9; Alexander, *op. cit.*, Table I.
10. Cross, *op. cit.*, tables.
11. See map; for monastic origins see BI, Bp, Dio. 2, 195–7.
12. E. Kerridge 'The movement of rent 1540–1640', *EcHR*, 2nd series, VI (1953–4), 16–34.
13. Heal, 'The Tudors and church lands', 210–11; Haigh, *op. cit.*, 161–3, discusses the use of entry fines on Chester rectory estates.
14. See below, p. 103.
15. BI, CC.Ab. 3/2, Frewen received £19,684 6s. 2d. from entry fines between 1661 and 1664.
16. LPL COMM/XII a/17, fos. 6–7, 40.
17. BI CC. Ab. 8/2, fos. 4, 126.
18. Dickens, *op. cit.*, 19; BI Bp. Dio. 2.
19. In these dioceses the bishops were able to extend their limited patronage by indirect means: W. J. Sheils, 'Some problems of government in a new diocese: the bishop and the puritans in the diocese of Peterborough, 1560–1630' in O'Day and Heal (eds.), *op. cit.*, 171–2; R. Houlbrooke (ed.) *The Letter Book of John Parkhurst, 1571–5* (Norfolk Record Society, XLIII, 1974–5), 35–7.
20. Quoted by Hill, *op. cit.*, 150.
21. *Ibid.*, 144–53, 317–28, but see also 245–74.
22. BI Chanc. AB. 9, f. 212-v; YML Wb, f. 96v; Hill *op. cit.*, 292.
23. Based on evidence from visitation court books 1567–1584 at BI. For Keyingham see J. S. Purvis, *The Conditions of Yorkshire Church Fabrics 1300–1800* (1958), 17.
24. BI V. 1567–8/CB. 1, f.186v; V.1571–2/CB, fos. 127v–128; V.1604/CB, f.89v
25. E.g. *ibid.*, V.1575/CB.1, f.42; V.1600/CB.1, f.237v.
26. P. Tyler, 'The status of the Elizabethan parochial clergy', *Studies in Church History*, IV (1967), 76–97; M. R. O'Day, 'The reformation of the ministry' in Heal and O'Day (eds.), *op. cit.*, 55–75; for Neile see A. Foster, 'The career of Richard Neile, Archbishop of York' (D. Phil. thesis, University of Oxford, 1978).
27. BI V. 1567–8/CB.1, f.162v; V.1571–2/CB, f.93.
28. R. A. Marchant, *The Puritans and the Church Courts in the Diocese of York, 1560–1642* (1960), 269–70, 290, 293–4; for Hoby see *The Diary of Margaret, Lady Hoby*, ed. D. M. Meads (1930), *passim*.
29. BI V. 1575/Papers; Doncaster DAB, 1575; *Archbishop Grindal's Visitation, 1575*, ed. W. J. Sheils (1977), 34–5, 38–9; Marchant, *op. cit.*, 27–8, 258.
30. YML Wc. fos. 77–8; for Huntingdon see M. C. Cross, *The Puritan Earl* (1966), *passim*.
31. E.g. YML Wd. fos. 119v–120; Hugh Aveling, *Northern Catholics* (1966), 169, 181–3; 394.
32. E.g. BI CC.Ab 8/3, f.68–9. Toby Matthew to tenant of Kilburn rectory, 1627.
33. For Grindal see C. Cross in G. E. Aylmer and R. Cant (eds.), *A History of York*

Minster (1977), 207–9, 222; for Hutton see the same author's *The Puritan Earl* (1966), 265–6, and P. Lake, 'Matthew Hutton–a puritan Bishop?' *History*, LXIV (1979) 203ff.

34. Kerridge, *op. cit.*, 34.
35. YML Wb., fos. 58–9.
36. See *DNB* under names of archbishops.
37. Dickens, *op. cit.*, 5–9, 17. The leases were recorded in YML Wb., fos. 27v–29, 53v–54, 55v–62, 64–65, 71–73, 75, 82v–83, 147v–148; for Dakyns see D. M. Smith and J. M. Horn (eds.), *Le Neve; Fasti Ecclesiae Anglicanae 1541–1857*, IV (1975), 16–17, 25, 34.
38. YML Wb., fos. 87–8, 111–13, 119v–120.
39. *Ibid.*, fos. 175–281 records all Grindal's leases; those noted here are at fos. 175 and v, 203 and v, 207v–208v, 218v–219v, 223–225, 238v–240; Alexander, *op. cit.*, 137.
40. YML Wb, fos. 326v–327, 331v–332, 336, 341v, 355 and v, 357–358, 360–361v, 364v–367. He was also forced to make a reversionary lease of the valuable rectory of Doncaster to the Crown, fos. 298–9.
41. BI, Bp. C. & P. xx, gives details of leases and grants of offices made by Sandys to members of his family.
42. The leases to the Sandys family are at YML Wc., fos. 15v–16, 37 and v, the others noted are at fos. 50 and v, 53v–54v, 75v–76.
43. For the Sandys family see YML Wc. fos. 105, 111v and North Yorkshire County RO, Za Z (Nottinghamshire Deeds), Askham. For the other leases see YML. Wc., fos. 94, 121v, 149, and for Durham connections see A. Raine (ed.) *The Hutton Correspondence* (Surtees Society XCII, 1843).
44. YML Wc., fos. 122, 157v–158; Wb., fos. 58–9.
45. *Ibid.* Wc., fos. 164v–360v; Wd. fos. 1–120; BI CC. Ab.8/3; LPL Comm/XII a/17.
46. BI CC. Ab 8/3 fos. 50–51, 71a; LPL Comm/XII a/17, fos. 8–9, 12–13, 18, 20–23, 33.
47. YML Wc., fos. 327 and v, 344v–345, 359v–360; Wd., fos. 4v–5.
48. *DNB*; BI CC. Ab. 8/3, f. 77.
49. YML Wd., fos. 118–43 and see for example BI CC. Ab 8/3, fos. 64–65, a grant of Brafferton tithes to John Dodsworth of York, son of Matthew Dodsworth.
50. J. T. Cliffe, *The Yorkshire Gentry; From the Reformation to the Civil War* (1969), 100, noted in Lake, *op. cit.*, 204.
51. See, for example, the recurring litigation over tithes at Sheriff Hutton, BI CP. G. 2649, 2776, 3118, 3148.
52. A notable exception here was the Fairfax family of Gilling, which held Sheriff Hutton from 1550 to 1641 at least.
53. See Smith and Horn (eds.), *op. cit.*, 24 for a kinsman of Young, and Heal, 'Economic problems of the clergy', 111, for the response of neighbouring laity to the economic policies of Sandys.
54. Lake, *op. cit.*, 192–5.
55. Hill, *op. cit.*, 21; Hembry, *op. cit.*, 171.
56. J. Hurstfield, 'Political corruption in modern England; the historian's problem', *History*, LII (1967), 16–34, esp. 18.
57. G. E. Aylmer, *The King's Servants* (1961), 178–81, but see his concluding remarks on p. 468; for an assessment of a particular institution see J. Hurstfield, *The Queen's Wards* (1958), 214–17, 348–9.

5

The Elizabethan episcopate: patterns of life and expenditure

Joel Berlatsky

A quarter of a century ago Christopher Hill focused attention on the economic impact of the Reformation upon the established English Church. Hill saw the Elizabethan era as a time in which the wealth of the Church was plundered and felt that the bishops in particular had their resources reduced. The consequences of this reduction in wealth was an end to 'the great days of hospitality' and a decline in the prelates' social prestige. Though the Church still held a great many assets the decayed condition of the hierarchy made the ecclesiastical establishment an easy target for Puritan critics and other 'land-hungry magnates and of businessmen great and small'.[1]

Since the presentation of Hill's broad interpretation a whole generation of scholars has paid increasing attention to the social and economic repercussions of the Reformation, with special reference to the financial solvency of the episcopate. The bishops have attracted attention despite their revised role in the community because they are an easily identifiable group who had significant possessions to be monitored by official record and private prying.

For the most part, studies of episcopal economics in the late sixteenth century have dealt with the very important issues of how well the bishops maintained revenues, especially in the light of inflation. Concern has also been shown toward the bishops' accumulation of riches and the endowment of their children. The picture that has emerged is somewhat blurred. Some sees held on to their assets quite well, while others were impoverished from the outset, with matters only getting worse. The total decline in value of English sees was not as great as Hill thought,[2] though in an era of inflation any loss was a serious matter. Similarly, some bishops died in debt, while others amassed substantial fortunes with which to endow their progeny. Further research into details of prelatical balance sheets is unlikely to alter this portrait of mixed prosperity and poverty.

One area of inquiry which Hill hinted at, but which has received less attention, is the question of just what Reformation meant to the life-style of bishops. As leaders of the Church prelates were expected to maintain a lordly standard of hospitality and display largesse on a lavish scale. Part of the need to keep up estate was a function of a profession which required the accumulation of books, plate and vestments to carry out the duties of scholarship, entertainment and ceremonial. The extent to which the episcopate did, or did not, live up to traditional expectations and obligations can help explain contemporary attitudes and criticisms of the hierarchy, as well as giving a direct view of what religious changes meant in the lives of churchmen.

The general thesis of this essay will be that the life-styles and living standards of the Elizabethan bishops were lowered, but that this decline cannot be judged exclusively by looking at changes in income as compared to price statistics. Rather, what most prelates did was to attempt to maintain their traditional lordly life style, no matter what the cost. Attempts to keep up estate were a function of the nature of the profession as well as individual desires. Such efforts caused financial difficulties for some bishops. Whatever decline in life-styles developed during the Elizabethan era was thus a matter of degree not a change in kind. The models of the English prelates of the late sixteenth century were the pre-Reformation bishops, not the reformed clergy of continental Europe. Proof of the character of the English Church from the European standpoint is to be found in the letters of various reformers expressing disappointment with the continuance of traditional forms and practices. The failure to undertake a more thoroughgoing reform of episcopal life-styles was lamented by Englishmen such as Thomas Sampson who refused elevation to a bishopric because 'so much expense must always be incurred for their equippages.'[3] Indeed the whole first generation of prelates, influenced by the experience of exile, was uncertain about taking up office, how to carry out their function and how to survive financially.[4] By the end of the queen's reign such doubts were vanishing, erased by time and Whitgiftian discipline.

No assessment of the episcopal life-style is reducible to a statistical table, but by examining several facets of the bishops' households an impression, if not a chart, can be formed. The houses inhabited, hospitality maintained, number of servants, funerals and goods inventories are used in this essay to sketch the daily circumstances of the Elizabethan diocesans. In a few instances detailed accounts of yearly expenditures can pinpoint more specifically the life-style of the prelates. To be used carefully are the wills of the bishops, which while numerous, are often examples of wishful thinking rather than of the actual estate available for distribution. When these factors are examined separately and then woven together an estimate of the bishops' life-style can be presented.

To understand what changes took place in the late sixteenth-century episcopal way of life there must be some basis of comparison. In some ways the wealth, power and estate of the episcopate peaked just prior to the Reformation. Indeed that overweening prelate, Thomas Wolsey, helped to make reform a popular ideal. At his peak Wolsey had an income of over £35,000 *per annum* drawn from the rich sees of York and Winchester, the Abbey of St Albans and numerous other livings. Wolsey was thereby able to build Hampton Court and Whitehall (York Palace) and generously endow colleges.[5] Vast revenues were also allocated to the maintenance of a magnificent mode of living. Wolsey's household numbered at least 500 people.[6] He was able to have 300 attendants at the Field of Cloth of Gold while Archbishop Warham and the attendant dukes could only muster 70 servants. Even Wolsey's cook was able to wear damask, satin or velvet with a gold chain around his neck.[7]

Wolsey was the extreme example of the kind of medieval bishop-statesman who set a standard of living which even a king might have had trouble rivalling. Lesser men of the same rank could not compete, but they still lived in a lavish fashion:

> Nicholas West, Bishop of Ely, in the year 1532, kept continually in his house an hundred servants, giving to the one half of them 53s 4d the piece yearly; to the other half each 40s the piece yearly; to every one for his winter gown four yards or broad cloth, and for his summer coat three yards and a half: he daily gave at his gates, besides bread and drink, warm meat to two hundred people.[8]

Cuthbert Tunstall of Durham added to his castle at Durham and Auckland while erecting a town hall in Durham city. His hospitality and charity were extensive as he maintained a sumptuous table – and at every Easter giving 'a peck of pennies' to the poor.[9] In 1546 Robert Holgate of York travelled to court with 70 horses and spent over £1,000. The same prelate expended over £4,000 on war and charity from his own money. Holgate's palace at Bishopthorpe was 'sumpt-uous' and an inventory of his goods while he was in prison showed the archbishop with £300 in gold coin, £400 in good debts, 1,600oz. of plate as well as much else in the way of worldly possessions.[10]

Probably the last of the truly princely prelates was Stephen Gar-diner of Winchester. With four great palaces Gardiner rode 'in his velvet and satin, aloft upon his mule trapped with velvet and golden stirrups and bridle ...'. His retinue was at least 140 and 'what a many idle bellies daily feedeth he.' As an ambassador to France, Gardiner 'hath a great number of servants in their velvet and silks, with their

chains about their necks, and keepeth costly table with excessive fare.'
Gardiner's will was an expression of his style of life: £200 was left for
funeral liveries, £500 for a chantry and £300 for a tomb. The total
money distributed at Gardiner's death was almost £2,400 and he had
just given 4,000 ducats to the see of Winchester.[11]

However, not all Henrician bishops could maintain such magnifi-
cence, and they offer a preview of the Elizabethan era. Thomas
Cranmer had 11 residences including Lambeth, Croydon, and Knole;
but by exchanges seven were lost and when the palace at Canterbury
burned in 1543 the archbishop did not rebuild. Indeed, Cranmer
spent the first part of his primacy short of money and sold wood to
keep out of financial trouble.[12] While he still kept an extensive household and dispensed alms, Cranmer's lack of building and more restrained demeanour was a precursor of things to come. Like his
Elizabethan successors Cranmer was reduced from a princely to a
noble style of life.

A more typical case of a Henrician bishop in reduced circumstances
was that of Robert Sherburne of Chichester. At his death in 1536 the
prelate had less than £300 in goods to be disposed of, though he had
some money owed to him.[13] Richard Rawlins of St David's was even
less affluent. His inventory still showed a substantial library but his
parliament robes were 'rat and moth eaten'. The total value of
Rawlins's goods and debts was only £487 13½d. When funeral
expenses and other bills had been deducted the bishop's estate at his
death in 1536 was but £307 13d, hardly indicative of a magnificent
existence.[14]

In searching out the degree to which bishops' lives changed, it is important to affirm how often perception of wealth is a relative
question. Compared to Wolsey the Elizabethan hierarchy were poor
imitators of a past not to be recovered. But to the eyes of his own
tenants, the holder of the most meagre see was rich beyond imagining.
When compared to the contemporary nobility Elizabethan prelates
had incomes which were slightly below average for peers. In 1559 the
mean gross income for peers was £2,380 *per annum*,[15] a sum which
could be equalled by only three or four bishops at Canterbury, Winchester, Ely and perhaps Durham. Three Welsh bishoprics offered
their incumbents less than £200 a year.[16] By the seventeenth century
the gap was widening. In 1602 the mean income for nobles had risen to
£3,360,[17] while as late as 1615 Canterbury was still valued at only
£2,816 17s. 6d.[18] although it yielded somewhat more. Clearly Elizabethan bishops could not keep up a life-style equal to that of the greatest peers, but almost all could attempt a mode similar to the gentry and
lower echelons of the peerage. The trappings of episcopal living were
pulled away more slowly than the revenues, as prelates tried to live up

to an image of their place in society, which their incomes were not always adequate to uphold. The result was that some Elizabethan diocesans were able to live lavishly while accumulating a fortune, but others were reduced to debt and died in penury. The key, however, is that all attempted to live in a style which they and those who watched them assumed was correct for men of their station.

One legacy from the medieval past was the attachment of palaces to most sees. The justifications for mansions were three-fold: to maintain the required estate, to allow the prelate to travel about and supervise his diocese, and to provide a suitable residence for the conduct of necessary business in London.[19] By the Elizabethan era such houses were often a liability: the laity cast covetous eyes on the possessions of the Church while many prelates lacked the means to keep up such houses and allowed them to fall into disrepair. Frequently mansions were poorly situated for the prelates' needs, being concentrated in one corner of a large diocese. Nonetheless the reason for the covetousness of the laity can be seen in the reaction of a foreigner to the bishop of Salisbury's residence, 'so spacious and magnificent that even sovereigns may, and are wont to be suitably entertained there.' Attached was 'a most extensive garden, kept with especial care, so that in the levelling, laying out and variety, nothing seems to have been overlooked.' Overall this visitor felt himself, 'transplanted into the magnificent abode of a prosperous individual,'[20] which was obviously expensive to maintain and an object of envy by some. Even so poor a prelate as John Young at Rochester had a handsome palace at Bromley, a 'many chimnied, two storied building' located on the main road to London, with an 'ample park' and 'fine vistas'.[21]

Richard Cox at Ely spent much of his time trying to protect his mansions at Holborn and Somersham, but in the end was forced by covetous laymen to compromise his position.[22] Cox's two main adversaries were Lord Roger North for Somersham and Christopher Hatton for Ely House. The latter dispute may have cost Cox his final chance of being archbishop of Canterbury.[23] To resist such pressure was not easy, as when Cox was accused by Thomas Smith of having made over leases to his wife, children and friends while denying them to queen and courtiers. On that occasion the prelate was reminded that it was the queen, 'who hath given you the whole, and now requireth but part in lease.'[24] Cox's defence consisted mainly of arguing that it was his duty not to spoil the Church and put his successors in a hopeless position.[25] Contests similar to Cox's woes led to at least 67 of 176 palaces being granted or leased away by the end of Elizabeth's reign.[26]

The loss of traditional residences was accentuated by a general failure to construct new palaces. Whereas late fifteenth-century dio-

cesans either built new mansions or repaired what they already possessed, the Elizabethans were not builders. Parker did make repairs at
Canterbury but no new official residences were erected. Some did put
up personal homes, but these were not on the grand scale of palaces
meant for public use.[27] Fairly representative was the case of Anthony
Rudd at St David's who found his mansions 'so ruinated and decayed
for want of reparation that they were not fit for any man especially a
bishop to dwell and keep hospitality in.'[28] The failure to build anew
and the problems of upkeep are in contrast to the great rebuilding of
Elizabethan England undertaken by lay magnates in the period after
1570.[29]

Nonetheless, the covetousness of the laity towards remaining episcopal properties can be understood by looking at Bishop Cox's
possessions at the mansion of Somersham. An inventory of 1569
enumerated 27 featherbeds, 2 down beds, 35 bolsters, 12 fine
tapestries and 22 carpets. Adding to the surroundings were 24 curtains of taffeta, sarsanet and damask. Amongst the furnishings were
20 'turkey-work' stools and chairs to complement 57 wall hangings
including new panels of 'beast and fowl'.[30] Much else might be listed
to illustrate a degree of affluence which might well lead the enemies of
the bishop to ask if he could not, in fact, get along with one house less,
as the inventories show Cox's other houses to be equally well provided.

The size of episcopal mansions is again well illustrated by Cox's
house at Downham which had no less than 31 rooms plus a gatehouse
chamber and porter's lodge, brewhouse, bakehouse and other outbuildings. At Fen Stanton the house had at least 23 rooms plus a cellar
and a 'tyled barn' filled with household goods and implements. Other
residences belonging to the bishop of Ely were Somersham, 28 rooms,
and Dodington, 14 rooms, a beehouse, storehouse, corn chamber and
lodge. Ely House had well over 30 rooms plus a wine cellar, wash-
house, bakehouse, porter's lodge, housekeeper's chamber and two
armouries.[31] Such a scale of living was not available to all the prelates
but it is an example of a life-style which laymen viewed with acquisi-
tive eyes.

A much poorer man was Hugh Bellot who served at Bangor and
then Chester. Christopher Haigh has shown that Chester was a place
which was under-endowed and likely to lead the incumbent into
poverty.[32] Yet Bellot lived in a mansion of 20 rooms with a wine cellar,
stable and bakehouse. His house was reasonably well furnished,
though not much more elaborately so than some well-equipped lesser
clergy.[33] Thomas Bentham was a first-generation Elizabethan bishop,
whose financial troubles and ultimate bankruptcy are well-
documented. Yet Bentham had two houses at Hanbury and Eccle-

shall, which were both habitable if somewhat dilapidated. The bishop also had a palace at Lichfield which he was not able to occupy because it was in disrepair. The inventory of Bentham's goods at his death amounted to £394 6s. 2d. which was insufficient to cover the money he owed, mainly to the government. The goods inventoried show little in the way of luxury, partly because much of the manuscript is illegible, but Bentham did have over 200 books, a sign that his condition was not that of the average debtor.[34] The inventory taken of Richard Curteys of Chichester also reveals little wealth. The goods at his two residences at Aldingborn and Chesworth were valued at just under £500. Like Bentham, Curteys had a substantial library but his silver was worth only £42. Some of the plate had to be pawned to keep Curteys financially afloat.[35]

William Morgan is an example of another type of impoverished bishop serving the queen in Wales. When his goods were inventoried they totalled only £110 1s. 2d., scattered in a house with only a dozen or so rooms. Morgan was living on a scale much below that of even Bentham and Curteys. The silver, damask and taffeta goods noted elsewhere were conspicuous by their absence amongst Bishop Morgan's plain possessions.[36] Welsh bishops were hard pressed 'to maintain state and hospitality appropriate to their station on their miserably inadequate incomes.' The result was 'they cut down on overheads like residence repairs and hospitality' which led to the decay of palaces and cathedrals.[37] Nevertheless in the Welsh countryside a man possessed of over 14 pages of inventoried goods was still a substantial figure. Welsh squires were in fact little more than substantial English yeomen. In 1569–70 the largest native Welsh estate, of the Gwydir family, had rents of less than £150 per annum which only rose slowly later in the century. An impoverished bishop thus remained an imposing figure in a poor society only superficially anglicized.[38]

Another type of poor bishop has been pointed out by W J. Sheils in his discussion of the new diocese of Peterborough which had a small endowment and no mansion house.[39] Small wonder that Richard Howland was another prelate who died in debt. Howland lived in a house with only ten rooms plus a brewhouse and stable. He also maintained a residence at the parsonage of Castor with another dozen rooms plus a dairy, 'cistern house', corn chamber, malt chamber, and stable. The goods at Castor amounted to £205 0s. 6d. and the total for both locations was a meager £262 12s. 5d. Howland was one of the poorest English bishops, rivalling the penury of the occupants of Welsh sees amidst the much more prosperous countryside of eastern England. The gentry who knew Howland must have held him in disdain. Howland was not able to keep up his estate and this contributed to his inability to 'combat the growth of Puritan activity' in his

diocese. Howland's substantial library was not unusual for clerics
and was not a substitute for silks, plate and a palace.[40] Another new
see at Oxford also left the bishop with no mansion. Hugh Curwen was
forced to plead that he might 'have an house for me and for my family,
and some land withal to find my cattle and geldings upon a reasonable
rent.'[41] It should not be a surprise that such a poor place was left
vacant for long stretches after Curwen died.

From the above cases, it is clear that the conditions in which Elizabethan bishops lived varied widely, but only in extreme circumstances
falling much below the level of the gentry while in a few instances
rising to high standards of material comfort. The long-lived Tobias
Matthew of Durham and later York lived in a truly noble fashion. He
had a residence of over 25 rooms plus outhouses at Cawood, almost
35 rooms at Bishopthorpe, 16 rooms at Southwell and 17 at York. All
of these were furnished in a luxurious fashion, as in Matthew's bed-
chamber at Cawood where there stood a bedstead, tester, valance and
'curtains of green say' with the 'valence fringed with silk'. In the same
room was a 'mattress, featherbed, boulster, 2 down pillows, 3 spanish
blankets and a green rug' valued at £4 10s. Also at Cawood Castle was
the archbishop's wardrobe which included seven gowns valued at
£49, 'his parliament robes, and convocation robes of scarlett' (£30),
'a mourning gown, a chimere, a trayne and a hood with all his apparel
of all sorts both cassocks and other things (£38 8s. 4d.).' Linen alone
was valued at £30. Perhaps most impressive was the valuation of
Matthew's books 'both divinity, humanity etc.' at £600, which in
itself represented a major accumulation of wealth. The inventory of
Tobias Matthew, though compiled at his death in 1628, is a reflection
of an Elizabethan attitude to the appropriate estate for prelates to
maintain.[42]

Bishopthorpe seems to have been the palace at which Matthew kept
his plate, including 630½ oz. of double gilt (£167 18s.),409½ oz of
gilt (£105 15s. 2d.), used gilt (138oz.) valued at £34 13s. 8d. and white
plate (1,278oz.) assessed at £308 4s. 6d. There were lesser amounts of
plate at York where the totals were about £150 in value.[43] Without
belabouring the point it is clear that Tobias Matthew lived on a scale
that was equalled by few in the kingdom and surpassed only by the
greatest men of the realm. Between him and the prelates who died
impoverished lay a huge gap, almost as large as the chasm between
most bishops and the common man, to whom palaces, plate and
libraries were quite foreign.

The sources of the lordly wealth of Tobias Matthew and those like
him are not completely clear. John Still and some others brought their
wealth with them by marriage or similar means. Some gained
affluence by husbanding their resources and exploiting their oppor-

tunities. Some riches were drawn from perquisites obtained by men who had the opportunity to dispense modest favours and patronage. These latter sources are impossible to document in detail and their role can only be surmised from a familiarity with the workings of Elizabethan society. Certainly one key factor in gaining wealth was longevity in a see to clear away the debts attendant upon entry and gain a familiarity with the local resources.

The houses and furnishings of the bishops were outward symbols of a style of life amongst the most elegant in the land. But there was a reason why a prelate needed such trappings, and at least in part this was in order to fulfil traditional duties of hospitality. Already we have observed that in the early sixteenth-century prelates did entertain lavishly; however, by the Elizabethan era bishops found themselves in an awkward situation regarding entertainment. If they were too expansive Puritans attacked them and covetous courtiers saw them as ripe for pruning; but, should the prelates skimp on providing hospitality, critics asked why they should be endowed and questioned if too much was being siphoned off to care for episcopal families.[44] Burghley felt that one reason the prelates lacked credit was their failure to entertain the influential in the fashion required.[45]

Matthew Parker in his stay at Canterbury managed to keep a good table. He maintained a retinue of 100 liveried servants, gave the queen expensive gifts and entertained Her Majesty as she expected. This he could well afford for his income was never much below £3,000; when he died Parker left a substantial fortune despite a funeral which cost over £1,000, even after having paid taxes during his time at Canterbury of well over £6,500.[46]

John Whitgift was the Elizabethan prelate who won the most favour for his entertainments. While still bishop of Worcester Whitgift was already in the habit at 'Assizes and Sessions ... to give the Judges and Justices entertainment.' After moving to Canterbury Whitgift was well known for living in splendour with lavish hospitality. Each year he hosted the queen, in some years more than once, a burden which few diocesans could have borne even had they so desired. The queen was always pleased because all was done in good order. But a welcome was also provided for 'strangers according to their several qualities and degrees ... at Christmas especially, his gates were always open, and his hall set twice or three times over with strangers.'[47] Such an open-armed policy can be documented from the few remaining fragments of the archbishop's accounts showing substantial expenditures for fish and wine.[48]

Archiepiscopal expenses cannot, however, be considered typical. Only a few others at Worcester, London, Ely and Winchester were burdened with entertaining the queen.[49] Such visits were a great impo-

120   Joel Berlatsky

sition, as when Robert Horne of Winchester wrote to Parker that his
deer herd was badly reduced by 'the Q Majesty being at Farnham this
last year'.[50] Horne held a wealthy see but in the year ending 28
November 1568 he spent £1,488 11s. 1½d. for provisions out of a
total revenue of £2,380 2s. 4d. When taxes, annuities and reparations
were added, total costs for the year were £2,603 3s. 6d. so that 'the
payments and charges of this year doth surmount the receipts as it
appeareth by the som £223 13s. ¾d.'. Provisions were 63 per cent of
revenues and 57 per cent of total expenditures. Included in the provisions were £82 6s. 6d. for the materials to brew beer, over nine tons
of Gascon wine, 2 butts of sack, 16 gallons of muscatel, 21 gallons of
malmsey costing £80. There were similarly substantial consumptions
of eggs, domestic fowl, fish and rabbits, the detailed accounting of
which would only reinforce the clear impression that the bishop entertained on a large scale. To make such hospitality possible Horne spent
£111 16s. 8d. for yearly wages to his servants as well as £81 6s. 6d. for
liveries.[51]

One of Horne's successors at Winchester, Thomas Cooper, illustrates well how difficult it was for bishops to maintain the liberality
which was required. On first coming to his diocese he found himself
burdened with many charges for 'tenths, first fruits, annuities etc; and
shall have to spent £300 a year in repairs, the county having complained to the justices of session of the decay of farm houses, mills,
bridges etc. I have little left for hospitality, finding of servants, furniture.'[52] A short time after he wrote this lament Cooper drew up an
account which he sent to Brughley in which he showed clear revenues
of only £398 9s. 2d. for 1587.[53] Many of the charges were the result of
coming to a new see and the threat of war which cost Cooper a subsidy of £250. When Cooper died his position was much improved, so
that he left at his death almost £2,500 in ready money, plus a great deal
of plate, indicating that he recovered from the early financial strains at
Winchester.[54] To achieve solvency the bishop must have reduced hospitality from the extravagant levels of Horne's accounts, if only for a
time.

Edmund Scambler was a prelate notorious for his lack of cordiality
and accumulation of wealth at the expense of the Church, both at
Peterborough and later at Norwich. In 1588 he spent only £144 on
food,[55] which would have taken care of his family but left little for
entertainment. Yet this same man passed on a substantial legacy to his
children, laying himself open to charges of dilapidating his sees while
failing to keep the proper estate. Bishop Howland sued Scambler for
dilapidations of £1,351 19s. 11d. at Peterborough of which Scambler
had to pay 400 marks plus £20 in goods.[56] Later Bishop Redman at
Norwich sued for dilapidations. One house at Ludham was found in

good repair but at St Bennet's 'the mansion houses, churches and all the walls and building about that place was utterly ruinated and wasted', though this was mostly the case before Scambler arrived and he escaped legal responsibility – although he was not absolved by public opinion. Such was the prelate's reputation that formal investigations were required to confirm that he had not ruined one see as he had the other.[57]

Much poorer men than Scambler spent much more lavishly to provide hospitality. William Redman from an income just in excess of £977 spent £292 19s. 10d. for 'the maintenance of my house servants wages liveries etc.' Redman felt that his see was already so spoiled that he could not even find 'by half great portion to my expenses of household.'[58] Others also felt embarrassed and pressured by household expenses. John Young of Rochester was accused of keeping a 'near and miserable house' yet he claimed to have spent £250 of his meagre £340 income on meat and drink. He felt that he had surpassed the minimal requirements for hospitality, as 'Some are of opinion that no man can well uphold his state, if he spent above third part of his yearly revenue in meat and drink'.[59]

Edwin Sandys, who later became archbishop of York and carved out a fortune for his family, incurred large expenses while bishop of London. London was an especially difficult place because it lacked the demesne lands which might allow a prelate to escape some of the ravages of inflation. Sandys' predecessors had seen the bishoprics real income whittled to a point where 'the bishop could no longer maintain his "place" or show that hospitality and liberality which was expected of him.'[60] Despite such circumstances, on an income officially valued at £1,110 8s. 4d. Sandys never spent less than £1,057 in a year and his average expenditures over seven years was in excess of £1,200 a year.[61] At least two-thirds of the spending went to cover household costs.[62]

In the absence of more numerous and detailed household accounts it is difficult to judge fully how well the prelates lived up to the universal expectation that they should maintain an open house. The credit which Whitgift won for his generosity may be a sign that most did not keep a very good table. Scambler's ill name was perhaps an exaggeration resulting from living in a region where the episcopal structure was little appreciated.

One outwardly visible symbol of efforts to keep up an élite life style was the number of servants the bishop's household contained. The size of episcopal households is not always easy to assess since enemies inflated or deflated estimates for their own purposes. At Canterbury Parker kept 100 liveried servants and expected a good deal of ceremony wherever he went. He was more concerned to preserve the

symbols and substance of his position than simply to husband resources and revenues.[63] More committed to reform, the second Elizabethan primate, Edmund Grindal, was not noted for his retinue or
liberality – contributing to the queen's conviction that she had made a
mistake in the appointment. John Whitgift was the standard by which
other Elizabethan prelates were judged. He was known for his
'Orderly troops of Tawny coats' at times numbering as many as 200
men.[64] At 'divers times [he] had one Hundred Foot and Fifty Horse of
his own servants mustered, and trained'. To meet such needs Whitgift
kept 'likewise for the exercise of military discipline, a good armory
and a fair stable of great Horses.'[65]

Below the archiepiscopal level the size of retinues varied by both
taste and wealth. John Jewel at Salisbury fell in the middle ranks of
income but he was well known for keeping up the estate of a great man
and had a household which numbered no fewer than 40 retainers. To
these servants Jewel felt a loyalty giving gifts in his will of from £1 to
£10.[66] Here we are reminded that part of the purpose of having a large
household was to provide employment and support for the poor of the
community.[67] At Chester, the impoverished Bishop Downham
claimed he could not get along with fewer than 40 servants, perhaps in
part because like the Jacobean bishop Arthur Lakes, he kept his servants 'not so much for state or attendance on his person, but pure
charity, in regard their private needs.'[68] Not all bishops were moved
by motives of charity or even desire to impress the community. John
Jegon of Norwich was generally not felt to be liberal with his money,
having only about two dozen servants, while gaining a reputation for
personal wealth. Jegon is of particular interest because his secretary,
Anthony Harison left behind the single best documentary evidence
as to the nature of episcopal households at the dawn of the seventeenth
century. Two lists, dated 1603 and 1608, show a household of modest
size. Jegon's servants were seemingly put to practical use, for included
were a butler, an usher, a gardner, two carpenters, two cooks, three
scullions, a baker and an assistant baker as well as husbandmen who
doubled as footmen. There was even a trumpeter. Of greater significance were the several bailiffs who looked after the prelatical
estates.[69] Harison's lists reveal that Jegon lived a comfortable existence, surrounded by a staff who kept daily life running on an even
keel. Yet, in his will, Jegon, in contrast to many other prelates, made
not a single mention of his servants.[70]

John Aylmer, the rather unpopular bishop of London, kept a large
household noted for hospitality which contained 60 to 80 servants.
Aylmer's Puritan critics felt that this was evidence of Aylmer seeking
'the favour of the world' more 'than the glory of God'. He accumulated a substantial portion of land for his children whilst felling trees

and leaving his see in a state of disrepair which his successors were unable to recover from his family. In his pursuit of his own profit Aylmer was in conflict with another quarrelsome proud prelate, Edwin Sandys, Aylmer's immediate predecessor at London. Sandys was not a particularly generous man; yet he too was known to keep a goodly number of servants appropriate to his station.[71]

Unfortunately only Jegon left precise records as to the extent of his retinue. From the meagre evidence it would seem that some Elizabethan bishops tried to keep up medieval traditions but severe shortages of funds inevitably, if reluctantly, led to reduced establishments. Symbolic of the consequences of such a situation was Bishop Redman of Norwich, who died in debt but kept a household with 32 servants.[72]

Keeping traditional episcopal living standards was largely a function of wealth. Discrepancies between rich and poor sees were not only evident in life but could easily be carried over into death. Lavish funerals were a time-honoured episcopal tradition. As noted, Stephen Gardiner spent over £1400 on his entombment, a sum beyond the reach of Elizabethan bishops and indeed most of the nobility.[73] Late Tudor bishops did in some cases manage to put on a good display after death. Robert Bennett, the little known, though prosperous, bishop of Hereford, bequeathed £500 for burial expenses and asked that his tomb be of white alabaster showing a man lying in a white sheet on an altar. Bennett also selected the preacher for his funeral and how much cloth at what price should be used for the cloak of each relative participating in the ceremony.[74] Martin Heaton of Ely made his inhumation a prime concern, requesting that all his goods be sold to provide a 'moderate' funeral and a convenient monument in the cathedral church at Ely. Only then was his estate to be divided amongst his heirs.[75] Henry Rowlands was a Welsh prelate whose very detailed will included careful instructions for his burial and 100 marks to buy gowns for poor men and women at his funeral.[76] One of the most prosperous prelates was John Still of Bath and Wells. He wished 400 marks be spent on the ceremony plus an additional £30 for a decent monument. Always a careful man with his money, Still outlined the fashion in which funeral expenses should be incurred.[77] The most elaborate interment for an Elizabethan bishop was that of Matthew Parker, who was buried in a grand fashion, the expenses exceeding £1,000, a sum worthy of his medieval predecessors.[78]

Elaborate funerals were one aspect of traditional church practice of which Puritans were critical. Since inhumation was no longer a sacrament, extreme Puritans called for a complete elimination of burial rites. Less radical reformers merely wished to see the pomp of Tudor interments reduced.[79] The Puritan call was for greater simplicity, a message embraced by at least some of the episcopate. Anthony Rudd specifically asked for a ceremony 'without pomp',[80] while Edmund Scambler's only request was that £10 be given to the poor who attended his burial.[81] Peculiarly, traditionally minded Richard Bancroft laid the greatest emphasis on having a plain burial. He forbade any monument except a plain stone and asked that his body be not laid open, but committed in one piece. Bancroft also wanted the inhumation within 40 or 50 hours of death and asked no needless expense, as such charges were 'idle and absurd'.[82] As Bancroft was not poor it is clear that his reluctance to spend money on his entombment was a matter of conviction or emotion and not resultant from want of means.

Funerals provide an illustration of what the Reformation meant to the episcopate. The Elizabethan bishops were not as wealthy as their predecessors and inflation compounded their economic shortages. However, it was still possible for some, though certainly not all, bishops to maintain a style of death and life which approached that of the nobility. Indeed, the very richest prelates lived like peers, with lavish hospitality, several houses, crowds of retainers, fine clothes and, if desired, sumptuous burials. The middling ranks of the episcopate managed to live as comfortable gentry. Though some might die in debt, in life they owned plate, slept in feather beds, and stocked their libraries. Only the very poorest diocesans, especially in Wales, lacked the means to live comfortably.

The picture that emerges from looking at the possessions and expenditures of Elizabethan bishops is less gloomy than that provided by a narrow focus on episcopal incomes. Bishops were often cushioned from inflation and lowered receipts by the use of their demesne lands. Price indices compared to income therefore are only partial elements in the equation which yielded a style of living. It is impossible to argue that the prelates of the late sixteenth century were not reduced from the splendour of Wolsey, Gardiner and the more distant medieval past. But the Elizabethan episcopate still lived at the apex of a hierarchy with considerable resources. The acceptance, indeed often avid pursuit, of prelatical places and promotion is testimony that the episcopal life-style was one which most were ambitious to emulate.

NOTES

1. C. Hill, *Economic Problems*, 25–9, 41–3.
2. R. O'Day, *Economy and Community: economic and social history of pre-industrial England, 1500–1700* (1975), 110.
3. *The Zurich Letters*, ed. H. Robinson, (1845), II, 2.
4. *The Letter Book of Thomas Bentham, Bishop of Coventry and Lichfield, 1560–1561*, eds. R. O'Day and J. Berlatsky, *Camden Miscellany*, XXIII (1979), *passim*.

5. A. F. Pollard, *Wolsey: Church and State in Sixteenth-Century England* (New York, 1966 repr.), 320–5.
6. G. Cavendish, 'The life and death of Cardinal Wolsey' in *Two Early Tudor Lives*, eds. D. S. Sylvester and D. P. Harding (1962), 22.
7. Pollard, *op. cit.* 327; Cavendish, *op. cit.*, 20.
8. Stow, *A Survey of London* (1965 repr.), 81.
9. C. Sturge, *Cuthbert Tunstal: churchman, scholar, statesman, administrator* (1938), 265–7.
10. A. G. Dickens, *Robert Holgate, Archbishop of York and President of the King's Council in the North* (1955), 16–28.
11. J. A. Muller, *Stephen Gardiner and the Tudor Reaction* (New York, 1970 repr.), 43–4, 76, 290–1.
12. J. Ridley, *Thomas Cranmer* (1962), 132–41.
13. *LP*, X, 1232.
14. *Ibid.*, X, 431.
15. L. Stone, *The Crisis of the Aristocracy, 1558–1641* (1965), Appendix IX.
16. BL Lans, MS. 683/, fos. 8–10; Gonville and Caius College MS 197/, fos. 388–90.
17. Stone, *op. cit.*, Appendix IX.
18. F. Godwin, *A Catalogue of the Bishops of England Since the First Planting of Christian Religion in this Island* (1615), f.180.
19. P. Hembry, 'Episcopal palaces, 1535 to 1660', in *Wealth and Power in Tudor England: Essays Presented to S. T. Bindoff*, eds. E. W. Ives, R. J. Knecht and J. J. Scarisbrick (1978), 150.
20. *The Zurich Letters*, I, 149–51.
21. A. C. Judson, *A Biographical Sketch of John Young. Bishop of Rochester with Emphasis on His Relations with Edmund Spenser*, (1934), 14–15; *idem*, *The Life of Edmund Spenser* (1945), 49.
22. F. Heal, 'The Tudors and church Lands: economic problems of the bishopric of Ely during the sixteenth century', *EcHR*, 2nd ser, XXVI (1973), 204–6.
23. P. Collinson, *The Elizabethan Puritan Movement* (1967), 161.
24. Gonville and Caius College MS 53/f. 32b.
25. BL Lans. MS., 19/63/f. 142.
26. Hembry, *op. cit.*, 159.
27. *Ibid*, 154–5, 163.
28. W. T. Morgan, 'Two cases concerning dilapidations to episcopal property in the diocese of St David's, *National Library of Wales J.*, VII (1951), 149.
29. M. W. Barley, 'Rural housing in England', in *The Agrarian History of England and Wales*, ed. J. Thirsk, IV (1967), 703–11.
30. Gonville and Caius College MS 53/f. 3.
31. Gonville and Caius College MS 53/ fos. 3, 4b–29, 45b–49.
32. C. Haigh, 'Finance and administration in a new diocese: Chester, 1541–1641', in *Continuity and Change: personnel and administration of the Church in England 1500–1642*, eds. R. O'Day and F. Heal (1976), 145–66.
33. G. J. Piccope (ed.), *Lancashire and Cheshire Wills and Inventories From the Ecclesiastical Court, Chester* (Chetham Society, LIV, 1861), 1–8; R. O'Day, *The English Clergy: the emergence of a profession, 1558–1642* (1979), 185–9.
34. PRO E178/2082. See R. O'Day, 'Cumulative debt: the bishops of Coventry and Lichfield and their economic problems', *Midland History* (1975), 77–115.
35. Sir H. Ellis, 'Notices of Richard Curteys, Bishop of Chichester, 1570–1580', *Sussex Arch. Collections*, x (1858), 56–8.
36. PRO E178/254/2–4 James I.
37. G. Williams, 'Landlords in Wales: the Church', in J. Thirsk (ed.) *op. cit.*, 393–4.
38. P. T. Jones, 'Landlords in Wales (the nobility and the gentry)', in J. Thirsk (ed.), *op.*

cit., 371, 376.
39. W. J. Sheils, 'Some problems of government in a new diocese: the bishop and the puritans in the diocese of Peterborough', in O'Day and Heal (eds.), *op. cit.*, 168–9.
40. PRO E 178/1703/7–17; Sheils, *op. cit.*, 187.
41. State Papers Ireland, Eliz. XX, 29, in M. Ronan, *The Reformation in Ireland under Elizabeth, 1558–1580* (1931), 228.
42. BI.
43. *Ibid.*
44. F. Heal, *Of Prelates and Princes: A study of the economic and social position of the Tudor episcopate* (1980), 279–80.
45. PRO SP 12/184/50.
46. J. I. Daeley, 'The episcopal administration of Matthew Parker, archbishop of Canterbury, 1559–1575', (Ph. D thesis, University of London, 1967), 322, 362; V. J. K. Brook, *A Life of Archbishop Parker* (1962), 311.
47. G. Paule, *The Life of John Whitgift, Archbishop of Canterbury in the Times of Q. Elizabeth and King James I* (1649), 103–4.
48. LPL MS CM/V/11a, 11b, CM/VI/84/1.
49. Hembry, *op. cit.*, 158.
50. Corpus Christi College MS 114/art. 150/ p. 437.
51. Guildford Muniment Room, Loseley MS 927/4/ fos 1–6.
52. *CStP Dom* 1595–1597, 47.
53. J. Strype, *Annals of the Reformation* (1820–40) II, *ii*, 26.
54. PROB 11/44 Dixy.
55. Heal, *Of Prelates and Princes*, 257.
56. BL Add. MS 18769, f. 62.
57. PRO E 178/1607.
58. Norwich RO. Har. 1 Box 896, f. 197.
59. Hill, *Economic Problems*, 40; Judson, *John Young*, 31.
60. G. Alexander, 'Victim or spendthrift? The bishop of London and his income in the sixteenth century', in Ives *et al.* (eds.), *op. cit.*, 141, 145.
61. PRO SP 12/149/22.
62. P. Collinson, *Archbishop Grindal, 1519–1583: the struggle for a Reformed Church* (1979), 299–300.
63. Daeley, *op. cit.*, 322, 343.
64. J. Harington, *Nugae Antiquae:* (1804), 22–3. J. E. Neale, *The Elizabethan House of Commons* (1963 repr.), 24.
65. Paule, *op. cit.*, 97.
66. W. M. Southgate, *John Jewel and the Problem of Doctrinal Authority* (Cambridge Mass. 1962) 67; Heal, *Of Prelates and Princes*, 258; PROB 11/43 Horney.
67. Heal, *Of Prelates and Princes*, 261.
68. C. Haigh, *Reformation and Reaction in Tudor Lancashire* (1975), 225; Thomas Fuller, *The History of the Worthies of England*, ed. John Nicholls (1811), I, 407.
69. T. F. Barton (ed.), *The Registrum Vagum of Anthony Harison* Part II (Norfolk Record Society, XXXIII, 1964), 238–41.
70. PROB 11/29 Meade.
71. J. Strype, *The Life and Acts of . . . John Aylmer* (1821), 127. Hill, *op. cit.*, 20, 97; R. G. Usher, *The Reconstruction of the English Church* (New York, 1910), 114–15; PRO Del. 5/2/144.
72. Hill, *op. cit.* 40.
73. Muller, *op. cit.*, 290–1; Stone, *op. cit.*, Appendix XXV.
74. PROB 11/122 Welden.
75. PROB 11/32 Wingfield.
76. PROB 11/90 Cope.

77. PROB 11/33 Windebanck.
78. Brook, *op. cit.*, 341.
79. J. New, *Anglican and Puritan: the basis of their opposition, 1558–1640* (1964), 76ff; Collinson, *op. cit.*, 370–1.
80. PROB 11/32 Rudd.
81. PROB 11/50 Dixy.
82. PROB 11/96 Wingfield.

6

Archbishop Laud revisited: leases and estate management at Canterbury and Winchester before the Civil War

Felicity Heal

'The king and the priest', wrote William Laud in 1639, 'must be careful of the church's maintenance . . . else the bees shall make honey for others, and have none left for their own necessary sustenance, and then all's lost.'[1] It became a primary concern of Laud as archbishop that the Church should retain or reacquire the financial resources necessary to strengthen its ministry and to establish it once more as a powerful institution within English society. Constantly before his eyes was the objective of 'the Church Triumphant', a body which would have transcended the spiritual crises of the preceding century and which would provide the true ecclesiastical counterpart to divine right monarchy. But the Church which Laud actually inherited upon his translation to Canterbury in 1633 was far from such an apotheosis. Its creaking mechanisms of administration and finance were still fundamentally those of medieval Catholicism, imperfectly adapted to the demands of a Protestant polity. Its clergy possessed more formal educational qualifications than their predecessors, but were still alarmingly dependent upon the goodwill of the laity and often influenced by the theology of Geneva which was in some ways so abhorrent to the archbishop. The Church needed to be strengthened at every level, nowhere more so than at the height of authority among the bishops. The episcopate was the exemplar: if the bishops showed themselves united and strong in the face of the hostility of certain sections of lay society then the lower clergy could follow them. One hundred years of reformation had, however, gravely weakened the authority of the episcopate and left many of its members without the power or resources to command the respect of the rest of the community. Laud sought to restore the ecclesiastical strength of the hierarchy with the assistance of such weapons as the Court of High Commission and to remedy its economic weakness by strict discipline and the effective use of such wealth as still remained to it after the depredations of the Tudor period.[2]

It was, in Laud's eyes, essential 'to see the bishops decently supplied ... according to their place and dignity', to reverse the pattern by which the hierarchy had lost economic strength relative to the nobility and gentry of the realm and had been allowed to organize its affairs for the advantage of its individual members and their families rather than for the benefit of the Church at large. No archbishop, no English monarch indeed, had the power to recall the property that had been dispersed: the contest between the Marian government and the laity about the monastic lands was sufficient proof of that. Instead Laud had to focus upon a strict supervision of the remaining resources of the English and Welsh sees. In general royal letters circulated to all bishops in 1629 and 1634 the details of this supervision were adumbrated. The prelates were to reside in their sees, unless specifically required to attend upon the Court, they were to live in their own episcopal residences, they were to preserve the timber growing upon their estates, to prepare adequate surveys of their lands and not to make or renew any leases after their nomination to a new see. Above all, they were to establish a tighter control over leasing policy so that the property of the bishopric might not be exploited for the private advantage of bishop or tenant. This involved limiting the length of lease grants as far as practicable to 21 years, rather than encouraging the three-life grants also permitted by law. In the royal letter of 1634, already quoted by W. J. Sheils, Laud correctly pointed out that the three-life lease almost always lasted longer than one for 21 years and that his prohibition upon the translation of years into lives upon renewal was therefore a first step towards changing a system by which 'the present bishop puts a great fine into his own purse, to enrich himself ... and leaves his successors ... destitute of that growing means which else would come in to help them'.[3] The general royal letters were supplemented by specific commands to individual bishops or deans and chapters: the Bishop of Bristol was ordered to keep the lease of Abbots Cromwell in his own hands to maintain hospitality, the Bishop of Bangor was particularly reminded of the importance of taking a survey of his lands and in 1637 the Bishop of Winchester was told not to allow his tenants their customary rights within his woodlands unless they had good claims in law. Laud's general reports on the state of his province, compiled from the information of his diocesans, allowed him to check regularly upon the progress of these royal initiatives, to apply his policy of 'thorough' to his weaker episcopal brethren.[4]

This approach to the financial problems of the bishops is already well known to students of early Stuart history, especially from the work of Christopher Hill. Laud emerges from the pages of his study as the tenacious proponent of a policy that was sound enough in purely fiscal terms, but which failed to take account of the sensibilities of the laity and which ran counter to the social and political direction of English history. What is missing in Hill's account is a detailed investigation of the success or failure of Laud's policy at diocesan level. Such an investigation can throw valuable light not merely upon the mechanisms of enforcement, but upon the appropriateness of the archbishop's remedies for the woes of his Church. Our perceptions of the religious history of the 1630s are still perhaps too much dominated by the confrontation between Laud and the forces of Puritanism, too little by the reality of local relationships which writers on the politics of the period have long recognized as of great significance. The archbishop was influenced by a variety of factors, including his own religious ideology, his perception of the weakness of the Church at the centre, the austerity of his personal life and his knowledge of the manner in which his own dioceses were organized, to argue that all prelates should behave in a similar way. This essay will attempt to study how suitable it was to the circumstances of the English Church to urge such uniformity of direction on the bishops through a detailed comparison between Laud's own diocese of Canterbury and the diocese of Winchester.[5]

Since the issue of leasing policy lies at the heart of the attempts to stabilize and improve episcopal finances it is important to be aware of the possible advantages and disadvantages to the bishops of any change in the *status quo* that existed before the 1630s. Almost all property vested in the prelates in the early seventeenth century was in lease: only a limited area of home farm, parkland and woodland usually remained under direct exploitation and some sees had everything demised; 'to the very mill that grinds his corn', as the Bishop of Bangor remarked gloomily in his 1638 report to Laud.[6] Rectories and tithes were granted out on the same terms as manorial property and could, as W. J. Sheils has shown for York, be a very important part of the assets of some sees. In these circumstances it was of great importance that there should be some form of inter-generational equity, that each bishop should have adequate profit from his leases, either in the form of rent or of fines. Since the beneficial lease, with its low annual rental and higher renewal fine, was universally established upon the property of the Church and custom made any significant shift towards rack-renting almost unthinkable, equity needed to be assured by a reasonable distribution of fines upon renewal. Hence Laud's conviction, enshrined in the 1634 letter, that leases for 21 years, renewable after seven to ten years, were of greater benefit to the bishops than three-life leases, which might yield a larger fine, but whose terms were indefinite. But there was more to the issue than equity within the bench. When the archbishop was questioned at his trial about his orders on leases, he pointed out that he did not overturn the Elizabethan legislation allowing either type of grant, but he went on, in a tone that must surely have been bitter, to complain that the laity already had more than five parts of the lands of the Church 'and shall it be yet an eyesore to serve themselves with the rest of their own?' The attempt to change to a system of leases more profitable to the Church was also a demonstration that the clergy could still assert their independence within their own sphere. Indeed, Heylyn suggests that the main reason for the attack upon leases for lives was 'that the Gentry and Yeomanry (and some of the nobility also) holding Lands of those Churches, might have a greater respect to the Church and Churchmen, when they must depend upon them from time to time for renewing of their said estates.'[7]

Thus expressed, the arguments in favour of changing to a tighter system of leasing sound almost irrefutable. Yet in the context of seventeenth-century society it was likely that such a rationalization could only be achieved at some cost in good relationships or individual profit. A bishop, in making leases of his lands, had to balance a variety of considerations: he had an obligation to be a good lord to his tenants and to treat them with customary justice, he often had responsibilities towards his own family and friends that were not easily gainsaid, he had to accept an inherited pattern of leasing arrangements that were often far from ideal and he had to evaluate the needs of the Church at large and of his own local part of it. Each of these considerations might run counter to the insistence of the archbishop that there should be rationalization. It has been argued, for example, that one of the most important features of the beneficial lease was that it provided a legitimate 'private' profit of office both because the fine became the personal possession of the bishop and because it offered invaluable patronage for the family and friends of the incumbent. The whole concept of the personal advantage that a prelate might take from his office is an interesting one: the early seventeenth century is noted as a period when the boundaries between legitimate profit-taking from office and exploitation were very poorly defined and the ecclesiastical hierarchy was peculiarly troubled by this issue. The austerity of Laud's own life and his total commitment to his office left him with little sympathy for the problems of a bishop who had a growing family to support, a family to whom he could give either leases or his additional 'windfall' income from fines. The fact that a number of prelates abused their position to enrich their children does not disguise the existence of a real and abiding problem created by a family who had to be provided for from a life-office.[8]

But perhaps the main argument against the Laudian position upon leases was that the economic advantages of change were not so clear-cut as to merit possible conflict with influential local laymen to implement them. After the Restoration John Cosin argued in favour of the three-life lease, claiming that it was advantageous to the Church at large, and recalling that in the 1630s Richard Neile had always felt the same 'though he displeased Archbishop Laud by it'.[9] While three-life leases could be very slow to fall in and could leave a bishop with little regular help from fines, we shall see below that in practice they were often renewed, presumably with some reasonable profit to the prelate. At the same time they were recognized as somewhat more advantageous to the tenant than the grant for years and thus gave the lord the opportunity of discriminating in favour of some of his farmers. If such a system was already in operation before the 1630s, as it certainly was in a number of dioceses, it might be one small element in the complex business of ensuring harmony between the bishops and men of property; if it was dislocated by order from on high, it would almost certainly be a point of disharmony and possibly of actual conflict. Did Richard Neile, more adept than Laud at securing his spiritual aims by tact and persuasion, see the pressure upon leases as an unnecessary irritant in the struggle to win the laity over to the cause of Arminianism?[10]

The issue of leases is a paradigm for other aspects of the economic and social life of the bishops. Constraints such as the inherited pattern of relationships with the laity of their dioceses, the pattern of office holding by their secular administrators and the attitude of the Crown towards them as individuals could all serve to complicate the behaviour of the prelates. Laud was, of course, aware in a general sense of this local diversity: he had himself risen in the Church through the dioceses of St David's, Bath and Wells and London before reaching Canterbury. Moreover, the annual diocesan reports continued to remind him of the complexity of the Church over which he presided. Nevertheless, his disposition was to ignore the special pleading of individual cases and to press for an ideological norm consonant with his general view of the direction and purpose of the Church. It is to the relevance of this norm to the conditions of the localities in the 1630s that we must now turn.[11]

II

It is unlikely that William Laud had a particular diocese in mind when constructing his orders for the better financial governance of the Church, but his own see of Canterbury in practice seems to have approximated to the pattern of governance for which he argued. Between 1583 and the Civil War the archbishopric of Canterbury was occupied by only four men, at least three of whom were deeply concerned with the need to stabilize the finances of the English Church. Earlier in the sixteenth century, under Archbishop Cranmer, the see had suffered its share of general dislocation as the original landed endowment was gradually appropriated by Henry VIII and his courtiers. By the end of the 1540s half the manors of the see had been lost, though they were replaced by new lands, principally by property formerly held by Kentish monasteries in the east and south of the county. A further round of exchanges under the Elizabethan Act of 1559 left the archbishops with a large number of rectories and tithes within Kent and with an income at least a third of which was drawn from spiritualities, that is from the wealth of other parts of the Church. The consequence of these exchanges was that in the early 1590s the rental income of the see stood at between £2,700 and £3,000, as compared to the 1535 estimate of £3,224. These figures make no allowance for the effects of inflation which could in theory have reduced the real value of the 1590s totals by a factor of three. Such a static money income in a period of inflation would always have been a problem but it was particularly difficult for the archbishops who, as leaders of the Church, were obliged to maintain an elaborate life-style and to be the equals of the nobility in their pattern of entertainment. Even before the Reformation the Canterbury household had consumed almost all the available revenues of the archbishopric: William Warham used so much of his income upon hospitality, charity and the care of his buildings that he died with very little money in hand.[12]

Given the earlier difficulties of the archbishops one might *a priori* assume that their Elizabethan successors would have been tempted to make what profit they could without too tender a care for the future of the see. There are some signs of such an attitude under Parker, who was accused of exploiting his woods for the benefit of his children and who certainly took a passionate interest in establishing his son in Kentish society. Nevertheless Parker also cared deeply for his see and for the discharge of his proper duties of hospitality and charity. He cultivated his connections with the county of Kent and was responsible for the first attempts at rebuilding on the Kentish manors since the Reformation. This local involvement did not survive into the troubled incumbency of Parker's successor Grindal, who, despite his general concern for the souls under his care, seems never to have resided in Kent, nor to have worked particularly hard to foster his relationships with the leaders of county society. It was left to his successor John Whitgift to search for a balance of local and national influence and to provide a close care for his own property that in certain ways approximated to the Laudian ideal. The reassertion of the authority of the Church within the localities was one of the aims of

Whitgift's ecclesiastical policy. Within the confines of his own diocese
he sought political influence through parliamentary elections, tried to
renew archiepiscopal claims to authority within the cathedral city and
endeavoured to increase the number of episcopal residences in regular
use. His visits to the county of Kent were solemn occasions, attended
by elaborate ritual more reminiscent of the medieval Church than of
the behaviour of some of his immediate predecessors. His biographer,
George Paule, describes his reception by the local gentry as a great
triumph: 'and surely the entertainment which he gave them, and they
him, was so great, that, as I am verily persuaded no shire in England
did, or could, give greater, or with more cheerful minds, each unto
other'.[13] The degree of harmony between the archbishop and the
Kentish gentry can be questioned: the radical laity were certainly not
enchanted by his attempts to enforce conformity in 1583 and there is
evidence of conflict between the ecclesiastical and lay authorities in
the 1590s on purveyance and joint musters. Nevertheless, Whitgift
was able to reassert the influence of the clergy, and the archiepiscopal
see in particular, without the total breakdown in contact with the
gentry that was to afflict Laud in the 1630s.[14]

Whitgift was able to sustain this strong presence in his diocese, as in
his main seat of government at Lambeth, partly because of the care
which he lavished upon the finances and administration of his see.
Again his behaviour seems to be a vital demonstration of the principles Laud asserted, though it is impossible to discover if he provided
any direct exemplar for his Caroline successor. Many of Whitgift's
measures can be characterized as 'good housekeeping' rather than as
major attempts to change the organization or financing of his possessions. While still bishop of Worcester he had recorded carefully all
the rents in kind and food from the demesne available to him, and had
gone to law to recover food-rents from two of his rectories. He had
urged on his officers to investigate rights which had been allowed to
lapse since the Reformation and also reduced the costs and arrears of
the bishopric, effecting a net increase in income of between £100 and
£200. Armed with this experience he arrived at Canterbury and at
once began to show a close interest in the finances by keeping his own
account book in which he noted all casualties as well as the formal
income from rents. At Canterbury as at Worcester some modest
savings were made in fees and wages during Whitgift's incumbency
and once again his officials were urged on to inquire into the rights of
the see. He was fortunate to inherit a very able steward, John Boys,
who identified the interests of the archbishopric closely with his own
and showed a sophisticated awareness of possible financial improvements. It was Boys who led a defence of episcopal leasing policy in the
Commons in the 1590s. It is difficult to overestimate the importance

of zealous central estate officers: the inertia of a large estate organization was almost impossible to overcome unless a bishop had time or
experience on his side. The archbishops, with their national role and
wide commitments, were particularly dependent upon their officers
for the sustained care of their see and the stability of Canterbury may
owe as much to the service of Boys under four masters as to the initiative of particular prelates.[15]

But Whitgift was more than a 'good housekeeper', since in two
areas he seems to have presided over important developments in episcopal finance. First he gave attention to the subject of food-rents
which were particularly valuable in the inflationary period of the
1590s. Under the terms of his leases 204 fat wethers, 194 quarters of
wheat and 251 quarters of barley were supplied annually by the
tenants, the vast majority of the produce being intended for consump-
tion in the episcopal household. Some of these leases seem to be survi-
vals from the time when parts of the Canterbury estates were in
monastic ownership, but Whitgift extended his demands for food
beyond those made by Matthew Parker, who in his turn seems to have
searched for the opportunity to increase rents in kind. The archbishops of Canterbury had very little farming activity on their own
account, in contrast, for example, to the archbishops of York who still
managed quite large flocks of sheep and some arable, but the food-
rents from Kent must have been a major factor in enabling them to
maintain their lavish household on reduced real revenues.'[16]

Even more interesting for our purposes is the archbishop's
approach to the problem of demesne leases. He embarked upon a
thorough policy of lease renewal which was in marked contrast to that
of his immediate predecessors. Between 1583 and 1600 he made 105
grants of the Canterbury demesnes, and in almost every case the lease
was renewed within five years. Whitgift was fortunate to arrive in the
see at a time when some of the long grants made in the mid-Tudor
period were beginning to fall in: his situation contrasts with that of
Parker, who lamented the difficulty of profiting from his demesnes
and who only had 12 leases confirmed by the dean and chapter
between 1567 and 1575.[17] The principle of renewable leaseholds,
combined with the legislation of Elizabeth I restricting those leases to
21 years or three lives, obviously lent itself to systemization of the sort
initiated by Whitgift. Since the ancient rent bore so little relationship
to the true value of the estates some compensation had to be available
to the archbishops through the renewal fines. When a tenant surrendered with a number of years still in being the fine which could be
asked of him was not large: the scattered evidence from Whitgift's
accounts suggests that payments varied between two and four times
the annual rental. Since only a few fines are recorded it is difficult to

extrapolate from these figures to the yearly value of the Canterbury fines, but a crude guess would be that the archbishop probably derived in excess of £1,000 from this source. The value of the system, as Laud was to perceive later, lay not only in the regular increase of income that it guaranteed to the archbishops, but in the closeness of the relationship which it engendered between lord and tenant. When John Boys defended Whitgift's policy in the parliament of 1601 he described it as of mutual benefit to the bishops and their tenants: its dislocation, he suggested, would advantage only those outsiders who wished to take undue profit from the lands of the Church. By 1601 he could also describe the pattern of renewals upon the Canterbury estates as common practice: 'I myself am farmer to a bishop, and I speak this as in my own case (on my knowledge) to the house, that it is ordinary upon every grant after four or five years, ever to fine and take a new lease.'[18] How common the practice in fact was is debatable. Many sees were still caught in the long leases made under Henry VIII and Edward VI, and others such as Winchester and Durham lost much of their property in further long grants made under the provision of the Elizabethan legislation that exempted the Crown from the general restriction upon length of leases made by the bishops. There are signs, however, that other efficient administrators of Whitgift's generation followed a policy similar to that of the archbishop: Bishop Still of Bath and Wells was renewing his leases regularly in the 1590s and at London one of the most efficient diocesan administrations had also commenced a regular review of grants. The reaction of the Commons also suggests that changes aimed at increasing the independence of the bishops were afoot in this decade and that they were viewed with some alarm. In the parliament of 1597 a bill was read 'concerning leases made by bishops and archbishops', but was rejected on a second reading. During the next session the bill was revived, now clearly identified as a measure to prevent the bishops renewing leases until they were within three years of expiration. This was the occasion on which Boys deployed his eloquence to urge the House to reject the bill. Even this rejection did not dampen the enthusiasm of the opponents of the bishops, for similar legislation was introduced into the parliaments of 1604 and 1610: in 1610 the matter was pursued with sufficient energy for a bill to be sent up to the Lords. The Upper House amended this so substantially that the Commons rejected the revised version and no more was heard of the issue. All this suggests that the problem was not one of critical concern to the members of the House, but that there were men who had a strong vested interest in resisting the attempts of the Church to strengthen its financial position.[19]

Whitgift may therefore be said to offer a model of efficient financial administration to which Laud could refer. He even converted some of the three-life leases of the archbishopric back into 21-year grants. The survey of the archbishopric initiated in 1606 shows that, although some three-life leases were still in operation, at least three had been converted in the 1590s: for example, Northborne rectory, leased to the Smith family, was renewed for 21 years only in 1591. Evidence for the estate administration of Whitgift's two successors, Bancroft and Abbot, is much less full, but indicates that the pattern established in the late Elizabethan years persisted into the 1630s. John Boys remained the presiding genius of archiepiscopal estate administration under Bancroft and in 1606 either he or his master initiated an elaborate 'view' of all the property of the see. Here we find another of the devices advocated by Laud as necessary for the proper control of the wealth of the Church: the upheavals of the mid-Tudor years had left many sees ill-informed upon the details of the property formally in their possession. The later years of Elizabeth's reign saw a number of bishops initiating full rentals and surveys for the first time since the Reformation: it may be that Whitgift ordered such a survey, but the evidence has not survived, and the comments of the two Jacobean investigations indicate that this may be one area of estate control that he neglected.[20] Abbot's period in office was marked by one major development in Canterbury estate administration. In 1616–17 a royal commission was established to survey all the lands of the see in great detail, since it was claimed that the lands which had come to the archbishops in the great exchanges of the Henrician years had never been adequately investigated and that the rights of the see were therefore being infringed by the tenants. Only two returns survive: those for the Dover priory lands and for the rectory of Whalley in Lancashire, and it seems unlikely from the document that any more was ever completed. It would be interesting to know if Abbot himself was the inspiration behind the commission: both the Dover lands and Whalley were still on long leases which were scheduled to expire in the 1620s and there was therefore every incentive to investigate the rights of the see before any new grants were made. If the archbishop did initiate the survey we have here a very interesting example of the increased collaboration between Crown and bishops that characterized the early seventeenth century. A survey of the detail and depth of that made in 1616 was both costly and complex, involving the convening of juries, the supervision of local men of substance and endless work for secretaries and scribes. Such an operation would have strained the resources of the archiepiscopal organization, especially on a distant estate such as Whalley, and it was greatly to the advantage of the see if it could invoke royal support and the mechanisms of royal administration. Unfortunately, the loss of Canterbury leases for the 1620s makes it difficult to assess what use Abbot made of the survey: the Whalley evidence suggests that the archbishop proceeded cautiously, for the rectory there was leased out for lives to the Ashton family and nothing in the later lease details indicates that there was any unusual attempt to tighten the terms by which the archbishop controlled his tenants.[21]

Abbot's years at Canterbury also offer us some insight into the economic pressures upon the archbishops and into their need to increase the basic revenues of the see. His excellent household accounts show that the Canterbury establishment always cost in excess of £2,000 *per annum* and that it only required some unusual event, such as a visitation of the diocese, to increase this figure to £2,500. Although the rental income of the see was increasing slowly in the period, until in the early 1640s it stood at c. £3,300 gross, the archbishops must have needed an income well in excess of £4,000 to meet all their additional expenses such as taxation, fees and works of charity. The image of Abbot that emerges from his accounts is an interesting one: his most lavish expenditure was consistently reserved for his visits to his own diocese, which suggests that he continued Whitgift's policy of generosity to his neighbours in order to strengthen the Church in his own locality. Like Cranmer and Parker before him he was a fascinating example of a firmly Protestant prelate who nevertheless felt it important to maintain the dignity of his office according to the lavish social conventions of his age: several of the revisions of the household ordinances of Cranmer date from his archiepiscopate and show a strong adherence to a formal, hierarchical pattern of household governance. The evidence from the early years of Abbot's archiepiscopate, before the problem of his accidental homicide clouded his labours, suggests that he endeavoured to continue the best of the traditions of his predecessors involving collaboration with the laity without any loss of dignity to the Church.[22] One final point needs to be made about William Laud's predecessors: all the archbishops between Grindal and Laud were unmarried. Although they were not averse to providing some support from their lands for their extended families – Whaddon manor was leased to George and John Whitgift in 1601 and the rectory of Rochdale to Richard Bancroft, brother of the archbishop, in 1606 – the tensions between their duties to the Church and their private obligations to their kin rarely seem to have been acute. Even their wills and bequests reveal a judicious balance between the protection of family interests and charitable endeavours. Whitgift, Grindal and Abbot all endowed schools or almshouses that were among the most important episcopal foundations of their century.[23]

At Canterbury, we may therefore conclude, there was in operation a system of ecclesiastical finance and administration that was acceptable to Laud, albeit that the laity still profited from the Church more

than they should do in the age of the 'Church Triumphant'. The surviving evidence suggests that Laud continued the financial policy of
his predecessors in his role as diocesan: the Commonwealth surveys
show that only four leases for lives still remained on the Canterbury
estates, and that the 1630s had marked the point when several others
previously held by this form of tenure had been converted. Laud
renewed only one lease on the Kentish lands for lives and he maintained many of the food-rents that can be traced from Whitgift's
tenure of office onwards. The loss of the original leases makes it impossible to judge if his officials were renewing grants at
regular intervals, but it is almost certain that they were doing so since
by the 1630s such renewals had become commonplace in other sees.
Although no details of any general land survey from these years survives there are careful surveys of the woodlands still available to the
archbishops. Woods were a particular concern of Laud's; after leases
they are the topic most often raised in the Crown's orders to the
bishops and higher clergy that they conserve the resources of their
estates. But if Laud continued the policies of his predecessors towards
their lands, he neglected another key dimension of their social and political role. The goodwill between the gentry of Kent and the archbishops, so carefully fostered by Abbot's visits, was dissipated by the
drive for conformity to Arminian practice and also perhaps by the
high-handed methods of an absentee prelate. Alan Everitt has chroni-
cled the process by which the Kentish gentry moved from a quiescent
acceptance of Jacobean Protestantism to a reluctant radicalism that
rejected the concept of episcopacy. Given Laud's national policies this
was almost inescapable, but there is no evidence that the archbishop
tried to moderate the impact of his changes by any appeal to the sensibilities of the local community.[24]

The same lack of local sensitivity lies at the heart of the one estate
problem of the 1630s that is well documented: the case of Whalley
rectory. We have seen that, despite the careful survey of 1616, the
rectory was leased for lives to the Ashtons in the 1620s. Since the lives
were all in being Laud would normally have had no grounds for intervening or forcing a renewal in the 1630s. However, he found technical
grounds to challenge the grant and, as he said in his defence at his trial,
took the case before the High Commission 'for the invalidity of the
document and the unworthiness of the tenants'. The tenants were presumably unworthy in his eyes because they espoused a form of back-
woods Puritanism that he found repellent. The threat of legal
proceedings was sufficient to persuade Sir Ralph to make a renewal,
paying a fine of £1600, which was claimed to be little more than one
year's improved rental, an increase in rent to provide for the curates
and supposedly changing from three lives to 21 years. The dilemma in

this case was that what served the immediate economic interests of the Church was not necessarily to its best long-term advantage: the Ashtons were an influential and ubiquitous local clan whose loyalty was important to the Church. Laud's clash almost ensured, as Christopher Hill has indicated, that Sir Ralph should end by leading a troop of parliamentary horse in the Civil War. And this was despite the fact that, under the strong urging of Orlando Bridgeman, the son of the bishop of Chester, Laud did modify his principles to the extent of allowing Sir Ralph a lease for lives.[25]

III

The Whalley affair reveals the difficulty of trying to apply a fixed series of social and economic ideals to the changing circumstances of the Church in the localities. The same dilemma can be demonstrated at large by looking at another diocese that had a history very dissimilar to that of Canterbury in the half-century preceding the Civil War. The relative success of the archiepiscopate owed much to the efficiency of its prelates, and their concern for their office, but much also to the internal stability of the see and the absence of pressure upon it from Crown and laity. The story of Winchester was a much less happy one. From the beginning of Elizabeth's reign the see was subjected to a series of dislocating events that reduced it from its once proud position as the wealthiest English bishopric. Between 1559 and 1573 the Crown held in its own hands the bailiwick of Taunton, meanwhile exacting a rent payment of £400, supposedly in lieu of the lands. John Watson, the second Elizabethan prelate, surrendered a large number of the estates of the see to the Crown on long lease, making many of the properties totally unimprovable for the next 60 to 80 years. The early Elizabethan prelates all found themselves in financial difficulty: Robert Horne died in debt to the queen for clerical taxes and Thomas Cooper alleged that he only had £300 per annum after the payment of all his fixed costs. Cooper also found himself embattled, surrounded by tenants who could not be controlled and who were 'encouraged and emboldened to enter suits of law against me by most unjust causes'. This sense of conflict was common enough in other sees, but the number of Winchester bishops who complained about their tenants seems almost unique: Horne, Watson, Day and Bilson all echoed the general sentiment expressed by Cooper. It may be that the conservatism of Hampshire society is some explanation for this tension: although none of the Winchester bishops challenged their Catholic laity as zealously as Bishop Curteys in neighbouring Sussex, they were not popular for their enforcement of the principles of reformed Protestantism. The energetic rule of Thomas Cooper at least seems to have stabilized the financial administration of the diocese, but after his death troubles began in earnest once again. Within three years between 1594 and 1597 three prelates were appointed. William Wickham died before he could be consecrated and his successor, William Day, survived his promotion by only a few months. Then Thomas Bilson was appointed, and he outlived Queen Elizabeth, dying in 1616.[26]

Rapid changes of this kind can have done little to secure respect for the authority of the see. The Winchester tenants were forced to pay recognizances at the entry of each bishop and in the 1590s these payments appear to have fuelled the resentment already felt on some manors at the behaviour of the episcopal officers. The change of rulership also allowed a resurgence of lay demands for the estates. Sir Francis Carew saw in the appointment of Day an opportunity to press an inexperienced bishop for long leases. He asked Elizabeth to arrange that property worth 2,000 marks *per annum*, or approximately one-third of the rental value of the see, should be transferred to him. Day had the courage to resist Carew, even with the full weight of royal approval behind him, for he argued that no bishop could afford this alienation since 'by long leases he cuts himself and his successors from more than the bare rents'.[27] The queen's response was chilly: she denied the bishop his temporalities until May 1596 in the hope that he would yield, with the consequence that he had no time to order his finances before his death in September of the same year. The next bishop undoubtedly found it expedient to be as pliant as Day had been obdurate: Bilson lost no time in agreeing that he would yield to Carew, provided that he was allowed to enter his see first to avoid the taint of simony. The transaction still bore a remarkable resemblance to simony in practice if not in theory and Carew gained five of the major manors of the see for a term of 60 years. In return Bilson gained some of those short-term concessions which show a placing of personal advantage before the interests of the see: the rents for the summer before he was eligible to have his temporalities restored and a long period in which to pay his first fruits.[28]

As Bilson surveyed his depleted inheritance there must have seemed much less opportunity to stabilize episcopal finance than that available to his colleagues at Canterbury. In addition to the long grants made through the Crown there were the 99-year grants from the mid-Tudor years, some of which did not expire until after the beginning of the Civil War. The results can be observed in the episcopal lease-book for the years 1619 to 1640. Although in some years the prelates were able to make as many as 20 leases, the range of property involved was small in comparison to the total number of estates owned by the see. In the 1630s grants could be made on only nine manors, two rectories and five parks or warrens, although the bishopric still held title to 39 estates. On the eve of the Civil War one or two extra properties, such as the manor of Hambledon, were released from long lease, but on the whole the bishops had to depend upon the renewal of a small group of lands, most of which were firmly in the hands of the same tenants throughout the period.[29]

The constraints upon the bishops of Winchester were increased by the behaviour of the Crown. Even after the death of Elizabeth, and James's moratorium on long leases made by the bishops to the monarch, there was a continuing interest in the rich manors of the see. James demanded a lease of Farnham Castle in 1608 in order to pass it to Viscount Haddington: Farnham and its two parks were one of only three properties that the bishops still held in hand. Bilson took a slightly stronger stand against the royal will than he had done in 1597, mindful perhaps that he had already paid his pound of flesh, but in the end he yielded grudgingly, saying: 'I am very willing to give his Majesty all contentation, and shall be glad if he so interpret my care for the church'.[30] Farnham was only one of several estates upon which the bishop was ordered to make leases: Bentley and Henley were passed to Sir Roger Aston via the Crown, and Hambledon Chase went to Haddington at the same time as the Farnham property. Bilson's successor, Lancelot Andrewes, was noted for the lavish entertainment that he offered to James: on one famed occasion in 1620 he spent £2,400 in three days when he acted as host to the entire Court. The interesting feature of this visit was that it took place at Farnham Castle, which had only been leased away from the bishopric for the duration of Bilson's occupation of the see. Given Andrewes' known concern to preserve the property of the Church there must surely have been a fixed policy behind this lavish display: the demonstration that church wealth and church property could be put to good use for the support of the Crown.[31]

Even the death of James I did not mark the end of royal intervention in the affairs of Winchester. Bishop Neile still found himself acting as host to the king in 1630 and offering lodgings to the great on their travels. In 1629 the Earl of Clare was a guest of the bishop's, and in the subsequent year the Countess of Castlehaven favoured him with her presence. More important as evidence that Charles had not entirely eschewed the behaviour of his predecessors is the case of Thomas Cary. In January 1632 the king wrote to Neile requesting the office of High Steward for Cary, with an annuity of £100 to accompany it. The bishop was so affronted by this blatant exercise of royal authority that he specifically recorded the letter in the patent book 'to avoid the distaste that any of my successors may perhaps conceive of me for granting this following patent'.[32] Neile also recorded that he actually waited upon the king to plead against the appointment, but that Charles was adamant, merely offering the bishop the bland consolation 'that Himself would be both High Steward and a gracious Patron to the See and Bishopric and Church of Winchester'. Such indirect control of episcopal offices was perhaps the last resort for a Crown which had effectively excluded itself from any influence over lands and leases. Its consequences for the bishops are difficult to evaluate: offices such as that of the steward had already become largely honorific in some dioceses. Effective power was often vested instead in hands of the receivers, surveyors and auditors, or even with some close confidant of the bishop such as the secretary. However, administrative continuity and efficiency was obviously best ensured when all the episcopal officers had some commitment to the see. Thomas Cary was *a priori* less likely to serve his lord with enthusiasm than John Boys had been to serve Whitgift.[33]

Royal demands upon Bilson presented problems for his successors, but the bishop may also have compounded them by his own moves away from 21-year leases towards three-life grants. The Winchester lease-books show that in the mid-Elizabethan period the predominant form of lease was for 21 years, although some of the most attractive manors such as Downton in Wiltshire were already granted out for lives, in this case to the Herbert family. There are signs of change under Cooper: for example, the manor of North Waltham, previously demised for years, was surrendered in 1594 and renewed for lives on the same terms. Bilson accelerated the process of conversion and by the end of his episcopate a majority of the new grants being made were for lives. It is interesting to compare this process with events elsewhere: while Whitgift continued to resist life leases at Canterbury some other diocesans were moving in the same direction as Bilson. At Ely it was Martin Heaton, bishop from 1599 to 1609, who standardized the practice of offering three-life leases, and at Chichester a similar transition occurred in the early Jacobean years. A possible explanation lies in the closing of the opportunity of granting long leases through the Crown after 1604. Bilson, whose concern for his family places him among those prelates who found it difficult to delimit private gain from public profit, certainly used the royal leasing exemption before 1604 and three-life grants to his kin thereafter. Leonard Bilson received an assignment of the tithes of Meon manor for 50 years from 1617 in a long lease made via the Crown in 1599. When this avenue for profit was closed, Osmund Bilson was given property in Southwark manor for three lives. But a more general explanation seems to be needed for a move which appears counter to the economic interests of the Church. It was, on the whole, the manorial sites at Winchester, or the more attractive of the parkland, that were converted to three-life grants. These provided valuable patronage for the bishops, an opportunity to secure good relationships with local families as well as members of the ruling elite.[34]

The pattern of estate management that Andrewes, Richard Neile and Walter Curle inherited at Winchester, was therefore very different from that of Abbot and Laud at Canterbury. Andrewes and Neile were as interested as the archbishops in strengthening the Church, but their local methods reflect an awareness of problems other than those that preoccupied Laud. Andrewes accepted the lease pattern of his predecessor, though according to Dean Young he was very cautious in making renewals, only once granting a concurrent lease and that 'for the good of the see'. In one or two cases Andrewes actually allowed the conversion of a grant to lives. The more important example, the lease of Adderbury in Oxfordshire, shows Andrewes' sensitivity to the value of lay support; this was granted to Sir Arthur Wilmot, a key figure in local politics and subsequent adherent of the royalist cause. It is, however, with the arrival at Winchester of Richard Neile in 1628 that we have the clearest evidence of the positive role that the bishops could play even within the constraints of the three-life lease. We have Cosin's word that Neile did not think it necessary to change the manner in which church property was leased, and his behaviour at Winchester bears this out. Grants continued to be converted into lives on some of the smaller estates within the bishop's gift and there is no hint that Neile contemplated change in the other direction, even after the royal orders of 1629 made it clear that life leases were no longer favoured. The bishop seems to have seen his property as primarily a means of supporting his friends and winning influence. When the Earl of Castlehaven was given a grant of the Wiltshire manor of Fonthill in 1629 he was allowed three lives, all of whom were adolescents, and the terms of his lease were generous on issues such as repairs and the use of timber. Also well treated was George Browne, the recorder of Taunton, who had lands within the Taunton bailiwick for lives. He was an influential local figure with whom the episcopal adminstration no doubt found it valuable to keep cordial contact.[35]

Neile also regarded as legitimate the support of his friends and *familia*. He had already given his immediate family and members of his household a number of grants from his previous offices as dean of Westminster and bishop of Lincoln and Durham: indeed at Durham his activities had been questioned when he issued nine concurrent leases to his dependants. Although Neile has recorded no formal defence of his conduct it seems reasonable to assume that he saw these grants as the natural fruits of office, as a means of livelihood for that inner group of confidants who were so important in his attempt to change the direction of the Church. At Winchester, where his Arminian views brought him into conflict with the dean, John Young, Neile found his attitude to church property questioned as well. In 1630 the dean challenged the bishop when the latter sought the ratification of four concurrent leases. Young believed that Neile only had personal profit in mind in making the grants which 'might prejudice our reputation'. It is difficult to ascertain from Young's account exactly what is at issue in this dispute: the implication is that it was the number of leases to which he most objected, since he professed himself willing to confirm one or two grants if it was the only way to persuade the tenants to offer a reasonable fine. A subsequent entry in his diary suggests that he may have been objecting to the insertion of new tenants by these means: in 1636 when some London tenements were due for renewal, Young accepted the concurrent lease since it was 'granted to the same Tenant'. The tension between the two men on ecclesiastical grounds probably does something to explain the dean's opposition to a pattern of issuing renewals that does not appear to be revolutionary. It is interesting that in 1631 Young was again opposing the bishop in chapter, this time over the confirmation of patents. This time we have a glimpse of Neile's loyalty to his dependants in the comment of his chaplains that 'the patents ... were not urged by my lord, but to pleasure his men'.[36]

Neile's objections to Laud's enthusiasm for 21-year leases must also be seen in the light of what he and his fellow-bishops were able to achieve within the existing pattern. The Winchester lease-book shows that the major objection to grants of three lives, that they were of uncertain length and could not readily be renewed in order to levy a fine, is not borne out in the practice of this diocese. Life leases were renewed at frequent intervals, usually of course when a new life needed to be inserted, but sometimes also on surrender when there was no evident need for change. Lord Wilmot's lease of Adderbury, for example, was renewed in 1634, from the original lease of 1622, not because any of the lives were actually dead, but to clarify some confusion in the earlier grant and to insert a younger life. This in turn was renewed again in 1639. The Downton grant to the Herbert family was renewed at least four times between 1610 and the Civil War, twice because a life had died, on the other occasions to insert new lives. By the time of Neile's episcopate at the latest the bishops of Winchester were not allowing all the lives in the lease to die before insisting upon renewal and the tenants presumably found it in their interest to accept a system which gave them considerable security in their property in return for a fine almost as regular as that taken on 21-year leases. Of the level of the fines taken we know nothing: in the period after the Civil War it had become customary to ask one year of the improved value of the manor for inserting a new life and half a year for a renewal, but Neile and Curle are more likely to have operated from some multiple of the existing rental value.[37]

The lack of enthusiasm that the Winchester prelates showed for Laud's priorities extended to the issue of their woodlands. In 1637 they were specifically forbidden to provide wood for their tenants by lease covenant in any greater quantity 'than the laws in those cases allow'. The rebuke to Curle followed upon complaints made to the Crown about the waste of timber at Winchester, a misuse of resources that cannot be verified by the surviving accounts, but which would be in the well-established tradition of the see. At the end of Elizabeth's reign a commission had found the woodlands of the bishopric to be severely depleted and Bilson was accused of taking timber from Farnham before he agreed to lease it to the Crown. Curle dutifully entered the royal letters in his lease-book as required, but there is no evidence that it made the slightest difference to the timber clauses that he included in subsequent leases. The legal right of tenants to enough wood for their own repairs, and often some access to fuel as well, were so well established that it would probably have been folly for the bishops to challenge them. From a national perspective the concern of Charles and Laud about the preservation of woodlands may well have been better founded than their preoccupation with leases: but in the localities it must have been the legal and political claims of tenants that often bulked most large in the minds of the prelates. The political costs of denying timber to the Earl of Pembroke, or even to Anthony Bruning, esquire, would have been greater than any medium-term gain to the bishopric from such a move.[38]

To understand the resistance of the bishops of Winchester one might compare their stance with that of their Chichester neighbour, Richard Montagu. Montagu arrived in his diocese in 1629 full of the enthusiasm of a Laudian new broom. He told Secretary Dorchester (with some exaggeration) that he found Chichester 'miserably depopulated, especially by my last two predecessors; amongst the rest, all things but one lease for lives, and all burthens laid upon successors.'[39] He therefore began to find technical faults in his leases so that he could either force his tenants into renewing on new terms and at increased rent, or in the last resort replace them. The attempt to raise rents at Chichester made more sense than it would have done at Winchester, for the fixed income of the former was only about £600 as compared to the figure of nearly £4,000 for the latter. However, the hazards of Montagu's approach were manifold. The challenge to existing leaseholders almost certainly involved extensive litigation to establish the faults in the grants and ensure that no one had an estate of freehold in the property. Litigation was costly and any attack upon existing prop-

erty rights was so sensitive that a bishop needed lay support to undertake it. In Montagu's case he offered both Secretary Dorchester and
Endymion Porter grants of episcopal property if they would 'try' the
leases. Moreover, raising rents was so contrary to the accepted practice upon church lands that even when leases came up for normal
renewal it could be very difficult to effect. In 1632 Montagu tried to
increase his income from the London rents by inserting new covenants
into his lease renewals. Maurice Scull, gent, was permitted to retain
his tenement in Chancery Lane at the old rent, but had to agree that
within two years the reserved rent should be increased from £2 13s.
4d. to £100. Two years later the lease was renewed, but at the old rent,
and Montagu's accounts for 1636–8 suggest that the new sum was
never raised. Instead between 1633 and 1636 the bishop was busy
renewing other Chancery Lane tenements on the old terms: in 1636
they yielded fines of £180 to the see. Although we cannot reconstruct
the whole of the Chichester case from the surviving sources enough
remains to indicate that Montagu's zeal brought little tangible
benefit. Since he was, according to his accounts, able to live in some
comfort and style within his means, he might have been better
employed in using his patronage to gain some support for his high
church policies within the county community. Instead, in Anthony
Fletcher's words, 'he preferred to cosset himself in the remoteness of
his palace at Aldingbourne' out of contact with the political realities
of his see.[40]

Archbishop Laud's assumption that the higher clergy only realized
a small percentage of the value of the property nominally under their
control was undoubtedly correct. When the commissioners for the
commonwealth came to survey the lands of the bishops and chapters
they concluded again and again that the old rents were only a tithe of
the improved annual value. The returns for Norwich show that most
manors were rented at between 10 and 15 per cent of their improved
value and Canterbury was scarcely better, with the proportion of
rental income to value ranging between 1:6 and 1:12. Nor is it easy to
contest the second Laudian assumption that some wealth was a
necessary concomitant to social and ecclesiastical power, or at least
that poverty was liable to breed contempt of those who claimed to rule
the Church. Hence some of the orders of the 1630s, annexing *commendams* to the poorer Welsh sees for example, or encouraging the
bishops of Oxford and Bristol to provide adequate homes for their
successors, were by any standards prudent measures for the protection of the hierarchy. From the perspective of Lambeth it can even be
argued that Laud's attack upon the abuses of the beneficial lease was
an appropriate response to the dislocation of a hundred years of lay
encroachment upon the Church. The archbishop did so argue, and

some of the firmest of his rebuttals at his trial came in response to criticisms of his defence of the finances of the hierarchy. In his own diocese he had an example of the benefits of a financial system that had for two generations conformed to the ideal that the Church needed to be economically strong and that a tight control upon leasing was an essential prerequisite for such strength.[41]

The bishops in their corners of the realm did not find it so easy to command this magisterial view of their economic situation. They confronted instead very different local circumstances, bred of the history of the previous decades, of the relationship between Church and laity and of the general level of resources which they each inherited. We have shown that the particular circumstances of Winchester lent themselves better to the intelligent exploitation of the three-life lease than to the sort of change envisaged by Laud. W. J. Sheils has shown that the different situation of York led to the continuing use of rectories as a major form of patronage, albeit largely on 21-year grants. This continuing conception of lands of the Church as available for the private profit of the bishops and their families and friends could be damaging to the long-term interests of the institution, but must also be perceived as part of the legitimate profits of office considered appropriate in the early seventeenth century. Insensitivity to these local nuances, and especially to the importance of collaborative relationships with the gentry and others who were episcopal tenants left the Church more rather than less vulnerable to the attacks of the laity. A zealous Laudian such as Bishop Wren could earn merit in the eyes of the Court by ostentatiously refusing to renew a lease for lives, at which 'the King was mightily pleased and told the Bishop he had done like an honest Churchman'. But an honest churchman might have been better employed in making intelligent use of the traditional pattern of resources handed to him; in balancing the advantages of collaboration with his tenants against his own need to command adequate revenues. The study of Canterbury and Winchester, and even our brief excursus into Chichester, suggests that such a balance was being achieved without the politics of confrontation so readily accepted by Laud.[42]

NOTES

I would like to thank Andrew Foster, Clive Holmes and Rosemary O'Day for their comments on an earlier draft of this paper. I acknowledge with gratitude financial support from the British Academy that enabled me to undertake this research.
  1. W. Laud, Works (1847–60), II, xii.
  2. On Laud and his economic policy see C. Hill, Economic Problems; H. Trevor-Roper, Archbishop Laud (2nd edn., 1962); N. Tyacke, 'Puritanism, Arminianism and counter-revolution', in The Origins of the English Civil War, ed. C. Russell (1973).

150   Felicity Heal

3. LPL MS 943, f. 329; BL Stowe MS 119, f. 13; Laud, *Works*, VI, 601–2.
4. LPL MS 943, f. 329; Laud, *Works*, VI, 389–90. Hants. RO, Ecc 155642, 172; Laud, *Works*, V.
5. Hill, *op. cit*. Some investigation of the impact of Laudianism can be found in the county studies for the 1630s, esp. P. Clark, *English Provincial Society* (1977); A. Fletcher, *A County Community in Peace and War* (1975).
6. Laud, *Works*, V, 359.
7. *Final Report of the Select Committee on Church Leases* (1839), 8–9; Laud, *Works*, IV, 192; P. Heylyn, *Cyprianus Anglicus* (1719), pt ii, 46–7.
8. On the problems of the episcopal family see J. Berlatsky, 'Marriage and family in a Tudor elite', *J. Family History*, III (1978); F. Heal, *Of Prelates and Princes: a study of the economic and social position of the Tudor episcopate* (1980), ch. 10.
9. A. Foster, 'A biography of Archbishop Richard Neile, 1560–1642' (D.Phil.thesis, University of Oxford, 1978), 262; J. Cosin, *The Correspondence of John Cosin, D.D.*, ed. G. Ornsby (Surtees Society, LIV, 1871), 240. I am very grateful to Dr Foster for drawing my attention to this letter.
10. Foster, *op. cit.*, 262–4.
11. Laud, *Works*, V.
12. F. Du Boulay, 'Archbishop Cranmer and the Canterbury temporalities', *EHR*, LXVII (1952), 19–36; Heal, *op. cit.*, 267–8; LPL MSS 1415–19.
13. J. I. Daeley, 'The episcopal administration of Matthew Parker, archbishop of Canterbury, 1559–1575' (Ph.D.thesis, University of London, 1967), 337; P. Collinson, *Archbishop Grindal, 1519–1583* (1979), 224–5; J. Strype, *The Life and Acts of . . . John Whitgift*, II (1822), 373; G. Paule, *The Life of John Whitgift* (1612), 78, Canterbury Cathedral Library (hereafter cited as CCL), Railton Papers, Misc. Corr., AC fos. 357, 394.
14. Clark, *op. cit.*, 182–3, argues that relations between Whitgift and the gentry were very strained. In so doing he almost ignores Paule's account, which may be biased, but which has the merit of being by a close witness of the progresses described. LPL MS 2009, f. 34.
15. Worcester RO, CC 900/1, nos. 43693–7; LPL MS 807 (I); Sir Simonds D'Ewes, *Journals of All the Parliaments* (1682), 623, 625; Heal, *op. cit.*, 309–11. Even Boys did not on occasion match up to Whitgift's exacting standards. He was accused of failing to defend the liberties of the see in the cathedral city: Strype, *op. cit.*, II, 425–6, 460–1.
16. PRO SP 12/277; CCL V2; BI Chancery, 1569, 1628.
17. PRO SP 12/277; *The Correspondence of Matthew Parker*, eds. J. Bruce and T. T. Perowne (Parker Society, 1853), 454; CCL V2.
18. LPL MS 807 (I); D'Ewes, *op. cit.*, 623, 625ff.
19. P. M. Hembry, *The Bishops of Bath and Wells, 1540–1640* (1967), 199–200; Guildhall MS. 11,927. H. Townshend, *Historical Collections* (1680), 186–7; *LJ*, 1578–1614, 327, 503, 532, 620; *CJ*, I, 237, 277, 421, 432, 441, 449.
20. LPL TC/1; Heal, *op. cit.*, 309–10.
21. LPL TC/2.
22. LPL MS 1730, MSS 1415–9; PRO SC 6/Car. I/494; Heylyn, *op. cit.*, 230–1, describes Abbot feasting the Kentish gentry at Lambeth; LPL MS. 884.
23. *DNB*; PRO SP 12/277; LPL TC/1; CCL Reg. Y, 149; PROB 11/103/45; Collinson, *op. cit.*, 280–1.
24. LPL Comm XIIa/22, fos. 147, 277; Comm XIIa/23, f. 328; LPL TS/1; Clark, *op. cit.*, 361–71. A. Everitt, *The Community of Kent and the Great Rebellion, 1640–60* (1966), 56–66. Orlando Bridgeman's motives for supporting the Ashtons emerge clearly from the information that in 1929 Ralph Ashton sold his paternal estate of Great Lever, Lancs., to John Bridgeman, bishop of Chester. I am grateful

to Dr Holmes for this reference.
25. LPL Comm XIIa/22, f. 147; Laud, Works, IV, 147; C. Haigh, Reformation and Resistance in Tudor Lancashire (1975), 293; Hill, op. cit., 329.
26. BL Lans. MS 52/61; Surrey RO, Guildford Muniments, Loseley MSS 8/26; HMC Salisbury MSS, VI, 64–5; CStP Dom Eliz., 1595–7, 215; R. B. Manning, Religion and Society in Elizabethan Sussex (1969), pts II and III.
27. HMC Salisbury MSS, IV, 31; BL Lans. MS 79/38.
28. HMC Salisbury MSS, VII, 220–1; Hants. RO, Ecc 155642, 22.
29. Ibid., Ecc 155642.
30. CStP Dom Jas. I, XLVII, XXXII (docquets); HMC Salisbury MSS, XX, 58–60; XXI, 48.
31. CStP Dom Jas. I, VI, XXVIII (docquets), PRO SP 14/94/13; 14/116/82, 92; H. Isaacson, The Life and Death of Lancelot Andrewes (1829), 47, provides a conventional picture of Andrewes' personal austerity amid his lavish hospitality.
32. I owe the first two references to Dr A. Foster; Hants. RO, Ecc 155655.
33. See, for example, Norwich, where Anthony Harison, the episcopal secretary, exercised a close control over the estates: Registrum Vagum of Anthony Harison, ed. T. F. Barton, 2 vols (Norfolk Record Society XXXII III, 1963–4).
34. Winchester Cathedral Library, Ledger Books 9–10; Book 9, fos. 63v, 74; Ely Diocesan Records, CC 95577; West Sussex RO, Cap/I/27/2; Hants. RO, Ecc 155642, 20.
35. The Diary of John Young, Dean of Winchester, ed. F. R. Goodman (1928), 88, Hants. RO, Ecc 155642, 28–9, 51, 59, 70, 41; T. G. Barnes, Somerset, 1625–1640: A County's Government during the 'Personal Rule' (1961), 258, 297.
36. CStP Dom 1628, cxxiv, 82. Foster, op. cit., 92. Goodman, op. cit., 88–91, 95, 118.
37. Hants. RO, Ecc 155642, 28, 144, 202; Ecc 155642, 111, 186, 188; Ely Diocesan Records, CC 95577.
38. Hants. RO, Ecc 155642, 172; PRO E178/3100; HMC Salisbury MSS, XX, 58.
39. CStP Dom, 1629–31, 122.
40. See, for example, his attempt to regain the manor of Selsey, CStP Dom, 1631–5, 206; 1629–31, 123: West Sussex RO, Cap I/27/2, fos. 374, 400v; Dean and Chapter Act Book, 1618–42, ed. W. D. Peckham (Sussex Record Society LXVIII 1959), 254; 'Bishop Montagu's accounts', ed. F. W. Steer, (Sussex Archaeological Society, XCV 1957), 28–41. Fletcher, op. cit., 79.
41. CUL, Mm/2/19; LPL, Comm XII a/22; XIIa/23; Laud, Works, IV, 177.
42. C. Wren, Parentalia, or Memoirs of the Family of the Wrens (1750), 51.

7

Parliamentary army chaplains: pay and preaching

Anne Laurence

The intention of this article is to show how the pay, service, and appointment of chaplains in the parliamentary forces differed from that of clergy in benefices or lectureships and that these conditions militated against radicalism. Information about chaplains' service comes mainly from the Commonwealth Exchequer Papers (SP 28) in the Public Record Office. Much of this material consists of pay warrants, but it is also possible to discover something of the conditions of service, equipment, and methods of appointment of chaplains. There is some material for most of the armies paid by the Parliament. This emphasizes the differences between the armies of Essex, Manchester, and Waller, the New Model army, and the provincial armies and garrisons. To some extent these differences in character and organization are reflected in the chaplains appointed to the individual armies.

Chaplains were in a peculiar position. They fitted uneasily into the hierarchy of the army and were quite outside the control of the Church. Serving as an army chaplain seems to have been something which individuals would do for a short period, as an interruption in a career of lectureships and benefices. Some of the men who served as chaplains in the parliamentary army had served as chaplains to English forces fighting in the Netherlands and elsewhere.[1] But it was not a career in the way that being a soldier could be. Chaplains were essentially members of the clergy doing something slightly different for a few years.

Most people who served as parliamentary army chaplains made their careers as clergy. Of those old enough to have been clergy before 1642 a very high proportion had held benefices or lectureships, although many had also fallen foul of the ecclesiastical authorities. The majority also held benefices or lectureships after their service in the army, though few conformed in 1660–2. Most chaplains went to university, though by no means all took degrees. An army chaplaincy, then, was not seen as a way of entering a clerical career through the back door. Most of those chaplains whose first clerical appointment was a chaplaincy were amply well qualified to hold a benefice if they chose to do so. The lack of ecclesiastical tests and the lack of supervision by any ecclesiastical superior did make it easier for those who had been in exile in the Netherlands and America to come back and take up a post. Radical sectaries seem not to have believed that army chaplaincies were analogous to benefices. A number of people, especially Baptists, who objected to a ministry maintained by tithes did not extend these objections to chaplaincies.

The pay, appointment, and services of chaplains in the parliamentary army were quite outside the control of the Church. They were the province of the army command. There has been a tendency amongst historians to treat chaplaincies as analogous to lectureships: a refuge for those whom the Church could not accommodate. Patrick Collinson has concluded that 'lecturing as practised in the combinations may have had effects quite opposite to those often alleged. It favoured the enhanced dignity and advancement of the beneficed, parochial clergy of seventeenth-century England, on whose labours these lectures very largely depended.'[2]

It is possible to make a similar, though less emphatic case for chaplaincies. Army chaplains were no more clerical tribunes or raving revolutionary fanatics than lecturers were agents of subversion. This is not to say that there were no extremists in either position, but rather that the majority were orthodox and did not use either chaplaincies or lectureships as a means of evading ecclesiastical control. The case for chaplains is best demonstrated by examining the pay, appointment and service of parliamentary army chaplains. These clearly demonstrate that men with conventional clerical qualifications were preferred, even though there was always a severe shortage of chaplains. Royalist army chaplains are not examined here, since no claims have been made for their importance as propagandists, and there is no reason to suppose that any but orthodox members of the established Church were appointed.

The parliamentary army for which most information survives is the New Model army. Much less is known about the organization and structure of the armies formed before the New Model or about the provincial forces, for it is important to remember that even as late as 1647 there were more forces in arms for Parliament outside the New Model army than within it. The provincial forces are the least well documented. Fewer pay warrants survive for them than for any other force and the intricacies of the administration of the individual counties have rarely been studied closely.

The surviving pay warrants for the armies of the earls of Essex and Manchester are incomplete, but some of the account books of the treasurers, or their deputies, remain. These not only fill in the information for the missing warrants but indicate that about two-thirds of the total number of warrants seem to have survived. These account books provide information about a number of aspects of chaplains' army careers. They indicate that it was common for a regiment to have no chaplain for long periods of time. This was particularly so in the cavalry, which was not, at first, organized in regiments.[3] The troop was really too small a unit to have its own chaplain unless its commander held some other command in the army, like colonel of foot or general, which warranted his having one. For the first few months of the war, troops of horse were not served by their own chaplains. They seem to have used the chaplains of the foot regiments whose commanders they shared, for it was common in the early months of the war for individuals to have several commands. With the successive reorganizations of 1643 and 1644 most troops of horse were incorporated into regiments and the amount of pluralism amongst commanders was reduced, though it was never completely eliminated. Most regiments aspired to having their own chaplains, but there was always a shortage, especially after those who had joined in the first months of the war had returned to their parishes.

The first regiments were raised in July 1642. These were the regiments originally intended for the expedition to Ireland under Philip Lord Wharton, raised by the Adventurers for Irish lands. These troops were then diverted to the use of Parliament in England. At this stage all payments were made through Nicholas Bond, paymaster of the army. The Earl of Essex began to sign individual warrants in early August 1642. These were chiefly for paying whole regiments and enumerate the members, showing that many then lacked chaplains. By October 1642 chaplains were being paid by individual warrants signed by Essex. There seems to have been no particular reason for this. The army list of December 1642, which gives some chaplains' names, is actually of some date between August 1642 and November 1642, when Sir John Merrick's regiment, which it mentions, was disbanded. Apart from a few odd warrants from the Earl of Warwick and Sir William Waller, the first large group of payments not authorized either by Essex himself or by Nicholas Bond, are from the Earl of Manchester and the Eastern Association, starting in January 1644. Here, too, the chaplains were usually paid by separate warrants.[4]

These warrants are the most important source of information for the administration of the armies fighting for Parliament before the formation of the New Model army. There is some supplementary information in the accounts drawn up in spring 1645 to show the arrears due to men then being disbanded. The warrants show roughly when a chaplain was with the army and with which regiment he served. Sometimes it is possible to discover when he received his commission and the precise date at which he was disbanded, though no chaplains' commissions seem to survive. It is unlikely that it will ever be possible to pin down periods of service, for many chaplains took a somewhat unprofessional view of their work in the army. Many still held benefices or lectureships and had to return to them in order not to lose them through absenteeism. Some subsequently returned to the army, others did not and it was often some time before they were replaced.[5]

The normal rate of pay for a chaplain was 8s. a day. In addition to this he usually received, on joining the army, a lump sum of £20. This was described as being 'By way of advance for the providing of necessaries for his attendance'.[6] It was apparently an *ex gratia* payment equivalent to a month's wages, rather than literally a month's pay in advance. This rate of pay could not be sustained. By May 1643 chaplains were being paid by debentures.[7] These were presumably just promises of payment on the public faith, rather than anything resembling the systematically issued certificates on delinquents' or Crown lands of later years.

Some element of organization was introduced by the ordinances of 20 January 1643/4 and 26 March 1644. The first was for recruiting, maintaining and regulating the forces of the Eastern Association. Amongst its provision was the clause that all officers and specialist personnel who were paid more than 10s. a day were to receive half pay, and all officers whose pay was between 5s. and 10s. were to receive two-thirds, with the exception of regimental ministers.[8] The same arrangement was made for Essex's officers, without the exception of ministers, by the second ordinance.[9] Certificates promising repayment 'on the publique faith' when the war ended, were issued for the respited sums, but some of these arrears seem to have been paid off on the disbanding of Essex and Manchester's armies. Chaplains in both armies had their pay respited, and were paid 5s. 4d. a day.[10]

In the early years of the war, chaplains received an allowance of 8d. a day for a servant. To begin with this was paid to the chaplain. After about 1644 the servant, if there was one, was paid with the ordinary soldiers, and often seems to have been a soldier himself, rather than someone brought along by the chaplain.[11] Chaplains were also provided with transport when with a marching army. Some brought their own horses, but they were otherwise provided with either a horse or a waggon, which sometimes they had to share with the surgeon. The sums allowed for horses varied from £6 to £13.[12] The standard rate allowed as waggon money seems to have been £20. William Benn, chaplain to the Earl of Bedford's regiment, was allowed £20 waggon-money in 1642, and the following year the chaplain and surgeon of Skippon's regiment were allowed £40 for a waggon which they shared.[13] The only references to chaplains being armed suggest that chaplains were not normally expected to carry arms and that if they wished to do so they might provide their own. Colonel Henry Marten certified that Thomas Gilbert had attended his regiment as chaplain between April and August 1643 and had brought his own horse and arms. Patrick Levington, who was chaplain successively to the regiments of James Kerr and Hans Behre in 1643 and 1644, provided his own horse, arms and quarter.[14] Many accounts and receipts for billets for ordinary soldiers survive, but there seem to be none for chaplains, nor are there any records of the payment to them of billet money. As they were commonly treated as staff officers they probably arranged their own billeting and free quarter, like other staff officers.

New Model chaplains were paid by warrant in the same way as chaplains in earlier armies. Unfortunately there is nothing comparable to the treasurers' account books for Essex and Manchester's armies, so there is no check on the survival of the warrants that were issued. Initially the majority of warrants were signed by Sir Thomas Fairfax (from April 1645), but the committee for securing the £80,000 lent by the City of London, which was created in March 1645, also issued some. By October 1645 this committee was known by the name of its most active member, Robert Scawen, who was a moving spirit until 1647 when it was reorganized, having disbanded a large number of garrisons. By early 1648 the new Army Committee seems to have taken over much of the financial administration of the army and issued an increasingly large proportion of warrants, the number issued by Fairfax being commensurately reduced. By mid-1649 the committee did little more than administer garrisons. The Act of 14 May 1649 transferred the responsibility for garrisons from the county committees to the Army Committee, but allowed for the appointment of county commissioners as well as the central government officials.[15] Cromwell, Bradshaw (president of the Council of State) and the Council itself signed warrants for the forces in Ireland. Fairfax and Lambert issued a few warrants for the forces in England until June 1650 when Fairfax resigned as commander-in-chief of the army. Cromwell signed most of the pay warrants for the forces in Scotland, while Ireton and the committee for Ireland issued them for the troops in Ireland.

New Model chaplains were provided with horses, but not with arms.[16] They probably still had servants, though they are not mentioned on the pay warrants. Their pay was still officially 8s. a day. The New Model ordinance of 17 February 1644/5 ordered that officers' pay should be respited on the terms laid down in earlier ordinances and no exemptions were mentioned.[17] On 5 March 1644/5, however, the House of Commons ordered 'That notwithstanding any former order, the chaplains employed in this army, upon the New Model, shall have full allowance as formerly during the time of their employment.'[18] There is no reference on the pay warrants of the New Model chaplains to any of their pay being respited. Their pay did fall into arrears for a number of chaplains' names appear on the lists of debenture certificates.[19] There appears to have been another payment made to chaplains to which only one reference survives. In Fairfax's order book the following note was recorded in December 1649: 'Order Colonel Wetham to cause Capt. Pitson and others to pay their dues to the minister or to dismiss them from the army.'[20] In Elizabethan armies chaplains were paid from a levy made on all the soldiers in the regiment, but some time in the early seventeenth century the central army administration took over the responsibility for paying them. It seems unlikely that a supplementary charge was made on the soldiers for the maintenance of a minister since he was comparatively well paid.

It is difficult to discover how much garrison chaplains were paid, since they were often paid for a local benefice or lectureship as well, or were just paid a fee for each sermon they gave. Chaplains in the provincial armies also supplemented their incomes this way. Indeed it would probably be more accurate to say that these were local clergy who supplemented their incomes by occasional duties as a chaplain. Nathaniel Lancaster, chaplain to Sir William Brereton and the Cheshire regiment, was apparently also chaplain to the garrison of Nantwich and received £12 for three months.[21] He also received various gratuities and had his board and lodging in Chester paid by the county committee. The county committees, or the treasurer in counties where military finance was separately administered, seem to have been responsible for paying chaplains in garrisons and provincial forces until 1649. These officials were often responsible for supplying vacancies in local lectureships and benefices and for augmenting the incomes of local clergy. These functions were often combined with providing for the local troops. After the fall of Chester to Parliament, the local committee paid a number of godly divines to come to the city to preach. There were then hardly any clergy there since Chester had been held by the royalists since the beginning of the war.[22] The clergy appointed preached both to the local civilian population and to the garrison and no separate garrison preacher was appointed. In spite of the vigilance of some local committees, many garrisons were not provided with chaplains. The garrison of Edgbaston under Captain John Fox had no minister or surgeon in April 1646, neither had the garrison at Warwick in November 1646.[23] The central government took note of

this negligence. In 1650 the Council of State wrote to Colonel Which-
cott, governor of Windsor Castle: 'We are informed that there are no
sermons in the castle for the garrison and prisoners, and desire care
may be taken for a supply; meantime we desire you to speak to Mr.
Symons and Mr. Batchelor to preach there in turns.'[24] Another
instance of their concern occured in May or June 1650 when a fast was
ordered. Chaplains or commanders were ordered to report to headquarters upon its progress. Many of these reports simply say that the
fast went well. Others mention the amount of drunkenness in the
army, say that the Presbyterians would not join the fast (which was for
the success of the forthcoming expedition to Scotland), express
sorrow at the lack of participation from the citizens in Exeter, and
invoke God to destroy Babylon and Antichrist and to exalt Zion.[25]

Chaplains' pay, at 8s. a day, £146 per annum was high for clerical
pay. Of course it was rarely paid in full and it was uncommon for
people to serve for more than two years as chaplain. But any benefice
which paid over £100 per annum was considered a good living and
some benefices paid as little as £20 per annum. This high rate of pay in
the army might have been intended to compensate for the lack of
alternative sources of income. Many beneficed clergymen took on lectureships as additional sources of income and before 1642 cathedral
offices commonly supplemented clerical incomes. The army chaplain
was prevented from seeking advancement in his career whilst serving.
On the other hand, especially at the beginning of the war, the majority
of chaplains had benefices or lectureships which they did not resign on
joining the army. The composition of the army was unstable, soldiers
came and went with great rapidity, and the majority of chaplains
served for less than a year. Many of them returned to their benefices.
Some clearly left because, as members of the Westminster Assembly,
they believed that the future would be better secured by the work of
the Assembly than by the army.

Chaplains received commissions on their appointments to regiments in much the same way as other officers. These were probably
issued by the general, although the actual appointment was made by
the colonel of the regiment in which the chaplain was to serve. Colonels seem to have had much the same freedom to appoint chaplains as
lay patrons had to make presentations to benefices. They seem sometimes to have sought the advice of the members of the regiment, or of
such bodies as the Westminster Assembly or the Presbyterian classes,
where they existed. A detailed study of the chaplains appointed to
regiments in Essex and Manchester's armies does not reveal any
pattern to the appointments made by particular colonels. Those colonels who had been in the forefront of the opposition to the king in the
Long Parliament tended to choose divines distinguished for their op-

position to the Laudian innovations. Several had also made their views known in fast sermons to Parliament. The chaplains to Essex's regiments of foot and horse were respectively Stephen Marshall and Cornelius Burgess. Marshall had, during the elections for the Short Parliament, preached throughout Essex on behalf of the Earl of Warwick, and Burgess, also a client of Warwick's, was accused of stirring up the London apprentices.[26]

In the New Model army there was no single method of appointing chaplains. In addition to regimental chaplains there were usually two chaplains at headquarters who seem to have been appointed by the general. Both regimental and headquarters chaplains seem to have been connected to the individual who chose them to the extent that when that commander left the army, his chaplain left too. In March 1645 the House of Commons resolved, 'That it be recommended to the Assembly of Divines to present the names of some godly learned ministers to Sir Tho. Fairfax, that he may thereby be better enabled to furnish his army with able and godly ministers.'[27] In January 1648 the Council of the Army intervened, 'having information of the willingness and readyness of diverse godlye men of the ministry to bestowe theyr paynes to preach the ghospell of Christ in the Armye, it was resolved by the Councell that some of them whose hearts God should most incline to that worke should be desired to come to the Army for that purpose and bee assured for the Councell of all incouragement thereto and good Acceptance of theyr paynes therein.'[28] Neither of these seems to have resulted in many vacant chaplaincies being filled. Indeed, in July 1649 four officers wrote to Fairfax asking that a chaplain be allowed them.[29] In the end it seems that those colonels who wanted chaplains went out and found them and others just left the position vacant.

Chaplains in garrisons were usually appointed by garrison commanders, unless there was any reason for the local committee or corporation to be particularly influential, as in Chester after its fall to Parliament. The element of clerical patronage in garrisons and provincial armies was as great as it was in Essex and Manchester's armies. It was not reduced by any centralization of appointments as had tended to happen in the New Model army. The religious complexion of the garrisons and provincial forces was different from that of the New Model. In the first place the provincial forces were never purged of Presbyterians. In the second place the religious views of local forces were subject to local pressure. Efforts would be made to ensure that the views of the soldiery did not differ too sharply from those of influential local divines. Many townsmen were unsympathetic to religious radicals, often on grounds of keeping the peace. The mayor and aldermen of Coventry took a very firm stand against the Ranters in 1650, and in Newcastle the disputes between Independents and Presbyterians left little room for sectaries to gain a foothold.[30]

As has been shown, most chaplains had the qualifications that one would expect of someone holding a benefice. There seems to have been a definite preference for chaplains who were not wildly unorthodox. Chaplains seem, then, to have reflected the views of the army command. In the New Model army they seem to have spoken against popular religious radicalism and to have identified themselves with the grandees. In the provincial forces they seem to have been virtually indistinguishable from the local clergy.

Nowhere are the functions of the chaplain in any of the parliamentary armies laid down. Even Essex's *Laws and Ordinances of War*, which remained the only disciplinary code for the parliamentary armies, say little. They contain only injunctions against blasphemy, unlawful oaths and scandalous acts, and imply that sermons and public prayers were to be given, since members of the army who absented themselves were to be penalized.[31] There is no mention of chaplains or their duties, although the establishments for the various armies always mention chaplains. The royalist ordinances are much more specific. Not only do they say what a chaplain should do, but they lay down penalties for failing to fulfil his duties.[32] They also lay down how many chaplains there are to be and how they should be appointed and paid. For the parliamentary forces we have to rely upon the accounts of such writers as Richard Baxter and Thomas Edwards. Clearly they preached a great deal, especially before and after engagements. But they faced increasing competition from the spread of lay preaching, especially in the New Model army after 1647. Sects gained adherents in spite of the work of the chaplains, not because of it.

Chaplains performed many other tasks besides their religious duties. They were actually expected to do little else, though their activities encompassed a wide range of fields. By 1645 there were few Presbyterian divines left in the New Model army so the Westminster Assembly was not a distraction, as it had been to the chaplains of Essex and Manchester's armies. The most important task performed by the New Model chaplains, apart from their religious duties, was that of liaison officer between the army and Westminster. Edward Bowles, chaplain to Fairfax, took the news of the victory at Naseby to Parliament; Robert Stapylton, chaplain to Cromwell, took the news of the battle of Worcester, and Hugh Peter the news of the fall of Bridgewater (amongst many other letters).[33] Often the bearer of a letter was entrusted with verbal instructions by his commander, as can be seen by Fairfax's words: 'Besides the general account I have already given by one of my servants whom I sent to London yesterday, I thought fit to send this bearer Mr. Boles, who may more particularly inform you.'[34] Acting as a messenger to Parliament carried with it the perquisite that if the bearer brought particularly joyful news he might well be granted a substantial sum of money. Chaplains often returned to the army with messages from Parliament and the Council of State. They also sometimes carried money. Robert Stapylton received Cromwell's pay on his behalf in May 1649.[35] Some chaplains took the initiative in spreading news and even, like Simeon Ashe and William Goode, Thomas Case and Edward Bowles, had their letters to London printed as newsletters. The opportunities offered by the confidential position which a number of chaplains held were not missed. Hugh Peter is the chaplain best known for his political involvement, but others engaged in political activities of one sort or another. Robert Fogg, for example, signed the articles of surrender for Ruthin Castle in April 1646.[36] Other chaplains confined their positions of confidence to less public matters. Robert Stapylton played an important part in the marriage negotiations between Richard Cromwell and Dorothy Mayor.[37]

Garrison and provincial army chaplains also performed a wide variety of duties. Of course many of them were not far from their own congregations and continued to serve them as well as acting as chaplains. The correspondence between Sir Samuel Luke, governor of Newport Pagnell, and his chaplain, Thomas Ford, gives a good idea of the variety of duties which a chaplain might perform. From time to time Ford left the garrison to preach elsewhere; in about 1644 he went to Rockingham, whence, he said, the well-affected people would not allow him to depart until he had explained that his engagements to Newport were greater than they were in Rockingham. Sir Samuel Luke used him to take messages, especially to his brother. Ford also kept a watchful eye on the officers of the garrison while Luke was away. In January 1645 Ford wrote to Luke, 'You may do well to keep an eye on him [Captain Pinkney] for I much doubt him, having heard so much of him I no way like.' In the same letter he reported that 'This garrison cannot stand unless a better course is taken to pay it.' He also gave advice on the appointment of ministers to local benefices, saying of one man; 'Without any prejudice or disparagement to any man's gift or parts I conceive him not a man to do good here.'[38] John Bryan, rector of Coventry and minister at Warwick garrison, did much work outside his ministerial duties. He was garrison paymaster and gave evidence at the enquiry held in February 1646 as to whether Major Bridges, then governor of Warwick, had embezzled a quantity of goods stored in the castle after the battle of Edgehill. Bryan also petitioned Parliament for the relief of the soldiers wounded at Edgehill and sent to Warwick. He tried to pacify the garrison soldiers after a man was killed at a muster of the militia: 'their zealous Preacher of the Castle (Master Bryan) made a sermon, wherein hee endeavoured to reconcile the business; adding that hurt was done through mistake; and not wilfully.'[39] The ministers and gentlemen of the county of Warwickshire, amongst whom were the chaplains of several garrisons, raised a company of dragoons in 1646 and nominated the officers.[40] The garrison of Nottingham was defended by a troop of horse raised by a local rector.[41] John Warr, chaplain to Colonel Edward Prichard's regiment in the garrison of Cardiff, was one of the largest agents for the sale of Crown lands. He may also have been the legal reformer of that name.[42]

Most of the accounts of chaplains who held military rank, or who fought in battle, occur before 1645. Samuel Kemme and Francis Cheynell acted simultaneously as field officers and chaplains.[43] Hugh Peter seems also to have had charge of a regiment, though it is unlikely that he ever actually commanded it.[44] Henry Denne was a minister who became a cornet in one of the New Model regiments, though he is probably better known as 'Judas' Denne at Burford.[45] Paul Hobson, major of Hesilrige's regiment garrisoning Newcastle, assumed the duties of a Baptist minister. He eventually left the army to devote himself to the ministry full time.[46] Joseph Salmon, later a Ranter, received arrears for his service in Ireton's regiment as a soldier and as a chaplain.[47] George Downing, scoutmaster-general, was probably the same person as the chaplain of Okey and then Hesilrige's regiments.[48] No specific references survive to chaplains acting as schoolmasters, but it is likely that they did perform some sort of educational function.

It has been shown that chaplains in the parliamentary armies did a variety of jobs, sometimes combining them with ordinary ministerial duties. Each colonel who appointed a chaplain acted much as a lay patron appointing to a benefice, though the relationship between colonel and chaplain was close enough for the chaplain rarely to remain in the army after the colonel had left. This exercise of patronage meant that men with respectable clerical qualifications were appointed to chaplaincies. As a rule chaplains made their careers in the Church, in benefices or lectureships. Thus it was uncommon to find radical sectaries in chaplaincies and it was uncommon to find people who made their careers as chaplains. For most service in the army was an interlude in a conventional clerical career. That that interlude meant transferring to a military organization from an ecclesiastical organization seems not to have mattered to those who became chaplains.

NOTES

1. Cornelius Burgess, for example, was chaplain to Sir Horace Vere in the Palatinate.
2. P. Collinson, 'Lectures by Combination', *BIHR*, XLVIII (1975), 213.
3. G. Davies, 'The parliamentary army under the Earl of Essex', *EHR*, XLIX (1934).
4. *A List of the Army of his Excellency Robert Earl of Essex* (1642); Davies, *op. cit.*; PRO SP 28/144, Account Book for the Eastern Association.
5. Letter from William Goode to Simeon Ashe, 6 May 1644, 'you desired libertie to leave us awhile that yourselfe might supply your lectures at London and provide for them' (*A Particular Relation of the Several Removes*, 1644).
6. PRO SP 28/1A, f.213.
7. PRO SP 28/7, f.144; SP 28/8, f.100.
8. C. H. Firth and R. Rait, *Acts and Ordinances of the Interregnum* (3 vols., 1911), I, 369–70; C. Holmes, *The Eastern Association in the English Civil War* (1974), 143.
9. Firth and Rait, *op. cit.*, I, 400.
10. PRO SP 28/18, f.54; SP 28/133, f.356; SP 28/15, f.266.
11. William Dell, minister to Colonel Hobart's regiment and his man 'who serves in Quartermaster Generall's troop'; PRO SP 28/24, f.360.
12. PRO SP 28/146, f.147; SP 28/24, f.335; SP 28/147, f.299.
13. PRO SP 28/3A, f. 277; SP 28/7, f.8.
14. PRO SP 28/47, f.24; SP 28/22, f.47. The minister captured by Sir John Byron's royalist forces at Cirencester in 1642, who was armed 'back and brest with swords and pistills' was subject to comment and Oliver Calderwood, chaplain to Sir William Balfour's regiment, 'never had any free quarter wherewith the state can be charged, ever had either horse or Armes delivered him by the state, neither did hee or any other to his use levy or take any money or other goods of the countrey' (*A Particular Relation of the Action before Cirencester*, 1642; PRO SP 28/34, f.465).
15. Firth and Rait, *op. cit.*, II, 63.
16. 'To Mr. Dell as a gratuity from the generall to by him a horse having lost his own the 2nd of September 1646 £10' (PRO SP 23/140, f.49).
17. Firth and Rait, *op. cit.*, I, 619.
18. *CJ*, 5 March 1644/5.
19. PRO E. 121/1–5. These are lists of the members of the army who held debentures for their arrears which were to be paid off by the sale of Crown lands.
20. Worcester College, Oxford, Clarke MS 69, Fairfax's Order Book 1648–9 (unfoliated).
21. PRO SP 28/30, f. 722; SP 28/42, f.698.
22. PRO SP 28/39–42, 144.
23. PRO SP 28/123, fos.294, 607–8.
24. *CStP Dom*, 1649–50, 52.
25. Worcester College, Oxford, Clarke MS 18 (unfoliated).
26. *DNB*, Stephen Marshall; D'Ewes' Diary quoted in V. Pearl, *London and the Outbreak of the Puritan Revolution* (1961), 219.
27. *CJ*, 21 March 1644/5.
28. Worcester College, Oxford, Clarke MS 110 (unfoliated).
29. PRO SP 28/61, f.386.
30. Worcester College, Oxford, Clarke MS 18 (unfoliated); R. Howell, *Newcastle upon Tyne and the Puritan Revolution* (1967), 232, 251.
31. *Laws and Ordinances of Warre established for the better conduct of the Army by his Excellency the Earl of Essex* (1642).
32. *Military Orders and Articles established by His Majesty for the better ordering and Government of His Majesty's Army* (1643).

33. *LJ*, 16 June 1645; *CJ*, 5 September 1651; B. Whitelocke, *Memorials*, IV (1853), 345; *Sir Thomas Fairfax's letter to ... William Lenthall ... or all the Particulars concerning the taking of Bridgewater* (1645).
34. *LJ*, 16 June 1645.
35. PRO SP 28/60, f. 660.
36. *Three Victories in Wales ... And a Coppy of the Articles for the Surrender of Ruthin Castle to Major General Mitton (1646)*.
37. Thomas Carlyle, *Letters and Speeches of Oliver Cromwell*, ed. S. Lomas I, (1904), 418, 420.
38. *The Letter-book of Sir Samuel Luke*, ed. H. Tibbutt (Bedfordshire Historical Record Society XLII, 1963), 341, 327, 423, 417.
39. PRO SP 28/33, f. 457–8; SP 28/39, f.254–6; *CJ*, 31 July 1643; *Mercurius Aulicus* 24 May 1643, 276–7.
40. PRO SP 28/41, f.163
41. A. C. Wood, *Nottinghamshire in the Civil War* (1937), 56.
42. I. Gentles, 'The sales of Crown lands during the English Revolution', *EcHR*, 2nd ser. xxvi (1973); C. Hill, *The World Turned Upside Down* (1972), ch. 12.
43. *DNB*.
44. *CStP Dom.* 1649–50, 349.
45. *DNB*.
46. Howell, *op. cit.*, 248.
47. PRO E. 121/3/4.
48. *DNB*.

8

Augmentation and amalgamation: was there a systematic approach to the reform of parochial finance, 1640–60?

Rosemary O'Day and Ann Hughes

Very little serious work has been done on the attempts to reform the finances of the State Church in the period 1642–60 since the monumental but in many respects unsatisfactory work accomplished by W. A. Shaw at the turn of the century.[1] Shaw's treatment of the available sources was not very precise and as a result his account of the work of the various bodies appointed by Parliament and Protector is often confusing and sometimes actually misleading. While this essay does attempt to outline the manner in which the various committees worked, with particular reference to the augmentation of livings in two counties – Derbyshire and Warwickshire – it has wider aims. The attempt to augment church livings from a central vantage point might, on the surface, be viewed as a part of the centralizing trend of government in England. The study of the growth of 'national policy' and of central attempts to enforce it is of especial interest at a time when seventeenth-century historians are exploring anew the whole concept of *county* as against *national* feelings and loyalties.[2] Do we have in the work of the committees of Parliament or, later, of the Protector the culmination of the centralizing, bureaucratizing efforts of the Tudor governments or not? Only a close examination of the working papers of the individual committees can either prove or give the lie to the contention that in the attempt to augment church livings throughout the nation we have an example of modern, centralized, bureaucratic government at work, implementing a well-thought-out, systematic policy with regard to one aspect of the nation's life. And, moreover, only such an examination can ascertain whether what was ordered on paper was ever implemented in reality. A study of the work of these committees can, therefore, contribute significantly to our knowledge of the character of seventeenth-century government by committee and should enable us to see how far contemporaries were able or willing to break away from the shackles of medieval concepts and procedures of government. Secondly, such a study may offer some clues as to the character of Cromwell's State Church.[3] Thirdly, and not least significantly, it may enable us to assess the extent to which the Church's economic problems were solved for the short term at the parochial level by the committees of the Civil War and Interregnum.

The counties of Warwickshire and Derbyshire were selected for this study for a variety of reasons: the authors were well acquainted with the counties concerned; the available documentation was relatively plentiful; and it was felt that the two counties concerned had been relatively neglected by seventeenth-century historians and that the study of the same would provide the basis for further comparative work. It should be admitted that the choice of these counties has both its advantages and its disadvantages. Both counties contained a good deal of royalist property which was sequestered. The financing of the local ministry was, therefore, in both cases an organizational rather than an economic problem. In counties such as Essex and Norfolk where there were few royalists, the problems facing those who sought to finance the ministry from local resources were probably of an entirely different nature. In view of this, it is clear that any conclusions which we may reach regarding the success of augmentations in Derbyshire and Warwickshire should not automatically be taken to apply to other counties. Yet in so far as this essay is concerned with evidence of the development of modern bureaucratic government, it may be advantageous to look at two counties where organizational efforts were not automatically undermined by financial exigencies.

In 1640 plans for improving the incomes of the parish clergy were not unprecedented. From the early days of the Reformation prominent ecclesiastics and laymen had believed that the poverty of the parish clergy was one of the root causes of the insufficiency of the ministry. Attempts to improve the incomes of ministers had ranged from the private efforts of patrons to augment the livings in their gift (either with cash or a settlement of tithes or with board and lodging for the minister) to the more ambitious proposals for the purchase of advowsons and impropriations and the resettling of impropriate tithes on the clergy. The plans of archbishops Bancroft and Laud are perhaps the best known among the latter. By now we all know that the main opposition to any such scheme came from laymen (and churchmen) whose property rights were threatened thereby.

With the 1640s the situation was somewhat changed. Although lay supporters of parliament still guarded jealously their own property rigghts in advowsons and impropriate tithes, they were less respectful of those of the royalists and not at all of those of the ecclesiastical hierarchy. Before the Civil War broke out, parliament was in fact considering the reformation of ecclesiastical finances. But with the coming of the war, such plans were rapidly submerged in the need to make *ad hoc* arrangements for the serving of cures vacated by delinquent clergymen. If we examine the history of discussions pertinent to church augmentations during the Long Parliament, we become aware that concern was directed not at the issue of the impoverished state of parishes within the State Church as a whole but at the plight of ministers who had suffered at the hands of royalists. The Commons had set up a Grand Committee for Religion in November 1640 which received many petitions from Puritan clergymen and parishioners against so-called Laudian incumbents. This committee set up a sub-committee of 24 on 23 November 'to discover the sufferings of ministers by ecclesiastical proceedings', and a second committee on 12 December – the Committee for Scandalous Ministers – to discover a way to remove scandalous ministers and establish a godly preaching ministry.[4] This committee dealt directly with the individual ministers concerned and did little to prevent Laud and the other bishops from presenting to benefices, until war broke out and disaffected ministers were sequestered by whichever side controlled a particular area. On 22 December 1642 the Lords voted that ministers who were in royalist camps should be sequestered and that they should be replaced by refugee ministers in London. A collection was ordered to assist 'mere ministers'.[5] Then, on 31 December, a committee was set up to discover how the plundered ministers might be helped, using the profits from sequestered livings. This became the Committee for Plundered Ministers.[6] At first the committee only had powers to give relief. In July 1643 it was ordered that its nominations to benefices had to be approved by the Assembly of Divines. At the same time it was ordered that the committee might itself sequester scandalous ministers.[7] In October 1643 it was directed that all processes for sequestration of ministers were to enter the House of Commons via the Committee for Plundered Ministers.[8] During 1643–4 the committee acquired a more general oversight over church affairs.[9]

Quite clearly we would be wrong to assume that parliament was attempting through the Committee for Plundered Ministers to stage a complete overhaul of the financing of ministers of the word. It was committed, rather, to the relief of ministers who had suffered by supporting an anti-Laudian religious stand or the parliamentary stance in the war and, in a rather more confused manner, to establishing a godly ministry at the expense of royalist/Laudian clergy and patrons. The Committee was not well-equipped to accomplish even this limited goal. Royalist and church property was not sequestered initially in order to establish a godly ministry. Both the royalists and the hierarchy were the enemy and Parliament was seeking to pay for the war with the spoils of war. Any money which was spent on improving the maintenance of ministers would have to be taken away from funds intended to enable Parliament to pursue the war successfully. At first the Committee for Plundered Ministers had no funded income of its own: the revenue of a sequestered living was received by a parliamentary nominee; when an impropriation was in the hands of a delinquent, the committee made an order that the cure be served and an allowance arranged, which was enforced by a local sequestration authority.

There were, however, early signs that Parliament wished to put the work of the Committee for Religion on a more systematic footing and perhaps extend its responsibilities towards the future character of the State Church. As early as 30 October 1641 an abortive act for impropriations was introduced into the Commons to improve maintenance. In April 1642 the Committee's representative, Mr Crewe, reported that

> The Lords and Commons do declare, that they intend a due and necessary reformation of the government and liturgy of the church; and to take away nothing in the one or the other, but what shall be evil, and justly offensive, or at least unnecessary and burdensome: And, for the better effecting thereof speedily to have consultation with godly and learned divines. And because this will never of itself attain the end sought therein, they will therefore use their utmost endeavours to establish learned and preaching ministers, with a good and sufficient maintenance throughout the whole kingdom; wherein many dark corners are miserably destitute of the means of salvation; and many poor ministers want necessary proovision. Resolved upon the question, that this House doth assent unto this declaration.

The committee considering this declaration probably envisaged using dean and chapter lands as well as impropriations as a source of necessary revenue, but nothing came of this plan.[10] These declarations on the part of parliament were a mere remnant of her initial concern for the state of the Church as a whole, a concern which had been all but erased by the emergency of war.

From 1643 onwards Parliament was making some piecemeal provision for the betterment of the maintenance of particular ministers. It seems, however, that July 1645 marks the beginning of a more systematic approach to the problem, probably because Parliament now had more time to apply to it. Thus on 7 July the House of Commons received and considered a petition from Middlesex appealing for better maintenance of ministers and asking Parliament to consider how to establish 'a competent maintenance for settling a good ministry in such counties' beginning but not ending with Middlesex.[11] Grants for augmentation began in 1645 although 1646 saw the most active period for the Committee in making initial grants.[12] The first known grants occur for Middlesex (in response to the petition) but there is one for a Derbyshire living as early as August 1645.[13] Parliament was no longer required to give separate authorization for each individual grant. In March 1645 the Committee proposed to the Commons that it use dean and chapter revenues for its work and an ordinance of 13 October 1646 exempted advowsons, appropriate tithes and other ecclesiastical revenues of bishops, deans and chapters from general (secular) use. This exemption was included also in the later sales Acts and ordinances. These ecclesiastical revenues became the basis of a fund for the maintenance of ministers.[14]

There are certainly grounds for believing that Parliament concerned itself with the general state of the Church well before the years of the Commonwealth. It is true that Parliament produced no general legislation for the augmentation of benefices until the Act of June 1649, but proposals for the establishing of an adequately endowed preaching ministry occupied some of its time before this. Some of the more important 'general' proposals are the bill of October 1641; the proposals of April 1642; the report of the Committee for Plundered Ministers to Parliament in March 1645 (mentioned above) and proposals before the House of Commons in April 1645 and April 1646. The first ordinance establishing a general fund for the augmentation of benefices was introduced in November 1646 but it did not become law until 1649.[15]

Prior to the passage of this ordinance in 1649 the Committee for Plundered Ministers was not acting in accordance with any clearly stated central policy regarding church benefices, although discussions in committee and in Parliament presumably influenced its activities. The Committee augmented 65 Derbyshire and 57 Warwickshire livings before 1649. One should ask several basic questions about these grants. How did the Committee decide which livings to augment? From what revenues were the augmentations drawn? To what extent were payments actually made?

What criteria did the Committee employ in awarding grants? Did it have a set of objective criteria, which it imposed from above or not? The Committee's simultaneous responsibility for the removal of scandalous ministers and their replacement by the godly, and the wording of the various proposals for augmentation schemes, might lead one to assume that the chief criterion employed it in selecting benefices for support would be the presence of a worthy and preaching minister. But in fact this seems far from the case. Only one augmentation order from the two counties mentions the character of the minister as a factor in the grant.[16] There was, however, an attempt to check that the recipients of such grants were not actually deficient. In August 1646 the Committee ordered that a county committee and some 'Godly ministers' should testify to the 'ability and desert' of any minister who requested an augmentation.[17] But a minister might be acceptable to one faction and unacceptable to another: 13 of the Derbyshire ministers mentioned in the 1650 survey as being in receipt of augmentation were noted as scandalous and one of these, Thomas Foulkes of Bolsover, had been presented to the living by the Committee. Such ministers may have been Presbyterians with whom the local surveyors were now out of sympathy.[18] The incumbents of three other Derbyshire parishes (and of three Warwickshire benefices) were ejected after receipt of an augmentation.

The application of another objective criterion to the task in hand may well have been intended by the Committee but was hindered by the weaknesses of the system. Certainly examination of the grants made suggests that the Committee wished to augment the most populous and impoverished of the benefices, but it could not bide entirely by such criteria because its fact finding machinery was so defective. Until 1649–50 there was no survey of Derbyshire livings; no Warwickshire survey survives. The Committee relied upon information provided from a number of sources and in a random fashion.

There seems little doubt that the Committee acted not with reference to a set of objective criteria (no matter how much it may have wished to do so) but to local initiative. Prior to June 1646 many ministers were seeking aid, as is evident from the wording of an order of 27 June 1646 whereby the Committee asked county committees to report on the value of such livings as had been 'or are endeavoured to be augmented'.[19] In other words, the Committee was not seeking an objective report on the values of all benefices but rather information concerning livings which had already been augmented or nominated for grants. It also suggests that the Committee did intend to use the current income from a benefice as the basis for its decisions when judging petitions. Everything points to the Committee acting upon petitions presented by the ministers and parishioners themselves, rather than on information supplied by the local committees. There was indeed no machinery for providing the central committee with information on when revenues for augmentation were available. Parishioners and ministers, however, made it their business to discover this information and to petition the Committee on the strength of it. For example, in August 1646 the parishioners of Duffield, Derbyshire, petitioned that the £38 *per annum* Sir Edward Leech had paid to the dean and chapter of Lichfield out of the rectory of Duffield be used to augment the living; a month later the augmentation was granted.[20]

Petitions from Bolsover, Bakewell and St Peter's Derby also prompted grants.[21] It is, therefore, not surprising that there were frequent discrepancies between the valuations of livings recorded in augmentation orders and their values as in the 1650 survey.

Ralph Josselin's reaction to the rumour that Parliament was about to increase ministers' incomes may have been typical. In November 1644 he was sufficiently encouraged to inquire when he would receive some supplement, only to have his hopes dashed for the moment: 'Concerning the increase of our living by the Parliament, there was no hope from them for the present, all that was to be done was to be expected from the Impropriator' and, as the impropriator was a supporter of Parliament, his rectory was not at the disposal of the Committee.[22] Josselin did not let the matter rest. In 1646 he was advised by a local M.P. and member of the Committee for Plundered Ministers, Harbottle Grimston, who suggested that the impropriation of Feering Berry, sequestered from the bishop of London, might possibly be used to augment Earls Colne. Josselin proceeded to draw 'up a petition for augmentation of our means. It was presented to Mr Grimston who promiseth all fair respect. This was October 9 and 10, God in mercy prosper our desires.' On 31 October Josselin heard that the augmentation had been granted and received the details on 27 November when the local landowner returned from London. On 22 December 1646 he saw the order itself.[23]

On occasion this local initiative may have by-passed the Committee altogether. Daniel Eyres of Hasely, Warwickshire, even seems to have arranged his own augmentation. He appropriated rents due to the prebend of Tachbrook (in the vicarage of which he preached) until in August 1647 he was ordered by the Committee to repay them because the prebend was not sequestrable.[24]

Yet from this evidence we should not infer that the Committee simply rubber-stamped local decisions. There does not appear to be any evidence that local committees themselves initiated grants although it is possible that local M.P.s had considerable influence on certain cases. The nature of the documentation militates against the possibility of pointing to cases when the Committee turned down petitions – what survive are orders for augmentation and Committee accounts rather than minutes of the Committee's deliberations. But the surviving documentation suggests that the first priority of the Committee was to augment large, populous parishes or the chapelries within them. The Committee clearly concerned itself not only with the value of the living but also with the value of the living in relation to its pastoral responsibilities. So we see Bakewell parish (at over £50 *per annum* the wealthiest Derbyshire living to be augmented) receiving a grant as well as each of its nine chapels of ease. The chapels of other geographically large parishes were also augmented – Chesterfield (2), Dronfield (2), Duffield (2), Glossop (at least 2).[25] This concern parallels and complements the concern of Parliament for the maintenance of a worthy pastoral and preaching ministry, and outweighs in significance for the future of the Church the desire to reward or assist ministers who had suffered at the hands of the royalists.

The extent to which the Committee could adequately supplement parishes of this type depended upon the availability of revenue and the degree to which the Committee was made aware of the need by local agencies. Under the Ordinance for Sequestring Notorious Delinquents' Estates of 27 March 1643, delinquents had their lands confiscated and put under the administration of the local committee. A delinquent's dependents were allowed a fifth of the revenue from the estate and the county committees often allowed a delinquent to lease back his own estate. In 1645 the proceeds of compounding were ordered to go to the central committee in London, but county committees appear to have reached an arrangement with the central committee by which they retained half the proceeds of compounding. From 1644 onwards a formal policy of composition was under way, whereby some royalists might recover their estates after the payment of a fine. In these ways the revenue available for augmentation was constantly being whittled away.

Similarly, the obligation laid upon the Committee to provide for the dependents of sequestered clergymen reduced the amount of money drawn from the sequestration. Nevertheless, on paper, the Committee for Plundered Ministers seems to have been reasonably successful in augmenting the very poorest livings (three-quarters of the livings valued at less than £10 in the Derbyshire survey of 1650). Its success rate fell dramatically with regard to those livings valued at between £11 and £20 – only one-third of these were awarded grants.

The failure of the Committee to augment all impoverished livings may be attributed in part to its inability to collect accurate information through its own bureaucratic machinery; in part to a confusion of purpose; in part to its commitment to aid parishes which were both populous and poor; in part to shortage of money. The Committee was understandably reluctant to fund the augmentation of a living in one county from property in another. Historians have commented on the localism of the county committees and the county militia but, although localism may have had its part in preventing the Committee from pooling its available revenues and centralizing the augmentation of benefices in a meaningful sense, there were other and more persuasive reasons for not so doing. In the absence of a centralized and efficient bureaucracy of its own, it would have been impossible either to collect the necessary information about available revenue on a national scale or to ensure collection of those revenues, transferral to a central fund, or payment. The Committee machinery would have ground to a halt had it engaged in extensive cross-county financing. Such confusions as did occur in the making and payment of grants often arose from augmentations made out of one parish to another.

Table 7: *Augmentations granted before 1654*

A. DERBYSHIRE

Grants

77 livings received some kind of augmentation
65 received their first grant on an order of the Committee for Plundered Ministers
7 received their first grant through a composition settlement
3 received their first grant on an order of the Committee for the Reformation of the Universities
2 augmentations are mentioned only in the survey of 1650 and have been excluded from further analysis.

Sources of revenue

(1) 46 received their augmentations solely from revenue raised from delinquents' impropriations (28 of these were raised on revenue arising in the same parish, including all from composition settlements)
total amount of these 46 grants: £2084 16s. 8d. per annum
(2) 19 received their augmentations solely from ecclesiastical revenue (including all those granted by the Committee for the Reformation of the Universities)
total amount of these 19 grants: £559 2s. per annum
(3) 10 livings received grants from both sources of revenue, either because a combination was used in one grant, or because the source of the grant was changed (3 of these received part of their grant from revenue charged on the sequestered tithes of the parish)

Total annual sum granted to Derbyshire livings prior to 1654:
£3039 18s. 8d.
but not all these grants were in operation at the same time; where the value of an augmentation changed, the sum finally decided upon has been counted.

B. WARWICKSHIRE

Grants

63 livings received some kind of augmentation
57 received their first grant on the order of the Committee for Plundered Ministers
5 received their first grant through a composition settlement
1 received its first grant on the order of the Committee for the Reformation of the Universities

Sources of Revenue

(1) 42 received their augmentations solely from revenues raised from delinquents' impropriations (22 of these were charged on revenue raised in the

same parish, including 4 of those granted as composition settlements)
total amount of the 42 grants: £1859 per annum
(2)   12 received their augmentations solely from ecclesiastical revenue (including that granted first by the Committee for the Reformation of the Universities
total amount of these 12 grants: £446 per annum
(3)   9 livings received grants from both sources of revenue; 3 of these received part of their grant from revenue arising from delinquents' impropriations in the same parish (including 1 of those receiving grant as part of composition settlement).
total amount of these 9 grants: £474 10s. per annum

Total annual sum granted to Warwickshire livings prior to 1654:
£2779 10s.

From what revenues were the augmentations drawn? All the revenue, including the ecclesiastical, used for Derbyshire augmentations until 1650 arose in Derbyshire itself. Over half the grants from delinquents' impropriations in both counties were charged on revenues arising in the same parish.[26] When the Committee awarded a grant, there can be no doubt that the parish, or even the chapelry, where the revenue arose had priority. For example, both Bolsover and Dove chapel, Dronfield, were augmented out of Bolsover rectory and Bolsover was to be augmented first. Honiley, Warwickshire, was granted an augmentation out of Stoneleigh rectory on condition that Stoneleigh was first adequately provided for.[27] Some of the better livings received augmentations simply because they had first call on the income of their sequestered rectories: Lullington, Derbyshire, and Aston, Kingsbury and Stoneleigh, Warwickshire, are all examples.[28] This apparent deviation from the wish to supplement the incomes of the poorer parishes resulted in part from the manner in which the Committee came to hear about the case in the first place: through a petition from people who knew of locally available sources of revenue. It was encouraged by the complications of cross-country finance. But it was also acceptable in terms of tradition. Earlier schemes had suggested the resettlement of impropriate tithes upon the vicar concerned. If parishioners objected to paying tithe to the cleric who served *them*, they would object yet more vociferously to paying tithes to an unknown outsider. That such a policy of restoring tithes to the local vicarage did not necessarily benefit the neediest livings and might simply perpetuate existing anomalies was apparently accepted. Impoverished rectories which had not been impropriated were cases in point. In view of the past history of parochial finance, one should not be surprised that this pattern prevailed: it is the exceptions to it which should appear remarkable. A very few non-local grants were made out of delinquents' impropriations, as when £50 of the tithes of

Alfreton and Hucknall, Derbyshire, were granted to the minister of Ramsey, Huntingdonshire, and when Grandborough, Warwickshire, received a Worcestershire impropriation.[29]

The priorities of the parish were recognized also when grants from ecclesiastical revenue were made prior to 1650. (Tithe income from appropriate rectories and prebendal stalls was used for grants, although it provided rather less than a quarter of the total revenue used for augmentation by the Committee before June 1650.)[30] Several Bakewell chapelries were augmented out of the rent which Edward Leech paid for Bakewell tithes to the dean and chapter of Lichfield.[31] The Committee actually revised the augmentation order which benefited Wilne out of the rent reserved from the rectory of Wilne to the prebend of Wilne, when the Committee discovered that the rent originated from Sawley and Wilne, and included Sawley in the new order.[32] When Stratford and two Warwick benefices were augmented from ecclesiastical properties outside the county belonging to the dean and chapter of Worcester, this may have indicated the extreme anxiety on the part of the respective corporations to shift the burden of the augmentations which they were obliged to pay under their Edward VI charters to another party. But the Committee had great difficulty in enforcing orders which crossed county lines. The Warwick clergy petitioned in July 1648 that the Worcestershire authorities had refused to pay the grant awarded in August 1646. The Committee unsuccessfully tried to have the tenants pay the ministers directly, in an attempt to circumvent the resistance of the Worcestershire committee. Eventually, the Committee for Plundered Ministers had to acknowledge tacitly the validity of the local committee's contention that this revenue should not be used outside the county and cancel the grant to Warwick.[33]

Were the orders of the Committee for Plundered Ministers implemented? Were the grants paid? The nature of the available sources makes it difficult to answer such questions definitively. When the county committee received an order for an augmentation from the central committee it normally ordered the tenant who leased the sequestered rectory or other tithes to pay the grant and to deduct it from the rent due to the committee, thus cutting down the administrative work of the county committee. Where there was no lease in force or where it was impossible to lease the tithes for a sum sufficient to cover the cost of the grant, the committee simply granted the profits of the rectory or other property to the minister concerned. The Warwickshire treasurer's accounts include direct payments to 16 ministers: only two of those mentioned received more than half the sum named in the grant over three years and 6 received less than 10 per cent. Yet the same ministers may have received some money from lessees of parts of the rectories concerned or the profits of some tithes directly without a county committee order.[34]

There are, however, other and numerous indications that many grants were not paid in full, if at all, and that there were many slips twixt the cup of the Committee and the lip of the cleric. Only 28 out of a possible 52 grants are mentioned in the Warwickshire Order Book as being implemented in any way, and only 37 of the 67 Derbyshire augmentations are mentioned in the parochial survey. It seems probable that local jurors would have known if augmentations were being paid, although it is possible that in some cases the amount of the grant is included in the 1650 survey without specific mention. But there is evidence in the records of the Committee for Plundered Ministers itself of difficulties regarding the payment of 21 Warwickshire grants (one-third of the total of 63) and of 27 Derbyshire grants (rather over one-third of the 67). Nineteen of the 27 Derbyshire grants occur in the survey. In some cases ministers petitioned that the grant was not being operated at all, or was in arrears; in others the Committee ordered the payment of arrears or repeated orders to local authorities to pay the grants.

Such difficulties did not always arise out of either the unwillingness of the county committees to co-operate or the resistance of tenants. One very common problem was that the revenue upon which the augmentation was charged was simply insufficient. Honiley in Warwickshire was granted £50 *per annum* out of the impropriate rectory of Stoneleigh in July 1646; in November the Warwickshire Sequestrations Committee could muster only a payment of £16 to the minister out of the Michaelmas rents but promised that at Lady Day he would get 'what more this committee can receive'. In 1647 the minister leased the rectory himself, presumably to ensure that he reaped some benefit from it.[35] This suggests that the tithes were not worth as much as the Committee had believed in making the grant – perhaps because of war damage not taken into account by petitioners, other burdens on the rents or the effects of poor harvest. On occasion the Committee seems to have used the same revenue twice. In April 1648 Parliament appointed trustees to receive all the revenue of Lichfield Cathedral (out of which several augmentations had been ordered earlier) and to pay £300 to two ministers at Lichfield. At this the ministers of Sawley, Wilne, Fairfield in Hope, Bakewell and many of its chapelries, (all in Derbyshire) and Cubbington, Warwickshire, complained to the Committee that their own augmentations out of Lichfield Cathedral had now ceased. The problem was not resolved until the general augmentation Act of June 1649 came into effect.[36]

The Committee had no really precise information on the worth of rectories at its disposal – it made the necessary grants and hoped for

the best. Its problems were compounded by the fact that impropriations were available for use by the Committee only until the delinquent died or compounded. On 8 December 1646 the House of
Commons had ordered the Committee to consult with the Committee
for Compounding to try to prevent augmentations lapsing when delinquents compounded.[37] As a result some delinquents settled their
impropriations on trustees, usually prominent M.P.s or county commissioners, to provide an annual sum for the ministers of specific
parishes. In return, the composition fine was lowered, usually by ten
times the amount settled. But this attempt to retain the revenue from
compounded delinquents' impropriations was not successful on a
large scale. The removal of impropriate tithes from the Committee's
use made many grants redundant and made a more reliable source of
funds imperative for any long-term reorganization of the Church's
finances.

The refusal of local bodies to obey the Committee's order was a
source of concern. Sir Edward Leech had to be reminded several times
to pay the grants due to Wilne, Duffield and Ashford and Chelmarston in Bakewell out of the rents he had paid previously to Lichfield.[38]
Sequestered delinquents would not always comply with the committee's orders. For instance, the minister of Edgbaston complained
that the sequestered recusant impropriator of the rectory was still in
receipt of its profits.[39] More difficult still was the misappropriation of
revenue by the county committees themselves. When the exigencies of
war demanded it the committees made clergymen wait for their
money: so the Warwickshire committee made the minister of Tachbrook await payment because 'they have long since by virtue of the
ordinance of sequestrations received the said arrears and disposed of
them for the payment of the soldiery at their disbanding before their
receipt of this committee's order for allowing unto them which said
certificate doth give this committee no satisfaction', and in June 1648
promised to spare the sum due 'when they can spare the money, the
treasury being now wholly exhausted, there being at present great
want of money for the carrying on of the state's service.'[40]

When a sequestration ceased because the delinquent died or compounded, the information was not brought to the attention of the
Committee automatically. Unless the minister concerned petitioned it
directly, the Committee could do little to remedy the situation. In
other words, the Committee had no regular machinery for checking
on the enforcement of its orders or the continued existence of revenue.
If the energy and initiative of the minister were often responsible for
the issue of the grant in the first instance, they were of equal importance in ensuring payment. Ralph Josselin, for instance, expended considerable personal effort before any of his grant was paid, in 1650,

four years after he received the order. Alan Macfarlane estimates that he received only about a quarter of what was due to him under the original order.[41] Probably ministers who lived further from London were doomed to yet poorer returns on their initial success in obtaining an order for augmentation.

II

In June 1649 a piece of general legislation was passed regarding the authorization and payment of augmentations.[42] In theory this Act should have clarified matters; in practice, it added to the confusion. Under the Act for Maintenance of Preaching Ministers a new body, the Trustees for the Maintenance of Ministers, was created which was to administer those augmentations drawn from ecclesiastical revenues as opposed to delinquents' impropriations. In May 1650 the Trustees took over this work and a month later the Committee for the Reformation of the Universities became the authorizing body for augmentations administered by the Trustees (in the stead of the Committee for Plundered Ministers).[43] Until 1653, however, the Committee for Plundered Ministers continued to authorize augmentations out of delinquents' revenue.[44] Until 1650 this class of augmentation was paid by the local county committees but they were then replaced by local commissioners under central control.[45] Thus an extra stage was introduced into the proceedings: the Committee for Plundered Ministers sent their orders to the Commissioners for Managing Estates under Sequestration who in their turn authorized payments by the county commissioners.[46] In 1653 the Committee for Plundered Ministers was abolished but not replaced, which threw the payment of augmentations from delinquents' impropriations into chaos. Not until 1654 was some order brought out of this chaos.[47]

The Committee for the Reformation of the Universities was ordered to make a thorough review of all augmentations ordered by the Committee for Plundered Ministers arising out of ecclesiastical revenue. Parliament was later to criticize the committee for not fulfilling this obligation. The criticisms seem to be substantiated to some extent by the figures for Derbyshire and Warwickshire. Twenty-nine Derbyshire grants required confirmation by the Committee; 19 were reviewed. Of 21 Warwickshire grants needing review and confirmation, only ten were ordered to continue. In addition the Committee did make three new grants in Derbyshire and one in Warwickshire.[48] When the Committee for Plundered Ministers took over briefly between February and April 1653, it too did very little business.[49] There were, however, some signs of a more systematic approach to the question of augmentation on a national scale after the execution of the king: in 1650 a survey was made of the values of church livings.[50]

A Cromwellian ordinance of 1654 placed the responsibility for authorizing and paying all augmentations (from whatever source) in the hands of the Trustees.[51] This was the first body both to order and enforce grants. The Trustees had a central treasury and bureaucracy. They also had at their disposal a central fund – the monies collected from first fruits and tenths – in addition to local revenues from ecclesiastical and delinquents' estates. Although technically this fund had been theirs since 1650, the Trustees do not seem to have had access to it until 1654. The Trustees also had far better sources of information at their disposal than had their predecessors. Their more exact information on the character of ministers, the value of livings, and the revenue available was thanks both to the survey of 1650 and the work of the Commissioners for the Approbation of Public Preachers.

It is interesting to compare the machinery used by the Trustees with that of earlier 'offices' of the Crown which dealt with ecclesiastical matters. After 1650 the parochial survey played an equivalent part in the procedure of the Trustees to that of the *Valor Ecclesiasticus* in the workings of the Lord Keeper's patronage office. The Lord Keeper's registrar of benefices was made aware of a vacancy by a petition from a suitor; only then was the *Valor* consulted to establish whether or not the benefice was truly in the Lord Keeper's gift. The Lord Keeper had no other way of knowing how much patronage was in his hands at any one time. Similarly, the Trustees apparently did not examine the survey and initiate proceedings for augmenting particular livings – proceedings were begun as a response to individual petitions; the Trustees acted on these petitions only if the information in the survey seemed to justify augmentation according to certain criteria which had been adopted by the trustees. This comparison suggests that the Trustees for the Maintenance of Ministers were simply continuing the bureaucratic procedures developed by Late Tudor and Early Stuart administrators and innovating very little. The Committee for Plundered Ministers, with its much more restricted short-term purpose of compensating ministers who had suffered as a result of royalist depredations and its status as a central liaising committee in the rather oddly federal structure of the parliamentary war effort, represented an aberration from the true line of bureaucratic development. Whatever intentions this committee may have had to reform the parochial finances of the national Church were developed rather late in the day and were not part of its original function.[52]

In a petition to Protector and Council in 1655 the Trustees declared their policy: they intended not to overcharge their revenues, to ensure that augmentations awarded would be paid; they intended to grant improvements in maintenance to 'the most deserving and godly mini-

sters of the nation who were worst provided for.'[53] A glance at the
graph below will demonstrate that the Trustees augmented far fewer
livings than did the Committee for Plundered Ministers before it. The
Trustees worked largely within the framework provided by that committee. The number of new grants seems to have varied regionally: for
instance, while nearly one-fifth of the post-1654 Warwickshire grants
were to livings not augmented previously, only one entirely new
Derbyshire grant was made by the Trustees. And the number of grants
was smaller in absolute terms also: 34 Derbyshire grants (:77) and 28
Warwickshire grants (:63) were in force sometime between 1654 and
1660. Why was it that there was such a chasm between what the
Trustees were created to do and what they actually did?

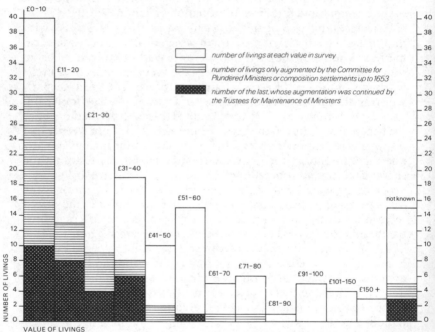

Derbyshire livings augmented by the Committee for Plundered Ministers and the
Trustees for Maintenance of Ministers

The activities of the Trustees cannot be explained adequately in
terms of comparative statistics. They have to be seen within the
context of other developments. One aim of the church survey of 1650
had been to discover which parishes might be united and which
divided.[54] The ordinance of 1654 empowered the Trustees to implement such proposals.[55] There were three main categories to be
treated: those parishes where hamlets were legally linked to mother

churches that were remote geographically; neighbouring small parishes with low population and small means which might profitably be united, thus improving the maintenance of a single minister; and geographically large, populous parishes, containing many settlements, which might be divided so that everyone was within easy reach of a parish church. Proposals under this last category often included plans for new churches where no chapel existed. The inhabitants of

Table 8: *Continuation and alteration of grants by the Trustees for the Maintenance of Ministers after 1654*

A. SOURCES OF REVENUE IN PRE-1654 ORDERS

Derbyshire	Number	Number carried on by Trustees*
Delinquents' impropriations	35	7†
Delinquents' conveyance	11	9
Ecclesiastical revenue/delinquent	10	6
Ecclesiastical revenue	19	11
Total	75	33

Warwickshire	Number	Number carried on by Trustees*
Delinquents' impropriations	33	8†
Delinquents' conveyances	9	4
Ecclesiastical revenue/delinquent	9	4
Ecclesiastical revenue	12	7
Total	63	23

* The source of revenue and the amount granted were not necessarily the same.
† Only two of these were still augmented out of revenue from delinquents' impropriations.
Grants found only in LPL Comm VIh/2 have not been included.

B. CHANGES IN THE AMOUNT OF GRANT

	Derbyshire	Warwickshire
Augmentations raised	2	2
Augmentations reduced	12	10
Augmentations unchanged	19	11
New grants	1	5
Discontinued grants	42	40

Beard, Glossop, stated that they were willing to build their own church if their hamlet could be made a parish of itself.[56] Such proposals obviously faced problems with the vested interests of incumbents, patrons and impropriators. The whole project depended for its feasibility on the augmentation of livings which had already been accomplished. Only thus could chapelries survive independently as adequately endowed parishes.

For some areas the Trustees ordered new surveys to be made especially with this proposal in mind, but plans for unions and divisions in other areas, such as Derbyshire, were based on the 1650 survey information alone.[57] From 1655 on the Trustees ordered that proposals should be followed up unless local objections were encountered. There were no orders for Warwickshire but several Derbyshire projects were raised in the months following 10 June 1655.[58] There is no evidence that any of the orders were implemented: a proposal made in April 1657 to unite Morton and Shirland was scrapped after both sides had been heard in June 1657.[59] Derbyshire proposals were not heard again until July 1658, when they concerned Bakewell and her chapelries. On 25 January 1659 the chapelries of Chelmarston, Monyash, Buxton, Ashford and Sheldon, Longsdon, Baslow and Taddington were all made parishes in their own right, and the council approved the division on the same day. This division was only possible because all the chapelries concerned were already in receipt of augmentations, as the Trustees had declared that no further grants would be made to divided parishes.[60]

Our present interest in the scheme for the union and division of parishes is dictated less by its intrinsic interest than by its effect upon the strategy of the Trustees. As the graph on p. 182 shows, the Trustees were slightly less consistent than their predecessors about augmenting the poorest livings. But this was because, on the basis of the 1650 survey, they appear to have avoided grants to small parishes that were marked down for union with other parishes and to have favoured chapelries destined to become parishes. The Trustees were regarding their work in augmenting livings as part of the wider strategy of the government for the future shape of the Church of England.

In 1655 the Trustees showed their awareness of the fact that although many augmentations had been ordered by their predecessor, relatively few were being paid. The decline in available funds which we noted under the Committee for Plundered Ministers continued under the Trustees. The records allow us several glimpses of the way in which the Trustees lost the revenues from delinquents' rectories. For example, when Sir Edward Moseley compounded for Etwall the augmentations of £30 apiece which were charged against it for Etwall and St Warburgh's Derby were lost.[61] Other augmentations failed on the death of the delinquent. The minister of Astley, Warwickshire, lost the grant of £50 obtained in 1646 when the delinquent's grandson claimed for himself in 1656.[62] Although it is possible that some grants continued without oversight and approval from the Trustees, the figures suggest that large numbers of rectories were

successfully compounded for by delinquents and their children and
that a huge well of funds for the augmentation of livings was thereby
removed. Derbyshire augmentations out of delinquents' revenues in
the 1650s amounted to only one-quarter of the 1640s total; Warwickshire augmentations from the same source amounted to only one-
tenth of the 1640s total.[63] It is true that the Trustees held more money
from such sources than they spent in Derbyshire but, even so, only
one-third of the monies available in the 1640s was available in the
1650s in Derbyshire (and in Warwickshire, one-fifth).

On the restoration of the Rump in 1659 and of the Committee for
Plundered Ministers, Parliament was to criticize the Trustees, among
other things, for not using local revenue to pay augmentations to local
ministers.[64] Was this a fair criticism? Given the depletion of the funds
of local revenue, it is not surprising that the trustees had to draw on
other sources of revenue to a far greater degree. Even so, table 9 suggests that only six Derbyshire augmentations were supported from
central revenue (first fruits and tenths) and that almost four-fifths of
the resources used were local. The Warwickshire picture is different
(although we have no information for a larger number of grants)
because there was less revenue available within the county from ecclesiastical or delinquents' estates. Local sources accounted for only
two-fifths of the revenue used. Three parishes were supported from
revenue in Gloucestershire, Derbyshire and Berkshire. But it seems
equally obvious that the Trustees departed from the normal procedure of providing for local grants from local monies only when necessity demanded it.

The Trustees seem to have been as careful as they themselves
claimed not to overcharge their revenues: the amount received for
both counties far exceeded the amount handed out in grants. The
Trustees were anxious to cut their coat according to their cloth. But
while payment under the Trustees was probably more certain than it
had been under the Committee, the Trustees were certainly not
without their accounting problems. At Christmas 1658 the local
revenue over the nation as a whole was some £50,000 in arrears,
although this situation was not as bleak as it sounds, as some revenues
were received direct by ministers and never entered into the central
treasury and as some arrears were either very recent or were already in
the hands of receivers.[65] The central revenue presented its own problems. The Trustees had to catch up with the activities of past receivers
and legal proceedings were begun against some.[66] In November 1656
the Trustees were offered £11,000 p.a. for the lease of first fruits and
tenths but decided that they did not have the power to farm the tenths.[67]

Partly as a result of the old problem of enforcement, some augmentations were not paid, although the Trustees paid the arrears upon

petition.[68] But, more often, the local revenue simply did not cover the grant. This was often because the revenue from tithes was a fluctuating commodity. There are indications of problems over payment in six Warwickshire and 11 Derbyshire augmentations.[69] For the minister who petitioned for arrears or for renewal of an original augmentation order, the delays involved were often as burdensome as the absence of

Table 9: *Revenues used in augmentations by the Trustees for the Maintenance of Ministers*

A. DERBYSHIRE

Revenue charged	Number	Total per annum
Ecclesiastical (Derbyshire)	15	£346 14s. 0d.
Delinquents (Derbyshire)	11	£491
Ecclesiastical (central)	6	£220
Not known	2	£59 14s. 8d.
Total	34	£1117 8s. 9d.

B. WARWICKSHIRE

Revenue charged	Number	Total per annum
Ecclesiastical (Warwickshire)	4	£205 9s. 0d.
Ecclesiastical (other counties)	3	£110
Delinquents (Warwickshire)	4	£161
Ecclesiastical (central)	8	£240
Not known	9	£225 6s. 8d.
Total	28	£941 15s. 8d.

Augmentations found only in LPL, Comm VIb/2 have not been included: it is uncertain whether these grants ever operated in practice as there are no formal grants or payment orders.

payment itself. Buxton chapel, Bakewell, did not have its grant confirmed until 1659 and other chapelries of Bakewell suffered similar delays.[70] Council approval of such orders was a long-winded affair – it could take up to one year after the order had been made.[71]

III

If we try to force the activities of the various bodies which granted augmentations to livings during the period 1643–60 into the straitjacket of a twentieth-century model we discover that this is not easily done. For instance, there is some confusion concerning the aims of the various committees. While it is true that the Committee for Plundered Ministers was more concerned with the plight of individuals who had suffered at the hands of the royalists than were the Trustees, who took a more long-sighted view of the problem, it is true nevertheless that both committees shared to some extent a concern for the Church as a whole. The aims and activities of the Committee for Plundered Ministers were certainly circumscribed by the needs of the war effort but attempts to produce a new valuation of all benefices were mooted throughout the 1640s. The policy with regard to augmentations shifted with changing circumstances: the plight of plundered ministers appeared much more pressing in the mid-1640s than did the long-term welfare of the pastoral ministry and any movement to press the urgency of the latter upon the rest of the government would have met with nothing but opposition; in the early 1650s the whole question of the necessity of a maintained and settled ministry may have thrown the issue of augmentations into the melting pot; under Cromwell there was an attempt to look at the problems of the State Church anew and integrate the approaches of the various authorities towards them. It would be a mistake, then, to treat the augmentations of 1643–60 as a single scheme. Certainly, the Trustees for the Maintenance of Ministers worked to a great extent within the framework provided for them by the Committee for Plundered Ministers, but there were significant differences of policy, emphasis and procedure.

The various authorities were, without doubt, aware of their own inadequacies as agents for their own policies. Petitions from ministers (and their families) who had not received promised grants, the difficulties in collecting due revenues, the impact of a changing political situation on particular sources of money all made their impression upon the committees and trustees. Whether this caused as much frustration to seventeenth-century contemporaries as it would to twentieth-century bureaucrats is a moot point. The system in operation did not appear by seventeenth-century standards to be malfunctioning at all. Many of the defects which we have noted – the absence of a detailed and uniform body of information from which to work; the unreliability of revenues because of the extreme dependence on changing commodity retail prices and harvests; the awarding of grants on receipt of personal petition rather than on the basis of an impersonal and objective survey of the situation from above – did not appear strange. Indeed, had contemporaries so reflected, they would have appeared essential to the functioning of the system. Seventeenth-century bureaucrats had no twentieth-century ideal of the virtues of administrative centralization to live up to; no twentieth-century model to measure themselves against.

What is true is that the creation of the Committee for Plundered Ministers was motivated by the realization that the problem of an impoverished, loyal ministry in England was a national problem. The Parliament could not allow its adherents to suffer for their support.

Parliament needed the pulpits of England. The Committee had, to some extent, a central mission. But it had no initial conception of the need for a centralized machinery in order to accomplish its goal. The Committee was little more than a central clearing house for petitions from suffering ministers, which ordered that the counties provide for individuals who had been approved by the Committee. The plundered ministers of each county would be provided for out of local funds. To the extent that Parliament's central committee realized that centralization of funding and enforcement was desirable, and dependence upon the machinery of local government for information and enforcement anathema, this emerged through painful experience. The attempt to initiate and implement a central policy for the augmentation of and reorganisation of benefices was the result of both the Committee's and the Trustees' effort to put into practice much more limited policies. The sensitivity of the Committee for Plundered Ministers to the extent of their problem dates from no later than March 1644–5, when their report to the House of Commons proposed the use of dean and chapter revenues for the augmentation of 'every poor vicarage or parsonage that hath cure of souls'; the need for additional resources to permit this to be accomplished; the bringing up of clerical incomes to a level of £100 *per annum*; the co-operation of the office of first fruits and tenths in this work; the union and division of livings and, significantly, the making of a survey of all the livings in each county, using again the county committees, the members of the assembly and the office of first fruits. W. A. Shaw argued that nothing more was ever heard of this report. This in itself might suggest that while the Committee was arguing for a wholesale attack on the financing of the ministry, Parliament, absorbed in the issues of the war, refused to take such a scheme seriously. Yet we know that from July 1645 the Committee was actively augmenting livings and that, contrary to the impression which Shaw gives, it was using reserved revenues of the bishops, deans and chapters to finance the operation. It seems clear that, while the Committee did not obtain all that it had urged from Parliament, it did get some satisfaction and that it clung to a wider conception of its responsibilities than that which Shaw suggests.[72]

The Committee for Plundered Ministers was led, by hard experience, to realize that it could not work effectively through committees whose prime *raison d'être* was managing the county war effort. It desired a new framework for action. The response of Parliament was less than satisfactory: it was reluctant to give the Committee adequate finance for the task of augmenting the incomes of all ministers and so the Committee never had access to the funds of first fruits and tenths during the 1640s. In itself this restrained the activities of the Committee but the conservatism of the body is evident both in its policy and in its methods. The attempt to restore alienated tithes to vicarages was not a novel policy – there is no hint in the proceedings of the Committee that it wanted to pay all revenues from tithe to a general fund and mete this out to needy livings. Theirs was, rather, a traditional Tudor/Stuart proposal designed both to further the Reformation and to ease the late medieval system of clerical finance.

The Trustees for the Maintenance of Ministers approximated more closely to the model of a central department of state, with its own treasury and bureaucracy, which sees itself as responsible for policy formation and declaration; collection of relevant information; decision making and issue of orders; and enforcement. Although one would not wish to exaggerate Cromwell's commitment to centralized government, it would be hard not to attribute the changed characteristics of the body in charge of augmentations in 1654 to the changed character of the régime. Even at this point, he was building upon the work of the Committee for Plundered Ministers. The parochial survey of 1650, the nearest that seventeenth-century Englishmen had come to revising the out-dated *Valor Ecclesiasticus* in accordance not only with inflation but also a post-Reformation view of the ministry as primarily concerned with pastoral care, was drawn up in order to permit the Committee for Reformation of the Universities to implement a policy similar to that broached by the Committee for Plundered Ministers in March 1644/5. But it was only in September 1654 that the remodelled Trustees for the Maintenance of Ministers were given access to this survey in order to augment needy livings and order the union or division of certain parishes. The work of the Trustees suggests that Cromwell's State Church was to have been more than a chimera. The years between 1654 and 1660 see the Trustees trying to implement a policy which dovetailed both the need to augment the meagre maintenance of many English and Welsh clergy, and also the more far-reaching proposals to bring the parish provision into line with changed population movements and, perhaps more pertinently, changed conceptions of the ministry. Cromwell gave the Trustees the authority to order and administer such reforms, the necessary access to such information as existed, and continued access to central funds. There can be little doubt that, had the Trustees succeeded in their two-pronged attack on the deficiencies of parochial finance, the situation in the Restoration period would have been far more equitable as between parish and parish, diocese and diocese, than it was in fact to be. The work of the Trustees presaged that of Queen Anne's Bounty and the Church Commissioners in more ways than one.[73]

Yet we should not be carried away. The trustees, despite their more bureaucratic and centralized approach and official recognition of their work, still relied upon petitions from the needy to initiate new grants and renew old. They still were cursed by deficiencies of collection and accounting techniques. Their funds were insufficient to permit them to do more than scratch the surface of the financial problems of the parochial ministry: that they appear to have appreciated this fact and set themselves realistic limits is true. Moreover, the Trustees still continued the age-old practice of augmenting most incomes from local tithes. This is a committee which, at most, represents a transitional stage in the evolution of the modern, centralized department. And those aspects of Cromwell's church financing policy in the 1650s which heralded a move away from 'federated reform programmes' authorized by central committees and implemented by local commissioners were themselves thrust aside at the return of the Committee for Plundered Ministers with the Rump. The Rump deprecated the Trustees for deploying central funds and called for augmentations to be paid exclusively from local resources; it criticized the Committee for the Reformation of the Universities for failing to review all augmentations, despite much evidence that the efforts of the Plundered Ministers' Committee had far outstripped the available revenues.

The evidence suggests a gradual move towards an interest in the problems of church finance as a whole on the part of those entrusted with the task of augmenting clerical incomes. Any suggestion that the legislation of 1649 represents a sharp break in this respect should be rejected. What is true is that the Commonwealth and Protectorate governments were able to treat this interest more sympathetically than had the war-worried Parliament of the 1640s. The extent to which the Trustees' continued reliance on income from local tithe as a source for local augmentation should be viewed in the context of the contemporary debate over the continuance of tithing is an intriguing question. It certainly appears significant that at least some central funding was envisaged and that this was drawn from clerical sources: in other words, the suggestion was that clerical income should be distributed more equitably and that income from clerical taxation should be invested in the clergy. The Trustees, by trial and error, developed a system which utilized available, and increasingly limited, resources to reorganize English parochial life and make the maintenance of ministers more equitable, while taking account of the sensitivities of lay patrons and impropriators, and the need to return to normal conditions of life after long years of war and disruption. The work of Cromwell's Trustees was not, therefore, devoid of significance for later church reformers and it certainly contributes a good deal to our knowledge of Cromwell's attitude to the State Church.

NOTES

We would like to express our appreciation to the following scholars for their valuable criticisms of this essay when it was in draft: Gerald Aylmer, Molly Barratt, Felicity Heal and Clive Holmes.

1. W. A. Shaw, *A History of the English Church During the Civil Wars and Under the Commonwealth*, (1900); W. A. Shaw (ed.), *Minutes of the Committee for the Relief of Plundered Ministers and of the Trustees for the Maintenance of Ministers, relating to Lancashire and Cheshire, 1643–1660* (The Record Society of Lancashire and Cheshire, 2 vols., 1893, 1896.)

2. J. S. Morrill, *The Revolt of the Provinces* (1976) contains the best general discussion of the issue. For more specialized contributions see A. M. Everitt, *The Community of Kent and the Great Rebellion* (1966), and *Suffolk and the Great Rebellion* (Suffolk Record Society, 1960) and *The Local Community and the Great Rebellion* (Historical Association Pamphlet G70, 1969); J. S. Morill, *Cheshire, 1630–1660* (1974); D. Underdown, *Somerset in the Civil War and Interregnum* (1973); P. Clark, *English Provincial Society from the Reformation to the Revolution: Religion, Politics and Society in Kent, 1500–1640* (1977); A. Hughes, 'Militancy and localism. Warwickshire politics and Westminster politics, 1643–1647' (Alexander Prize Essay, 1980, to be published in *Trans. Royal Hist. Soc.*).

3. C. Cross, 'The Church in England, 1646–1660', in *The Interregnum: The Quest for Settlement*, ed. G. Aylmer (1972); for a further discussion of Cromwell's State Church see the forthcoming Open University correspondence units for *Seventeenth Century England: A Changing Culture*.

4. *CJ*, II, 21, 28, 54; Shaw, *English Church*, ch. 4, *passim*; Dering's notes of the proceedings of the sub-committee of 24 appear in Camden Society, LXXX, 45, 52, 80–100. Refer to I. M. Green, 'The persecution of "scandalous" and "malignant" parish clergy during the English Civil War', *EHR* (1979), for a discussion of the work of the Committee for Scandalous Ministers.

5. *LJ*, V, 510.

6. *CJ*, II, 909.

7. *CJ*, III, 183.

8. *CJ*, III, 270.

9. Shaw, *English Church*, II, 198. Shaw claims that a similar committee sat in Kingston, Surrey.

10. *CJ*, II, 510, 515, 549, 574.

11. Bodl. MS 322, p. 411.

12. At least in the case of Derbyshire.

13. BL Add. MS 15669 gives earliest Middlesex grants. The earliest Derbyshire augmentation is for Bakewell: Bodl. MS 322, f. 5r.

14. BL Add. MS 15669. The recommendations of the Committee for Plundered Ministers, 17 March 1645, on the method of augmenting poor livings are printed in Shaw, *English Church*, Appendix X, 601–2.

15. Shaw, *English Church*, II, 202–3; *CJ*, II, 510, 515, 549, 574; Shaw, *English Church*, II, Appendix X, 601–2; *CJ*, IV, 113, 119, 502; Shaw, *English Church*, II, 214–15; Act of 8 June 1649 printed in C. H. Firth and R. Rait, *Acts and Ordinances of the Interregnum* (3 vols., 1911), I, 142–8.

16. This was the award of £50 to John Rowlandson jr to assist his father at Bakewell on 22 April 1648: Bodl. MS 325, f.57v.

17. Bodl. MS 323, no folio.

18. The ministers of Allestree, Beely and Chelmarston (Bakewell chapelries), Tissington (Bradbourne), Brimington (Chesterfield), Elmton, Stony Middleton (Hathersage), Hognaston, Hucknall, Norton, Scarcliffe, Caldwell (Stapenhill), and

192 *Rosemary O'Day and Ann Hughes*

Barlow (Staveley) are recorded as scandalous or, in the case of Roger Cook, curate of Hognaston, 'honest but weak' in the 1650 survey: LPL Comm. XIIa/6, fos. 347–478.

19. Bodl. MS 323, no folio.
20. *Ibid.*, fos. 66r, 67r.
21. *Ibid.*, f. 64r, Bolsover; Bodl. MS 325, f. 57v, Bakewell, April 1648; PRO SP 22/3/568, Derby, April 1647.
22. Alan Macfarlane (ed.), *The Diary of Ralph Josselin, 1616–1683* (British Academy, Records of Social and Economic History, N.S. III (1976), 26.
23. *Ibid.*, 72, 74, 76, 80.
24. BL Add. MS 35098, fos. 114v, 66r, 45v.
25. Bodl. MS 322, fos 5r–v, 6v (Bakewell); f. 6r; Bodl. MS 325, f. 59v (Chesterfield); Bodl. MS 323, fos. 63v, 64v (Dronfield); Bodl. MS 323, fos. 65v, 66r, 67r (Duffield); Bodl. MS 323, f. 68r, Bodl. MS. 327, 155, 157 (Glossop).
26. See table 7.
27. Bodl. MS 323, fos. 63r, 64r, 290v; PRO SP 22/3/536.
28. In the respective augmentation orders Aston was valued at £80, Kingsbury at £40 and Stoneleigh at £60 (although the latter had been disrupted by the war): Bodl. MS 323, f. 348r (Aston); *ibid.*, f. 293v (Kingsbury); *ibid.*, f. 349v (Stoneleigh).
29. Bodl. MS 328, 133 (Hunts); Bodl. MS 323, f. 349r (Grandborough); PRO SP 22/1 f.99v (Harborne).
30. Shaw asserted that *no* ecclesiastical revenue was used for augmentations prior to 1650; his error arose from the fact that the committee treated tithe income from appropriate rectories as if it were simply revenue drawn from delinquents' impropriations.
31. For example, Bodl. MS 322, fos. 5r–v: Ashford, Beely, Chelmerston and Moniash all in December 1645.
32. Bodl. MS 325, f. 56v, November 1647. The original order to augment Wilne was in February 1647.
33. I owe this suggestion to Dr Molly Barratt of the Bodleian Library. Bodl. MS 323, fos. 308r, 325, 243v–244v.
34. BL Add. MS 35098, Order Book; PRO SP 28/136, 201: Accounts of Thomas Basnet, Treasurer of the Warwickshire County Committee.
35. BL Add. MS 35098, f. 18r; Bodl. MS 323, f. 290v gives the original augmentation order.
36. Bodl. MS 323, f. 64v (Dore); Bodl. MS 328, 153–4 (Dronfield); *LJ, X,* 178–9; Bodl. MS 326, fos. 76r–v, 77v.
37. Bodl. MS 323, no folio.
38. For example, Bodl. MS 323, f. 68v, October 1646.
39. Bodl. MS 327, 536, February 1649.
40. Bodl. MS 325, fo. 243r; BL Add. MS 35098, f. 101v.
41. *Diary of Ralph Josselin, op. cit.*, 135, 193, 178; A. Macfarlane, *The Family Life of Ralph Josselin* (1970), 35.
42. Firth and Rait, *op. cit.*, 142–3.
43. According to *CJ*, VI, 388, this had been decided on 29 March 1650.
44. For examples, see Bodl. MSS 327–9.
45. For examples, see Bodl. MS 327, 536 (Edgbaston, Warwickshire order, July 1650); Bodl. MS 328, 128 (Alfreton, Derbyshire order, April 1651).
46. See PRO SP 23/22: The Order Book of the Commissioners for Managing Sequestered Estates, 1652–5.
47. This took place against the background of the proposals for the abolition of tithes which, of course, provided the chief source of revenue available for augmentations.
48. LPL Comm VI a/ Augmentations Orders Books 1650–60/ 2 & 3. The new grants

were to Chellaston, Chesterfield and Wirksworth, Derbyshire, and to Bishops
Tachbrooke, Warwickshire: Comm. VI a/3, 83, 399, 528; Comm VIb. Lists of
Augmentations; Comm VIb/2, 26 (Wirksworth).

49. LPL, Comm VIa/ Augmentation Order Books . . . /4, being the Order Book of the
    Committee for Plundered Ministers during the brief period when it took over again
    from the Committee for the Reformation of the Universities, Feb.–Apr. 1653.
50. LPL Comm XII a. VI, fos. 347–478, covers Derbyshire.
51. Firth and Rait, op. cit., II, 1000–6.
52. See R. O'Day, 'The ecclesiastical patronage of the lord keeper', in Trans. Royal
    Hist. Soc. (1973).
53. LPL Comm VI a/11; see table 8.
54. Firth and Rait, op. cit., II, 142–8.
55. Ibid., 1002–4.
56. LPL Comm XIIc/4, 29.
57. LPL Comm XIIc/1, Register of the appointment of commissioners to survey
    parishes (this contains nothing for Derbyshire).
58. For example, LPL Comm XIIc/2, 10 July 1656, 107: an order to proceed with
    uniting Little Ireton and Kedlestone according to the survey, unless shown to the
    contrary by 9 October 1656.
59. LPL Comm XIIc/4, 208, 220.
60. LPL Comm XIIc/3, 221; Comm VII/4, Register of the Orders of the Council, 8 May
    1656–29 January 1659, 44; Comm XIIc/2, 369, December 1657 contains the
    Trustees' declaration that no further augmentation would be made after division.
61. PRO SP 22/3/597, October 1651, an order granting a new augmentation to St
    Warburgh's because the earlier grant had lapsed with Moseley's composition.
62. LPL Comm VIa/13, 205–6.
63. See tables 7 and 9.
64. Shaw, English Church, 243–4.
65. LPL Comm XIa/6.
66. LPL Comm VIa/12, 115.
67. Ibid., 255, 257.
68. LPL Comm VIa/10, 4 5.
69. LPL Comm VIa/9, 471; Comm VIb/3 f. 134, Comm VIa/8, 6 (1656), Derby;
    Comm VIb/3, 2–3, Comm VIa/9, 422 (1657 original grant, taken over by Steele in
    1658), Chesterfield.
70. LPL Comm VIa/11, 94, Buxton.
71. E.g. Chesterfield, where augmentations to the minister and the lecturer were
    granted by the Trustees in August 1655 and approved by the Council in June 1656,
    LPL Comm VIb/2, 24.
72. P. Styles, Studies in Seventeenth Century West Midlands History (1978), 81–3.
73. For some discussion of the Trustees see G. E. Aylmer, The State's Servants (1973),
    267–70, 44–5.

9

The clergy as money-lenders in England, 1550–1700

B. A. Holderness

R. H. Tawney, in his celebrated introduction to Thomas Wilson's *Discourse upon Usury* in 1925, had much to say about the nature of credit transactions in a peasant society. So far as he was concerned his investigation was pathological, for money-lending, otherwise usury, was a disease that deformed social relationships.[1] Nevertheless, he set out to discover the character of the money-lenders who provided the casual or contingent credit of villages and small towns in sixteenth-century England. Without revealing his sources, he drew a picture of the money-lenders who came to dominate the peasants and craftsmen of these communities:

> Generally they are quite unpretending people, farmers who are a little more prosperous than their neighbours, and see in their diffi-culties the chance of turning an honest penny, innkeepers, who gradually worm themselves into the affairs of the unwary custo-mer, give long credit, and at the critical moment foreclose, tailors, drapers, grocers, mercers, who have a little money laid by, and take to lending it in order to eke out the earnings of their trade. In country districts the character most commonly found advancing money is a yeoman, *and next to him comes probably the parson*; for both are slightly if only slightly better-off and better educated than the humbler cottagers. The outstanding debts are commonly articles such as grain, cattle, clothes, and household furniture.[2]

Through Tawney spoke both the radical conscience of Edwardian Britain and all the outrage of the preacher and moralist of an age of faith. His views upon the supererogatory, and not infrequently evil nature of credit in agrarian societies seem, however, to have been much exaggerated and often misplaced. Money-lending played a part in pre-industrial England that was more positive than the mere entrapment of humble men in the toils of the bloodsucker. Tawney acknowledged the ubiquity of credit, and his discovery that among the leading lenders were clergymen not only deserves recording but makes a convenient launching-place for the present essay.

Because his schedule of references is incomplete, Tawney fails to establish a logically convincing case either for the extent of credit transactions or for the participation of particular social types in its provision. Yet there is no doubt that he was basically correct in his assumptions. Rural credit was not negligible in medieval England, and it increased steadily in volume and extent in the century or more after 1550. Wills, which as a source Tawney seldom used, and testamentary inventories, of which he was largely unaware at the time, confirm his observations, and incidentally disclose something of the changes which occurred through the passage of time. Money-lending and sales credit were not the same thing as usury, for one can make out a good case to support the former even in the kind of society described so bleakly by Tawney. But behind any positive or beneficial aspect of money-lending was always the darker, malignant aspect of usurious extortion, from which not even the clergy were exempt.

It was this recurring social disorder which caused divines and magistrates so often roundly to condemn all kinds of lending, and adverse public opinion apparently outlasted widespread public resort to the amenities of credit. This placed the parson, whether medieval priest or reformed minister, in a difficult and delicate situation. The sanctions against money-lending were widely ignored by their peers; yet the stigma of antisocial or unclerical behaviour still attached to the implication of the clergy in what was obviously a profitable by-employment. Usury, as both excessive and sometimes even permissible interest-taking was called, was so repeatedly and unimaginatively comminated in sermons and writings that men of good conscience had to perform prodigies of casuistry or self-justification to counter such powerful public repugnance, especially in the sixteenth century. Usury was an offence triable in the church courts, and in due course by magistrates or judges in prerogative courts or in Chancery. It may be argued that one reason for the weakening of antipathy against usury was the fact that it was a cause appropriate to the increasingly unpopular and contemptible consistory courts: yet the action even of magistrates in quarter sessions during the early seventeenth century in trying and convicting usurers rather suggests that there were many who still found the practice repulsive whatever the prevailing opinion of ecclesiastical jurisdiction.

Nevertheless usury was a rare offence so far as legal records are concerned. If we turn from the preachers to look for evidence of cases in the courts or of pleas to the Crown against extortion of high interest rates, few can be excavated from the mass of documents surviving for the period. Among the tens of thousands of disputes brought before officials principal, archdeacons, or magistrates, the cases of usury are numbered in dozens, and in many records feature not at all. Only in the voluminous and still largely unpenetrated records of Chancery and other prerogative courts of the Crown do disputes over debts form a noteworthy segment of juridical business. And even there – so far as I can tell – excessive interest charges were an issue much less often than defaulting or than technical problems related to the constitution of particular debts or loans.[3] Tudor legislation, responding to changed customs or expectations, in 1571 permitted the taking of interest, providing that the rate did not exceed 10 per cent, although in some of the cases tried subsequently men were summoned for lending at interest within the legal maximum.

Medieval priests had lent money at interest, for several were duly haled before the courts for usury. The number of cases was very few, but in view of the evidence that money-lending in peasant communities was almost as widespread before 1500 as afterwards, the contribution of priests may have been a good deal greater than is suggested by the surviving tally of cases and admonitions.[4] The medieval Church acted ambiguously over the treatment of money-lending, even though the principle had been established by the twelfth century of ostracizing and excommunicating usurers presented to ecclesiastical courts. Although usurers could have been rendered virtual outlaws by the Church, and men in orders caught in the act were required to be summarily dismissed from their clerical offices, the fact, firstly, that cases recurred generation after generation, and, secondly, that much casual lending even by priests apparently continued without provoking reprisals from above, suggests that the medieval Church had already lost the struggle to enforce obedience in this part of its jurisdiction.

By the sixteenth century, therefore, official tolerance even of clerical money-lending was in contrast to popular feeling, and in the few cases where incumbents were at odds with their congregations over credit transactions, the offending clergy were apparently not even rebuked by their archdeacons or bishops. The best example is that of Dr Bennett who was preferred to the best parochial benefice in the city of Hereford. The rumour of Bennett's appointment incensed the burgesses of the city, who were in any case very active in the harrying of suspected usurers. They appealed to the Crown, protesting that 'Dr Bennett is a great taker of advantages', meaning, among other things, that he had a reputation for taking a penny in the shilling.[5] In Essex earlier had occurred the indictment for usury of Mark Simpson, rector of Pitsea, the only known example of a clerical money-lender brought before the archdeacon of Essex after the Reformation, even though his court was one of the most active and busy in the country. Simpson admitted that he had made loans at 10 per cent, but claimed that the addition to the principal which he had received had been by way of a gift from the grateful borrowers. Even though he had broken no law in 1578, and could not be convicted of the offence, he was still required to do penance and to give 5s. to the use of the poor.[6] Other Essex parsons were tried and punished for a variety of criminal, moral or civil offences, and some were notorious for disreputable conduct, yet none was even accused of usury as part of the litany of complaints against him. Proceedings in Chancery add a little to our knowledge of parsons active in making loans or allowing sales credit to accumulate, but it seems unlikely that more than one in a thousand disputes over debts brought into equity related in any way to clergymen. It is, however, a field of research which requires further investigation, and so far none of the cases inspected by this writer has been of any interest for the present purpose.

It should be obvious from the discussion above that the study of money-lending in the early modern period cannot be accomplished by searching through the administrative and juridical records of the age. Law cases can be interpreted either as evidence of scandalous abuse by clergy unmindful of traditional sanctions or popular distaste for their transgression or, more probably, as evidence of the infrequency and unimportance of credit transactions implicating men in clerical orders. The only source which can supply some statistical material, and at the same time offers a corrective to the bias of evidence drawn from legal proceedings, is to be found in the immense mass of wills and testamentary inventories that have been preserved in the probate registries of English dioceses since the sixteenth century. Their use by historians during the past 20 years has become such a commonplace that it is now probably unnecessary to explain the form, content and drawbacks of the probate records. The inventories, in particular, are so useful as a window upon the everyday lives of comparatively humble folk that no scholar seeking to interpret economic change and continuity in the pre-industrial past, to sketch the profile of occupational structure and comparative wealth in defined social categories, or to illustrate the theme of daily life, can afford to ignore the myriad of lists and appraisals exhibited for ecclesiastical approval. In the past few years a number of collections of inventories has been printed and published, although among the hundreds of documents made accessible in this way there are very few inventories of clergy.

Even so, F. W. Brooks, in a pioneering essay 30 years ago, demonstrated that probate records could be used successfully to indicate some of the features of the social position of the clergy in sixteenth-century Lincolnshire. He, like most other writers in the field, discovered that the economic position, that is to say the personal wealth, of parsons improved during the course of Elizabeth's reign.[7] Clergy in 1600 were, for the most part, still poor and humble by comparison with later ages, but Brooks implies that not only were they more comfortable but that clerical expectations had simultaneously been rising with the modest accession of material possessions. Unfortunately he paid little attention to the data of debts recorded as owing to the deceased in some of the inventories he inspected. This is only to be expected, for until recently evidence of credit in probate records has not been fully exploited. Inventories, even more than wills, which are eccentric in the matter, record among the personal possessions of testators monies owing to them by way of credits. In some instances, the appraisers of the goods also listed debts owed by the deceased. This latter practice was very common in the accounts of intestate estates, since the administrators were required to exhibit a balance-sheet of the personalty of the dead at the conclusion of their labours. Unfortunately comparatively few administration accounts survive beside the testamentary inventories, and the number of clergy estates thus evaluated was minute.

Some examples of clergymen who died with money owing to their estates can be found in the collections already printed. Thus of the half-dozen parsons whose inventories have survived among the few Devon inventories to escape bombing in the Second World War, two, Nicholas Downey of Modbury (d. 1640) who left £100 worth of bad debts and £20 of good debts out of £296 of personal effects, and Robert Hart (d. 1680) who left £163 out of which £27 5s. 4½d. were in debts owing to him, can be accounted money-lenders. They are fairly typical examples of clerical creditors. Henry Clarke, vicar of Stoke Gifford, Gloucestershire, who died in 1620, left only £36 10s. 3d. worth of chattels but he held one bond in £20, 'wherein William Smith and John Taylor of Stoke Gifford stand bound to the Deceased for payment.' When Thomas Coller, rector of Malpas, Cheshire, died in 1623 he was owed £218 7s. 6d. out of £462 3s. 1d. Fewer sixteenth-century inventories of clergy have been printed, but there is the interesting case of Christopher Pennell, vicar choral of Southwell, Nottinghamshire, (d. 1567) whose credits amounted to £6 17s. 4d., but who was recorded as owing £11 11s. 2d. to others at the time of his death.

Mortgage lending was apparently rare before the late seventeenth century, perhaps because the term of a mortgage was too long for a comparatively poor man who might need his money on call, for mortgages could not legally be assigned until the later seventeenth century. Nevertheless, Giles Ailiff, vicar of Heversham, Westmorland, as early as 1588 devised to his wife 'all [those] morgaiges, tackes, leases and grantts of ground which I have within the parishe of Heversham [or] anye other place elswhere', and Joseph Hall, bishop of Norwich (d. 1654), held mortgages on land in Norfolk and Leicestershire which, before his death, he had converted into freehold property to be devised to his sons. In the higher reaches of the clergy, from the sixteenth to the eighteenth centuries, the connection between money-lending and land-buying was often so close as to be indistinguishable.[8] But to get a picture which is not distorted by special circumstances, by individual characteristics or by an insufficient sample, a much more extensive analysis of testamentary material, covering both a longer period and a coherent area, is desirable. What follows is based on such an investigation.

Without burdening the reader with excessive detail, it is necessary that he should know something of the nature of inventories. Inventories recorded only movable possessions (personalty by contrast with realty), which included money, plate and apparel, household furniture, books, pictures, weapons, linen, livestock and farmyard equipment, crops sown or in barn, the value of tillage or meadowground, stock and tools of trade, and all debts owing to the deceased, whether 'sperate' (good or hoped-for) or desperate. The schedule of goods was drawn up and evaluated by one or more appraisers or 'prizers' as soon after death as it was possible to arrange. In theory, but perhaps not always in practice, goods owned by the deceased but in the hands of others at the time of the assessment were included by the appraisers, and dispersal sales had to wait for the machinery of probate to complete its course. Inventories, as a statistical source for quantitative historians, are fallible on several counts. Their accuracy depended much upon the skill and interest of the man or men appointed to make the valuation. Some are incredibly detailed with appraisal of even the least item of a man's possessions; others scorn to offer values for even substantial goods and chattels. Some were apparently comprehensive, others cursory and neglectful, for the work of appraisement relied upon co-operation with members of the family who might be tempted to begin dividing their inheritance before legal proceedings could be opened. Individual inventories are generally interesting, but cannot be taken as accurate in their details. The best we can hope for is that by analysing a considerable number of inventories we may overcome the deficiencies of each document. The process of averaging is, in any event, the only avenue open to the historian attempting a survey of the credit system in the rural setting of sixteenth- and seventeenth-century England.

Clerical inventories naturally form a small portion of the whole collection preserved in particular archives. There were probably only about 20,000 men in orders in the reformed Church by 1600, when there must have been about one million households in England and Wales, and it is not surprising that parsons' wills and inventories should be fewer than those of the gentry. The clergy can be expected to have left wills disposing of their worldly possessions more often than unlettered peasants, but a comparison of surviving clerical inventories in dioceses such as Lincoln, in which probate administration from 1560 to 1640 was efficient, with known clerical deaths suggests a high degree of intestacy even among the priesthood. Half or fewer of the parsons believed resident in the archdeaconry of Lincoln between 1570 and 1603 are to be traced in the index of wills and inventories, though a few others, possibly non-residents, proved their wills in the Prerogative Court of Canterbury.[9] This proportion was perhaps twice as good as the proportion of yeomen and husbandmen who left wills, but many clergy whose wills it would have been a pleasure to inspect left no hostages to fortune, even in late Elizabethan times when the probate courts were apparently functioning at their most efficient level.

Turning from the general problem of using inventories as a source of information to the specific question of credit as it is answered in the probate records, we are hedged about no less by dense thickets of doubt and uncertainty. It is possible to say how many of the clergy in particular parts of the country died with money owing to them, as a proportion of those who left inventories, in the later sixteenth and during the seventeenth centuries. It is seldom, however, that we can identify the debtors or place them topographically or socially. Interest, too, is rarely if ever mentioned in the inventories, or in the wills, which is not to say that it was not expected, merely that the appraisers were concerned only with the sum of the debts owing not with their composition.

In considering the system of credit as it operated in England before the eighteenth century, the chief technical problem facing us relates to the types of debt recorded in the inventories of the period. Three categories are commonly mentioned, mortgages, bonds and bills (or notes), the first two of which were alternatively described as 'debts upon specialty', and the last as 'debts without specialty'.[10] When all or any of these descriptions are employed it seems fair to assume that the testator was, in some sense, a genuine money-lender, if not necessarily a professional 'usurer'. Few clergy in our period had the means to lend sums of money on mortgage, since conjoint investment in loans and the practice of assignment were still illegal. The bond, which in essentials was a formal, contractual loan against security other than real property, is, however, commonly mentioned in our batches of clerical inventories. That it was a weapon in the money-lenders' arsenal is evident from the formulation of the bond, which was a written document specifying the sum advanced, the term of the loan and, generally, the rate of interest charged. As a rule it was an instrument of credit employed when loans were arranged to run for periods of months rather than of weeks. The term 'bill' is more ambiguous, but its commonest meaning was synonymous with 'note of hand' or 'promissory note', and as such it again was a customary device of the accredited money-lender to secure his loans. When these terms are found in contemporary documents they leave no room for doubt about the institutional nature of credit transactions, at least by the early seventeenth century.

More problematical are the references to unpaid debts for goods or services rendered. Sales credit formed a major element in the indebtedness of the period, and the parsons who were farmers or dealers had as much opportunity to give or take credit as their peasant or artisan neighbours. Moreover, even in their official functions, clergymen handled money or goods from their parishioners in the form of tithes or fees payable to their office, and delay in meeting their obligations caused defaulters to be numbered among the parsons' debtors. Now whether we should admit such outstanding dues as credit in our analysis is doubtful. When so many payments to the clergy were made under protest and dilatoriness could be explained as a political act of will, indebtedness can be described neither as a voluntary transaction nor as the consequence of *economic* necessity. On the other hand, the person withholding payment of tithe or mortuary might thereby gain an economic respite or advantage in his own business, so that the effect of deferred settlement could be similar whatever its cause.

Table 10 presents the data of clerical inventories collected by the author from the archives of Norwich and Lincoln. Whether the data are representative of the whole country in the period from 1560 to 1700 is not certain. Even within these two large bishoprics it has not been possible to examine every archdeaconry or subsidiary district. The basis of the table is evidence from the archdeaconries of Lincoln, Norwich, Norfolk and Sudbury, although no breakdown of the data from each district has been attempted, owing to the comparatively small number of inventories from each archdeaconry and the homogeneity of the sample.

The periods chosen are not significant. Each represents roughly a generation except the last which has been prolonged because the number of inventories drawn up, or preserved in the records, after 1660 was much lower than before the Civil War.

It may be inferred that between one-quarter and one-third of the English clergy were, in some sense, creditors of relatives, friends or neighbours before the eighteenth century. None of our sample appears to have driven a large money-lending trade, though of course the evidence from inventories may mislead in disclosing only the material circumstances of men who, upon the point of death, may have retired from, or given up any such activity. Eighteenth-century clergy were often rich enough to possess diverse interests in lending or investments. Not a few apparently owned portfolios of loans, shares, annuities, mortgages and promissory notes apt to spread their risks to avoid drawing fire upon them from discontented opponents of clerical affluence. Indeed, according to the authority on corporate financing in eighteenth-century Britain, much of the funds provided for

Table 10: *Clergy inventories analysed to reveal money-lending (select parts of Lincoln and Norwich dioceses)*

	Inventories	Valuation of personal effects (£)	Clergy with debts A	B	Valuation of credits (£)	Valuation of known loans (£)
1560–90	58	2,784	28	13	342	32.67
1615–45	60	7,080	42	23	1,084	138.40
1670–1720	47	6,533	32	17	869	197.55
Total	165	16,397	102	53	2,295	368.62

Note: Columns 4 and 5: 'A' refers to the total number of clergy with debts owing to them at the time of death in the sample; 'B' refers to those clergy whose estates included 'credits' of at least one quarter of the aggregate valuations of their personal effects. In column 7 'Loans' relates to credits designated by terms such as Bills & Bonds, Debts upon Specialty, etc. which are to be interpreted as deliberate loans; most 'credits' recorded are unspecified.

Sources: Inventories deposited and calendared in the Lincolnshire Archives Office, Norfolk and Norwich Record Office, and the (former) Bury and West Suffolk County Record Office. The items are calendared and boxed by year and were extracted from the mass of probate inventories by the technique of rapid searching – i.e. the details of each inventory were largely ignored in preference for collection of aggregate valuations and the valuation of debts owed to the deceased. Where possible administration accounts were also searched.

shares or debentures was drawn out of English parsonages. It is doubtful whether such clerical investors existed in Elizabethan England; the social milieu of the Anglican clergy changed almost beyond recognition between 1580 and 1780. But the inventories also disclose no sign of the Dr Bennetts of the contemporary scene. They suggest that the clergy who held 'credits' were very like the farmers and tradesmen of equivalent wealth. Thus whereas 14 per cent of clergymen's personal wealth was classified as credits, the proportion in a sample of farmers' inventories of the seventeenth century, for roughly the same geographical area, was 9 per cent and of tradesmen's inventories, 13 per cent. Moreover, in each case only one-third or two-fifths of the group possessed 'credits' in their tally of personal wealth. The resemblance between clerical and 'plebian' inventories was much closer than that between clerical and gentry inventories. None of these figures takes account of debts owed by the deceased, although it is certain that some at least of the clerical testators, like those among the agriculturalists and tradesmen, were actually insolvent when they died. Not enough of the surviving documents are in the form of balance-sheets for us to ascertain the actual financial standing of the clergy, but it is significant that when a detailed account of both assets and liabilities is provided, it shows that most creditors were also debtors to other people. To some extent this is simply the result of the suddenness of death, for among both credits and debts were bills unpaid for comparatively recent transactions that have nothing to do with any system of credit, but enough survives, however fragmentarily, to indicate that some individuals were both borrowers and lenders, deliberately and according to some rational principle difficult now to interpret; for among the many thousands of inventories and administration accounts inspected by the present writer are a few dozen listing both bills and bonds owed by the testators and bills and bonds owing to them.

Table 10 above corroborates the evidence of Brooks, Hill and others that some increase in clerical wealth, and presumably of clerical incomes and standards of comfort, took place before the Civil War. Set in the context of the so-called 'price revolution,' however, the improvement was not spectacular, though it is apparent that the clerical accumulation of property more than kept pace with rising prices. The explanation is complex, but seems to have owed more to the non-clerical avocations of the parson than to any major improvement in value of his benefice. The rise in agricultural prices, which far exceeded the increase of wages or industrial prices, profited the clergy as farmers, but it also raised the value of some livings substantially by enlarging the incumbents' expectations from tithes, especially when parish clergy were able still to enjoy the profits of the great tithes, for grain prices were particularly elastic. Additionally the clergy who owned land, or who could let the glebe of their livings on short leases, gained a good deal from the upward pressure upon land rents in the same period. But since the majority of country parsons were husbandmen, often possessing farm goods and livestock equivalent to the stock in trade of passing rich yeomen, they gained most from the profitability of agriculture in Tawney's century.[11] But even in the seventeenth century the range of clerical wealth exhibited in the inventories was very wide, rising from less than £5 altogether (two cases) to more than £700 of personalty. The median valuations, however, seem to have reflected general conditions quite faithfully, for the modes in each period are very close to both means and medians. Many clergy left goods valued at around £50 in the 1570s and at around £130 in the

1680s, and the cases which were far outside the standard of deviation can be interpreted as *sui generis*. The very poorest were apparently aged priests, the richest (those with personal estates in excess of £400) were gentlemen, prosperous graziers or well-endowed pluralists. They were already men of higher standing in the agrarian community than the common run of parsons, in spite of the fact that many, perhaps a majority of them, had reached the high plateau of social influence by their own efforts as place-seekers or entrepreneurs.

There remain problems of interpretation affecting the 'deep structure' of pre-industrial systems of credit. Given that borrowing and lending were immanent in agrarian societies – even in those which were not fully monetized – whether the nature of this credit was malignant, as Tawney tended to believe, or positive and perhaps benign, as the present writer avers, it is still to be proved that the instruments of credit available to our ancestors before 1750 were used to the full extent of their potential as agents of capitalist transformation. Leading merchants and financiers were clearly capitalistic in outlook, but the attitude of gentry, clergy and peasants is much more problematical. Among the clergy, indeed, the tensions engendered in the doctrinal prohibition of usury at a time when its practice was being extended almost certainly induced or reinforced hesitation and ambiguity. The parish priests of the age, being of the people, were sensitive to popular feelings. On the other hand their plebeian origins placed the clergy in a setting in which they readily understood both husbandry and trade. Parsons who sprang from peasant or mercantile stocks not only fell easily into non-sacerdotal avocations of a commercial character, farming, manufacturing, commodity dealing, or in the case of the poor, labouring and menial service also, but clerical by-employments were indistinguishable from those pursued by the laymen in their congregations. The common ground of worldly experience among clergy and lay-folk was further enlarged by the habit of clerical marriage, and by the fact that very many of the clergy before 1600, and a substantial minority in the seventeenth century, were ill-equipped by education or propensity for learning and contemplation. Scholarly detachment as much as breeding severed clerk and people in later ages of the Anglican Church. It may even be true that the Protestant emphasis upon the priesthood of all believers undermined the particularity of the clergy, despite the protracted attempts of the Church to maintain its ecclesiastical jurisdiction, and despite the strenuous new demands of the reformers for a godly and exemplary ministration of the Word. When parsons were recruited as often from serving-men as from scholars, and more often from farmers' sons than from the gentry, their economic and social position coincided with the outlook, and as far as one can discern, with the social behaviour of peasants or petty bourgeois.

This is important because the background in which clerical money-lending was set was filled with figures whose economic behaviour had already outpaced traditional or doctrinal tabus. As William Harrison expressed it in the 1570s, 'Usury [is] now perfectly practised almost by every Christian and so commonly that he is accounted but for a fool that doth lend his money for nothing.'[12] Harrison, moreover, was not only a clergymen of Puritan predilections, but had served as an official in the Essex archidiaconal court, and his knowledge of human behaviour in matters affecting public morality was both subtle and extensive. Some social anthropologists have questioned the institution of ubiquitous interest charges in primitive, pre-industrial or agrarian credit systems, on the grounds that men and women who borrowed, or made their savings available for others to use, in societies in which the links between individuals were founded upon kinship, affinity or neighbourhood, expected not a monetary penalty or reward, but some other service as their lot in discharge of the obligation. This makes it difficult to assume that parsons and other men acted on rational principles of judicious cupidity throughout the period about which we write. For the anthropologists, however, self-interest cannot always be expressed in terms of money. Instead of interest, the money-lender might prefer to receive less tangible benefits in return for his liberality, the hope of future help or accommodation, good will, family loyalty or family honour; and his service to the neighbourhood might even be interpreted as a branch of good works or as the emblem of familial piety. For the clergy, acting both on their own behalf and as the voice of conscience in the community, such reflections of social duty accorded well with Biblical teaching and theological tradition, which emphasized not only the spirit of charity but the reciprocity of human relationships.[13] Nevertheless, cogent as are the arguments of the anthropologists, they are not entirely supported by evidence from modern pre-industrial societies, where forms of interest charges have often be devised even in communities not familiar with the use of money. And even in sixteenth-century England, there is no direct evidence that men expected *not* to pay in cash or in kind for the amenity of a loan. Bonds which do not mention rates of interest almost always contain provision for swingeing penalties of up to twice the value of the principal, in the event of repayment out of time. The custom of receiving an additional payment by way of a gift for the use of a loan was also widespread, though this was frequently a fiction to cover the taking of fixed interest, when, as in the case of Mark Simpson in Essex, it was thought expedient to offer excuses for an unpopular transaction.[14]

The idea of interest, however, was already fixed in the management of undertakings close to the parson's earthly orbit. The custom of lending funds to worthy men, to give them a start in life or to help them in temporary crisis, had long been a feature of the administration of parochial stocks dispensed by churchwardens or other parochial officials, sometimes including the incumbents themselves. Among activities such as the hire of cattle or sheep to villagers, or the operation of a common brewhouse, which at a very simple and local level resembled the agricultural credit societies of modern peasant economies, the churchwardens also frequently lent out parish money at interest. John Aubrey recalled a tradition, moribund or dead in his day, at Frensham in Surrey where a great 'kettle' or cauldron was kept in the church, which, if anyone 'went to borrow a yoke of oxen, money, etc. he might have for a year, or longer, so he kept his word to return it.'[15] The Twelve Men of St Columb, Cornwall, drove a flourishing business in money-lending out of parochial funds, receiving goods in pawn or issuing notes of hand to the debtors. In 1590 the rate of interest charged was 5 per cent, much below the rate regarded as usurious, but accepted by those who took part in the scheme as just recompense for the use of parish money.[16] Similar practices were found elsewhere and had been in use so for a long time before the sixteenth century, as the early series of churchwardens' accounts for St Michael's, Bath, testify.[17] Whether churchwardens as money-lenders were ubiquitous in England before the early seventeenth century is unknown, because so few of their accounts have survived or have been published, but there is no reason to believe that this part of their activities was restricted to the few examples available to us. The point of the discovery that parish vestries or individual officials traded in loans at interest is that it proves an institutional credit system close to the heart of the parson's living was thoroughly established at the time when evidence for clerical money-lending is readily to be found in contemporary records. The connection is circumstantial or contingent, but quite probable none the less.

By the eighteenth century the Anglican clergy were acknowledged to be useful as a source of credit or investment. Parsons and their immediate families were frequently to be found making loans, giving sales credit or entrusting their savings to public utility investments, into bank stock, Consols or insurance stock. There were clergy among those ruined in the South Sea Company mania, and others who contributed significantly to the building of canals and turnpikes.[18] Many, however, among whom were the 'investors', used their spare cash for personal loans. Men like Samuel Whiting or John Willan in eighteenth-century Lincolnshire were significant links in a long, rather unarticulated chain of credit in the region.[19] But for every clergyman who drove the business himself, there were two or more who preferred to put their savings at the disposal of provincial attorneys whose skills and knowledge of the trade were extensive and, by 1750, unparalleled, at least in the matter of negotiating 'middle-class' loans. The parson who gave credit compassionately or in neighbourly fashion to kinsfolk or fellow-villagers casually and at haphazard – a man who was neither a John Bennett nor a Samuel Whiting – was still a familiar character in the scenes of village life, and so remained at least so long as his kind was not distanced by superior wealth and gentility from the village community whose cure he served. More research needs to be done on the subject of rural credit and the social groups which made use of its facilities, but there can be no doubt that the parson – though not all parsons individually – played a modest but important part in its development and organization between 1550 and 1700.

NOTES

1. R. H. Tawney (ed.), *Thomas Wilson's Discourse upon Usury* (1925), 17–30 and *passim*.
2. Tawney, *op. cit.*, 22 (*my italics*); the theme is elaborated in his *Religion and the Rise of Capitalism* (1922), which is more diffuse but otherwise very like the introduction to *Thomas Wilson*.
3. Proceedings relating to 'debts', which was a term more embracing than the modern use of the word implies, are to be found in several classes of judicial records at the PRO, e.g. C131,239 (Extents for debts, 1320–1649), C103–14 (Chancery Masters' Exhibits) and 6117–26, C1–3, 5–13 Chancery Proceedings, REQ. 1–2 (Court of Requests Documents) and WARDS 9 (Debt cases before Sheriff Courts), many of which have not yet been fully listed or even sorted. The intractable nature of this material has deterred the present author from anything other than a cursory examination. For some background information the introduction to A. Conyers (ed.), *Wiltshire Extents for Debts, Edward I – Elizabeth I*. (Wiltshire Record Society, XXVIII, 1973), is useful.
4. A few examples are found in W. Hudson (ed.), *Leet Jurisdiction of City of Norwich* (Selden Society, V, 1892), 35; A. T. Bannister (ed.), *Registrum Thomae Spofford* (Canterbury and York Society, 1919), 52; W. Brown (ed.), *Register of Thomas of Corbridge, Archbishop of York (Surtees Society CXXXVIII, 1925), I, 187–8. See also the volumes published by the Surtees Society of The Acts of Chapter of the Collegiate Church of Ripon*, LXIV (1875); and *Ecclesiastical Proceedings from the Courts of Durham*, XXI, 1845, *passim*.
5. *CStp Dom* Eliz. CCLXXXVI, 19–20.
6. F. G. Emmison, *Elizabethan Life: morals and the church courts* (Essex County Council, 1973), 73. The whole book is useful to set the context of usury in the framework of ecclesiastical jurisdiction.
7. F. W. Brooks, 'The social position of the parson in the sixteenth century', *J. British Arch. Assoc.*, 3rd ser., x, (1945–7), 23–37.
8. The printed sources of clerical inventories cited here are M. Cash, *Devon Inventories of the Sixteenth and Seventeenth Centuries* (Devon and Cornwall Record Society, N.S. XI, 1966), 55–6, 146–7; J. Moore (ed.), *The Goods and Chattels of our Forefathers* (1976), 52–53; J. P. Earwaker (ed.), *Lancashire and Cheshire*

Wills, II (Chetham Society, XXVIII, 1893), 31–2; P. Kennedy, *Nottinghamshire Household Inventories* (Thoroton Society, XXII, 1967), no. 118; Earwaker, *op. cit.*, 45.

9. An estimate of my own, *marrying* the data of clerical benefices and incumbencies in C. W. Foster (ed.), *The State of the Church* (Lincoln Record Society, XXIII) with the Calendars of Inventories and Wills for the period in the Lincs. AO.

10. This is in fact something of an over-simplification, for the term 'bill' is really very ambiguous, referring apparently to several different species of debt from a bond to an unpaid invoice for goods, but the distinction between 'bonds' and 'bills' was generally maintained in the way suggested in the text.

11. The wider context is discussed in Hill, *Economic Problems*, pt II, esp. ch. IX. See also J. H. Pruett, *The Parish Clergy under the Later Stuarts* (Urbana, Ill., 1978) esp. pp. 100ff.

12. William Harrison, *A Description of England* ed. G. Edelen (Ithaca, N.Y., 1968), 203.

13. My attention was drawn to this by Dr Alan Macfarlane. Monographs of economic anthropology, however, are much more ambiguous concerning the development of lending at interest: see, for example, R. Firth and B. S. Yamey (eds.), *Capital, Saving and Credit in Peasant Societies*, (1964); M. J. Herskovits, *Economic Anthropology* (New York, 1960), 225ff.

14. A little light is thrown upon this aspect of borrowing by H. R. Trevor-Roper in his dispute with Lawrence Stone in, 'The Elizabethan aristocracy: an anatomy anatomized,' *EcHR*, 2nd ser., III (1951), 279ff., which relates obviously to an altogether more exalted social plane.

15. J. Aubrey, *Natural History and Antiquities of Surrey* (1719 edn.), III, 366.

16. T. Peter (ed.), 'St Columb Green Book', *J. Roy. Inst. Cornwall*, XIX (1912).

17. See, for example, *Churchwardens' Accounts of St Michael's Bath* (Somerset Arch. and Nat. Hist. Society, 1878) *passim*. Other examples and a discussion is to be found in J. C. Cox, *Churchwardens' Accounts* (1913).

18. See, e.g. G. H. Evans, *British Corporation Finance, 1775–1850* (Baltimore, 1936), 35–8.

19. For Whiting see Lincs. AO, Dallas-Yorke Deposit, S. Whiting's Diary etc.; for John Willan, see A. H. Tindal Hart, *Country Counting House* (1962), xii–xiii, citing W. A. Pemberton, 'An Eighteenth Century Lincoln Clergyman', *L.A.A.S. VII/2*, 1957. Most clerical daybooks or accounts are still reticent about private financial affairs in the eighteenth century, but parsons do appear as clients in certain solicitors' papers, e.g. in the ledgers of David Atkinson of Louth, Benjamin Smith of Horbling and George Tennyson of Grimsby whose business papers have been in part preserved and are deposited at Lincs. AO. As a rule the parson is lender rather than borrower.

10

Episcopal incomes and expenses, 1660–c.1760

D. R. Hirschberg

Although historians have long pondered the financial underpinnings of the Church of England from the Reformation to its abolition in the 1640s, they have been slower to examine the economic foundations of Anglicanism in the late seventeenth and early eighteenth centuries. This may stem in part from the fact that Norman Sykes in his seminal work did more to give us realistic answers to older questions about institutionalized Church-State relations than to formulate broader ones about the relationship of Church and society. It may be due too to a feeling that a supposedly greater stability in the early eighteenth century rendered obsolete questions derived from an age of greater religious strife. For whatever reasons, the more explicitly economic questions asked of earlier Anglicanism seldom crossed the historiographical gulf separating the Laudian from the Restoration Church. Until quite recently, when commentators did notice the 'sordid' business of clerical getting and spending, they tended to repeat the jibes of contemporary critics against a supposedly greedy and sybaritic upper clergy; or at best they engaged in a form of economic antiquarianism, unearthing random information about clerical incomes or lifestyles and serving it up in general, rather formless works.

This essay has two aims: first, to gather and explicate in a more complete and coherent way the surviving data about the incomes and expenses of Anglican bishops between the Restoration and the mid-eighteenth century, and second, to derive from our discussion of the sources of and restraints on episcopal profits some broader theories about the duties and performance of bishops in particular, and the State Church in general. Some of our concerns are similar to those of authors of other essays in this volume, and we will note where their points seem useful for our period too.

The first task is to ascertain the value of the various bishoprics. This is more difficult than it might sound, for the only complete official valuation, the *Liber Valorum et Decimarum* of Ecton, is worthless for practical purposes. Although this was used right up to 1760 as the guide for the payment of first fruits and tenths, its sixteenth-century values provide little clue to either the absolute or relative income of sees. Indeed, some bishoprics were worth even less in the eighteenth than in the sixteenth century.[1]

There do exist, however, scattered accounts of revenues that may be pieced together, and this has been done in table 11. Ideally it would be possible to reduce all values to a uniform basis, but this proves to be unworkable. Some of the figures, including all those from a series of years, are taken from detailed account books of episcopal receivers. These we assume to be fairly accurate, and we have stripped them, whenever possible, to the base revenue – i.e., minus entry and renewal fines and supplementary offices held *in commendam*. For two points in time – listed as c.1710 and 1762 – there are fairly complete lists of values. The 1710s list is from the Wake MSS and the 1762 list is to be found in the correspondence of George III.[2] The other valuations appeared at random in correspondence and diaries.[3] For both the lists and random figures we are at the mercy of the documents, and must wonder whether fines or commendams are included. Certainly it is naive to think that by piling dozens of imperfect estimates on top of each other we can somehow transcend the weaknesses of the individual figures. Still, the valuations are consistent enough with the more reliable evidence we do have to establish at least a broad order of magnitude. Ecton values are given in parentheses, and all figures are rounded off to whole pounds.

There are at least two striking aspects to these figures. The first is the relative lack of very high base episcopal revenues. Even if we take only the highest valuation for each bishopric (knowing that these may well include some fines and commendams), before 1714 16 out of 25 bishoprics had £1,000 or less a year; 21 had £2,000 or less; only 3 had over £3,000. Between 1714 and the 1760s, 17 out of 26 were reported at best to have £2,000 or less; 14 to have £1,500 or less; and 5 to have £1,000 or less. To be sure, most Englishmen would have been deliriously happy to have the bishop of Bristol's yearly £500–600 and prelates were hardly paupers, but clearly few had the incomes of princes.

The second notable point is the great variation among bishoprics. To use presumably consistent data, in the 1762 list the richest see (Canterbury at £7,000) was rated at 15.5 times the poorest (Bristol at £450); the mean for the top five sees (£4,300) was 8.1 times the mean of the bottom five (£530). Even in the c.1710 list, which regrettably excludes many of the richest sees, the top five still averaged 3.3 times

Table 11: *Annual episcopal revenues*[4]

Diocese	Date	Value (£)	Comments
9 Poorest			
Bangor	c.1671	120	Clear, no commendam
(Ecton Value			
132)	c.1680	150	
	c.1710	400	
	c.1715	520	
	1721–2	1277	
	1729–31		
	1733–7	1348	Mean
	1737	1000	Clear
	1755	1522	
	1762	1400	
Bristol	c.1680	342	
(327)	c.1680	341	Rents
	c.1680	300 or less	Clear
	c.1688	350	
	c.1710	400	
	1737	600	
	c.1762	500	
	1762	450	
	c.1762	c.300	Clear
Exeter	c.1670	584	Without commendam
(500)	c.1710	500	Reserve rents
	1747	1300+	
	1762	1500	
Gloucester	c.1710	600	
(315)	1762	900	
	1781	900+	
Llandaff	1660	400+	Includes commendam
(155)	1675	365	Plus commendam
	c.1680	344	Plus commendam
	c.1710	300	
	1718	680	
	1729	581	
	1762	500	
Oxford	1690 or		
(382)	1699	700	
	c.1710	600	
	1752–57	542	Mean, without fines
	1762	500	
Rochester	c.1663	500	
(358)	c.1710	600	
	c.1721–2	500	
	1737	631	
	1738	1283	
	1762	600	

Diocese	Date	Value	Comments
St Asaph	c.1685	800	Maximum
(188)	c.1685	700	
	c.1690	500+	
	c.1705	300	Without the annexed archdeaconry or 3 sinecures
	c.1710	800	
	1721	1000–2000	
	1732	1300	Plus annexed archdeaconry
	1735	839	
	1762	1400	
St David's	1683	600	
(426)	1684	c.500	
	c.1688	405	Rents and pensions
	1707	450	
	c.1710	700	
	1720	681	
	1723	544	
	c.1744		
	–52	542	Without fines
	1752	c.700	
	1762	900	

9 Middling

Diocese	Date	Value	Comments
Bath and Wells	c.1665	1800	
(533)	c.1688	850	
	c.1710	1400+	
	c.1710		
	–25	1600+	Perhaps less
	c.1721	1500–1800	
	1762	2000	
Carlisle	1688	713	Rents and pensions
(531)	1707	755	
	c.1710	800	
	1734–5	825	
	1739	802	
	1743–4	791	Without fines
	1762	1300	
Chester	c.1663	473	
(420)	c.1680	744	
	1704	900	
	1707	900	
	c.1710	1000	
	1722	1295	Gross
	1762	600	
Chichester	1666	1000	
(677)	c.1680	800	Plus procurations
	1688	770	
	c.1710	1000	
	1762	1400	

Diocese	Date	Value	Comments
Hereford	c.1710	1000	
(769)	1762	1200	
Lichfield and	c.1660	1200	
Coventry	1690		
(560)	or 1699	900–1000	
	c.1710	1400+	
	1762	1400	
Lincoln	1660	1193	
(828)	1705	1000–1100	
	1707	c.1200	
	1715	1100	
	1762	1500	
Norwich	1692–		
(835)	1706	1529	Mean
	1705	1404	
	1718	1200	
	1761	2160	
	1761	2500	
	1762	2000	
Peterborough	1688	630	
(414)	c.1710	800	
	early 18th	1000	Maximum
	century		
	c.1740	1150	
	1747	c.1100	
	1747	1300	Maximum, in a very good year
	1762	1000	
	1764	1050	Clear

8 Richest

Diocese	Date	Value	Comments
Canterbury	1663–4	4523	
(2683)	1677	4384	
	1681–2	4317	
	c.1688	c.4000	
	1694–5	4196	Without court fees
	c.1700	5784	Mean for 7 years
	1711–14	4775	Mean, without fines
	c.1715	6000	
	1761–7	5242	Mean, without fines
	1762	7000	
Durham	1662	3915	
(1821)	1664	3500	
	1664	1500–1600	Clear, according to a bishop
	1762	6000	attempting to justify high renewal fines

Diocese	Date	Value	Comments
Ely	1683	1089	
(2135)	1684	1106	
	c.1688	2000	
	c.1700	2283	
	1707–8	2300	Plus institution fines
	1762	3400	
London	1679	3000+	Without fines
(1000)	c.1710	c.2300	Somewhat less
	1762	4000	
Salisbury	c.1675	1920	Without fines
(1385)	1762	3000	
	1766	under c.3400	
Winchester	1663	c.2000	Gross, maximum
(3193)	1663–4	3900	Rents and dues
	c.1670	3563	Gross; net = 2977
	1762	5000	
Worcester	1762	3000	
(945)			
York	1692		
(1610)	–1700,		
	1702–4	2524	Mean, rents only
	1743	4500	
	1762	4500	

as much as the bottom five (£1,430 as against £440).

While it no doubt aggravates the intellectual misdemeanour to calculate rates of change from figures in which we have less than total confidence, such comparisons might be instructive. It seems that valuations were rising from the beginning of our period until the end. Indeed the mean net yearly increase in base revenues for all sees was 1.0 per cent; or an extrapolated increase of 103.2 per cent (without compounding) for the period 1660–1760. In other words, the figures might suggest that revenues doubled. For 16 dioceses for which we have two readings at least 20 years apart before c.1710, the extrapolated increase between 1660 and 1710 is 45.5 per cent. This is surely overstated since the c.1710 list highlights the dioceses with the lowest absolute base incomes in the 1660s and 1670s, and also because many bishops immediately after the Restoration understated their revenues to avoid criticism of high lease fines or of clerical greed in general. A similar figure for 21 dioceses (not necessarily including the same 16) for 1710–60 would be 66.7 per cent. We do not want to argue on too subtle a level, but it seems quite plausible that revenues were rising overall, that they were at least holding steady in the half-century after

1660, and that they may have risen more sharply after that. By comparison, the Phelps Brown indexes indicate that builders' wages in the 1760s were 37.4 per cent higher than in the 1660s, and a unit of consumables 2.7 per cent lower. To be sure, prices continued to fluctuate greatly, but it seems probable that episcopal incomes more than kept pace with changing costs of basic commodities.[5]

These figures have tried to exclude lease-fines, which are doubly important to us. Firstly, they represent real income, and we need to know by how much to correct our base revenue figures. Secondly, it is more than likely that fines were the main source of the increase of episcopal revenues. (As we mentioned, the later figures may be assumed to include fines to some extent.) As studies of York and Durham show, much of the effective revenue from episcopal lands – and much of the control over profits – came from entry and renewal fines.[6] The standard rule of thumb was one year's income for a seven-year lease. In actuality the fines seem to have been much greater than that. An examination of 12 episcopal account books, covering a total of 75 years spread out over our entire period, shows the mean fines to have been 35.3 per cent of base annual episcopal revenues.[7] Thus we may need to add about one-third to the estimates in table 11. What is more, when we consider that the base figures we used already include not only some fines, but also some commendams and non-leased fees, then fines as a percentage simply of leased lands and offices would be still higher. In only two cases out of the 12 do we find that our artificially low fine percentage is less than the one-in-seven guideline.

York leasing books for this and the period immediately before encourage a relatively benign view of leasing policies.[8] The restraints of custom and usage on reserved rents, coupled with a legacy of long-term leases from the sixteenth century in some cases, well-nigh forced bishops and their stewards to manipulate fines in order to get closer to fair market improved value for their lands. High and frequent fines are not necessarily a sign of rack-renting, of the irresponsible desire of a bishop to make a quick profit at the expense of his successors, or of lax supervision by higher church leaders. Marcombe suggests that lessees may well have received both social and economic value for their fines, that such fines still left room for tenants to make fair profit. After all, no-one forced generations of lessees to renew their lease from the local bishop.[9]

In spite of the apparent gains in real income and successful circumventions of inflexible reserved rents, contemporary churchmen constantly sought to increase overall episcopal revenues by piling additional offices, held *in commendam*, on top of the bishopric. We could, of course, simply assume that bishops were greedy and overseers (lay and ecclesiastical) were lackadaisical or collusive. To many, commendams appeared at least triply deplorable. Firstly, they were a sign that bishops were spending too much time (and were probably being too pliable politically) in the quest for glittering prizes. Secondly, these additional offices – some of which were not sinecures – would get only a pitiful fraction of the bishop-pluralist's attention. Thirdly, less fortunate clergy would have the bread taken from their mouths. In reality, commendams were given out according to plans more logical and less deleterious.

In a handful of cases a sinecure rectory or a cathedral dignity was annexed formally to a bishopric, as were the archdeaconries of Bangor and Anglesey to the bishopric of Bangor, and the treasurership of Llandaff cathedral to the see of Llandaff.[10] For the most part, though, commendams were granted by the king to each new bishop on an *ad hoc* basis, even if the actual commendam remained the same. Certain offices traditionally came to be paired. For example, a visitor to Rochester Cathedral will find few of the bishops buried there, since most claimed their rights as deans of Westminster to be interred in the abbey.

A study of commendams reveals that the bishoprics supplemented were almost invariably those commonly held to be the poorest.[11] Throughout our period the bishops of Bangor, Bristol, Chester, Exeter, Gloucester, Llandaff, Oxford, Rochester, and St Asaph always received commendams. From various times from the late seventeenth century on, all occupants of the sees of Chichester, Hereford, Lichfield and Coventry, Peterborough and St David's came to hold additional posts. By the mid-eighteenth century many Bishops of Carlisle, Lincoln and Norwich were granted temporary commendams at the beginning of their incumbency.

At first this might seem merely to support those critics who claimed that the eighteenth-century bishops increasingly became pluralists, and more at the mercy of politicians who dangled preferment before them. However, the actual composition of commendams and their equalizing effect on episcopal revenues soften such images. Admittedly the percentage of episcopal appointments made with long-term commendams (i.e., held for more than two years) rose from 46.7 per cent of all appointments before 1714 to 68.9 per cent afterwards. But only 22.7 per cent of these commendams before 1714 contained cures of souls, and 35.3 per cent afterwards. Furthermore, since these poorest bishoprics were the ones with most frequent turnover, even these figures overstate the percentage of bishops at any given time who would be holding a cure of souls. While it might still be argued that a bishop who was also a cathedral dignitary or college president might discharge his secondary duties less zealously than others, this is different from bishops depriving parishioners of a resident minister, or a worthy starving clergyman of a chance to tend a flock.

What is more, the fact that commendams were handed out in a logical way, to supplement the poorest sees, narrowed the gap between them and the middling sees. Thus there was less reason for such poorer bishops in the eighteenth century to covet a translation to a see that in the late seventeenth century would have been far richer than their own. Granted, some sees were simply more prestigious than others, and some of the poorest sees were despised because they were in undesirable parts of the country like Wales. However, the crude economic motive for promotion became less compelling as time went on.

From the commendams whose value we know for certain, coupled with our estimates of base revenues and fines, we imagine that the supplemented sees were worth £1,200 to £1,600 at the beginning of the eighteenth century and £2,100 to £2,800 by mid-century. The one notable exception was Llandaff, which lagged behind the others. Such values seem even more likely when compared with the reputed values of the poorest non-supplemented sees, which are close to our high estimates. Incidentally the earlier figure tallies nicely with the £1,300 offered by Gregory King in 1688.

How rich were bishops? In other words, how adequate were these gross revenues for the demands made upon them? In determining episcopal expenses we are blessed in having two complete sets of accounts that enable us to specify expenditures to the halfpenny. The personal account books of John Moore at Norwich and Thomas Secker at Oxford and Canterbury are detailed enough for us to separate their personal and official finances and to gain a view of the costs of a middling, a poorer and a rich see.[12] Moreover, these accounts seem quite typical when compared to other, partial lists of expenses.[13]

These books are cash books, so appropriate calculations have been made to transform them into general account books: duplicate transfer payments have been eliminated, and net ledger accounts have been restored to their gross receipts and allowed deductions. Payments to relatives were considered personal expenses, unless clearly specified to be church-related; thus official expenses may be artificially low. The yearly figures represent accounts cleared and not expenses incurred. Thus fluctuations from year to year may indicate irregularity in settling accounts, rather than wild swings in revenues and expenses. Both series are long enough for the mean figures to even out variations.

John Moore was named to the see of Norwich in 1691, to replace the non-juror William Lloyd. Late in 1707 he was translated to Ely, where he remained for the last seven years of his life. Thomas Secker was translated to Oxford in 1737, after three years at Bristol. His commendam with both sees was a small prebend of Durham cathedral and the prestigious rectory of St James, Piccadilly, Westminster. After 1750 he exchanged those places for the deanery of St Paul's. In 1758 Secker was raised to the primacy, which he filled until his death in 1768.

In tables 12 and 13, the so-called voluntary expenses in the last columns include charity by Secker and charity and books for Moore. The rationale for this disparity is that Moore was a notorious bibliophile who bought books for pleasure as well as the performance of his office. The figures for Secker at Oxford include his commendam. All figures have been rounded off to the nearest £.

Table 12: *John Moore's income and expenses, 1692–1707*

Year	Clerical income (£)	Clerical expenses		Clerical and voluntary expenses	
		Value (£)	% of income	Value (£)	% of income
Norwich					
1692	1844	1698	92.1	1851	100.4
1693	1837	1608	87.5	1770	96.4
1694	2954	644	21.8	807	27.3
1695	1780	1352	76.0	1435	80.6
1696	1735	1833	105.6	1913	110.3
1697	2355	2007	85.2	2067	87.8
1698	2090	1658	79.3	1789	85.6
1699	1987	2708	136.3	2889	145.4
1700	1958	1759	89.8	2005	102.4
1701	2526	2348	93.0	2719	107.6
1702	1952	2027	103.8	2313	118.5
1703	1206	1289	106.9	1406	116.6
1704	1370	1503	109.7	1652	120.6
1705	1708	1667	97.6	1812	106.1
1706	1437	1331	92.6	1443	100.4
1707	2309	2510	98.5	2605	112.8
Mean	1941	1746	90.0	1905	98.1

Clearly Moore was living closer to the break-even point than Secker was. Even without expenditures on books and charity, Moore was clearing only 10.0 per cent of his revenues, while Secker averaged 23.6 per cent at Oxford and 26.1 per cent at Canterbury. The revenue figures are within the range of those we might expect from the first part of this essay except for Secker's at Oxford, when he had his rich deanery too. If anything, the revenues and thus the net income may be a bit high. During the period of these accounts, Secker's lease fines averaged a spectacular 103.2 per cent of his base episcopal income at

Oxford and 57.9 per cent at Canterbury, while Moore's averaged only 24.4 per cent.

It would be instructive to see in greater detail where the money went: first, to understand why the net income is but a shadow of the gross; and second, because the expenses reveal much about the duties and performance of the Church and its prelates. In table 14 we have broken down Secker's expenses at Oxford for 1757. Every effort has been made to assign all expenses incurred during 1757 to that year. We traced accounts cleared years later, and deducted expenses cleared in 1757 but incurred much earlier. Naturally the final figure is different from the 1757 expenses in table 13. Secker's expenses in

Table 13: *Thomas Secker's expenses paid and allowed, 1757*

Type of expense	Value (£ s. d.)			% of all expenses
Household	1205	18	3¾	54.0
Wages and salaries	202	8	0	9.1
Household goods and expenses	200	4	0	9.0
Repairs and maintenance	94	10	4¼	4.3
Provisions	708	15	11½	31.8
Food	563	4	8	25.2
Liquor	145	11	3½	6.5
Professional	320	12	9	14.4
Travel	263	14	5	11.8
Coach and horses	225	16	11	10.1
Other travel	10	17	6	0.5
Books	15	0	3	0.7
Habits[14]	65	18	11	3.0
Miscellaneous church expense	2	19	2	0.1
Taxes and fees	298	0	1¼	13.4
Charity	196	9	11	8.8
Miscellaneous	210	14	8½	9.5
Medical	69	18	8½	3.1
Other and unaccounted	140	16	0	6.3
Total	2231	15	9½	

table 14 represent about 85 per cent of his mean yearly expenses at Oxford, partly because this was not a year for a triennial visitation (which always cost more than the extraordinary fees collected), and partly because maintenance expenses were atypically low that year.

To judge from Secker, the bishops of England were spending their money as they ought: on taxes, charity (and much of Secker's medical

222 *D. R. Hirschberg*

expense was charity), professional expenses, and most of all on maintaining a significant household. Long-standing traditions of episcopal hospitality continued throughout our entire period. A decent bishop lived as any great man should. He kept a proper table, repaired his palace and outbuildings, made lavish shows of charity (in many

Table 14: *Thomas Secker's income and expenses, 1747–67*

Year	Clerical income (£)	Clerical expenses		Clerical and voluntary expenses	
		Value (£)	% of income	Value (£)	% of income
Oxford					
1747	2582	2875	113.4	3031	117.4
1748	3629	2882	79.4	3259	89.8
1749	1612	2588	160.5	2777	172.3
1750	3614	2595	71.8	2886	79.9
1751	2923	2756	94.3	3085	105.5
1752	2948	1954	66.3	2124	72.0
1753	3694	1661	45.0	1818	49.2
1754	3630	2863	78.9	3052	84.1
1755	2821	1725	61.1	1976	70.0
1756	2926	1865	63.8	2100	71.9
1757	3678	2245	61.0	2442	66.4
Mean	3096	2364	76.4	2595	83.8
Canterbury					
1759	7264	6050	83.3	6226	85.7
1760	7421	5433	73.2	5983	80.6
1761	9318	7082	76.0	7613	81.7
1762	8234	5279	64.1	6043	73.4
1763	8611	7265	84.4	8550	99.3
1764	7718	5388	69.8	6017	78.0
1765	8290	6371	76.9	7452	89.0
1766	8103	5431	67.0	6469	79.8
1767	7722	5391	69.8	6733	87.2
Mean	8076	5966	73.9	6787	84.0

cases ritual displays), and provided accommodation to influential travellers. Much of this was simply good lordship, or the benevolent side of a quasi-theatrical social system of paternalism/deference in the countryside. To omit such shows would be a false economy, for much of the respect – and the notion that the Church was part of an organic English society – would be forfeited. As Bishop Richard Hurd stated: 'It is taken notice of, you know, if things about me are not, as they should be.'[15]

Immediately after the Restoration bishops often faced extraordinary expenses. The iconoclasts and almost two decades of disuse had ravaged cathedrals and episcopal palaces. Bishops often had to go to law to re-establish title to lands and collect arrears. The central government (king and church leaders) were concerned that the Anglican Church show itself to be the lavishly splendid and humane alternative to the sects: this meant a succession of 'voluntary' gifts to the king and more truly pitiful sufferers, and strong encouragement to patronize learning and the arts. But it was not only the late seventeenth-century bishops who were staggered to discover the costs of the style in which they were supposed to live – the wages of a large household staff, the furnishings that needed to be moved or bought from a predecessor. However, not to spend according to their position have been unseemly.[16]

Bishops were political personages as well, and their political duties could also prove expensive. The expense of going up to London for Parliament could be dear: indeed, residentiary canonries in London cathedrals were increasingly given as part of commendams in the eighteenth century so that bishops could have a London house for the session. This was a great boon to the majority of prelates who had lost their properties in the capital at the Reformation. In the countryside, entertaining local worthies added to the food and (especially) the drink bills. We can only wonder whether other bishops were less scrupulous than the notoriously upright Secker about using episcopal revenues at election time.[17]

Moreover, while the overall net profit from episcopal revenues seems low, all agreed that the expenses of coming into a new see would reduce it to zero or less.[18] The standard rule of thumb was that the first four years in a see would be profitless, with costs of setting up an establishment and paying first fruits (one year's value in Ecton). Thus length of tenure of office played a key role in determining the overall profitability of episcopal service. When we consider that the average age at first appointment to the episcopate was 55 in this period, and 52 even after 1688, we can see how limited were the chances to amass great wealth. Over the period, fewer than half of all bishops (42.3 per cent) has as many as ten 'profitable' years of office. Even if we take the fairly high figure of 16 per cent net profit (roughly Secker's net after charity), this equals only about 1½ years' gross revenue. Only 21.6 per cent of all bishops had as many as six profitable years in one of the best bishoprics, which would be worth about one year's gross.[19] Ironically, one of the reforms sought most vigorously by bishops themselves – namely, a more regular system of promotion by seniority – served, when established in the eighteenth century, to shorten the time bishops had in the richest sees once they attained them. While a greater percentage of bishops did come to hold a rich bishopric, more also spent time in a poor one at the start of their career.[20]

What does all this suggest about some broader issues of church finance and the behaviour of churchmen? Earlier essays have raised some important questions about the relationship between the personal and public aspects of office-holding. Clearly such thoughts are germane for our period too. Bishops in the late seventeenth and early eighteenth centuries were aware of the possibilities of abuse and concerned about the criticism it might draw. We must constantly remind ourselves, however, that the blurred distinction applied to expenses as well as incomes. If there was but one purse into which personal and official revenues were put, there was but one purse to dip into for money to cover official expenses.

The purse was often less full than we may have imagined. In fact, some bishops with private means were appointed precisely because they could support the dignity of the see. The best born bishops were if anything slightly less likely than others to hold a rich bishopric. Prelates such as Lord James Beauclerk, the Hon. Henry Egerton, Sir William Ashburnham, Sir George Fleming and Herbert Croft (son of Sir Herbert) toiled till the ends of their days in middling sees for (to their minds) lamentable profits. While all accounts indicate that pre-Civil War bishops were of somewhat meaner birth than their successors, a marked rise can only be observed from the mid to late eighteenth century. Perhaps the continued dominance of the middling sort of bishop is to be explained by the moderate rewards of episcopal service. Certainly private wealth was the handiest supplement to episcopal revenues.[21]

We must also be careful in our assumptions about officeholding morality. We may be too ready to accept that ill-defined boundaries between public and private will foster lower standards. Actually, it appears that bishops were not amassing outrageous fortunes from officeholding, and that those who did profited more from longer service than from misappropriation of revenues. The Secker and Moore profit margins are moderate at best and dangerously low at worst — all the more when we remember the unspectacular absolute value of bishoprics and the limited number of profitable years in office. Elsewhere we have calculated that only 35 per cent of bishops were able to leave portions of £2,000 or more each to their younger children.[22] While this is hardly pauperage, it is but moderate return for a lifetime of successful service in a profession.

It is harder to explain away nepotism and church leases in episcopal families. These were common. Fully 73.5 per cent of bishops who had a son or son-in-law had at least one in a church or church-related place.[23] Rent books suggest that leases were granted to family or to friends in trust for family with great frequency.[24] Clearly such practices were accepted more readily then than they are now. We must distinguish between the acceptance and the motive, though. Such places and leases formed a major part of the benefits of episcopal service. Necessity as well as greed can explain apparent abuses.

It is important to recognize the sources of restraints on episcopal profits. Clearly there were official and supervisory pressures on bishops to limit their incomes in some cases, help from above in increasing incomes in others, and some official encouragement to spend those incomes in certain ways. The long-lived nature of these and other financial imperatives is also significant when we compare the post-1660 period with its predecessors.

Laudianism, whatever else it meant, represented an attempt to find a realistic level of episcopal incomes.[25] This aspect of Laudianism did not die after 1660. The very people who ran the Restoration Church rose in the Laudian Church, and these Sheldons, Sancrofts and Wards successfully bequeathed to their late seventeenth- and eighteenth-century successors a concern for the proper use of church resources. Church leaders continued to feel that church wealth was an instrument to create a propitious image for the Church, that obvious greed and mismanagement would alienate and anger vital lay and clerical supporters, but also that incomes must be sufficient to attract talent into the Church.[26] The result was a greater effort to redistribute those revenues already available to the Church: for example, by striving for more equitable promotion by seniority and logical commendam policies.[27] This was in contrast to an aggressive policy of taking more from the lay sector. Anglican tithe policy, for instance, seems to have been fairly cautious. Even the success in raising incomes through manipulating lease-fines probably owes more to the rising value of the lands leased than to a radical new leasing policy. For example, Archbishop Gilbert Sheldon's circular letter to bishops in 1670 urging them to convert leases from lives to years was a continuation of pre-Civil War schemes, and at best spread out the existing rents and fines more evenly among bishops.[28]

If we see that we are not necessarily dealing with one bishop against a monolithic institution, but rather a number of bishops who were the institution, we can understand how so-called institutional checks might operate. At its best, this was a group of like-minded churchmen, often friends since student days, patrons and even in-laws to each other's families. Or, to take a less rosy view, with limited resources available, the excess income of one bishop came at the expense of another who could watch out for his own interests. No one pushed harder than the bishops themselves for fairer translation and commendam policies, to forestall such inequities. There were also grittier remedies: one bishop could sue his predecessor in a see for dilapidations if the palace and grounds were left in disrepair. Notably, such dilapidations suits practically disappeared from the late seventeenth century on, and cash settlements between old and new bishops were remarkably low.[29]

Restraints did not come only from within the Church, though. Custom helped to determine greatly the sources of and demands on revenues. Traditional attitudes toward leasing practices made it difficult to raise rents. Even if fines could be levied to compensate, each new bishop had to fight the battle afresh. Custom also dictated the proper behaviour of a bishop, especially his social duties as a great man. If we consider popular ideas of Christian behaviour to be another type of custom, we have another source of that costly social duty, charity. Certainly the Anglican Church in this period gained support because it portrayed itself as the customary Church, as opposed to the unlamented innovators of the Interregnum. Such support, however, was not to be purchased on the cheap.

Our study of bishops' finances hints at the sorts of insights to be gained from examining the economic underpinnings of the Church. The activities of bishops as important landlords, consumers and redistributors of wealth should lead us to ponder the economic functions of all the clergy. In this volume and other recent works we see clergy as holders of significant tracts of land; surely we can ask the questions about the social and economic basis of their power that we would of lay landlords. Bishops were also great consumers and employers in their localities. We might wonder, for example, about the impact of cathedral chapters on the social and economic life of small and middling cathedral towns. Perhaps most intriguing are the ways bishops redirected the wealth of the countryside into quasi-governmental channels. Watching bishops use their revenues to pay their own taxes, maintain themselves while serving as legislators, supplement welfare systems with charity, as well as simply to run normal episcopal administration, we glimpse some of the hidden taxation in early modern England.

We have seen the inaccuracy of many myths not only concerning prelates' economic behaviour, but also their stewardship of the Church. Bishops maintained higher standards for themselves and gained lower rewards than we have hitherto thought. Some ramifications of this are important for general views of the Church. It may still have been necessary for eighteenth-century clergy to choose between their pocketbooks and their piety. Thus the post-Restoration Church élite may not have differed so greatly in their zeal from their Laudian predecessors. The relatively low rewards enticed few of those fabled younger sons of aristocrats, and attracted in their stead the sons of the middling sort. In turn these prelates pushed their own sons and sons-in-law into church service, because patronage was the main part of their disposable assets. The resultant overlapping kinship and professional groups eventually formed the nucleus of the clerical dynasties of which the Victorians were so proud. This is not to deny that there was contemporary criticism of an imagined ecclesiastical El Dorado, or of exaggeratedly high and low episcopal birth. Indeed, bishops felt unfairly maligned, and when frustrated in making their own case heard, often turned to their political allies to silence criticism. Whether this close partnership between top clergy and politicians won support from the Church of England is an open question.

When we mention support for the Anglican Church, it is appropriate to return to the thoughts in our introduction. At first it might seem singularly ill-conceived to urge historians of the late seventeenth and early eighteenth centuries to apply questions usually asked of the early seventeenth-century Church. After all civil war scholars are ever more inclined to turn to tightly controlled local studies and away from the problems of disentangling rising, falling and dysfunctional gentry, and theological, social and political puritans. Strange to say, though, this may be just the historiographical moment to examine the relationship between economic behaviour and religious belief between 1660 and 1760. As political historians have attacked the Namierian concepts of ideological sterility and socio-political consensus, they have re-opened the question of the nature and basis of Anglican support. The Church of England is re-emerging as what it surely was: the primary focus for religion in the nation. Moreover, the attachment to Anglicanism appears often to have been quite fervid: we see this in continual bigotry, and acrimonious theological and political controversy. Thus it is quite pertinent to analyse the state religion with some of the tools we have used to study Laudianism and Puritanism.

It is also apparent that much of our received wisdom about Anglican supporters has always been couched in socio-economic terms, and thus needs be tested against social and economic histories of the Church. One of the hoariest theories says that squires and parsons formed an alliance to run life in the localities. Another proposes a 're-ligious sandwich' with Anglicans at the top and bottom of society and a generous layer of dissent in the middle. Old notions about commercial pursuits and dissent die very hard. Thus social and economic statements about Anglican attachment are hardly new, although carefully designed and thoroughly researched social and economic histories may be. We need not adopt Weberian, Marxian or Whiggish apriorism, or even anecdotal empiricism: we can learn the pitfalls as well as the pertinence of such approaches from those who have used them. But as we come to understand how far into the eighteenth century seventeenth-century religious attitudes survived, we can feel less comfortable about erecting historiographical barriers at 1660, 1689 or even 1714.

NOTES

1. John Ecton, *Liber Valorum et Decimarum* (1711).
2. [William Wake?] to [Thomas Tenison?], [c.1710], Christ Church Library, Oxford, Wake MSS, Arch. W. Epist. 19, fos., 393–4; 'A List of the Archbishops, Bishops, Deans and Prebendarys. In England and Wales, in His Majesty's Gift. With the reputed Yearly Value, of Their respective Dignities, 1762', in J. Fortescue (ed.), *Correspondence of King George III* (6 vols, 1927).
3. National Library of Wales, (hereafter cited as NLW), B/EP/428–36, 632; John Evans to Wake, 6 October [1715?], Wake MS 7, f. 437; Bodl., Tanner MS 146, f. 74; All Souls' College, Oxford, 244, no. 170; John Potter to Wake, 26 October 1721, Wake MS 9, no. 135; Bodl. Tanner MS 28, f. 110a; BL Add. MS 5811, f. 96; A. E. Baker, *Bishop Butler* (1923), 28; L. Twells (ed.), *The Lives of Dr Edward Pocock . . . Zachary Pearce . . . and of Dr Thomas Newton* (2 vols. in 1, 1816), II, 171; Bodl., Tanner MS 129, fos. 5–6, 48, 85; PRO C/111/65; LPL 1485, 239; E. Tenison, *The True Copies of Some Letters, Occasion'd by the Demand for Dilapidation in the Archiepiscopal See of Canterbury*, (2 pts, 1716), I, 8; LPL 1729, fos. 31–2; E. Carpenter, *Cantuar: The Archbishops in their Office* (1971), 244; BL Carte MS 244, f. 141; Bodl., Tanner MS 127, fos. 69, 87; Cumbria RO, D.Sen.Flem. 9, 44, 115; Carlisle Public Library, Nicolson diaries, XXVI, 3–4; *ibid.*, XIII, 107; C. M. Lowther Bouch, *Prelates and People of the Lake Counties* (1948), 311; William Dawes to John Sharp, 8 July 1707, Hardwicke Court, Gloucester, Lloyd–Baker Sharp MS 78, 4/L 122; F. R. Raines, Introduction to *Notitia Cestriensis*, by Francis Gastrell (Chetham Society *Remains*, XXI, 1850), 3; Bodl., Tanner MS 144, f. 13; Bodl., Gough MSS, Cheshire 2, fos. 11–12; Henry King to Gilbert Sheldon, 23 April 1666, Bodl., Tanner MS 45, f. 73; *ibid.*, 148, fos. 95–7; *ibid.*, 92, fos. 10–11; Guy Carleton to Sheldon, 25 November 1664, Bodl., Add. MS C 305, f. 114; White Kennett to Samuel Blackwell, 21 August 1714, BL Lans MS 1013, f. 199; CUL Mm. 6.61, fos. 123–38, 139–54; *ibid.*, CC 95577–8; Edmund Gibson to [——], 26 July 1747, BL Add. MS 32712, f. 343; Bodl. Add. MS C302, fos. 108–9; S. Rudder, *The History and Antiquities of Gloucester* (1781), 298; E. D., *A Letter to the Late Lord Bishop of Lichfield and Coventry* (1699), 7; Sharp to Dawes, [c.22 July 1707] L–B, 78, 4/T 29; Gibson to Nicolson, 17 December 1715, Bodl., Add. MS A269, 51; NLW. 101B, 70–1; Bodl., Tanner MS 146, fos. 163–4, 165–6; Browne Willis to [Wake?], [c.1718], Wake MSS, IX, nos. 25, 26; Bodl., deposited MSS, c. 234, fos. 27–8; Edmund Pyle to Samuel Kerrich, 19 November 1761, E. Pyle, *Memoirs of a Royal Chaplain, 1729–1763*, ed. Albert Hartshorne (1905), 358; Humphrey Prideaux to Wake, 30 May 1718, Wake MSS, 20, f. 547; CUL Mm. 6.61, fos. 155–44; *ibid.*, CC 95579; Bodl., St Edmund Hall MSS, 55; Daniel Gell to Gibson, 28 July 1747, BL Add. MS 32712, f. 345; Joseph Wilcocks, Jr. to Zachary Pearce, 11 February 1763, Westminster Abbey Muniments, 64508; Francis Atterbury to William Morice, 5/16 May 1729, F. Atterbury, *Miscellaneous Works*, ed. J. Nichols (ed, 4 vols., 1789–90), III, 23; R. F. Williams, *Memoirs and Correspondence of Francis Atterbury* (12 vols., 1869), I, 426; E. Lee-Warner, *The Life of John Warner* (1901), 57; NLW, SA/Misc/473, 543; M. J. Sommerlad, 'The historical and antiquarian interests of Thomas Tanner, 1674–1735, bishop of St Asaph' (D. Phil, thesis, University of Oxford, 1962), 89 and n. 2; NLW SD/ERA/11, 14, Thomas Herring to Lord Hardwicke, 21 November 1752, BL Add. MS 35599, fos. 83–4; NLW Ottley MSS 532;

Lawrence Womack to William Sancroft, 9 July 1684, Bodl.Tanner MS 32, f. 85; Womack to Sancroft, 17 September 1683, *ibid.*, 34, f. 136; E. A. O. Whiteman, 'The episcopate of Dr Seth Ward, bishop of Exeter (1662 to 1667) and Salisbury (1667 to 1688/9) . . .' (D. Phil. thesis, University of Oxford, 1951), 33; Bodl. Tanner MS 140, fos. 65–76; George Morley to Earl of Clarendon, 12 September 1663, Bodl. Clarendon MS 80, f. 198; L–B, 78, 4/Z(1); Herring to William Herring, 9 June 1737, Nottingham University Library, Portland MS PwV 120, no. 6; Duke of Newcastle to Thomas Secker, 8 August 1761, BL Add. MS 32926, f. 306; Richard Terrick to George Grenville, 5 May 1764, *ibid.*, 57819, f. 17; Nottingham University Library, Portland MS Pw2Hy 860; Newcastle to John Hume, 16 October 1766, BL Add. MS 33070, f. 393 and *ibid.*, Egerton MS 2181, f. 52; Herring to William Herring, 31 March 1743, Nott. UL PwV 120, no. 41; N. Salmon, *The Lives of the English Bishops from the Restauration to the Revolution* (London, 1731–3), 35 n. 4; N. Sykes, *William Wake, Archbishop of Canterbury 1657–1737* (2 vols., 1957), I, 158. I am grateful to the warden and fellows of All Souls', Col. A. J. Lloyd-Baker, the Church Commissioners, and Dr M. J. Sommerlad for permission to use their materials.

4. To bring some order to these data, we have divided bishoprics into three broad categories, according to common contemporary perceptions of their desirability. See D. R. Hirschberg, 'A social history of the Anglican episcopate, 1660–1760' (Ph.D. thesis, University of Michigan, 1976), 314–15.
5. E. H. Phelps Brown and S. V. Hopkins, 'Seven centuries of the prices of consumables compared with builders' wage-rates,' in *Essays in Economic History*, ed. E. M. Carus Wilson (1966), II 195–6. Comparisons are based on the means for the decades 1660–9 and 1750–9.
6. See above, pp. 96–7 and below, pp. 257–8.
7. Hirschberg, *op. cit.*, 378–9.
8. See above, p. 97 and Hirschberg, *op. cit.*, 386–8, which is based on BI MS Bp Dio 2.
9. See above, p. 263.
10. Hirschberg, *op.cit.*, 449, no. 7.
11. *Ibid.*, Appendix 3, and LPL, F/1 Index.
12. CUL CG 95579–80; Bodl. St Edmund Hall, 55; LPL 1483, with further information from LP, 1729.
13. Hirschberg, *op. cit.*, 395–406.
14. This is based on clothiers' bills, which include the cost of servants' livery.
15. Richard Hurd to Gertrude Warburton, 1 March [c.1777], BL Egerton MS 1958, f. 71. See also J. Britton, *The History and Antiquities of the See and Cathedral Church of Lichfield* (1820), 60; Pyle to Kerrich, 20 August 1752, Pyle, *op.cit.*, 178; Bodl. Tanner MS, 146, f. 127; J. Wilford, Preface to W. Dawes, *Works* (3 vols., 1733), I; xxiv–xxv; Salmon, *op. cit.*, 277; Nicholas Stratford to Ralph Bathurst, 21 November 1691, in T. Warton, *The Life and Literary Remains of Ralph Bathurst* (1761), 83–4,
16. BL Lans. 986, f. 136; Bodl., Bodley MS 898, f. 188; Bodl. Tanner MS 141, f.103; W. Hutchinson, *The History and Antiquities of the County Palatine of Durham* (3 vols., 1785–94), III, vii; Carleton to Sancroft, 16 April 1683, Bodl. Tanner MS 149, f.62; John Lake to John Milner, 10 April 1688, BL Birch MS 4274, f. 115; LPL 1729; Bodl. Add. MS C305, f. 200.
17. J. Cosin, *Correspondence*, ed. G. Ornsby (Surtees Society LII, LV 1869–72), *II*: 22–4; Cumbria RO, D.Sen.Flem. 9; Carlisle Public Library Nicolson diaries, XXV, 10; Lancelot Blackburne to Wake, 8 December 1716, Wake MS 20, f.240; Cosin to Sheldon, 26 June 1666, Bodl., Add. MS C 305, fos. 85–96; H. C. Conybeare,

230   *D. R. Hirschberg*

Conybeare Wills and Administrations (4 pts, 1911–14), III, 35; J. Pelham to
Herring, 24 December 1747, LPL, 1130/1/96; John Butler to Lord Onslow, Guild-
ford Muniment Room, 173/2/1/116; *An Examination of the Life and Character of
Nathaniel Lord Crewe* (1790), 38.

18. Thomas Newton to J. Dealtary, 1 May 1762, Bodl., English Letters MSS, d.122,
f.140; Prideaux to Wake, 30 May 1718, Wake MS 20, f.547; Robert Frampton to
Sancroft, 19 February 1680/1, Bodl. Tanner MS 37, f.256; P. J. Dunn, 'The political activities of William Nicolson, bishop of Carlisle 1702–1718' (M. A. thesis,
University of London, 1931), 118; Hugh Boulter to Newcastle, [18 February
1726/7], Carlisle Public Library Nicolson diaries, XXXI, 34; Boulter to Gibson
[c.18 February 1726/7], *ibid.*, 35; Sykes, *op. cit.*, I; 70–1; Sheffield City Libraries,
Bag. C. 330, no. 23.

19. Hirschberg, *op. cit.*, 406–8.

20. *Ibid.*, 314–16.

21. Salmon, *op. cit.*, 186, 311; Hirschberg, *op. cit.*, ch. 3, Norman Ravitch, 'The social
origins of French and English bishops in the eighteenth century, HJ, VIII (1965),
309–25.

22. Hirschberg, *op. cit.*, 417.

23. Ibid., 424.

24. Ibid., 418–19, and above, pp. 102–3.

25. See above, pp. 129–30.

26. John Nicholson to Sheldon, 10 February 1671/2, Bodl. Add. MSC 302, f.85;
C. Wren, *Parentalia* (1750), 31; Balliol College, Oxford, MS 342, f.14; T. S. Evans
(ed.), *The Life of Robert Frampton* (1896), 160; D. R. Thomas, *The History of the
Diocese of St. Asaph* (3 vols., 1908–13), I, 122; NLW 6717C, f.182; University
College of North Wales, Bangor, Penrhos MSS, I, 567; Humphrey Humphreys to
Anthony a Wood [c.1682], BL, Lans. 986, fos. 10–11.

27. Hirschberg, *op. cit.*, 342–4.

28. Gilbert Sheldon to all bishops and deans, 29 July 1670, BL Harl. MS 7377, fos. 16–
17.

29. Hirschberg, *op. cit.*, 401–3.

11

The first five years
of Queen Anne's Bounty

Ian Green

When it became known that Queen Anne intended to create an organization to help poor clergy and to endow it with her own money, the supporters of the established Church vied with each other in their praise of her generosity.[1] In the event their gratitude was well founded, for in the first century of its existence Queen Anne's Bounty raised over £2,450,000 from various sources and made over 6,400 grants to poor livings in England and Wales.[2] Although the largest strides towards the elimination of clerical poverty would be made in the nineteenth century, Anne's initiative undoubtedly marked the decisive first step: the perfecting of a workable and enduring system of relief after the repeated frustrations, piecemeal attempts and short-lived successes of previous centuries.[3]

What distinguished the Bounty from earlier projects for reform was the large measure of co-operation between the three elements most involved – the Crown, the clergy, and the most important members of the laity. This was most evident in Parliament where a series of enabling Acts was passed quickly and smoothly between 1704 and 1717,[4] but was also visible in the way in which interested parties pooled their financial resources. The Crown made the largest individual contribution, of course, but it has not always been appreciated that in the first 30 years of the Bounty's operation private benefactors from both laity and clergy gave almost as much to augmentations as the Governors – £195,000 as against £227,000.[5] This situation was atypical: the Governors had to devote much of their early revenue to clearing encumbrances on their income (see below) and to other initial administrative expenses; equally, private benefactions proved to be at their peak in these years. Nevertheless the figures are revealing, and one of the purposes of this essay is to ask why Queen Anne's scheme proved to be much more acceptable than previous ones.

A second feature of the Bounty's early history, the considerable length of time that it took its officials to come to grips with the administrative demands of the scheme, may seem to reduce the significance of its popular appeal. The fact that there was a gap of ten years between the setting up of the royal corporation in 1704 and the voting of the first augmentation was a source of concern to the Governors of the Bounty themselves; and another ten years would pass before the maximum possible number of augmentations was being made regularly each year.[6] But it must be stressed that this slowness was not due to lack of effort; between them the Governors and their staff could muster plenty of expertise and enthusiasm.[7] The delays were due largely to the complexity of the Church's financial system, the product of centuries of accretion, made more confusing by the effects of changes in religious aspiration, political interference, and the movement of population. The apparently simple task of finding out how many poor livings there were and what their income was would take the Governors and the Church's officials over 15 years and in most dioceses at least three surveys, each one different from the last in its scope and results – a clear indication of the difficulties under which church reformers worked in the early modern period. It stands to the Governors' credit that although they were delayed they spent their time wisely, and though they sometimes underestimated the difficulty of their task, they were prepared to learn from their mistakes and to use all of the means at their disposal to advance the Bounty's interests.

The essence of Queen Anne's original scheme was simple: the Crown handed over its revenues from two types of clerical taxation, first fruits and tenths, to a corporation charged with raising the values of as many poor livings as possible. First fruits (the first year's profits of a living) and tenths (an annual payment of 10 per cent of the value of a living as given in the *Valor Ecclesiasticus* of 1535) had been paid to the Crown by the richer clergy since the Reformation. Poorer rectories and vicarages, worth less than £6 13s. 4d. and £10 respectively, and curacies were exempt. At the beginning of Anne's reign the combined value of the two taxes was about £17,000 *per annum*, and it was this sum that Anne transferred to the Governors named in the charter of 1704 to be used to increase the income of poor livings.[8] It was also hoped, as the statute of 1704 confirming the transfer made explicit, that 'such well-disposed persons as shall, by her Majesty's royal example, be moved to contribute to so pious and chartable a purpose' would do so through the royal corporation, and to this end various temptations were placed before potential benefactors, as will be seen shortly.

Despite its simplicity, the plan faced immediate problems. The Governors found it difficult to extract their full income from first fruits and tenths, partly because previous monarchs had given away much of the revenue as pensions to courtiers and others, and partly because the system of collection was plagued by an inability to collect arrears properly.[9] It took several years, and sums of money that could have been devoted to better ends, to buy out the holders of existing pensions. Equally it took a series of measures between 1704 and 1717 to rationalize the system of collection to the satisfaction of the officials concerned.[10] In the process the Governors came to the decision that it was uneconomic to pursue the incumbents of livings that had been relatively prosperous in 1535 but which had since become impoverished, and so in 1707 they sponsored a bill to discharge all livings currently worth £50 or below from payment of first fruits and tenths. This was an enlightened move and in the interest of greater efficiency, though it had the unfortunate side-effect of reducing their income to about £13,700 *per annum*.[11]

Another thorny problem for the Governors was to decide how this income could be used to the best effect. What was to be the level below which all livings would be eligible for help? At different stages various figures were considered: £80, £40, £50, £10, £35.[12] Within the category of deserving cases, which should have priority: the poorest or the most populous parishes? At different times Burnet, Kennett and Tenison had all bemoaned the problems of market towns without decent maintenance for the clergy, but there must have been powerful lobbies on the side of the poorest livings of all, for they carried the day.[13] Finally, what was the best means of helping the poor clergy: gifts of cash that would bring immediate and widespread relief but not necessarily any permanent improvement, or the investment of capital in land, a system that would yield definite long-term benefits but would take many more years to implement? In the end two basic principles were agreed: each augmentation should consist of a capital sum of £200 to be invested in a piece of land, the rents of which would accrue to the incumbent of the poor living concerned; and the cardinal criterion for augmentation should be simple poverty. Initially the most deserving cases were deemed to be those worth £10 or less, and within this group the first benefices to receive help would be chosen by lot, until all the names had come up. Then the Governors would move on to livings worth £20 or below, until they too had all been improved; and so on until all livings worth £50 or less had been augmented. Given that each augmentation would bring in about £10 a year in rents or interest, it was possible for the poorest livings to receive two, three, or four augmentations eventually. Thus the 6,400 grants referred to in the opening paragraph were directed to only 3,200 livings.[14] One important exception to the £10 rule was suggested to encourage private benefactors: where an individual or a corporation was prepared to help a living worth £35 or less by matching the

Bounty's £200 with the same or a greater sum of their own, the Governors would, subject to the availability of funds, help that living *before* other cures for which no such offer had been received.[15] The Governors' proposals proved acceptable to the queen, and were incorporated into the second charter issued shortly before her death. Other measures were needed, however, before the Governors were satisfied. In the summer of 1715 they secured the passage of a bill to extend and clarify their powers, plug some loopholes, add some further inducements to benefactors, and generally tie up loose ends, and finally in 1717 they sponsored the Act to regularize the collection of tenths by bringing it into line with that already used for first fruits.

The relatively smooth passage of a series of Acts from 1704 to 1717 was in sharp contrast to the storms that blew over most ecclesiastical issues at that time.[16] The fact that the Tories were strongly represented in the government and in Parliament at the start of Anne's reign obviously helped the Bounty through its early stages of development, because they were anxious to bolster up the established Church against the twin threat of dissent and deism.[17] Between 1702 and 1708 the country was ruled by a combination of forces that it had not seen for three reigns and more – a monarch who positively liked the Church of England and a set of councillors who were both willing and able to do that Church some good. But the Bounty was the property of no one party in Church or state. It was a Whig bishop, Gilbert Burnet, who had pressed first William and Mary and then Anne to take the lead in helping the lower clergy. The idea was taken up by the more conservative Archbishop Sharp in 1703, and greeted with joy by churchmen as diverse as Kennett and Atterbury.[18] When it came to steering the scheme through Parliament, it was the moderate Tory Godolphin rather than the High-Church Nottingham who was most active; and it was a Whig government that passed the last pieces of legislation after the accession of George I.[19] It is fair to say that both Tory and Whig politicians were prepared to use the Bounty to curry favour among the parish clergy; it was no accident that the Whigs found time for the bill of 1715 in the middle of an invasion scare. But the fact remains that both sides had a hand in its success.

An examination of the political rivalry of the period and of the more altruistic concern for moral and spiritual regeneration evident in the numerous societies then being set up provides a partial explanation of the Bounty's ready acceptance. But for a complete answer one needs to look also at the details of the scheme iself; the final terms of the Bounty were very cleverly drafted. The Governors antagonized neither the propertied orders by suggesting that they return part or all of their impropriations to the clergy, nor the clergy by proposing to redistribute the wealth of bishops and dignitaries among the clergy at large.

On the contrary the Bounty had something to offer almost all sections of society.

For the queen herself it provided two opportunities: to end the scandal whereby ecclesiastical taxes were diverted to support cast-off royal mistresses and their offspring; and to render the Church she loved some permanent service. Given the limited size of the civil list from which she had to meet her personal needs and reward her friends, the loss of first fruits and tenths represented a real sacrifice, and as a recognition of this the Governors inserted special privileges for the Crown into their rules. In the second charter, for instance, it was stipulated that each year two Crown livings worth £10 or less were to be considered before those in the hands of other patrons.[20]

For the aristocracy and gentry the scheme had various attractions. If they already possessed a poor living, there was the possibility of a free increment for its incumbent. There were one or two strings attached to such an offer, but the Act of 1715 pointed out that a proprietor was under no obligation to accept an augmentation if he did not wish to abide by the corporation' rules.[21] If a patron was prepared to donate as much as the Governors, his living would be dealt with before other livings for which no such offer had been received. If he would rather make the gesture in his will, he was allowed to make a bequest without having to go through the bother and expense of obtaining the licence of mortmain that would normally have been required.[22] If a gentleman did not possess an advowson, the Bounty could remedy that. As clause VIII of the 1715 Act recognized, the acquisition of the 'Right of Presentation, or Nomination to small Livings . . . may be a great Inducement' to private benefactors to come forward; if they then reached agreement with the Governors, all such arrangements over patronage would have the force of law. This clause was probably designed to cover presentations to two types of living, those whose patronage was not clearly established, for example very poor or isolated chapels that had not had a minister for some time, and those whose existing patron was open to pressure, for example a bishop with an impropriate rectory, or the incumbent of a mother-church with the nomination to a dependent chapel, either of whom might be persuaded to part with their title for the greater good of the clergy. (G. F. A. Best does not tell the full story when he says that the form provided in Ecton's *State of the Proceedings* envisaged a knight's acquisition of the patronage of a bishop's impropriate rectory; it actually provided for the transferring of the nomination of a dependent curacy from the vicar to a lay donor with the approval of the bishop – or to be precise in the case cited, the bishops and chapter – concerned.)[23] The offer of presentations found a number of takers, which was predictable given the prestige attached to patronage and the fact that an increasing number of sons of the gentry and the well-to-do had been entering the later Stuart Church.[24]

The richer clergy probably breathed a sigh of relief when the final provisions of the scheme were known. There was to be no revaluation of the basis on which they paid their first fruits and tenths, and no other penal clauses aimed against them. Instead they merely had to continue paying those taxes as before. The process of payment was actually simplified, and the notorious 'fifth bond', a later Stuart device holding the threat of higher assessments over the richer clergy, was cancelled.[25] Perhaps as a gesture of gratitude as much as piety, a number of the wealthier clergy emulated the gentry in making donations to poor livings.

Finally, for the poor clergy and their parishioners there was the prospect of a decent maintenance in years to come. From their standpoint it was reassuring that the Governors had taken great care to see that the augmentation reached its intended object, and that where possible further improvements in revenue or legal security were obtained. Thus it was expressly forbidden for the impropriator of a living which came up in the lottery to deduct the value of the augmentation from the salary of the incumbent, or for the minister of a mother-church to reduce the salary of a curate in a chapel of ease that was being helped by the Bounty. Clause IV of the Act of 1715 reassured those people who doubted if livings with ambiguous legal status, such as chapelries, could hold land in perpetuity as the scheme envisaged: all such cures once augmented by the Bounty would become 'perpetual Cures and Benefices' and 'be esteemed in Law, Bodies Politick and Corporate'.[26]

The rules in the second charter and the Act of 1715 showed not only an awareness of the realities of life in many poor livings, but also a shrewdness in judging how much carrot and how much stick were needed to make the scheme work. They went straight to the heart of the problem, but also guarded against misappropriation of funds by less scrupulous proprietors. By the doubling clause for livings worth £35 or less, they appealed both to the charitable and the speculative instincts of the day, and encouraged large numbers of impropriators and parishioners to donate sums of money which, if there had been an element of compulsion, they would certainly have baulked at paying. A recent commentator has expressed surprise that the Governors did not try to do more, but it may be suggested that the Bounty struck just the right note: any lower and it could have been accused of being faint-hearted, any higher and it would almost certainly have run into trouble with one of the groups that was otherwise prepared to give it active support.[27]

Before the Governors could begin the work of augmentation in

earnest, they needed an accurate and up-to-date record of poor
livings. No such information existed in the hands of the central authorities, either in Church or State,[28] and the task of obtaining it was to
prove one of the most protracted of the Governors' first duties. In February 1705, as instructed in the first charter, they asked the bishops to
inform them of 'the true yearly value of the maintenance of every
Parson, Vicar, Curate and Minister, officiating in any Church or
Chapel' in their dioceses 'for whom a maintenance of the yearly value
of £80 is not sufficiently provided'. The bishops were also to 'ask the
distance of such Churches and Chapels from our city of London, and
which of them are in towns corporate or market towns, and which
not, and how the several Churches and Chapels are supplied by
preaching Ministers, and where the Incumbents have more than one
living.'[29] To these the Governors added a question that was not in the
Charter: how many families were there in each poor parish?[30]

The questionnaire was sensible and reasonably well drafted, but
the method of conducting the survey was rudimentary. Bishops
ordered their officials to ensure that the clergy answered the queries
and then forwarded the replies to London, often without even bother-
ing to append their seals.[31] The results were soon in the Governors'
hands, for early in 1707 a detailed summary was being prepared. This
document alerted the Governors to the scale of the problem: 5,082
livings were below £80 in value, they were told; a breakdown of this
total showed that over three-quarters (3,826) were worth less than
£50.[32] Unfortuately from our point of view the reliability of this
survey must be called in question. It is clear from the returns, most of
which survive in the Church Commissioners' records, that their
quality was very variable.[33] Some gave precise valuations, others
round or approximate figures. In some cases information was given
that had not been requested, such as the names of incumbents or the
number of sermons preached each week; in others at least half of the
questions had been ignored, especially those touching pluralism,
numbers of families, and whether a market town or not.[34] Most
serious of all, the replies concentrated heavily on rectories and
vicarages; a few dioceses either mentioned no lesser cures at all or only
a handful, and several others referred to curacies and chapelries only
under the mother-church and gave no separate indications of income
or size.[35] To some extent the neglect of these cures was accidental: the
printed form listing the questions in a tabular form was a misleading
document, the first column asking for the name of the parish church,
and the second for the name of any chapels. It was not at all clear how a
chapel with parochial status should be entered, or whether separate
details for chapels of ease were needed; and the variety of ways in
which respondents filled in these columns indicates the confusion

caused. It should also be remembered that virtually all episcopal
surveys in previous centuries had concentrated on rectories and
vicarages and that it would take time to break down the assumption
that they were all the authorities were really interested in.[36]

The first survey was barely over before another was ordered. By
1707 the Governors had decided to seek an Act discharging all livings
worth £50 or less from payment of first fruits and tenths, and that Act
ordered the bishops to certify, to the Exchequer this time, 'all Ecclesiastical benefices with Cure of Souls, not exceeding the clear yearly
value of fifty pounds.' Both the methods and the principles of this
enquiry were specified in great detail. Bishops and ordinaries of peculiars were to gather information through the oaths of 'two or more
credible witnesses' which either they or others 'duly commissioned by
them, under their hands and seals' were empowered to administer.
Hundreds of copies of printed commissions were sent out with blank
spaces where the names of the commissioners chosen by the bishops
and the time and place of their meeting could be filled in.[37] Thousands
of copies of three printed information sheets were also circulated:
'Directions for the better Execution of the Commission to Enquire
into the Value of Small Livings', 'Some General Considerations about
the Commissions to Enquire about the Value of Small Livings', and
'A Letter of Notice to be sent to the Clergy'.[38] Clergymen who thought
their living qualified for help were told to bring not only two witnesses
but also 'terrars, books of account, leases, contracts' etc, and the
bishops were enjoined to preserve the detailed findings of the commissioners after the net values had been returned to the Exchequer.

What distinguishes the 1707–8 survey even more clearly from that
of 1705–6 is its greater awareness of the need to define its terms of reference. In assessing whether a living was worth £50 or not, the commissioners should count only revenue that was 'perpetually annexed'
or could 'legally be demanded'; they should exclude 'voluntary Gifts
or Contributions, or any thing of that kind'. Where the value of a
living rose and fell, they should take an average over seven years.
Where the living had been leased, they should discover the fine as well
as the rent. Certain deductions were permissible, such as pensions,
procurations, and synodals, but others were not – taxes other than
first fruits and tenths, poor rates, and the cost of assistant curates
(unless there was more than one church in the parish).

This was a much more thorough exercise altogether, and it is not surprising that the time allowed by Parliament proved inadequate. Early
in 1708 a bill to allow an extension from 25 March to 25 December of
that year was rushed through, and even then one diocesan return
arrived after the deadline.[39] By the spring of 1709 lists of discharged
livings and of livings still 'in charge' (still liable to pay first fruits and

tenths) were being prepared for the Exchequer (which was still responsible for the auditing of the taxes before they were transferred to the Bounty), and in January 1710 the Governors were told that 3,839 'benefices' had been discharged.[40] As a guide to the number of livings worth £50 or less, this figure was remarkably close to the total of 3,826 livings that the survey of 1705–6 had found to be worth less than £50. However, the comparison is not straightforward for at least three reasons; the first figure is of livings *below* £50, the second of livings worth £50 and below; the first may include quite a few curacies, the second very few; and it should also be remembered that in some dioceses tenths were paid not to the Crown but to the bishop, and that technically poor livings in these dioceses had not been discharged from both first fruits *and* tenths by the Act of 1707.

The Governors had in fact taken three steps uphill and slid two paces down. By 1710 they had a reasonably accurate picture (not a perfect one, as will be seen) of the poor rectories and vicarages which in some parts of the country constituted the main source of clerical poverty. But their knowledge of the poorest cures of all, curacies and chapelries, which abounded in other areas, such as the North, Wales, and the north Midlands, was little greater than when they started. In the Act of 1707 and their instructions to commissioners, the Governors had spelt out the fact that the queen wanted to help chapels as well as parish churches, but no more than 50 curacies were listed separately in the returns.[41] Commissioners and witnesses may have been misled by the frequent use of the word 'benefices' in official documents. For most contemporaries that word had a fairly precise meaning. It almost certainly did not embrace chapels of case and it probably did not include perpetual curacies either. Chapels of case had developed to cater for scattered hamlets in larger parishes and in most cases lacked the fixed or independent income and the perquisites associated with a mother-church. Perpetual curacies usually derived from benefices which before the Reformation had been served by temporary curates sent out by the monastic patron, but which thereafter received a lay patron who could not serve the living himself and so appointed a permanent or 'perpetual' curate on a stipend. Perpetual curacies could count on fairly regular income and fees from baptisms, marriages, and deaths but received neither the greater nor the lesser tithes associated with rectories and vicarages.[42] Perhaps the commissioners were also misled by the fact that compared to the first survey the *main* purpose of the second one was limited – to freeing poor 'benefices' from payment of first fruits and tenths. Curacies and chapelries had never paid those taxes, so why bother to mention them in the returns?

There are signs that the Governors soon realized that the information at their disposal was incomplete. The Act of 1715 stated that in many dioceses the survey of 1707–8 had not been carried out 'with that exact Certainty of the yearly Values . . . as regularly ought to have been', and laid down machinery for late registration at the Exchequer of poor livings that had been accidentally omitted from the returns. More significant is the section of the Act which 'impowered and required' the bishops 'from Time to Time, as they shall see Occasion, and as may best serve the Purposes of the said Bounty' to carry out further enquiries.[43] As noted above, this Act was at pains to assure the public that curacies and chapelries *could* be augmented, which suggests an awareness of the omission of many of these cures from previous surveys. The Act of 1715 also differed from that of 1707 in saying that in future bishops should enquire not only into livings under their own aegis but also 'within any Peculiars or Places of exempt Jurisdiction within the Bounds' of their respective dioceses or adjoining them. Clause XIV went so far as to stipulate that exempt donatives augmented by the Bounty would thereafter be subject to the bishop.[44]

At last in the early years of the reign of George I more searching enquiries into the values of curacies and chapelries were undertaken in at least 20 dioceses, though the exact origin of these surveys is something of a mystery. The fact that the great majority of the surviving returns concentrate on curacies and chapelries alone and were made at roughly the same time, between 1716 and 1719, suggests that there was some direction behind the surveys.[45] On the other hand there is no clear evidence of such surveys being commissioned specifically, either in the Governors' minutes or in the returns; and the fact that six diocesans included some rectories and vicarages alongside the curacies and quite a few livings worth £80 alongside those worth £50 or less suggests that not everybody knew exactly what they were supposed to be doing. (Those who listed livings below £80 were probably misled by the pirate publication of a form which was clearly produced after the Act of 1715 had been passed but which otherwise conflates the forms of 1705–6 and 1707–8 and asks for the names of livings below £80).[46] The impetus for these surveys may have been no more than the more conscientious bishops acting under the powers of the 1715 Act and being followed by others. Alternatively it might have been that the bishops became tired of the flow of requests from head office for certificates of the value of individual livings then being considered for augmentation because a private offer of help had been received, and so decided to have a thorough survey.[47] Whatever the impulse, a number of careful returns were made and forwarded to London, so that when John Ecton prepared *A State of the Proceedings of the . . . Bounty of Queen Anne*, to describe the work of the Governors up to Christmas

1718, he could append a list of about 1,300 poor curacies and cha-pelries.[48] Adding these to the 3,800 poor rectories and vicarages dis-charged from first fruits and tenths the Governors had a total of at least 5,100 livings in need of help.

Even then a comprehensive picture of clerical poverty eluded them. In October 1718 the Board was told by its secretary that several bishops had 'not yet certified the value of the Curacys in their respec-tive Dioceses which may prove prejudicial to such as have been pro-posed to be augmented.' The secretary was ordered to write to the offenders and a few more replies trickled in. But both in February 1719 and May 1721 the names of dilatory bishops were given to the Board.[49] The second edition of Ecton's *State of the Proceedings*, published in 1721, would contain new or enlarged entries for 8 dio-ceses, adding about 200 names to those given in 1719, but would still underestimate the numbers of curacies in half a dozen dioceses (though to be fair most of these had no more than a handful of curacies anyway).[50]

The first relatively complete list of poor livings, gathering together the fruits of all the general and particular enquiries made by then, was that prepared in 1736 for Parliament. This was printed the same year as *The Return Made by the Governors of the Bounty of Queen Anne*, but since it is little known and its findings are of broader interest, its contents are summarized in table 15. The picture that emerges from the *Return* is depressing. Over half of the churches and chapels in England, over 5,600 out of about 11,000, were considered to be below the poverty line. Indeed, in two respects the *Return*'s totals are actually too low. Under the names of the mother-churches it mentions over 100 dependent chapels without giving them the separate valu-ation that at least some of them should probably have been accorded; and if they had been, their value would usually have been less than £50.[51] Moreover if one compares the *Return* with a later work, the *Liber Regis vel Thesaurus Rerum Ecclesiasticarum* of 1786 produced by a senior Bounty official, John Bacon, it is clear that a number of livings worth £50 or less had been omitted from the *Return*, either by accident or because they had not been reported by 1736.[52]

On the other hand there are number of ways in which the *Return* exaggerates the scale of clerical poverty. It accidentally incorporates a few livings that were acknowledged to be worth over £50; it includes at least a dozen livings alleged to be worth less than £50 but which were still 'in charge' at the Exchequer; and it gives the names of many more churches which had ceased to exist since the *Valor* of 1535 was made, either because they were surplus to requirements or because the congregation had moved away.[53] The total given in the *Return* is also inflated by giving separate entries to livings which at the time of the

Table 15: *Breakdown of the poor livings listed in the* Return *of 1736 by diocese, type, and value*

Diocese[1]	Rectories				Vicarages			
	A	B	C	Sub-total	A	B	C	Sub-total
Canterbury	16	16	–	32	21	19	1	41
Bath & Wells	69	29	–	98	45	46	–	91
Bristol	36	18	6	60	19	17	4	40
Chichester	32	16	5	53	34	24	4	62
Coventry & Lfd.	26	12	–	38	57	61	3	121
Ely	4	–	1	5	24	26	2	52
Exeter	34	32	3	69	57	18	5	80
Gloucester	21	16	4	41	26	30	6	62
Hereford	36	32	2	70	33	41	3	77
Lincoln North	85	75	7	167} 193	58	179	33	270} 393
Lincoln South	20	5	1	26}	63	56	4	123}
London	31	9	2	42	50	44	2	96
Norwich	267	157	20	444	79	146	17	242
Oxford	9	4	1	14	28	20	1	49
Peterborough	10	3	3	16	37	29	6	72
Rochester	6	6	–	12	15	3	–	18
Salisbury	19	12	1	32	49	28	1	78
Winchester	15	8	3	26	17	24	2	43
Worcester	18	9	6	33	30	16	3	49
Bangor	22	20	1	43	3	8	4	15
Llandaff	24	24	3	51	19	37	6	62
St Asaph	15	11	–	26	21	13	–	34
St Davids	18	58	4	80	27	76	12	115
York	32	32	5	69	73	163	24	260
Carlisle	8	7	1	16	9	11	3	23
Chester	16	14	1	31	21	36	2	59
Durham	4	8	3	15	9	11	–	20
Totals	893	633	83	1609	924	1182	148	2254

Total number in category A (rectories, vicarages, curacies, chapelries, and others): 1931; in category B 2589; in category C 1118.
* In the *Return* peculiars are usually listed under the diocese in which they were physically located rather than under the diocese which exercised jurisdiction over them. The diocese of Lincoln has been subdivided as follows: North comprises Lincolnshire and Leicestershire, South the rest.
† This category includes a number of livings which cannot be described with accuracy as a rectory, vicarage, or curacy (e.g. a vicarage united to a rectory), some which cannot be identified with confidence, and one or two miscellaneous items.
The totals given here are the same as the *Return*'s in 19 cases, but different in the other seven, for various reasons; in the case of Winchester, six rectories, nine vicarages, and one chapel are given as being below £50 but no precise valuation is recorded; in the case of four other dioceses, livings stated to be worth more than £50 or entered twice have been omitted; and on other occasions the difference is due to the fact that the compiler of the *Return* when faced with the names of two livings but only one valuation has counted names where the present writer has counted valuations.

Category A comprises livings worth from £35 0s. 1d. to £50; B from £10 0s. 1d. to £35; and C £10 and below

	Curacies and Chapelries				Others*			Total†
	A	B	C	Sub-total	A	B	C	
Canterbury	7	12	2	21	–	–	–	94
Bath & Wells	5	44	27	76	–	1	–	266
Bristol	–	3	5	8	2	–	–	110
Chichester	2	8	2	12	1	3	1	132
Coventry & Lfd.	5	87	116	208	4	1	–	372
Ely	–	3	4	7	–	1	–	65
Exeter	7	26	24	57	1	2	2	211
Gloucester	1	18	17	36	–	6	1	146
Hereford	1	31	38	70	–	2	1	220
Lincoln North	8	30	26	64 } 113	2	3	8	514 } 712
Lincoln South	7	27	15	49	–	–	–	198
London	3	10	11	24	1	–		163
Norwich	5	54	40	99	2	4	1	792
Oxford	–	10	2	12	–	1	–	76
Peterborough	1	7	3	11	–	3	–	102
Rochester	–	1	–	1	–	–	–	31
Salisbury	2	7	2	11	–	–	–	121
Winchester	1	4	4	9	–	–	–	78
Worcester	–	15	10	25	–	–	–	107
Bangor	1	13	20	34	–	1	1	94
Llandaff	4	23	40	67	2	1	–	183
St Asaph	–	13	13	26	1	2	–	89
St Davids	1	21	123	145	3	5	8	356
York	16	135	102	253	1	1	3	587
Carlisle	–	15	20	35	–	–	–	74
Chester	12	87	177	276	1	4	9	380
Durham	4	29	9	42	–	–	–	77
Totals	93	733	852	1678	21	41	35	5638

Valor or by the strict letter of the law may have been separate entities but which by the early eighteenth century were customarily held together. Thus the two moieties of the rectory of South Ottrington in Yorkshire, listed at £27 18s. 9d. each in 1736, had been held together since the reign of Elizabeth; and since their combined value was £55 17s. 6d. their incumbent was not in such urgent need of help as other clergy.[54]

There are a number of other reasons for suggesting that the Governors' figures give an unduly pessimistic picture. First of all, their figures make no allowance for the alleviate effect of pluralism (and here I refer to the temporary holding together of different livings rather than the regular or permanent uniting of livings mentioned in the last paragraph). Many ministers undoubtedly earned a competence by holding two poor livings or a poorer and a richer one together. The Governors' decision not to exclude pluralists' livings from the benefits of augmentation was a perfectly conscious one, since it is known that on various occasions they considered sanctions against pluralists. The enquiry about pluralism in the questionnaire provided by the first charter, a draft clause to exempt some pluralists from the benefit of the scheme to discharge small livings from first fruits and tenths, and Archbishop Tenison's proposed ban on the giving of augmentations to poor livings held in plurality with rich ones, all point in the same direction, but none was acted upon.[55] It may be that the Governors thought it unfair to ignore poor livings temporarily held together by a pluralist; when he died or resigned, the individual cures would still be as poor as ever. It may be that the returns of 1705–6 persuaded them that pluralism was not as common or as great an abuse as was often suggested.[56] In the countryside at least, a living might be poor because there were relatively few families in it. Where livings held in plurality were close together and the incumbent alternated regularly between the two, pluralism could be regarded as a necessary evil, and in such cases the granting of an augmentation was not an encouragement to vice, but a temporary expedient, a means of building up a poor living until it could support its own minister unaided.[57]

The figures produced by the Bounty's surveys also discounted sources of income of a professional or semi-professional nature: cathedral dignities, minor canonries or posts as vicars choral, preaching extra sermons on demand, acting in the church courts, school teaching, medicine, acting as a notary, money-lending, or farming the glebe for profit. If it is thought that not many of the poorer clergy could aspire to cathedral livings it should be remembered that in Lincoln and Sarum dioceses, according to Kennett, bishops appointed the ministers of poor urban livings to prebends or sinecures before other candidates, and the same may have happened in Bristol; and most of the other jobs listed here were open to a majority of the lesser clergy.[58]Inherited wealth and money acquired through a good marriage were also not considered. One would not have expected clergymen of means to stay in poor livings for long, but they might start their careers in one or hold a smaller with a greater living.[59] Certainly the first benefactors to poor livings included a number of clergymen who were actually serving in a living worth less than £50.[60]

Another reason for caution is that in all the surveys carried out under Anne and George I the valuations may prove to have been on the low side. In the case of the surveys of 1705–6 and 1707–8 it would appear from W. G. Hoskins's data that the price of grain, a major determinant of the income of many clergy, was well below average at that time.[61] As one report on a Yorkshire parish in 1708 pointed out, the living had been below £50 for some years, but would rise above it 'when the price of Corn mends'.[62] Even if commissioners took averages over seven years, the values they recorded would in many cases have been below the true one. In the case of the surveys of curacies and chapelries carried out under George I, it is clear that in some areas care was taken to exclude revenue that could not be demanded in law. While perfectly logical, this policy distorted the picture of clerical incomes severely, since voluntary contributions by parishioners were often substantial. In many cases they more than doubled a curate's income.[63] To give but one example, the total value of 30 curacies and chapelries in Carlisle diocese according to the *Return* was £419 5s. 6d., but the 'clear value' including contributions came to £1,101 15s. 0d.[64]

It was also the case that the clergy and ecclesiastical officials played a large part in the conduct of the surveys. It is not being suggested that they perpetrated major fraud, or even contemplated it; but there was room for manoeuvre. Of one Yorkshire parish it was said that the certain income was only £27, even though an additional £18 was available if the vicar was an M.A. and resident. Other petitioners claimed land tax or charitable donations as allowable deductions, or claimed triennial visitation fees as annual expenses, or made separate claims for livings customarily held together.[65] In 1705–6, the incumbent was sometimes the only witness.[66] In 1707–8 and 1716–19 the individual cleric was again a key figure, usually appearing in person, and bringing along two 'credible persons' of his choice to testify on oath as to the living's value. Often these witnesses were churchwardens, who were probably testifying more to their minister's trustworthiness than to the accuracy of the estimate, since even churchwardens did not know an incumbent's income to the last penny.[67] In none of the surveys were the incumbents themselves required to take an oath, as it was felt that to do so 'in a Case where their own Interest is concerned, may expose them to the Censure of many, who are apt to think and report their Livings to be better than they are.'[68] From 1707–8 clergymen appeared not only as petitioners but also (with laymen and ecclesiastical officials) as commissioners sitting in judgment on the petitions. Indeed, on many occasions the clergy formed half or more of the quorum of commissioners, though where an individual had to pass judgment on his own living he seems to have acted with probity.[69]

One should also allow for the possibility that some of the laymen involved in the surveys were not anxious to put too high a value on livings. The men who acted as witnesses were often yeomen or husbandmen who were probably not well versed in the subtleties of the scheme (a surprising proportion of them signified their assent with a mark rather than a signature).[70] Such men may have thought that if they suggested a low figure, good Queen Anne might save them the bother of paying their dues in full, or that the lower the estimate the better their church's chances of getting an augmentation. Certainly in the case of two parishes in Yorkshire in December 1707 the witnesses gave figures that were several pounds lower than those given by their incumbents.[71] The gentry and aldermen who acted as commissioners were presumably better informed, and were enjoined to be strict, especially in 1707–8, for if too many rectories and vicarages were exempted from first fruits and tenths there would be less income for the Governors to devote to the cases of greatest need.[72] But they too may have been aware of the personal or local advantages of putting a marginal living into the category of deserving poor. The Roger Talbot who acted as commissioner in Cleveland deanery in Yorkshire in December 1707 was almost certainly the same man who had a share in the rectory of South Ottrington mentioned earlier as an example of a living with a dubious claim to inclusion in the *Return*. His signature appears first in the list of commissioners who examined that living.[73]

As a broader example of how there may have been some under-assessment, especially in marginal cases, we may take a sample of 70 poor livings in the county of Warwickshire for which values are available both for the late seventeenth century and the reign of Queen Anne. The first thing that emerges is that the stricter enquiry of 1707–8 tended to produce higher valuations than the looser exercise of 1705–6, despite the fact that on the second occasion incumbents were urged to deduct legimate expenses from their estimates.[74] The second feature is that notwithstanding the higher valuations of 1707–8, many of the figures given in Anne's reign were lower than comparable estimates from the late seventeenth century. In about 30 per cent of the cases where valuations from the 1700s and the late seventeenth century survive, the valuations were virtually identical, and in a similar proportion of cases the values given under Anne were actually higher than the earlier ones. Nearly all of the livings in these two categories, however, were worth £50 or less and so automatically qualified for help under the Act of 1707 and the second charter. On the other hand, in the final 40 per cent the valuations given in the 1700s were lower than the earlier ones, sometimes substantially. Thus Ashow rectory, valued at £66 6s. 8d. in the 1690s, was given as £49 in 1707, and Caldecote, £60 before, dropped to £35. These drops may have been due to depressed grain prices, but it is apparent that in several other cases livings that had stood on or just above the cut-off point had been given lower values which put them safely inside the category of poor livings. Thus Ansley, valued at £50 in the late seventeenth century, was returned as £49 in 1707; Baxterley, also £50 before, was given as £48, and so on.[75] (A valuation of £50 did qualify a living for discharge from first fruits and tenths and, later, for help from the Bounty; but contemporaries may not have been certain of this, and perhaps regarded a figure below £50 as a safer guarantee of help.) Most of the valuations given to the Governors were probably fairly accurate then, but the existence of some doubtful cases provides another reason for not taking their figures too much at face value. The situation was bad, but not quite as desperate as the *Return* made it appear.

One final point to bear in mind about the Governors' figures, however, is regional variation: some areas were clearly worse off than others. If we add together the number of rectories and vicarages and the number of curacies and chapelries in each diocese, and then divide by the number of poor livings in each diocese we have a guide to the proportion of poor livings worth £50 or less.[76] The national average was approximately 52 per cent, but in the dioceses of York, Chester, St David's, and Landaff, well over two-thirds of the livings were classed as impoverished; and in the neighbouring dioceses of Carlisle, Bangor, and St Asaph the situation was only marginally better. Three other dioceses had well above the average share of poor livings: Norwich, with its unusually high number of poor rectories; Bath and Wells, which had both poor rectories and vicarages in abundance; and Hereford, which had a lot of poor curacies as well. The northern half of the diocese of Lincoln was also a black spot, with literally hundreds of impoverished vicarages. An even more sensitive indicator of poverty is the proportion of livings worth £35 or less, those on which the Governors planned to make their initial assault. Approximately one-third of all livings in the country at large fell into this category, and by this token two or three more dioceses would be added to those in greatest need: Coventry and Lichfield (well over one-third worth £35 or less), Durham (just over one-third), and perhaps Gloucester (slightly under).[77]

Market towns, despite the Governors' fears, were not at a particular disadvantage.[78] If one looks at the value of the livings in the 801 market towns which Alan Everitt found to be active centres of trade in the Stuart period, one finds that almost half of them – 389 – contained at least one living worth more than £50, much the same proportion as for the country at large.[79] (Only 300 definitely did not have a living worth £50 or less, but I have presumed that in the majority of the 75 cases where the value is unclear, it is because the value was probably small; in the remaining 37 towns there were probably no churches at all.) On the other hand the areas with the highest proportions of market towns with livings worth £50 or less, or even without a church, were again the North and Wales and some of the other dioceses mentioned above. In the Lake District, Northumberland, Durham, Yorkshire, Nottingham and Wales, well over half of the market towns with livings whose value is known were valued at £50 or less; in the counties which made up the dioceses of Norwich and Coventry and Lichfield the proportion was just over half.[80] As in the sixteenth and seventeenth centuries, the region north-west of a line from the Severn to the mouth of the Humber was by almost any standard the most deprived; but there were concentrations of poor livings, both urban and rural, south of that line, in parts of the Midlands, East Anglia and the West Country.

How far did the Bounty remedy this situation? The Governors started to augment livings by lot in 1714, but straight away were met by requests from potential benefactors anxious to match the Governors' doles of £200 with similar amounts of their own. Soon the pressure was so great that in 1718 the Governors had to alter two of their rules, enlarging the scope for private benefactions from livings worth £35 or less to those worth £50 or below, and increasing the proportion of Bounty funds reserved for livings above £10 from one-third to two-thirds.[81] By 1736 well over 1,100 grants had been voted, and of those only 234 had been by lot, the other 903 being by benefaction combined with Bounty grant.[82] Among the laity, benefactors varied from peers and peeresses through the gentry down to humbler parishioners making a contribution towards the improvement of their local church. Both Whigs and Tories can be identified among the donors, for example the Earl of Burlington, the Duke of Devonshire, the Earl of Rochford (Whigs), and the Earl of Thanet (Tory).[83] A number of the knights and baronets who made contributions represented a county in Parliament, for example Sir Thomas Wroth, Sir Thomas Hanmer, Sir Jacob Astley, Sir Justinian Isham, and Sir Edward Turner, and so there is a strong chance that many of *them* were Tories. Similarly, clerical donors ranged from archbishops, bishops, deans and chapters through individual dignitaries down to the incumbents• of the smallest livings. Again they included those who leant towards the Tories such as Dawes and Gastrell and those who leant the other way such as Wake and Kennett.[84] Clergymen may have contributed to as many as a third of the benefactions, either acting by themselves or (less commonly) in combination with members of the laity. Most benefactors were clearly giving money to a living with which they had a particular association: it was their place of birth, they owned or hoped to own the advowson or impropriation, or they had served there as incumbent for a while.[85] But by no means all contributions were tied to specific cures, as the generous open-ended gifts of Lady Elizabeth Holford, Edward Colston, and Henry Godolphin, Dean of St Paul's, bear witness.[86]

In general the greatest help was given to the areas of greatest need, such as the North, the north Midlands, and the Severn valley. This was particularly true of benefactions by lot, but help from private benefactions followed much the same pattern, with one or two exceptions: in the home counties and the dioceses of Winchester and Sarum donors were numerous despite the relatively small number of poor livings; on the other hand relatively little help was forthcoming in parts of Wales and eastern England which needed it badly, due perhaps to the relative poverty of the former and the greater number of nonconformists in the latter.[87] Market towns did quite well: although their poor livings comprised only one-ninth of the total, they received nearly one-fifth of the grants made in the first 23 years of the Bounty's effective operation.[88]

The Bounty proved to be such a success that it ran into trouble with some of the Whigs who, for reasons unconnected with the Bounty, had decided to take the Anglican clergy down a peg or two, and saw in it an easy target.[89] Some Whigs purported to believe that the clergy were abusing their position by securing death-bed grants for the corporation, with the result that soon most of the land of the kingdom would be in the Church's hands. To prevent this they passed a new Mortmain Act imposing the sort of restrictions that had been lifted in 1704.[90] But the work of the Bounty was not greatly affected. Bequests had never constituted more than one-sixth of the benefactions received, and the Whigs' attack led to only a temporary reduction of donations. Meanwhile the Governors simply increased the number of augmentations made by lot.[91] As a result of their efforts, and other factors such as rising prices and enclosure awards, the number of livings worth less than £50 in 1810 was only 1,000 compared to the 5,600 worth £50 or less in the early eighteenth century. Admittedly the clergy were by then demanding a higher minimum of £150 for every living, and the same survey showed that by this new standard one living in three was still unacceptably poor.[92] Nevertheless the proportion of one-third was better than the half suggested by the *Return* of 1736, and thanks largely to the efforts of the Governors and the co-operation and generosity of many laymen and clergymen, the basis for further improvements had been soundly laid. The early years of Queen Anne's Bounty thus illustrate not only the problems inherent in reforming the Church of England but also the positive support that it enjoyed. The success of the scheme should give pause to those who are prone to write premature obituaries of the eighteenth-century Church.

NOTES

1. *CJ*, XIV, 325, 329, 356–7; *CStP Dom*, 1703–4, 550–1; *London Gazette*, 3–7 August and 24–8 August 1704, and see n. 18 below.

2. *An Account of the Annual Produce of the Revenues vested in the Governors of the Bounty of Queen Anne . . . and . . . . of the Annual Application of the said Revenues* (1803), 6–10, copy bound in CC Records, 694.

3. For the nineteenth century, see G. F. A. Best, *Temporal Pillars Queen Anne's Bounty, the Ecclesiastical Commissioners, and the Church of England* (1964), chs. 5–10, and D. McClatchey, *Oxfordshire Clergy* (1960), chs. 2–6. For earlier failures, C. Hill, *Economic Problems, passim*, and A. Whiteman, 'The re-establishment of the Church of England, 1660–1663', *Transactions of the Royal Historical Society*, 5th ser., V (1955), 112, 128–9.

4. 2 and 3 Anne, c. 20 ('An Act for the makeing more effectual Her Majesties Gracious Intentions for the Maintenance of the Poor Clergy', 1704); 6 Anne, c. 24 ('An Act for discharging small Livings from their First Fruits and Tenths', 1707); 6 Anne, c. 54 ('An Act to inlarge the Time for returning the Certificates of all Ecclesiastical Livings not exceeding . . . fifty Pounds', 1708); 1 George I, c. 10 ('An Act for making more effectual her late Majesty's Gracious Intentions for augmenting the Maintenance of the Poor Clergy', 1715); and 3 George I, c. 10 ('An Act for the better collecting and levying the Revenue of the Tenths of the Clergy', 1717).

5. C. Hodgson, *An Account of the Augmentation of Small Livings by 'The Governors of the Bounty of Queen Anne'* (2nd edn., 1845–64), Appendix, cxxix–cli; A. Savidge, *The Foundation and Early Years of Queen Anne's Bounty* (1955), 86.

6. The first charter was dated 3 November 1704: PRO C 66/3446, no. 2; the first augmentations were voted in October 1714: CC, Minutes of the General Court of the Board of Governors of Queen Anne's Bounty, Minute Book 1, 196. For the Governors' concern at delays, see their 'Humble Representation' of 1710, *ibid.*, 108–10, 114, and J. Ecton, *The State of the Proceedings of the . . . Bounty of Queen Anne* (2nd edn, 1721), 6, 106–11 (all subsequent references will be to this edition unless otherwise stated).

7. CC, Minute Books 1 and 2, and the admirable accounts of the Governors and their officials in Savidge, *op. cit., passim*, and Best, *op. cit.*, ch. 3.

8. F. Heal, 'Clerical tax collection under the Tudors', in *Continuity and Change*, eds. R. O'Day and F. Heal (1976), 98; C. D. Chandaman, *The English Public Revenue 1660–1688* (1971), 116–17; Savidge, *op. cit.*, 32.

9. PRO QAB 1; Chandaman, *op. cit.*, 115–16, 348–57; Savidge, *op. cit.*, 32–42.

10. See the Acts of 1704, 1707, 1708, and 1717; and Savidge, *op. cit.*, 35–6, 42–51.

11. See Act of 1707; CC, Minute Book 1, 108; and Savidge, *op. cit.*, 46, 56.

12. All of these figures will be explained below, except for the second for which see CC, Minute Book 1, 39.

13. Best, *op. cit.*, 89.

14. *Account* (1803), 10.

15. Second charter, rule 4. These rules were subsumed into the second charter, dated 5 March 1714 (PRO C 66/2494, no. 3), but can be viewed more conveniently in Savidge, *op. cit.*, 140–2, or Best, *op. cit.*, 532–4.

16. There was some opposition in the Lords to the bill of 1704: Savidge, *op. cit.*, 21–2; but none of the bills underwent serious delay or modification.

17. G. V. Bennett, 'Conflict in the Church', in *Britain after the Glorious Revolution*, ed. G. Holmes (1969); G. Holmes, 'Religion and party in late Stuart England' (Historical Association, 1975).

18. Clearly described in W. Kennett, *The Case of Impropriations* (1704), 360–70, and

see Savidge, *op. cit.*, 4–5, 13–24.

19. *Ibid.*, 15, 17–22, 25, 48, 61.
20. Second charter, rule 10; and see clause XVI of 1 George I, c. 10.
21. 1 George I, c. 10, clauses XIV–XVI.
22. Second charter, rule 4; 2 and 3 Anne, c. 11, clause IV.
23. Best, *op. cit.*, 92 n. 1.
24. Savidge, *op. cit.*, 62, 101–2; Best, *op. cit.*, 91–3; J. H. Pruett, *The Parish Clergy under the Later Stuarts The Leicestershire Experience* (Urbana, Ill., 1978), 34–9.
25. Best, *op. cit.*, 24–5, 33–4.
26. This wording represents a strengthening of the same point made in clause V of the Act of 1707.
27. Best, *op. cit.*, 88–91; and see below for the hostility provoked by its relatively modest achievements in the first 20 years.
28. The most recent general survey, albeit of rectories and vicarages only, was the 'Notitia Episcopatum' of 1664–5, LPL, MS 923, but even that may not have been complete for all dioceses. The same was true of the parliamentary surveys of the 1650s.
29. Charter of 1704 (Savidge, *op. cit.*, 129–30; Best, *op. cit.*, 525).
30. See the printed forms in CC 637 and 638, and the letter of one incumbent detailing the questions: Lancs. RO, DRCh. 35 Blackburn. The printed form also adds to the charter's question about values the phrase 'how arising'.
31. CC 636–8; Lancs. RO, DRCh. 35; Cheshire CRO EDA 6/1/29–79; Lichfield Joint RO B/A.13.II; and St Helen's RO, Worcester, BA. 2616.721.031. At least two of the surveys, in Coventry and Lichfield and Sarum, may have been combined with visitations.
32. Loose folio in CC 637. Ecton prints a not dissimilar breakdown in *State of the Proceedings*, 249, but he must be mistaken in ascribing this to the survey of 1707–8; note for instance the reference to livings 'under £50', not £50 and under as in the Act of 1707.
33. As n. 31. Only for Durham among English dioceses does a return not survive either in the Church Commissioners Records or a local record office. I am very grateful to all of the archivists who replied to my questionnaire about surveys between 1705 and 1719. Among the Welsh dioceses I have found no trace of returns from Bangor and St David's, but am less familiar with the repositories.
34. See especially CC 637 and 638. Full replies were received from a dozen dioceses, and fairly full from another six.
35. Bristol, Norwich, and Rochester appear to list no curacies or chapelries at all (CC 637–8); for the approximate number of curacies in these dioceses at the time, see table 15 below.
36. Printed forms were used by 14 dioceses for their replies: CC 637–8. Surveys concentrating on rectories and vicarages included those of 1603 and 1664–5: BL Harl. MS 280, and LPL MS 923.
37. Copies of these printed commissions survive in various places: BI PL Ret. 1, fos. xxi-xxviii and *passim*; CUL, EDR A/4/1; Guildhall London MS 11248; St Helen's RO, Worcester, BA. 2613.721.031; and Lancs. RO Ben. 8.
38. BI PL Ret. 1, fos. ix-x, xiii-xvi, xviii-xix, and St Helen's RO, Worcester, BA.2613.721.031 preserve multiple copies of each of these. I have deduced the large numbers printed from the Governors' penchant for ordering forms on a grand scale: Ecton, *State of the Proceedings*, 4, 7, 8–9.
39. 6 Anne, c. 54; 1 George I, c. 10, clause XVII.
40. CC, Minute Book 1, 108.
41. Mainly in Gloucester and Worcester dioceses: PRO, E.332/1. Drafts or partial returns survive in various record offices (see n. 37 and Somerset and Sarum dioces-

an repositories).

42. R. Burn, *Ecclesiastical Law* (4 vols. 1797), II, 55.

43. 1 George I, c. 10, clauses I, XVII-XVIII.

44. Though the next clause defended the patron's rights by allowing him to refuse the augmentation.

45. CC 633, 634, and 636; BI PL Ret. 2; Lancs RO, DRCh. 33, 35; Cheshire County RO, EDA 6/4.

46. The six dioceses were Canterbury, Chester, Durham, Lincoln, Oxford, and Peterborough: Ecton, *State of the Proceedings*. Another bishop was under the impression that he had to report all livings worth £35 or less: Glos. RO, V/9/1.

47. This process can be seen clearly in CC 633-4.

48. 1st edn, 1719, 90-182: the calculation is complicated by the need to weed out those rectories and vicarages (usually the ones given in the surveys referred to in n. 46) included among the poor curacies.

49. CC Minute Book 2, 70, 101, 192; CC 633-4.

50. The new or enlarged entries were for the dioceses of Chichester, Exeter, Gloucester, Lincoln, Sarum, St Asaph, Carlisle and Durham: see the 1719 and 1721 editions of Ecton's *State of the Proceedings*.

51. The largest number of these were the 33 named in Sarum diocese and the 15 in Bath and Wells: *Return*, 174-7, 62-6.

52. Compare, for example, the entries for the dioceses of Peterborough and Carlisle in the two sources named.

53. See, for example, the entries for the dioceses of Lincoln, Oxford, Peterborough, Coventry and Lichfield, Norwich and Chester.

54. *Return*, 214; York Minster Library, Torre MS L1/9.

55. See above p. 237; Savidge, *op. cit.*, 150; and CC, Minute Book 1, 145.

56. CC 637-8.

57. For these reasons I would tend to disagree with Savidge's criticisms of the Governors for not taking a firmer line against pluralists: *op. cit.*, 105-6, 111-12.

58. Kennett, *op. cit.*, 408; Bodl. Tanner MS 129, f. 29. Clergy held lesser cathedral posts at York, London, and Lincoln; and probably elsewhere; and still acted in the church courts: B. D. Till, 'The administrative system of the ecclesiastical courts in the diocese and province of York, pt III, 1660-1883' (transcript in BI, 1963), 112-13, 158-64. For examples of the other activities, see Lancs. RO, DRCh. 35 - Aldingham, Cockey, Seathwaite, Todmorden; B. Varley, *The History of Stockport Grammar School* (1937), 172-3, 176-9; Pruett, *op. cit.*, 91-3, 126; J. L. Salter, 'Warwickshire clergy, 1660-1714' (D. Phil. thesis, University of Birmingham, 1975), 64-5, 124-33; and B. A. Holderness, '*The clergy as money-lenders in England, 1550-1700*', above

59. Pruett, *op. cit.*, chs. 3 and 4.

60. Various examples can be found in the list of contributors given in the *Return*, 28-50 (Henry Rix, John Gibson, Daniel Collyer, *et al.*) See also Savidge, *op. cit.*, 89-90.

61. W. G. Hoskins, 'Harvest fluctuations and English economic history 1620-1759', *AgHR*, XVI (1968), figs. 1 and 3.

62. BI PL Ret. 1, 36.

63. See Kennett, *op. cit.*, Appendix, 45-7 (contributions constituting £769 of the £913 total income of a number of parishes in late-seventeenth century Norwich) and *Return*, 165 (contributions of £40 and £50 in eighteenth-century Norwich); Lancs. RO, DRCh. 35; Cheshire CRO EDA 6/4.

64. *Return*, 227-9; Bacon, *Liber Regis*, 1194-1202.

65. BI PL Ret. 1, 17, 19; Lichfield Joint RO, B/A/13/II; Lancs. RO, DRCh.33; St Helen's RO, Worcester, BA.2613.721.031; Holme Cultram (worth £45) united to

Newton Arloish (worth £21 12s. 7d.) but presented as separate entities: *Return*, 227, 229, and Bacon, *Liber Regis*, 1193, 1195.

66. Sources as in n.31.
67. Sources as in n. 37. The commissioners could call their own witnesses, but there is little evidence that they did.
68. 'Directions for the better Execution', *op. cit.*, and Ecton, *State of the Proceedings*, 127–30. In some cases, usually where they had brought only one witness, or none at all, the incumbents did take the oath: e.g. CUL, EDR A/4/1; Lancs RO, DRCh. 33, f.4r; but on other occasions the clergy swore even though there were two witnesses present: BI, PL Ret. 2, fos. 1–3.
69. Clerical commissioners predominated in the deaneries of Barnstaple, Braughin, Rochford, Sampford, and Tendring in London diocese (Guildhall London MS 11248), and of Worcester and Warwick in Worcester diocese (St Helen's RO, Worcester, BA.2613.721.031); see also Lancs. RO, Ben. 8/39,41. For examples of probity, see BI PL Ret. 1, 35, 107.
70. For the status of witnesses, see Guildhall London MS 11248 (Lexden deanery); St Helen's RO, Worcester, BA.2613.721.031 (deaneries of Evesham and Pershore), and Lancs R.O., Ben. 8/34–56; and for marks rather than signatures, the same, plus CC 636 (Canterbury and Sarum).
71. BI PL Ret. 1, 19–20, 23.
72. 'Directions for the better Execution', *op. cit.* From a letter in Guildhall London MS 11248, James Rathborne to the bishop of London, dated 24 September 1707, it appears that the commissioners were nominated at the archdeacon's visitation and with his approval; this may have included lay as well as clerical commissioners.
73. BI PL Ret. 1, 147; York Minster Library, Torre MS, *loc. cit.*
74. Lichfield Joint RO, B/A/13.II, and St Helen's RO, Worcester, BA.2613.721.031 and BA.2616.721.031, supplemented by J. Ecton, *Liber Valorum et Decimarum* (2nd ed, 1723), which prints the information provided by the survey of 1707 8.
75. Sources as in last note, together with William Salt Library, HM. 36, and St Helen's RO, Worcester, BA.3965.712.1716093.
76. Numbers of rectories and vicarages have been taken from the *Perfect Catalogue of all the Archbishops Bishops etc* (1660), (copy in BL, 816.m.24); other information from table 15.
77. Method and sources as for previous calculation.
78. See the question asked in 1705, above p. 237; it was probably at this stage that the Governors acquired two copies of John Adams' *Index Villarum* (CC 683–4).
79. A. Everitt, 'The Marketing of Agricultural Produce', in *The Agrarian History of England and Wales*, IV, *1500–1640*, ed. J. Thirsk (1967), 468–75, compared with the *Return* supplemented by Bacon's *Liber Regis*.
80. Sources as in last note.
81. CC, Minute Book 2, 67, 75, 83, 87.
82. Figures derived from the *Account* of 1803 (see above, n.2); Savidge's figures, derived from Hodgson's appendix, are slightly different.
83. These and subsequent comments are based on an analysis of the donors listed in B. Willis, *Thesaurus Rerum Ecclesiasticarum* (3rd edn, 1754) and Hodgson's *Account, loc. cit.* For the political leanings of the peers mentioned, see *The Complete Peerage*, ed. Vicary Gibbs et al. (12 vols., 1910–59).
84. As previous note, except for the affiliations of the bishops named, for which see the relevant articles in *DNB*.
85. As n.83. Dr Thomas Gibson, a Presbyterian according to *DNB* but also a high-ranking army surgeon, gave to the parish in Westmorland in which he had been born; see also above, n.60, and Savidge, *op. cit.*, 88–90.
86. *Ibid.*, 89–90, 98, and sources n.83.

87. Sources as in n. 83.
88. Clearly visible in Willis, *op. cit.*, ix-xxxvi, where the names of market towns are printed in capitals.
89. Best, *op. cit.*, 93–110. Much of the hostility was against 'Walpole's Pope', Edmund Gibson, who among other things had become an active Governor of the Bounty in the 1720s and 1730s.
90. 9 George II, c.36, and above, p. 235.
91. *Account* (1803), 7-9; for the proportion of a sixth, see Savidge, *op. cit.*, 98.
92. *Abstract of the Returns of Livings under the value of £150 per Annum* (1810), copy in CC 694. W. R. Le Fanu's *Queen Anne's Bounty*, ed. F. G. Hughes (1933), 43–4, charts the gradual raising of the Governors' sights in the later eighteenth century; see also Best, *op. cit.*, 200–4.

12

Church leaseholders:
the decline and fall
of a rural elite

David Marcombe

In most English shires the Church was a very substantial landowner, and the tenants who leased its lands came to form an élite group in county society characterized by an economic independence and a degree of social aspiration not common to the English tenantry at large; the fact that this important social and economic group has been almost wholly neglected by historians is all the more difficult to understand when we remember that in the third and fourth decades of the nineteenth century the position of the church leaseholder provoked heated debate in and out of Parliament. Despite the remarkable strength of his position he was never a popular figure either with his landlord or with society in general. Indeed, when the Parliamentary Select Committee on Church Leases, proposed by Lord John Russell, reported in May 1839 it was stated that church leaseholds were in general terms 'disadvantageous' and in particular a great hindrance to agricultural improvement.[1] These conclusions, which were challenged by very few at the time, need to be tested in the light of historical evidence, and from the point of view of the tenant rather than that of the great landowning corporations. Consequently, this essay is a social and economic study of a section of the rural middle class rather than an assessment of the fortunes of the established Church. Because of this, certain difficulties have been encountered, particularly in framing generalizations about such a diverse group as the church leaseholders; certainly the concept of the 'average' leaseholder poses just as many difficulties as E. P. Thompson encountered in his fruitless quest for the 'average' labourer or the 'average' textile worker.[2] Moreover, whereas institutional history presents the historian with few technical problems the history of individual farming families is not always so easy to reconstruct; leasehold estates were only rarely of the size which required bureaucratic management on the part of the tenant and consequently much of the detail of their *modus operandi* is lost. In view of these difficulties my main emphasis has been on the reconstitution of one family, the distinctively named Boazmans, during the period between the Restoration and the Reform Bill, but to avoid too narrow a spectrum this has included not only the immediate family group but also the extended family, or cousinage, which played such an important part in eighteenth-century social alignments. There is no reason to suppose that in the years before 1812 these families were not typical of the majority of ecclesiastical tenants, and between them they give a fair indication of the place of the church leaseholder in society. Those who believe the eighteenth-century Church to be moribund – socially and economically, to say nothing of evangelism – should consider the inadvertent contribution it made to the fluidity of English society and agricultural improvement on the eve of the industrial revolution. Those who believe my sample to be unrepresentative should test the water themselves and help shed more light on a neglected area of English church history.

In the middle years of the nineteenth century the agricultural writer George Bell noted that 'the Church has two large tracts of land in Durham; 10,000 acres near the Tees (and) 10,000 acres between the Wear and Tyne.'[3] The income which the clergy derived from these estates was considerable, totalling £71,431 shared between the bishop and dean and chapter, which made the clerical hierarchy of Durham one of the wealthiest in the country.[4] Although the bishop owned important copyhold estates, the vast majority of this land was held on lease, about half being occupied by the lessees themselves and half by their under-tenants. Dean and chapter leaseholds formed the most substantial portion of the landed interest of the Church in Durham, and the evolution of this form of tenure is of considerable interest; certainly the 'classic' form of chapter leasehold, characteristic of the eighteenth century, took many years to evolve and its emergence was not without considerable crisis and trauma – problems, incidentally, which did not effect the episcopal estates to the same degree.[5] The system of renewable leaseholds had its origins on the estates of the prior and convent and after the refoundation of the cathedral in 1541 the 21-year lease became the accepted format. However, in the general atmosphere of social and economic upheaval which characterized the middle years of the sixteenth century, the chapter tenants became increasingly concerned about the question of security of tenure, especially in view of the fact that the new generation of married Protestant clerics was beginning to look on the chapter estates as a means of enriching their families. Under the influence of local agitators, such as Roland Semer, the tenants came to imagine that they had special security and privileges because of the vague and ill-defined local custom of 'tenant right'; basically, what they meant was that because of the military service they were liable to perform on the borders they should be guaranteed low rents and fines and the right of renewal.[6] The chapter, under the leadership of Dean Whittingham, vehemently denied these claims, though the government, with an eye to the preservation of social order and border service, was at least prepared to give the tenants a fair hearing. Thus, the 1570s were particularly difficult years, and in that decade the matter was discussed before both the Privy Council and the Council of the North.[7] Various compromise solutions were worked out. In 1575 the chapter devised a plan under which leases were to be transferable to personal representatives on payment of a fine of four years' ancient rent, but when this failed to receive widespread backing a new plan was devised in 1577, this time with the authority of the Council of the North. According to this scheme the right of succession was to be restricted to immediate relatives, but the fine was to be lower, no more than three years' ancient rent.[8] Therefore, after 1577 chapter tenants had two sorts of lease from which they could choose; those taken 'simply', according to the Chapter Act of 1575, or those taken according to the 'Lord's Order' of 1577. For a while the tension subsided, but despite the conciliatory approach of Dean Matthew the problem was far from solved.

The weak link in all this, so far as the chapter was concerned, was the level of fine; three or four years' ancient rent was a pitifully small sum, and, of course, it was decreased according to the number of years surrendered in a lease. On a seven-year renewal, for example, the chapter could receive as little as a year's ancient rent as a fine, though it appears from a list of leases renewed in 1611 that the majority of tenants did not renew until their leases were almost expired.[9] The reserved, or ancient, rents of the Church bore no relation whatsoever to the real value of the property, and many of them were to remain unchanged between 1541 and 1700. In the context of stagnant rents the low levels of fine established in the 1570s were obviously quite unsatisfactory from the point of view of the chapter, and in the early seventeenth century serious attempts were made, notably by Marmaduke Blakiston, to increase fines payable to the Church. Blakiston's idea appears to have been to base fines on the principle of the 'seventh penny', and in doing so he introduced a change of interpretation of the 1577 order which was to have profound consequences; what had really been intended, he suggested, was three years' *improved value* for a 21-year renewal, and thus, in effect one year's value every seven years.[10] For a while the chaos of the 1570s was recreated, with Blakiston, on occasion, demanding arbitrary fines far in excess of the 'seventh penny' principle, and the tenants, for their part, attempting to negotiate an agreed fine based on the old principle of ancient rent; there appeared to be no consistency in chapter policy, and accusations of favouritism and bribery were rife.[11] Eventually, in an attempt to clarify the situation and remove the worst scandals, the chapter decreed in 1626 that in future tenants were to pay one year's improved value as a fine every seven years 'which by true account is three years' fine for a lease of 21 years'; if this was accepted, it was agreed that tenants would be able to renew their leases 'without difficulty or delay'.[12]

The Chapter Act of 1626 was an important turning point in the leasing policy of the dean and chapter, but nevertheless it was not accepted without opposition. There were those, both prebendaries and tenants, who continued to insist that the action of the chapter was arbitrary and unjust in view of the 1577 order, and in the 1630s two more agitators appeared in the persons of George Grey and Anthony Smith. Although their complaints got as far as the Privy Council in 1640 their dismissal was hardly surprising considering the High Church prejudice of the central government at the time; indeed, both the Privy Council and the Commonwealth Commissioners of 1649 accepted the 1626 Chapter Act as a reasonable basis on which to proceed.[13] Despite this, the tenants still felt in need of some legal clarification of their position, and after the Restoration many of them insisted on renewing their leases according to the Elizabethan principle of ancient rent. When the dean and chapter refused, the whole matter was referred to Chancery where a long and complex lawsuit ensued. Eventually, judgment was given in favour of the dean and chapter in 1664, though the Privy Council, in a desire to keep the peace, advised the bishop and chapter 'to continue their ancient tenants and their heirs and representatives' and 'not to advance their rents or fines.'[14]

Even critics of the chapter accepted that in the years after 1664 the compromise was observed 'tolerably well', with tenants having the right to renew their leases on payment of one year's value every seven years. But by this time the emnity was too deep-rooted for good faith to be assumed on either side. In 1729 Spearman complained that following an investigation into improvements on certain tenements the dean and chapter had 'severely exacted arbitrary and excessive fines, rents and fees', and suggested that the tenants should petition the king and Parliament to have their ancient rights of tenure established.[15] Thankfully no-one rose to the bait, but it seems to have given the chapter a fright. Thereafter, what alterations there were to fines were undertaken 'stealthily' by the dean and chapter. In his evidence before the Select Committee of the House of Lords (1851) Mr. W. C. Chaytor, registrar of the dean and chapter, recalled that in 1790 fines had been increased to 1¼ years value and further raised to 1½ years value in 1810; he went on to explain that 'such increase .. was never intimated to the tenants, who may have supposed that a higher valuation than before had been put upon the premises.'[16] So the tenants were right when they claimed that there was a consistent history of double dealing on the part of the chapter, but at the same time they were less than honest themselves when, in petitions to the Privy Council, they portrayed themselves as an impoverished group of farmers unable to meet the demands of a rapacious landlord.[17] In fact, as we shall see, the church leaseholders were always a privileged group in rural society, well capable of meeting the comparatively modest demands placed on them by the dean and chapter.[18]

By 1700, then, the classic form of chapter leasehold was firmly established at Durham, and the mode of tenure was to endure virtually unchanged until the foundation of the Church Commissioners in the nineteenth century.[19] The tenants were bound by very few covenants. They paid a nominal reserved rent to the church every year, and an adjustable fine of one year's value every seven years; minerals, woods and quarries were reserved to the chapter, and the tenant was to procure a licence from the chapter if he wished to mortgage or sell his lease. Apart from this his only obligations were to plant a certain number of trees every year, to maintain existing tillage and to pay the corn tithe. Everything else was up to his personal discretion; this included questions such as the scheme of husbandry to be adopted, buildings, improvements and the payment of the land tax. By contrast, episcopal leaseholds were divided into two types, leases for lives and leases for 21 years.[20] Both were very similar to chapter leases with regard to covenants and obligations, though the episcopal tenant was even less controlled because he was not formally bound to plant trees, maintain tillage or pay the corn tithe. Episcopal leases for 21 years were renewed on the same terms as chapter leases, but there was, of course, a major contrast when it came to the archaic leases for lives. Here the custom was to propose a new life to be placed in the lease when an existing life 'dropped'; for this privilege a fine was charged from the lessee, which in some cases was adjusted according to the ages of the lives still surviving. Thus the system was in a real sense a lottery, prefaced by a battle of wits between the tenant, who wanted to prolong his interest as long as possible, and the bishop who wanted to see a reasonable return from his lands. One of the few social benefits of the system was that it gave a tremendous boost to life insurance companies – and, indeed, insurance was one of the major costs of the lessee – but according to some observers 'it is easy to procure three lives on whose existence a lease is of the same value very nearly as one for a term of 72½ years'.[21] Once in possession of his lease, it was virtually impossible to remove an ecclesiastical leaseholder so long as he upheld his very limited obligations; in fact, the mode of tenure had many of the characteristics of freehold, and leasehold lands could be mortgaged and settled in much the same way as estates held in fee simple. Grey summed up the strength of the position of the leaseholders very well when he said that 'they were never likely to be disturbed in their possession and might regard themselves more as proprietors, whose estates were subject to a certain charge, than in the light of tenants having a determinable interest only in their property'.[22]

Church leaseholders came from all social classes, and in the registers of the dean and chapter peers of the realm and poor tradesmen can often be found in close proximity to one another. However, the vast majority of leaseholders came from neither of these two extremes and are best placed in the rural middle class, though, as we shall see, social status was often something which was directly influenced by the possession of leasehold property. The Boazmans, who for our purposes can be considered fairly typical, originally came from north Yorkshire, a branch of the family having migrated to Durham at the time of the Civil War.[23] The family had always been of respectable yeoman stock, and George Boazman became tenant of a substantial non-ecclesiastical estate at Trafford Hill, Aislaby, in the 20 years or so after the Restoration.[24] He was a prosperous man and evidently had some social pretentions, because his daughters married well; one was married in Durham Cathedral to a gentleman freeholder of Long Newton, while another received a dowry of £150 when she married Edward Moorcroft, a Cambridge Master of Arts and vicar of Monk Hesleden.[25] However, there appears to have been a rift between George Boazman and his eldest son, John, who went to settle at Great Stainton and was completely excluded from his father's will; falling out with father proved to be a bad move, because John was reduced to making a living as a weaver with only a 'house and garth' to his name.[26] Thus, the senior branch of the family went into the doldrums for a while and only re-emerged in the eighteenth century due to the energy and determination of two of the weaver's grandsons, John Boazman I and his brother William. Originally three brothers, John, George and William had farmed an estate at Great Stainton, but after the death of George in 1758 the two survivors appear to have become more ambitious.[27] Over the next 30 years both men built up substantial estates, John with interests at Kelloe, Trimdon, Aycliffe and Sherburn, and William with interests at Grindon and Merrington, as well as some small freeholds in either case.[28] The estates were hybrids, scattered geographically and representing different modes of tenure, but both included substantial church leaseholds, comprising dean and chapter property at Aycliffe and Merrington and episcopal property at Sherburn.[29] Both of the founding fathers died childless, John in 1790 with an estate valued at £5,000 and William in 1807 with an estate valued at £1,500. Consequently their property passed to a number of nephews of whom the most important were John Boazman II and John Brown. In the years after 1790 a certain clarification took place. John Boazman II consolidated and developed an estate of chapter leasehold at Aycliffe, while his cousin, John Brown, did the same with an estate of episcopal leasehold at Sherburn. Thus, we are presented with two comparable estates within the same family group, both based on different types of church leasehold. Hopefully, through careful comparison and analysis we can learn more about the significance of leaseholds and the place of the leaseholder in society.

The first question which emerges concerns the way in which newcomers like the Boazmans managed to break into the charmed circle of church leaseholders. Whereas in the sixteenth century it had been almost solely as a result of inheritance, in the eighteenth century it came to be much more a matter of ready cash and influence in the right places. Cash was important because most leases were bought from sitting tenants, and church leaseholds always commanded good prices until the uncertainty about their future knocked the bottom out of the market in the nineteenth century. In 1649 five years' value was the accepted price, though in the nineteenth century Mr Percival Fisher said that he could remember leases selling for 17 years purchase;[30] in fact sitting tenants negotiated what they could get, and that depended largely on the desirability of the property in question and the way in which the prospective buyer viewed the future of land-owning ecclesiastical corporations. Specific examples of sales are difficult to come by, though we know that part of a 97-acre chapter farm at Aycliffe changed hands for £940 in 1793 and a similar lease for 40 acres cost £600 as late as 1847.[31] When sums like these were involved, the new tenant clearly had to be a man of some substance. Breakthrough for the Boazmans came in 1761 when John Boazman I bought his first chapter lease at Aycliffe from Francis Holmes, a Darlington merchant;[32] where he got the money from is uncertain, though by that time he had been a working farmer at Great Stainton for 30 years and by thrift and good management could well have saved up enough to buy himself in. Alternatively, his credit was perhaps good enough by that time to secure a loan, though he did not do what some new tenants did, and immediately mortgage the lease in order to pay for its purchase.

Once the initial breakthrough had been made progress became easier. Good management of a church leasehold should have provided spare cash to invest in others, and one's circle of acquaintances and contacts inevitably grew once one was a member of the privileged brotherhood. Contacts were very important in the gaining of the initial and subsequent leases, especially when leases which had fallen in were put out to tender by the bishop or chapter. As we have seen, the Boazmans had contacts with the dean and chapter going back to the seventeenth century, by way of the Moorcroft marriage, but it is unlikely that that connection carried much weight in the eighteenth century. More important was the fact that they were tenants of the Tempests, and apparently on good terms with their landlords.[33] The Tempests, who represented the city of Durham in Parliament from 1742 to 1800, were church leaseholders themselves who enjoyed considerable influence with the bishop and dean and chapter because of their political connections and High Church views.[34] However, as the contacts between the Boazmans and Tempests waned in the last decade of the eighteenth century, Arthur Mowbray began to replace them as an increasingly important factor in the equation. Mowbray was a relative of John Boazman II's wife – probably her cousin – and from middling origins he rose to become a very influential man in the locality.[35] Not only was he a church leaseholder of considerable importance, but also receiver-general and land agent to Bishop Barrington, amongst a host of other offices. In 1812 he achieved a remarkable social coup when his only daughter married Captain Archibald Cochrane R.N., a younger son of the ninth earl of Dundonald.[36] Mowbray's influence both with the bishop and dean and chapter was almost certainly used in support of his relatives; the fact that the Boazmans and other members of the cousinage prospered during his period in office is no mere coincidence.

What was the extent of these leasehold estates and what margin of profit could be expected from them? The Aycliffe estate grew steadily after John Boazman I acquired his first lease there in 1761. This lease had comprised about 100 acres of farmland, and in 1786 Boazman made a fortuitous purchase of a small freehold in the same area.[37] Thereafter, between 1797 and 1812 John Boazman II and III procured six more leases of farmland in Aycliffe, comprising in all about 376 acres. At its greatest extent, therefore, the family interest in Aycliffe comprised about 476 acres of choice farmland, in addition to a shop, a number of cottages and the local quarries.[38] By contrast, the Sherburn estate developed rather later. In 1786 John Boazman I, as part of a consortium which included Arthur Mowbray, purchased the important Sherburn Hall estate from John Tempest of Wynyard: Boazman's portion of the spoils – 157 acres of farmland – passed eventually to John Brown along with some small freeholds he had also bought in the area.[39] Like his cousins at Aycliffe, Brown was intent on expanding the estate and in 1812, in conjunction with William Clark of Ludworth, he purchased two leases comprising a further 283 acres. Thus, at its greatest extent, Brown's interest in Sherburn – shared with William Clark – was about 453 acres.[40] The cost of these holdings is best estimated by a consideration of the running costs of one particular lease, which, for the sake of convenience, we will take to be the first lease in each estate. For his 100 acres at Aycliffe leased from the dean and chapter in 1761 John Boazman I and his successors paid an annual reserved rent of £3 9s.4d. and a fine every seven years.[41] The level of fine rose with rising land values and clerical sleight of hand, the increase being predictably steep during the period of the Napoleonic Wars; in 1771, for example, the fine for renewal was £58 11s.2½d., though by 1814 this had risen to £178 4s.2d.[42] Looked at over a seven-year period from 1785 to 1792, this lease cost the Boazmans a total of £88 1s.2d., or approximately £12 *per annum*; over the seven-year period from 1807 to 1814 the overall cost had gone up to £126 4s. 11d. or approximately £18 *per annum*.[43] Brown, sitting on an episcopal holding, was even better off. For his 157-acre share of Sherburn Hall lease, granted in 1786, he paid a reserved rent of £2 11s.10d. *per annum*, and over the next 39 years paid three fines: Boazman paid one when the lease was granted, and Brown paid two in 1793 and 1795 when two Tempest lives 'dropped' in rapid succession, one of them aged only 25; this stroke of bad luck, which cost him £253 10s. 5d. in a mere three years, was evened out by a 30-year run without payment of a fine.[44] Over the 39 years between 1786 and 1825 the running costs of this lease were £444 11s.11d. or approximately £11 *per annum*.

Even when we remember that these basic sums were subject to charges such as legal fees, land tax and the costs of improvement, it is difficult to resist the conclusion that the church leaseholders enjoyed a peculiarly favourable position, with the episcopal leaseholders for lives doing best of all, given a reasonable run of luck. Both the Aycliffe and Sherburn estates were subjected to direct farming after 1790, but it is clear that the owners of these leases could make a tidy profit out of subletting if the fancy took them. An account has survived which shows how John Brown, acting as a trustee under the terms of William Boazman's will, administered a chapter farm at Merrington in the years between 1807 and 1822.[45] The farm was leased to William Grieve on a rack-rent which rose from £80 to £85 in 1810; that this sum was very closely related to the real value of the land is illustrated by the fact that the rent was reduced to £70 in 1816 in line with the economic depression that set in following Napoleon's defeat. Regular outgoings for the landlord included land tax, reserved rents to the dean and chapter, the cost of occasional improvements, and, of course, the septennial fine; but even when all of these charges were met there was still a comfortable surplus which in the ten years between 1807 and 1816 averaged about £40 *per annum*.[46] Of course, these circumstances did not represent a consistent pattern and the conditions of tenure for ecclesiastical undertenants varied enormously. In contrast to the plan adopted by Brown at Merrington, John Boazman I let out his first Aycliffe leasehold, discussed above, for £51 9s.10d. The rent was proportionally lower than that charged at Merrington, but in this case the tenant was responsible for the land tax and any assessments due.[47] With running costs for the leaseholder in the region of about £14 *per annum* the profit margin could again be considered a reasonable one.

The significance of these favoured conditions enjoyed by the church leaseholders only really hits home when we compare them to the lot of the average tenant farmer in Durham, or indeed, to the farmer of prebendal corps land rack-rented by individual members of the chapter. The corps lands always yielded an income out of proportion to their size, and this stemmed from the custom of leasing them at the going market rate compared with the long-winded process of reserved rents and fines favoured on the bulk of the cathedral estates. Sometime before 1785 John Boazman I procured a lease of the tithe corn of Sherburn, part of the corps of the first stall; it was his first toe-hold in the township, but ironically it was to cost him more than his extensive leasehold lands there. Boazman paid Dr Charles Cooper £40 *per annum* for the lease, but after his death John Brown was obliged to pay £45 *per annum* at which level it remained until Cooper's removal from the stall in 1804.[48] Thereafter, the new prebendary, Mr R. G. Bouyer, seems to have had more ambitious ideas. Brown's lease was cancelled and the corn tithe leased to the tenants of Sherburn jointly. In 1807 the lease brought the prebendary £101 15s. 4d., in 1811 £130 11s. 0d., and in the 1820s £147 12s. 0d.[49] Clearly, the removal of the middle-man brought obvious financial benefits to the clergy. Outside the clerical sphere conditions of tenure differed considerably, but a couple of examples will suffice to bring out the contrast. On the Tempest estate at Great Stainton, Hauxley Farm, comprising 178 acres, was leased to John Boazman – a cousin of the Aycliffe branch – for £120 *per annum* in 1799; the condition of his tenure was from year to year.[50] By 1819 the rent had been dropped to £100 and the surveyor lamented that 'the buildings are not in very good repair, neither is the farm in a good state of cultivation'. He went on to suggest that this was the fault of the tenant who was 'unequal to the management of it', but the blame must lie in part with the landlord for permitting a mode of tenure so obviously detrimental to improvement.[51] The Bakers of Elemore did rather better than this. Although much of their property was badly run down in the 1780s, the situation improved somewhat when Arthur Mowbray became estate surveyor to Mrs Judith Baker in 1788. Mowbray favoured three- or six-year leases 'with proper covenants and schemes of husbandry'; moreover, after 1790 there were regular allowances for lime and structural repairs.[52] But rents were still very high compared with the ecclesiastical holdings. Matthew Potts – John Brown's cousin – farmed 161 acres at Wingate Grange for a rent which rose from £60 *per annum* in 1783 to £84 *per annum* in 1809; allowances were made against these sums for land tax and improvements, so that in real terms the rent rose from £56 6s. 0d. in 1783 to £75 7s. 8d. in 1809.[53] A real increase in rent of £19 1s. 8d. between 1783 and 1809 could hardly be considered penal, particularly in view of a paternalistic encouragement of improvement, but nevertheless the profit margin here was considerably smaller than that available on the directly farmed church leaseholds. In 1809 the cost of Matthew Potts' Wingate farm was roughly seven times as much as John Brown paid for a comparable estate at Sherburn only five miles away.

It was these privileged circumstances, related to the lot of the tenantry at large, that caused resentment to grow against the church leaseholders. Dissatisfaction was voiced in a number of ways, but most persistently in the accusation that ecclesiastical tenants tended to be bad farmers, ruining the countryside by their short-sighted and selfish methods. In an age when 'improvement' was very much the watchword of the day such anti-social activities could not be allowed to pass without critical comment.[54] As early as 1729 Spearman was emphasizing the need to encourage improvement on leasehold estates and arguing that the present mode of tenure was detrimental to it.[55] Most of the criticism was directed against fines, which Bailey suggested acted as 'penalties on improvements' because of their 'oblique malignity.'[56] The argument was that church leaseholders, and their tenants, were reluctant to improve their estates because if they did, their fines would be raised at the next renewal: Bell summed it up by saying that 'though he possessed a lease, he knew that upon his expending money on the property he would upon the next renewal have to pay over again for his own improvements'.[57] Moreover, it was claimed that if freehold and leasehold lands were interdispersed, as they often were, a tenant could even suffer an increase in the level of fine because of improvements undertaken on the freehold portion – 'the fate of the one is too often dependant on the other'.[58] The state of buildings and of woodland was marked out for special criticism. Bell alleged that the buildings on church leaseholds were 'generally bad and barely what will serve for the occupation of the land', because tenants were reluctant to lay out money on property 'in which nobody felt possessed of any permanent interest'.[59] Granger, Bailey and Bell all lamented the lack of timber, 'for who will plant a tree, which, the moment it takes root, will no longer be his property?'[60] Even the Select Committee of the House of Commons appears to have convinced itself by arguments of this nature, though it was judicious enough to admit that the evidence on the subject had not been unanimous.[61]

Bailey, one of the major critics of church leaseholds, believed that on some farms in the area 'considerable improvements are going forward'; these he said were taking place on farms which were large enough to provide a surplus for reinvestment and which were held on secure enough terms to allow planning for the future.[62] It is difficult to see how both the Aycliffe and Sherburn estates, and many more church leaseholds, did not fit into these categories. Certainly to claim that church leaseholders had a temporary interest in their estates, as Bell does, is very far wide of the truth, and even when the property was not directly farmed the under-tenant was not much worse off than on some of the secular estates noted above.[63] The idea that fines prevented improvements assumes a chronic lack of ambition on the part of the tenants and a total indifference to long-term estate management on the part of the landlords, both of which are intrinsically unlikely. In the evidence before the Select Committee Stodard and Davison gave examples of some Durham manors, where, in their opinion, 'leasehold cultivation is superior to freehold', and it was also said that 'much of the South shore of the river Tyne has ... been ... reclaimed and embanked and rendered valuable at the expense of the tenants.'[64] Wise landlords did not take account of these improvements, for the purpose of fines, until they had had a chance to pay for themselves, and certainly at Durham a tradition developed whereby improvements were ignored for the renewal immediately following their implementation.[65] In fact, ecclesiastical landlords appear to have reduced fines on occasion in order to encourage improvements; in 1779, for example, the bishop of Durham remitted £10 of a £105 fine to John Rawling of Sherburn 'on account of his industry and great improvements'.[66] The criticism about the quality of buildings ignores the close interaction between freehold and leasehold in the eighteenth century and the fact that farmers often – and understandably – erected their buildings on the freehold portions of their estates; when this happened at Durham there is no evidence that tenants were penalized for so doing.[67] Hill House, the Boazman 'seat' at Aycliffe, stood on leasehold ground, yet in 1815 was described as 'a good dwelling house with excellent outbuildings and a thrashing machine' – hardly one of the run-down hovels envisaged by Bell.[68] The problem of lack of timber does not seem to have been confined to the church leaseholds. Marshall, one of the few writers to sympathize with the leaseholders, pointed out that the shortage was common to the whole county and that only one-third of it belong to the Church.[69] In fact, the dean and chapter probably did more than most landlords to enourage the supply of timber. Ecclesiastical landlords were more prone to governmental pressure with regard to timber and it was probably as a result

of representations from the Privy Council, during Charles I's rebuilding of the fleet, that the chapter took action. In 1631 it was decreed
that in all future leases there should be a clause binding the tenant to
plant 16 trees of specified type every year and that these should be
fenced off to protect them from animals.[70] In this way the standard 21-
year lease should have produced 336 trees. The clause was continued
into the nineteenth century and there is no reason to suppose that it
was not taken seriously. Therefore, it seems that in general terms the
complaints of the critics were often unjust.

A study of the Boazman estate endorses this conclusion. In about
1805 John Boazman II opened up a lime-works on one of his Aycliffe
leaseholds. The use of lime on fallow fields was recommended by
Marshall and others and it was one of the regular allowances made to
the Baker tenants at Wingate Grange.[71] Boazman, who made an
average annual profit of £33 0s.11d. from sales of lime over the period
1806–12, was clearly producing much more than he needed for his
own use and in one year, 1811, his declared profits topped the £100
mark.[72] Similarly, between 1815 and 1820 several new cottages were
built on Miss Mary Boazman's land, perhaps to house the workers
needed for this entrepreneurial venture.[73] In line with chapter policy
neither of these improvements was fined at the first renewal, though in
both cases there was a larger than average increase at the next
renewal.[74] Although these fines on improvements were not as malignant as is sometimes claimed, church leaseholders understood that
the only improvements for which they could not be charged, at some
stage, were those undertaken with a view to the quality of their stock.
In fact, the area around Darlington had long been famous for its cattle,
which, according to Marshall, were 'not inferior to any in England'.[75]
The interest in stockbreeding was encouraged by the patronage of
certain members of the gentry, such as George Baker of Elemore, and
by a number of local societies, such as the Darlington Agricultural
Society founded in 1783 and the Experimental Society formed at
Rushyford in 1803.[76] The principal breeders of shorthorn cattle were
the brothers Robert and Charles Colling of Ketton, but the practice
was widespread; indeed, it was the interaction of a number of
breeders with different strains of cattle which provided the key to
success. George Baker's catalogue of the sale of a notable herd of
shorthorns at Corbridge in 1817 gave the first indication of the involvement of the Boazmans in stock rearing: in it two cows and two
yearling heifers had their ancestry traced back to cattle bought from a
Mr Boazman of Great Stainton.[77] Soon after that sale, in 1822,
George Coates published the first comprehensive herd book of shorthorn cattle, and in it several lines are traced back to cows purchased
from John Boazman II in the 1790s. One of Boazman's cows, for

example, was matched with Charles Colling's bull Bolingbroke, which Coates thought was the best bull he had ever seen.[78] The fact that auctioneers and breeders thought it worth recording the name of Boazman in pedigrees implies that John Boazman II was a respected local breeder, rather than a man who had the good fortune to stumble across a couple of good cows; the 'ten fat steers' owned by John Boazman III in 1815 probably represented the last of his father's fat-stock.[79] Certainly all of the circumstantial evidence points to that conclusion. The Boazmans and Collings were close neighbours and fellow members of the Aycliffe Select Vestry, they shared mutual friends, and the amount of land kept under grass on the Aycliffe estate implies a considerable interest in stock.[80] Most telling of all, though, is a scrap of local legend which recalls how John Boazman II was bewitched by a woman whose daughter he had jilted; as a result of this we are told that his cattle were decimated and that he did not even have a single horse to remove their bodies from the foldyard.[81] He recovered from the disaster, but it must have been a cruel blow indeed for one who moved in the circle of the Collings. Therefore, the leasehold estate of the Boazmans at Aycliffe was far from moribund, and it could be suggested that it made a real contribution to the agricultural improvement of the area by releasing new supplies of lime and by assisting the evolution of shorthorn cattle. These developments were made possible by the position of the family as church leaseholders, because their favourable conditions of tenure provided spare cash to enable investment in both of these areas.

But possibly the most far-reaching consequence of being a successful church leaseholder was the transformation which it was likely to bring about in the matter of social status. English society had always possessed a certain element of fluidity, and we have already seen how the Boazmans aspired to gentility in the mid-seventeenth century only to collapse into complete oblivion fifty years later. Gentility was a vague and ill-defined concept, and the criteria by which it was judged in the eighteenth century were not generally agreed upon. Certainly, the old notion of 'ancient lineage' was by that time largely redundant, and the more fashionable interpretations were based on the stability of one's economic fortunes or Lord Chesterfield's notion of 'good breeding'.[82] It appears to have been on a combination of these ideas that prospective gentlemen were judged by society; the aspirant should at least have the rudiments of an education and should be in some vague sense considered 'comfortably off', ideally possessing freehold property or drawing an income from rents. What was beyond dispute was that the number of people claiming to be 'gentlemen' rose dramatically during the period of the Napoleonic Wars: Thomas Bewick, a shrewd observer of Northern society during the period, commented on the numbers of 'upstart gentlemen' from the farming classes, many of whom, he thought, acted the part 'very awkwardly.[83] Mr. Thompson is correct in relating this national disease to the increased prosperity of the farming community during the wars, but he did not explain that church leaseholds provided one important route for the fledgling gentleman. This did not mean that the transition was automatic. No-one had any serious doubts about Arthur Mowbray, who had the backing of his prestigious offices, but poor John Brown appears to have suffered a real crisis of identity during the difficult transitional stage; different sources refer to him as gentleman, yeoman and farmer at one and the same time, and the lack of general acceptance might have had something to do with the fact that people could remember that his father had been a day labourer.[84] The Boazmans appear to have been more readily acceptable, though even here there were inconsistencies of nomenclature as late as 1800. Broadly speaking, though, John Boazman I and William Boazman appear to have emerged from the 'yeoman' bracket in the mid-1780s, by which time the extent of their interests had made it plain that they were a cut above the average: John Boazman II was pretty consistently referred to as 'gentleman' and John Boazman III was described as 'Esquire' after 1810—for reasons which will be explained shortly.[85] The interest which John Boazman I and his brother showed in small freeholds is also probably best explained in terms of social status, though in itself the status of a freeholder did not automatically bestow the 'gentleman' accolade.[86] These freeholds often had little intrinsic value or usefulness, but what they did do was to enable the owner to vote, and voting was an important part of the contemporary social rigmarole. In the 1790 county election, which was a close-fought contest in which one of the sitting members was defeated, the votes of the 'devisees' of John Boazman I were eagerly sought. William Boazman, who was visited by the canvassers on his chapter leasehold at Merrington, said that he thought he would give Sir John Eden his undivided vote and if not he would split between Eden and Milbanke.[87] Either way he was backing a loser, but it was the least he could do since Eden was a co-lessee of his Merrington tenement. One suspects that the rising families made the most of all this; after all, many of them were being courted for the first time as politically articulate persons, and the ballyhoo of an eighteenth-century election put them in touch, for a while, with the rich and famous.

Although John Boazman I and II were both generally conceded to be gentlemen, social 'lift-off' only really came with John Boazman III. This was based on a very important marriage which he contracted with a Miss Mary Hodgson at Aycliffe in 1800.[88] The Hodgsons were a respectable, if not unduly rich, local family, but this was far overshadowed by the bride's connections. Mary Hodgson's maternal grandmother had been the sister of Sir William Dalston, sheriff of Cumberland, and she had married a brother of Fletcher Norton, Lord Grantley, erstwhile Attorney General and Speaker of the House of Commons. It was these impressive connections, coupled with the timely deaths of a number of relatives over the next few years, that led to John Boazman III inheriting the Westmorland manor of Temple Sowerby in 1808 in the right of his wife.[89] But before he reached these dizzy heights he sought to make his mark at Aycliffe. Immediately after his marriage he joined his father as a member of the Select Vestry, and in the following year – 1801–2 – served as a churchwarden, evidently laying out his own money on parish business.[90] The tendency of both John Boazman II and III to live beyond their means could well have been linked with a desire to impress as their social aspirations grew; certainly this second generation was financially less stable than the frugal yeomen who had laid the foundations of the family fortune, and they sometimes behaved in a way which earlier generations would have found difficult to comprehend.[91] In life, domestic comfort improved with up-to-date mahogany furniture and household luxuries which even ran to a harpsichord; in death, impressive and rather ostentatious family tombs advertised relationships with such local notables as the Nortons and Mowbrays.[92] As lord of the manor of Temple Sowerby Boazman's new-found wealth and status appears to have been more than he could cope with. Moving in the smart world of the Fancy he began to develop a racing stable and his uncontrolled gambling led to heavy debts; he is reputed to have lost £40,000 in the four years between 1810 and 1814, and not surprisingly, subsequent generations came to remember him as a 'bad lot'.[93] But this was the way in which gentlemen were expected to behave in the buoyant years of the Regency and the riotous extravagance of John Boazman III was a clear, if somewhat perverse, indication that the family had arrived; the russet-coated yeomen of the eighteenth century, with their vulgar frugality, had given way to the new genty of the nineteenth, with a life-style and debts to match. It should not be forgotten that 'gentry aspirations' were a general feature of the period, but in this case the transformation was in no small part the result of the family's interest in church leaseholds; after all, it was the dean and chapter estates which gave them their first steps up the social ladder and in particular made the wayward John Boazman III an acceptable husband for the well-connected Miss Hodgson.

Mercifully, John Boazman III died of apoplexy just in time to ensure that his family history would not be the classic case of clogs to clogs in three generations: however, although the family was saved from the ultimate humiliation of bankruptcy, it was forced to sell off large quantities of land after 1815 including the leasehold properties in Durham.[94] Thus, the Boazmans shed their leasehold interests at a time when the future of that style of holding was coming increasingly into doubt and the farming community was feeling the cold wind of the post-war depression. Church leaseholders were unpopular in rural society because certain churchmen and politicians believed that they deprived the clergy of the income which was due to them and because the mass of tenant farmers were jealous of their privileged status; the objectors often alleged failure to improve as the real reason for their concern, but this was, in fact, merely a thin disguise for self-interest. It was, perhaps, a sign of the times that after the death of Spearman very few writers reiterated the old complaint that the clerical involvement with estate management was 'a great prejudice to religion' and 'one great cause of the decay of Christian piety' – the Select Committee concluded that leaseholds were 'disadvantageous' for economic reasons rather than for ethical ones.[95] There is no doubt that the reform of ecclesiastical estate management would have yielded much more in terms of hard cash – the handling of the Durham corps lands proved that point – but was it fair also to allege that the system of church leaseholds was detrimental in a broader sense? At worst the under-tenants of ecclesiastical lessees could well have rated with some of the most underprivileged secular tenants, but Bell tells us that only half of the leasehold property was sublet, and the real figure may well have been smaller than this. Those ecclesiastical tenants who undertook direct farming were in a unique position to improve their estates, given their favourable conditions of tenure and regular surplus for reinvestment; the uncertainty about the future of leaseholds after the 1830s may well have effected improvement and morale, but in the earlier years some, at least, were rising to the challenge and were making a real contribution to the quality of local farming. Moreover, church leaseholds provided one important route of social mobility, and the gentleman-farmer of the eighteenth century was just as often a leaseholder as he was a freeholder. In view of this it would be difficult to argue that the system of leaseholds was intrinsically detrimental to agriculture or to rural society. But the benefits which church leaseholds brought to a few were to be forgotten in the consideration of the many, which was becoming an increasingly important political consideration after the passing of the 1832 Reform Bill. Squeezed between the governmental establishment on one hand and the mass of tenant farmers on the other, the leaseholders were largely bereft of support. John Boazman II left behind him one or two doggerel verses which described aspects of the society in which he lived; one of them records neatly both the confidence felt by the leaseholders during the boom years of the

272 *David Marcombe*

Napoleonic Wars but also the dangerous isolation which was to lead to their undoing in later years. In it he sought to make fun of the local rector, George Maclellan, and a tenant farmer, Antony Jordison, whose modest wealth he had far surpassed.

> Maclellan of Stainton has no corn,
> Jordison hasn't a shaff,
> Jack Boazman has got plenty,
> And that makes him to laugh.[96]

Boazman was doubtlessly still laughing when he died in 1812, though by then the days of the church leaseholders were numbered.

NOTES

I would like to thank Miss Barbara Boazman for her help, and especially for placing her family papers in my custody. They are now deposited at the University of Nottingham Centre for Local History (hereafter cited as UNCLH).
 1. *Final Report of the Select Committee on Church Leases* (1839), 22–3.
 2. E. P. Thompson, *The Making of the English Working Class* (1963), 213.
 3. Durham Cathedral Library (hereafter cited as DCL), Raine MSS 89, f. 8. See also T. G. Bell, 'A report upon the agriculture of the county of Durham', *J. Royal Ag. Soc.*, XVII (1856), 86–123.
 4. DCL Raine MS 89, f.140.
 5. The best (though partisan) account of the altercations between the Durham Chapter and its tenants is in the *Statement of the Defence Committee of the Tenants... to the Ecclesiastical Commissioners for England* (1871). For a discussion of the Elizabethan disputes see, D. Marcombe, 'The dean and chapter of Durham, 1558–1603' (Ph.D thesis, University of Durham 1973), 141–60: some evidence of similar problems on the episcopal estates is to be found in the handlist to the Weardale Chest, deposited at South Road, Durham.
 6. *Statement... to the Ecclesiastical Commissioners*, 15–17.
 7. *Acts of the Privy Council*, NS VIII, 318, 337; IX 90,140–2, 291–2, 313; X 151, 218–9, 281–2, 261, 337, II, 34, 71–2, 79 81, 84.
 8. Durham University, Dept of Palaeography and Diplomatic, Prior's Kitchen (hereafter cited at PK), York Book f. 40, Dean and Chapter Register C, fos. 148–9.
 9. BL Harl. MS 6853, f. 407.
10. Bodl. Rawlinson MS D. 821, fos. 14–15. I am grateful to Mr. M. J. Tillbrook for providing this reference and other useful information.
11. BL Harl. MS 6853, f. 444. Examples of extremes in chapter fining policy are to be seen in PK Dean and Chapter Act Book (1619–38), fos. 18,20.
12. *Ibid.*, f. 46.
13. W. Hutchinson, *History of Durham* (1785–87), II, 157; *Statement... to the Ecclesiastical Commissioners*, 31–3.
14. Hutchinson, *op. cit.*, II, 163–6, *Statement... to the Ecclesiastical Commissioners*, 36–52; J. Spearman, *An Enquiry into the Ancient and Present State of the County Palatine of Durham* (1729), 116.
15. *Ibid.*, 117–18.
16. *Statement... to the Ecclesiastical Commissioners*, 54.
17. *Ibid.*, 16.
18. Ralph Lever believed that it was the 'wealthier sort' who were the main opponents

of the chapter, and a petition of 1590 comments on the prosperity of the chapter tenants at Ferryhill. PK York Book, f. 36, P.D.M.R. (1590. Aycliffe).

19. There is a general discussion of the conditions of church leases in the *Final Report of the Select Committee on Church Leases*, 4–18: see also P.K., P. Mussett, Notes on the system of Church Leases in the post-Reformation period. Copies of leases are recorded in the Registers of the Dean and Chapter after 1541; counterpart leases have survived from the mid-eighteenth century. The Renewals Books (from 1660) and the Contracts Books (from 1734) record the fines. All of these are deposited at the Prior's Kitchen.

20. Copies of leases are to be found in the Registers of Leases of the Bishops of Durham and evidence of fines is provided by the Notitia Books. All of these are deposited at South Road.

21. *Final Report of the Select Committee on Church Leases*, 20.

22. W. H. Grey, *Church Leases; or the subject of Church Leasehold Property considered with a view to place it on a firmer basis* (1847), 9.

23. The family originated from Skelton-in-Cleveland and make frequent appearances in the parish register after 1570: several family wills are preserved at the Borthwick Institute, York. For early evidence of their habitation in Durham, see Newcastle Reference Library, Elton Parish Register Transcript (1645–56), *Royalist Composition Papers*, ed. Welford (Surtees Society, III, 1905), 35.

24. PRO E.179.106/27, 28, 245/27. His assessment was for three hearths.

25. BI Prob Reg 60, f. 34; Durham University, Dept of Palaeography and Diplomatic, South Road (hereafter cited as SR), Index of Durham Marriage Bonds (1662–87), 241, 388. Moorcroft was the grandson of a prebendary, and a brief notice of his career appears in J. A. Venn, *Alumni Cantabrigienses* (1924), III, pt I, 210.

26. Durham CRO, EP/GS/I (Baptisms, 1672, 1675, 1676, 1678, 1682), D/CH/E.207, 208.

27. Durham CRO, D/EL/Box 7: abstract of the title to estates at Great Stainton; SR, Probate, admin. of George Boazman of Great Stainton (1758).

28. *Ibid.*, Will of John Boazman of Sherburn West Moor (1790), William Boazman of Kirkmerrington (1807).

29. *Ibid.*, admin. of John Boazman of Aycliffe (1813), will of John Brown of Sherburn Grange (1834).

30. *Statement . . . to the Ecclesiastical Commissioners*, 33, DCL Raine MS 88, f. 139.

31. Ibid. Longstaffe MS 2 (transcripts of J. R. Ord's deeds, 1793, 1847).

32. PK CC 155/263230.

33. In 1759 John Tempest of Wynyard purchased a moiety of Great Stainton which had earlier been the property of the Chaytors. William Boazman was tenant of the best Tempest holding at Salter House, Wynyard, and John Boazman I was lessee of Tempest lands at Kelloe and co-purchaser of their Sherburn Hall lease in 1786.

34. E. Hughes, *North Country Life in the Eighteenth Century* (1952), 265.

35. For Boazman's relationship with the Mowbrays, see SR, Probate, will of William Mowbray of Littletown (1789).

36. Burke, *Peerage and Baronetage* (1975), 870.

37. PK CC 173/263890, Receivers Book 155, f. 173.

38. *Ibid.*, CC 250/266803, 266804, 299/225272, 300/225300, 298/225215, 301/ 225344, Receivers Books 132–198 (Aycliffe): for some surveys of the Aycliffe estate see CC 167047⅓, 1670117⅔, 167047⅓. UNCLH, Boazman MS.L/52, Durham CRO, Q/D/L, 46–53 (Aycliffe).

39. SR, DR/Lease Register 184980, fos. 463/66, 467/69.

40. *Ibid.*, Lease Register 184986, fos. 661/4, 665/8: for some surveys of the Sherburn estate see Durham Halmote Court Records, M.II, fos. 12, 13, 24. Durham CRO. Q/ D/L, 138–58 (Sherburn).

274   *David Marcombe*

41. PK CC173/263890.
42. *Ibid.*, CC 235426½ (Renewals Book), f.230,Contracts Book (1734–1829),1771 (John Boazman), 1814 (Gabriel Fielding).
43. *Ibid.*, CC 235426½ (Renewals Book), f. 230, Contracts Book (1734–1829), 1785, 1792,1799,1807 (John Boazman), 1814 (Gabriel Fielding).
44. SR, DR/Lease Register 184982, fos. 267/70, CC 54001 (Notitia Book), f. 401, CC 54011 (Notitia Book: Easington Ward, vol. I), f. 257.
45. *Ibid.*, probate/will of William Boazman of Kirkmerrington (1807).
46. UNCLH Boazman MS L/40, fos. 1/4.
47. PK CC235426½ (Renewals Book, f. 229.
48. *Ibid.*, S.R.A./I/I, 3.
49. *Ibid.*, S.R.A./I/5, 2.
50. Durham CRO, D/LO/E. 390, f. 17.
51. *Ibid.*, D/LO/E. 497, fos. 202–4.
52. SR,Baker MS 17/14, 23.
53. *Ibid.*, Baker MS.,16, 86,19, 84, 85. For examples of improvements see 18/79, 19/ 59.
54. *Final Report of the Select Committee on Church Leases*, 22–3.
55. Spearman, *op. cit.* 118–19.
56. J. Bailey, *General View of the Agriculture of the County of Durham* (1810), 53.
57. DCL Raine MS 89, f. 65.
58. Bailey, *op. cit.*, 53.
59. *Ibid.*, f. 139.
60. J. Granger, *General View of the Agriculture of the County of Durham* (1794), 47; Bailey, *op. cit.*, 53; DCL Raine MS 89, fos. 139–40. Bell mentions Sherburn as being of an especially 'naked appearance'.
61. *Final Report of the Select Committee on Church Leases*, 18, 22.
62. Bailey, *op. cit.*, 67–8, 71.
63. DCL Raine MS 89, f. 65. Bailey disapproved of short-term leases, whoever perpetrated them: *op. cit.*, 71.
64. *Final Report of the Select Committee on Church Leases*, 22; *Statement . . . to the Ecclesiastical Commissioners*, 54.
65. G. B. Hodgson, *The Borough of South Shields* (1903), 158; 'The tenants improvements were not included in the valuation for fine until the second renewal, nor the value of new premises until the third renewal after their erection.'
66. SR, CC 54001 (Notitia Book), f. 396.
67. See, for example, Boazman freeholds at Aycliffe and Brown freeholds at Sherburn, both of which were held in conjunction with leasehold estates the level of fine is no higher than at Merrington where no freeholds were owned: Durham CRO, Q/D/ L.49 (Aycliffe), 147 (Sherburn): UNCLH Boazman MS L/52.
68. Newcastle Reference Library, *Newcastle Courant* 25 March 1815, 1 April 1815. See also UNCLH Boazman MSL/52.
69. Marshall, *A Review of the Reports of the Board of Agriculture: from the Northern Department of England* (1808), 147.
70. PK, Chapter Act Book (1619–38), f. 99.
71. *Ibid.*, CC 300/225314.
72. *Ibid.*, CC 167011⅔, f. 35.
73. *Ibid.*, CC 167047⅔, f. 20,167047⅓, f. 42.
74. *Ibid.*, Contracts Book (1734–1829),1805 (John Boazman),1812 (Ann Boazman),1820 (Rev. George Horner);1808 (Mr. Miller),1815 (Mary Boazman),1822 (Mary Boazman).
75. Marshall, *op. cit.*, 153.
76. SR, Baker MS 19/19. For a general discussion of the early development of short-

horn cattle see, J. Sinclair, *History of Shorthorn Cattle* (1907).
77. SR, Baker MS 19/206.
78. G. Coates, *The General Short-Horned Herd Book* (1822), 164, 273, 299, 484, 510.
79. Newcastle Reference Library., *Newcastle Courant*, 11 and 18 February 1815.
80. CRO, EP/AY/7, fos. 52/78, P K, 167047½, fos. 5, 16, 22, 23, 24, 28, 34, 42. Colling's friend, Haigh Robson, was an executor of the will of John Boazman III: SR, Probate, will of John Boazman of Aycliffe (1815); *Darlington Telegraph and North Eastern News*, 17 January 1863.
81. W. H. D. Longstaffe, *The History and Antiquities of the Parish of Darlington* (1854), 328. Boazman's association with the family of the alleged witch, the Closes of Aycliffe, is proved in SR, Index of Durham Marriage Bonds (1765–75), 326.
82. Lord Chesterfield, *Principles of Politeness and the Polite Philosopher* (1792), 31–6; G. E. Mingay, *English Landed Society in the Eighteenth Century* (1963), 7.
83. Thompson, *op. cit.*, 180–1, 218; Mingay, *op. cit.*, 255; E. W. Bovill, *English Country Life, 1780–1830* (1962), 29–30.
84. Durham CRO, EP/PI/2 (Baptisms, 1803): SR, DR/Lease Register 184982, f. 267, Lease Register 184986, f. 661, PK CC 388/228414. His father, Henry Brown, had died at Great Stainton in 1764: Durham CRO, EP/GS/2 (Burials, 1764).
85. SR, DR/Lease Register 184980, f. 467, 184982, f. 293, Probate, will of John Boazman of Aycliffe (1815), PK CC173/263890, 250/266804, 233/266182.
86. John Boazman I purchased freeholds at Stockton, Sherburn, Great Stainton and Aycliffe, and William Boazman at Sadberge and Stockton: SR, Probate will of John Boazman of Sherburn West Moor (1790), William Boazman of Kirkmerrington (1807), Durham CRO, Q/D/L, 95 (Stockton).
87. SR, Baker MS 17–41, 9, 42v.
88. Durham CRO, EP/AY/5 (Marriages, 1800); SR, Index of Durham Marriage Bonds (1798–1808), 162: in the bond Boazman is designated merely 'yeoman'. UNCLH Boazman MS L/27, 28.
89. W. Whellan, *History and Topography of Cumberland and Westmorland* (1860), 733; F. Haswell, 'The family of Dalston', *Transactions Cumberland and Westmorland Antiq. and Arch. Soc.*, NS x (1910), 255; Boazman MSS., L/27, 28, C/63. For the career of Mr Speaker Norton, see DNB.
90. DCRO, EP/AY/7, fos. 58, 60, 63.
91. The will of William Boazman in particular gives strong hints of the financial unreliability of both John Boazman II and III.
92. Newcastle Reference Library, *Newcastle Courant*, 11 and 18 February 1815. The Boazman altar tomb can still be seen in Aycliffe churchyard. UNCLH Boazman MS L/47.
93. Boazman had some quality horses which traced their pedigrees back to such stars of the turf as Hambletonian and Cardinal York: Newcastle Reference Library, *Newcastle Chronicle*, 3 April, 28 May, 9 July, 13 August 1814. UNCLH, Boazman MS C/116, 127(i). L/47 records mortgage debts of £27,137 on the Westmorland and Durham estates.
94. Newcastle Reference Library, *Newcastle Courant*, 4 February 1815, Boazman MS L/42–51.
95. Spearman, *op. cit.*, 117.
96. W. H. D. Longstaffe, *The History and Antiquities of the Parish of Darlington*, 329.

Index